The Blood Libel Legend

Edited by

ALAN DUNDES

The Blood Libel Legend

*A Casebook
in Anti-Semitic Folklore*

The University of Wisconsin Press

The University of Wisconsin Press
114 North Murray Street
Madison, Wisconsin 53715

3 Henrietta Street
London WC2E 8LU, England

Library of Congress Cataloging-in-Publication Data
The Blood libel legend: a casebook in anti-Semitic folklore /
    edited by Alan Dundes.
        396 pp.   cm.
    Includes bibliographical references and index.
    ISBN 0-299-13110-6   ISBN 0-299-13114-9
    1. Blood accusation.   2. Christianity and antisemitism.
I. Dundes, Alan.
BM585.2.B58   1991
305.8'924—dc20   91-12592

Contents

Contents

Preface

The prospective reader should be warned at the very outset that the subject of this volume is not a pleasant one. This is not a study of a folktale like Cinderella or Little Red Riding Hood. Instead it is an assemblage of essays all treating one of the most bizarre and dangerous legends ever created by the human imagination: the blood libel legend. According to this legend, which goes back to at least the twelfth century in Europe, Jews murder an innocent Christian infant or child for the ritual purpose of mixing the victim's blood with their matzah around Easter time. Strange though this legend may sound to anyone who has not encountered it previously, it has a sordid history which has caused great grief to countless numbers and generations of Jews. It continues to be believed as true even in the twentieth century, and it has had a demonstrable effect on the perpetuation of the worst kind of anti-Semitism, that is, anti-Semitic behavior which has caused the death of Jews.

In order to better understand the blood libel legend, we should perhaps make several basic distinctions. *Ritual murder* is a general term referring to any sacrificial killing—of either animal or human victim for some designated reason, e.g., to place in a cornerstone so as to ensure a successful building or bridge. Jewish ritual murder, in particular, refers to Jews killing Christians for some alleged religious reason. The blood libel is a subcategory of Jewish ritual murder. Not only is a Christian killed—usually a small child, typically male—but the child's blood is supposedly utilized in some ritual context, e.g., to mix with the unleavened bread eaten at Passover.

One of the first reported cases of ritual murder allegedly carried out by Jews is that of William of Norwich in 1144. The first essay in this volume by Gavin I. Langmuir discusses this case in ample detail. The second essay, by nineteenth-century folklorist Joseph Jacobs, considers a more famous case in England, that of Hugh of Lincoln in 1255. From cases we move to more folkloristic or literary renditions of the legend.

Brian Bebbington's symbolic analysis of the ballad of Little Sir Hugh is followed by Chaucer's classic Prioress's Tale.

From cases and texts, we shift to surveys of ritual murder or the blood libel in different locales. Colin Holmes's review of modern English instances, František Červinka's account of a well-known case in Czechoslovakia, and Sanford Shepard's consideration of Spanish examples are representative. Charlotte Klein samples the many reports of ritual murder found in an important Catholic periodical sponsored by the Vatican. Then follow examinations of ritual murder reports in nineteenth-century Egypt by Jacob M. Landau and in the twentieth century in the United States by Abraham G. Duker.

After these cases, texts, and surveys, the final section of the volume concerns the analysis of the blood libel legend. Cecil Roth seeks an origin for the legend in the Christian misunderstanding of the Jewish feast of Purim, and Magdalene Schultz emphasizes the child abuse component of the legend in her essay. The last two selections by Ernest A. Rappaport and the editor attempt to bring psychoanalytic theory to bear upon the content of the blood libel legend.

One should keep in mind that these fourteen essays were written at different time periods and were addressed to very different audiences. So it was almost inevitable that there would be some repetition and overlap in the essays. On the other hand, taken as a whole, these diverse studies of the blood libel legend give a remarkably complete picture of the legend in all its complexity.

The intent of the casebook is to hold an evil legend up to the light of reason with the hope of nullifying its pernicious influence. To do so, I had to take the risk of introducing the legend to some who may never have heard it before. I would hate to think that this volume would in any way help spread the legend. On the other hand, the legend has existed for nearly nine centuries up to the present time and it has had dire consequences for many, many individuals. I believe the risk is worth taking because such an evil legend must be analyzed and shown to be the dangerous fantasy that it surely is.

Acknowledgments

I thank the diligent and resourceful interlibrary loan staff of Doe Library at the University of California, Berkeley, for their success in locating rare and arcane publications on the blood libel legend. I am also grateful to Simone Klugman of the reference department of the same library for carrying out a computer search on the subject. A number of specialized libraries were kind enough to send me photocopies of their card catalogue entries on the blood libel. I am indebted to the Blaustein Library of the American Jewish Committee of the Institute of Human Relations in New York City and to the Hebrew Union College Library in Cincinnati for such assistance. I am also obliged to the Library of the Jewish Theological Seminary of America in New York City for reproducing a copy of Louis Ginzberg's unpublished "Reply to Mr. Pranaitis" at my request. To the Simon Wiesenthal Center in Los Angeles, I express my thanks for sending me translated excerpts from General Mustafa Tlas's book *The Matza of Zion*. Finally to my dear wife, Carolyn, who is ever by my side, I wish to signal my heartfelt appreciation for her continued assistance and support during my research on this painful and unpleasant project.

The Blood Libel Legend

GAVIN I. LANGMUIR

Thomas of Monmouth:
Detector of Ritual Murder

In the case of custom and belief, or any item of folklore for that matter, it is difficult if well-nigh impossible to establish with any certainty the ultimate origin of that custom and belief. One cannot say just when the very first accusation that some other group committed a ritual murder was made. On the other hand, we can indicate with some confidence when the first such recorded accusation was leveled at Jews or at Christians. Moreover, since the blood libel legend seemingly came later in time than the more general ritual murder, we may be able to do more than speculate when the first case of blood libel occurred. Much evidence seems to point to the events surrounding the death of William of Norwich, which took place in 1144. Many of those who have written on blood libel believe this to be the first documented instance of such an accusation.

For this reason, it is appropriate to sample the scholarship devoted to the case of William of Norwich. Gavin I. Langmuir, Professor of History at Stanford University, has carefully reconstructed the case in the following essay. For earlier considerations, see S. Berger, "Le prétendu meurtre rituel de la Pâque juive (II)," Mélusine 8 (1897): 169–74; Joseph Jacobs, "St. William of Norwich," Jewish Quarterly Review 9 (1897): 748–55; and especially M. D. Anderson, A Saint at Stake: The Strange Death of William of Norwich 1144 (London: Faber and Faber, 1964).

Reprinted from *Speculum* 59 (1984): 820–46.

The detective story in which the investigator is an amateur without official standing is a peculiarly English genre. Perhaps the earliest example, telling of an investigation that was pursued unofficially by an individual who arrived on the scene after the crime, disagreed with the official stand, pursued his own investigation, and reported the results, is "The Life and Passion of Saint William the Martyr of Norwich," which Thomas of Monmouth started in 1149–50 and completed in 1172–73.[1] Book 1 of the *Life,* apparently completed by 1150, is a flowing narrative of the events of William's life and of his death in 1144 as Thomas had reconstructed them. And although books 2–6, written in 1154–55, consist primarily of descriptions of the translations of William's body between 1150 and 1154 and of the miracles attributed to him, Thomas devoted the first part of book 2 to a lengthy defense of the truth of his reconstruction of the crime, a defense in which he carefully marshaled the evidence or arguments that had led him to his conclusions. The last book, book 7, which was only completed by 1173, describes the further miracles attributed to William between 1155 and 1173.[2]

While the work obviously belongs to the genre of hagiography, the first two books are primarily a detective story— even involving international intrigue—because confidence in William's sanctity depended entirely on certainty as to who had killed young William and how they had killed him. The central drama of the *Life* is not William's heroic holiness—indeed he plays a singularly passive role—but the revelation of who murdered him and how and why they did so, as can be seen from the summary in a contemporary chronicle.

> In his [King Stephen's] time, the Jews of Norwich bought a Christian child before Easter and tortured him with all the torture that our Lord was tortured with; and on Good Friday hanged him on a cross on account of our Lord, and then buried him. They expected it would be concealed, but our Lord made it plain that he was a holy martyr, and the monks took him and buried him with ceremony in the monastery, and through

4

our Lord he works wonderful and varied miracles, and he is called St. William.[3]

This brief report in the final continuation of the *Anglo-Saxon Chronicle* was written in or immediately after 1155 at Peterborough, not very far from Norwich, and is the earliest extant trace of William's death. It is not direct evidence, however. Few copies of Thomas's *Life* seem to have been made (the only copy presently known, written shortly before 1200, was discovered by M. R. James in 1889), but elements of Thomas's story spread rather rapidly by word of mouth and were soon incorporated in other chronicles. Since the continuation of the *Anglo-Saxon Chronicle* depended on the rumors emanating from Norwich and was written after 1150, after Thomas had created his version of the story, it is not independent evidence. Indeed the Peterborough chronicler does not even know that William died on the Wednesday before Good Friday, according to the story at Norwich. Yet if the *Chronicle* is not independent or accurate evidence, it does confirm that the crucifixion accusation had been made by 1155; and it illustrates that what interested people then and long after was not William himself. What mattered was the divinely assisted revelation of the identity of his killers and what they had done. William's death had occasioned the first of the connected series of accusations from the twelfth to the twentieth century that Jews committed ritual murder.

Thomas's *Life* of William, which records that accusation, is a rich document. If it is an interesting reflection of ecclesiastical life and religious mentality, as well as our first evidence for the presence of Jews in Norwich, it is important above all for the general history of Jews, and of relations between Christians and Jews, for it is our most direct evidence for the first medieval accusation that Jews were guilty of ritual murder, a myth which spread, caused the death of many Jews in different localities, and influenced Luther and Hilter among others. It is not surprising, therefore, that it has been discussed at length by both Jewish and non-Jewish historians and mentioned by many more.[4] The fundamental question these historians sought to answer was whether Jews had

5

indeed killed little William, and how, or if not, who had. In this, they were pursuing the same goal as Thomas of Monmouth, who was also their only evidence. Yet the death of William was of little importance in itself. Even if he had been killed by Jews, that, like many other homicides committed by Jews, would have been of little historical importance. The event in twelfth-century Norwich that had broad historical ramifications was not William's death but the accusation—which many at Norwich at the time did not believe—that the Jews of Norwich had crucified him. The most significant question to be put to the *Life*, therefore, and one that is not directly answered by it, is not who killed William but who first accused Jews of crucifying a Christian child out of religious hatred, and why that accusation was made.

Since historians agree that Thomas of Monmouth's evidence is too unreliable or insufficient to determine with any certainty who killed William and have only been able to produce widely divergent hypotheses, we might expect that it would be even more difficult to establish from it who accused Jews of a crucifixion. In fact, the reverse is true. At the least, we know that Thomas himself accused Jews of a crucifixion; and if we keep our eyes fixed not on William's unknown murderer but on Thomas himself, we can reach a much firmer conclusion about how the enduring myth of Jewish ritual murder was created than we will ever be able to do about who killed poor William.

Before we locate the creation of the medieval and modern myth in twelfth-century Norwich, however, we must be sure that the accusation at Norwich was not merely the repetition of an older myth. Two accusations of ritual murder or something similar to it had in fact been made against Jews in antiquity, and Jessopp and James suggested that the historiographic transmission of one of these might have influenced the Norwich accusation.[5] Whether the idea for the accusation at Norwich came from antiquity or was a fresh creation of the twelfth century is a question of such importance for our understanding of what went on at Norwich that it must be examined at some length. All too often it has been assumed that confrontation with Jews has inspired similar reactions through the millennia, a perspective that foreshortens history and reads it backwards. From that perspective, it does not seem surprising that Jews in the twelfth century should have been accused of crucifying Christians. Yet if Jews had not been accused of anything resembling ritual murder for seven centuries, and if there was no knowledge of the accusations in antiquity, then the accusation at Norwich was an independent creation, and the myth which inspired deadly attacks against Jews for centuries to come was an expression of the distinctive culture of twelfth-century Europe.

The first known accusation of ritual murder against Jews is that recorded by the historian Posidonius in the second century B.C.E. He asserted that when Antiochus IV Epiphanes invaded and desecrated the Temple in 168, he found a Greek captive in the Temple who told him that every seven years the Jews captured a Greek, fattened him up, killed him, ate parts of him, and took an oath of undying enmity against Greeks.[6] Since the story is completely unbelievable, it has been suggested that it was fabricated as propaganda to justify Antiochus's desecration or was invented, probably in Alexandria, to express Greek hatred of Jews. Whatever the precise explanation, we can be sure that the accusation was not an immediate reaction of people on the spot at the time but was created afterwards, possibly by Posidonius himself.[7] It certainly circulated in literary circles thereafter.

The rhetorician Appolonius Molon repeated the story in Alexandria in the first century B.C.E., as did Damocritus, probably in the first century C.E.[8] It was also repeated by Apion in Alexandria in the first century with the modification that the ritual was an annual affair; and toward the end of that century, Flavius Josephus described the charge in *Against Apion* and denied it.[9] Josephus thereby ensured its preservation, yet the way he reacted to the charge indicates that he considered it a historical or literary fable rather than a belief widely current among Greeks in Alexandria that endangered contemporary Jews. And if the story had little currency in Alexandria, where anti-Jewish attitudes were strong-

est, it was apparently unknown outside of Alexandria, for no
Roman writer, not even Tacitus, repeats it. Charges of ritual
cannibalism were widely made against Christians in the second century, but not against Jews. And in the later centuries
of the Roman Empire, though Christian writers were familiar with Josephus's works, they never referred to Apion's
charge as preserved in Josephus.

Josephus was also well known in the Middle Ages, but if
much attention was paid to his *Antiquities* and *Jewish Wars*,
little was paid to *Against Apion*, even less to book 2 of that
work, and still less to sections 89–96 of book 2, which contain the discussion of Apion's charge. In the first place, all
extant Greek manuscripts of *Against Apion* derive from a
single manuscript of the eleventh century that lacks sections 51–113 of book 2;[10] none consequently contain the
accusation of ritual murder. Moreover, although Eusebius
quoted or referred to Josephus so frequently that he is a major
channel of transmission, he never referred to those sections;
indeed no one seems to have done so.[11] Our knowledge of the
sections missing from the Greek manuscripts of *Against
Apion*, like that of medieval scholars, depends entirely on
the Latin translation of Josephus's works commissioned by
Cassiodorus about 578.[12] Yet if all of *Against Apion* was
thereby available to medieval scholars, they were little interested in it and concentrated on the *Antiquities* and *Wars*.
Franz Blatt lists 171 Latin manuscripts containing the *Antiquities*, but only seventeen of these also contain *Against
Apion*, and one of these only contains the first book.[13] Moreover, of the twenty-six manuscripts containing the Latin
Against Apion that Karl Boysen listed for his edition of that
work, only five contain *Against Apion* by itself.[14]

Interest in *Against Apion* for its own sake seems to have
been very late. Of the seventeen manuscripts of the Latin
Antiquities listed by Blatt that also contain *Against Apion*,
only seven are dated before the fourteenth century. Only six
of the twenty-six manuscripts of the Latin *Against Apion*
listed by Boysen are dated earlier than the fourteenth century; and the five manuscripts that contain only *Against
Apion* without any other work by Josephus all date from

the fifteenth and sixteenth centuries. Manuscripts containing the complete *Against Apion* were apparently very rare in the middle of the twelfth century when the medieval accusation of ritual murder against Jews appeared; and in the manuscripts in which *Against Apion* did appear then, it was always accompanied by other works of Josephus which attracted all the attention. Thus Peter Comestor (died ca. 1179), who used Josephus more often and more explicitly than any other church writer, never referred to *Against Apion*.[15] Indeed, so far as Schreckenberg has noticed, the only medieval Latin author ever to cite the work, and that only for a single passage in book 1, was Sicard of Cremona, who died in 1215.[16] Nor is there any allusion to the story in Yossipon.

Since the first medieval accusation against Jews appeared at Norwich in England about 1150 and soon spread to northern France, the geographical dispersion of the manuscripts is also of interest, and one manuscript immediately attracts attention. It is an Italian manuscript in the Lincoln cathedral library which was given to the cathedral about 1150 by Bishop Robert of Chesney,[17] possibly a relative of John of Chesney, the sheriff of Norfolk who protected the accused Jews of Norwich. But the manuscript does not contain *Against Apion*. Indeed, none of the manuscripts that Blatt characterizes as the Anglo-Norman family does.[18] Similarly, in Boysen's list of five manuscripts of the work in English archives, our attention is immediately attracted to a manuscript of 1145 in the Bodleian Library, one of the best early manuscripts of the work.[19] But it came to Oxford from Italy in 1817 as part of the great Canonici collection. The only other one of these five manuscripts (now at Tübingen) that is dated before 1300 is also Italian and did not leave Italy during the Middle Ages.[20]

It seems reasonably clear that although Josephus was well known in the Middle Ages, copies of *Against Apion* were rare, particularly in the north, and of no interest. The absence of references to the work by medieval authors confirms that conclusion; and, so far as I know, there is no reference to Apion's story by any medieval writer in connection with a medieval accusation of ritual murder. The accusations of ritual cannibalism against Christians deemed heretical in the eleventh and twelfth centuries drew on an entirely different tradition.[21] So far as we can tell, there was a complete discontinuity between the first accusation against Jews in antiquity and the first medieval accusation.

The second and only other relevant accusation against Jews in antiquity is the charge against the Jews of Inmestar (Syria) about 415 in connection with the celebration of Purim. This is the charge that some have thought may have influenced the Norwich accusation. Before the alleged incident, Jews had been accused of burning an effigy of Haman that was made to resemble Christ, and in 408 Theodosius II had prohibited Jews from burning such an image or mocking the cross during the Purim festivities.[22] Moreover, at least according to a Christian writing much later, forcibly baptized Jews at Alexandria had crucified a statue of Christ, mocked Christians, and provoked a riot.[23] Then, about 415, drunken Jews of Inmestar allegedly took a Christian boy, tied him to a cross in place of an effigy of Haman, and so mistreated him that he died. Our only evidence for the incident is a contemporary Christian historian, Socrates, and modern historians have disagreed about the truth of his report. Parkes and Simon accept that the Jews were drunk and did kill the boy in this fashion;[24] Juster was suspicious of the story;[25] and Roth and Blumenkranz are hesitant to pronounce.[26] Given the bitterness of relations then, the incident might have happened, but it could equally have been imagined by Socrates or others.

Socrates' story about the Inmestar incident was available to the Latin West during the Middle Ages in the work known as the *Historia tripartita*, the translation of the histories of Theodoret, Sozomen, and Socrates commissioned by Cassiodorus. Manuscripts of the work were widely disseminated; yet of the 138 known manuscripts, only two early ones are found in England, and they date from the late twelfth or early thirteenth century.[27] The *Historia* was, however, cited or used by such universal chroniclers of the eleventh and twelfth centuries as Marianus Scotus, Hermann Contractus, Sigebert of Gembloux, and Otto of Freising, but none of them referred to the Inmestar incident. That may be because their treatment of fifth-century events in the Eastern Empire was very scanty and annalistic, and their attention was focused on major events of political and Christian history. Yet they did carry forward some stories of marginal events with miraculous implications such as the existence of a gigantic woman or Siamese twins.[28] Of this genre was the story about a Jew which comes right after the Inmestar story in the *Historia*. It concerned a Jew who, apparently about 416, got himself baptized by several Christian groups, presumably to collect the financial rewards offered adherents. But when he went to a church of Catholics to be baptized once more, the water in the font miraculously disappeared on each of the three times they tried to baptize him— thereby demonstrating the power of God and the bad faith of the Jew.[29] Now there was a story of religious significance, so Sigebert copied it, and through him it passed to the *Annals of Waverley*—but neither Sigebert nor the *Annals* mentions the Inmestar incident.[30]

Those who borrowed from the *Historia tripartita* did so sparingly and most selectively, and the Inmestar incident did not interest them. Marianus, Hermann, Sigebert, and Otto did not mention it, nor does it appear in other well-known early chroniclers, whether because they did not use the *Historia*, started their chronicle after 416, or were primarily concerned with Western or regional history. The incident is not mentioned by Prosper of Aquitaine, Isidore of Seville, Gregory of Tours, Bede (in *De temporibus* or *De temporum ratione*), the *Anglo-Saxon Chronicle*, or Hugh of Flavigny. In fact, Blumenkranz found no reference to the incident in any of the Latin Christian authors up to 1096,[31] nor does Yossipon mention it. And since the first medieval accusation against Jews appeared in England about 1150, it is significant that the incident does not appear in such Anglo-Norman or English chronicles as those of St. Edmunds, Florence of Worcester, Orderic Vitalis, Robert of Torigni, or Roger of Wendover. Moreover, to the best of my knowledge, the Inmestar incident is not mentioned in any medieval discussion of ritual murder. Certainly, Thomas of Monmouth does not allude to either the Inmestar incident or Apion's charge in his account of the Norwich accusation. Thus, to conclude our long digression, it seems as certain as such things can be that the two accusations in antiquity had no influence on the first medieval accusation. We can now return to the evidence provided by Thomas of Monmouth, secure in the knowledge that the accusation he recorded was an independent creation.

What we know of Thomas himself is limited to what he discloses incidentally in the *Life*. But because in book 2 he engaged in an angry defense of his reconstruction of the crime, he tells us more about how he acquired his information than do many medieval hagiographers. As his name indicates, Thomas of Monmouth was born in Wales and was, judging by his writing, a respectably educated man when he arrived at Norwich sometime after 1146 and probably not long before 1150 to become a monk in the cathedral priory. The city in which he settled was one of the largest in England, but its cathedral was recent, a consequence of the Norman Conquest.[32] In 1096, the see of Thetford and its bishop, Herbert of Losinga, had been transferred to Norwich. Herbert began the construction of the cathedral and, following English custom, established a priory of Benedictine monks as canons of the cathedral over which he presided until his death in 1119. He was succeeded by Bishop Eborard, who died in 1146 and was succeeded in turn by Bishop William Turbe, who was bishop when Thomas of Monmouth arrived. Another Norman innovation that confronted Thomas was the castle under the control of the sheriff of Norfolk, John of Chesney, member of a Norman family which supported King Stephen and provided him with three sheriffs and possibly a bishop of Lincoln.[33] The Conquest had also brought the settlement, beside the original Danish and Anglo-Saxon inhabitants, of a substantial number of French merchants, particularly in the new burgh beside the castle. More recent French-speaking residents—if it is true that no Jews resided outside of London before 1135[34]—were the relatively few Jews who lived primarily in the new burgh. Outside Norwich, on the opposite side from the new burgh, lay

Thorpe Wood; and it was there that the body of William, a twelve-year-old apprentice skinner, had been found on Easter Saturday, 25 March of 1144.

When Thomas of Monmouth arrived, William had been dead for about four years, and his alleged martyrdom had attracted very little attention. Thomas, however, was attracted by the story and became obsessed with William's sanctity. He collected all the information he could about William, was highly influential in the development of his cult, became sacristan of his shrine, and wrote his *Life*. Since the *Life* is our only independent evidence for that first accusation, which was probably responsible for the accusations that followed fairly soon after, and since it may well be also the longest and most detailed account of any medieval accusation of ritual murder by a contemporary at or near the scene of the alleged crime,[35] it is somewhat surprising that there has been little effort to analyze it to discover how the accusation appeared at Norwich. The few modern scholars who have examined the *Life* closely were distracted from that problem by their concern to decide whether the Jews had in fact killed William. Indeed, they were so seduced by the urge to play detective, or so influenced by cultural predispositions, that even after they had recognized that the evidence was entirely insufficient to determine guilt, they went on to make strange conjectures.

Thomas of Monmouth would have been grateful for their failure to pursue the emergence of the accusation, for he wanted his readers to take it for granted as manifest truth. Book 1 describes events from William's birth to his honorable burial in the monks' cemetery, but most of it is devoted to a closely woven, melodramatic recreation of what happened between 20 March and 24 April of 1144. We observe William's disappearance with a stranger who takes him to a Jew's house, we watch him being tortured and crucified by Jews, we listen to the murderers talking among themselves about how to dispose of the body, and we are told how they did dispose of it and how it was found.

Thomas thus ensures that his readers learn that William was crucified well before any of the protagonists, other than

13

the murderers and their victim, do. Consequently, when readers who shared Thomas's preconceptions read that the boy's family accused the Jews after the body had been found, they would not have been predisposed to ask why the family had suspected Jews of the crime, and it would seem only appropriate that the boy's uncle should accuse the Jews before an episcopal synod, and that the boy's body should be buried in the monks' cemetery. The crucifixion is thus presented as the fundamental and indisputable core of the drama.

Thomas does mention in passing that some elements of his story were not known until later, but there is only a single hint in book 1 that anyone in 1144 had doubted the basic accusation. The truth of the story is taken for granted, and the narrative is so dramatically circumstantial that it is easy to forget that Thomas wove it together out of hearsay at least six years later. Even when readers discover in book 2 that much of the story of book 1 was not known for some time after 1144, and that many people in 1144 and for years after did not believe the accusation, it is hard to abandon the perspective and chronology so compellingly imprinted by book 1, hard to set Thomas's convictions about the crime aside and view his words simply as data with which to establish, so far as possible, what did go on in Norwich in those years. It is much easier and seems more important to focus on the issue made central by Thomas himself. Did the Jews crucify William? Or—since credence in that myth has waned —did they do something else that explains why people then accused them of ritual murder, something that might justify, in some measure, all those who repeated that accusation later?

Granted that centuries of cultural conflict have made those questions important to many people for various reasons, the question the historian should first ask is: what events can be established with certainty or high probability from the data of Thomas's words? We only see events as they were refracted through Thomas's mind, and the first step is to determine how Thomas acquired his conception of what happened. We cannot accept that something happened just as Thomas asserts that it did; indeed, we should be most suspicious of the assertions he most wants us to accept. Thomas was a monk of the twelfth century, concerned with his status on earth and in heaven, and convinced that loyal service to William would benefit him in both realms. His primary purpose was to praise William and edify others. So far as was compatible with those aims, he probably tried to be honest in the sense that he wrote nothing that he knew was certainly false. But his standards of evidence and analysis were not those of a modern historian; he had no disposition to be skeptical of his story, and he accepted anything he heard that could be used to support his conviction that William was a saint. He was sure—and badly wanted to be sure—that he had discovered what had happened to little William. The *Life* tells us what he wanted to believe happened, but not necessarily what really did happen.

Fortunately for us, the exigencies of his narrative—and his fellow monks' criticism of it—forced Thomas to reveal things that enable us to question his reliability. Many of the events between 1144 and 1150 that had to be mentioned in any description of William's death and later fame were so much a matter of public knowledge that neither Thomas nor anyone else could falsify them in obvious ways without losing credibility. Thomas could wishfully distort them by vague rhetoric or avoid emphasizing them, but they could not be made to disappear entirely. An illuminating example is the body itself. Thomas would have us believe that the wounds indicated a crucifixion, but he cannot help revealing the manifest lack of concern with which the body was treated for a whole month until someone suggested its potential as a relic. Similarly, he may distort accusations or testimony produced in public to suit his thesis, but he cannot insert striking assertions that people knew had not been made. Chronology is particularly revealing. The only sequence Thomas was concerned to establish precisely was the drama of William's disappearance, death, discovery, and honorable burial as he had reconstructed it. He does, however, give dates or indications of chronology for many other events; and if we establish the sequence of the events we can be fairly sure happened, and disregard dubious assertions, a

15

very different picture from that of Thomas's reconstruction appears. The general picture of how events unrolled and of Thomas's role in them that emerges from this procedure is as follows.

A priest named Wulward had two daughters, Leviva and Elviva. In 1144, Leviva was married to a priest, Godwin Sturt, and had a son Alexander, who was a deacon, and a small daughter. Elviva had married one Wenstan and had two sons, Robert, who later became a monk at Norwich, and William. William had been apprenticed to a master skinner at age eight and was twelve in 1144. He lived with "a certain Wulward" (apparently not his grandfather) and had occasion to visit Jews in the course of his work. According to the Sturts, in Lent of 1144 Godwin and Wulward prohibited William from visiting Jews any more.[36] Then, on the Monday of Easter week, 20 March 1144, a man who said he was the archdeacon's cook came with William to ask his mother's consent to take the boy to work in the kitchen. Elviva, who can only have taken him for a Christian, consented after receiving some money. Then, according only to Leviva, a highly biased source as we shall see, the man and William briefly visited her, apparently on the Tuesday.[37] Thereafter, William disappeared from public sight until Easter Saturday, when his body was discovered in Thorpe Wood.

The body was first seen by a nun and a peasant, and the latter informed a forester, Henry of Sprowston, who came and saw the body on Saturday but decided to do nothing about it until after the weekend. The news spread, and other people came out from Norwich on Saturday and Easter Sunday to look at the body but also did nothing. On Monday, Henry of Sprowston came back and buried the body where it had been found. Meanwhile some friends of William who had recognized the body told Godwin Sturt. Godwin, his son Alexander, and William's brother Robert came out on Tuesday, dug up the body, and recognized it. Instead of carrying it back for burial in consecrated ground[38] and seeking justice, they reburied it on the spot and returned to tell Leviva. According to the Sturts, she immediately told Godwin about a dream she had had two weeks before, in which she was in

16

the marketplace when Jews ran at her, surrounded her, broke her right leg with a club, tore it off her body, and ran away with it. She then reminded Godwin that he had warned her that she would lose someone dear because of the Jews. When Elviva arrived and heard what the Sturts had to tell, she ran around crying that the Jews had killed her son, but she did not provoke an attack on Jews, nor did they seek refuge in the castle.[39] And although William's relatives must have talked a lot about it among themselves and with others, nothing worthy of note seems to have occurred for some three weeks thereafter.

Around the middle of April, Godwin arose in the synod being held by Bishop Eborard and accused Jews of the crime. Since Godwin spoke before many witnesses, some of whom were still alive six years later when Thomas wrote book 1 of the *Life*, Thomas could not falsify the accusation unduly. As Thomas has him speak, Godwin first exonerated all Christians from so cruel an act and accused the Jews. He justified the charge by referring to "the practices which the Jews are bound to carry out on the days specified," "the manner of the punishment inflicted and the character of the wounds," "the many confirmations of circumstances which agree together," his wife's "very remarkable warning vision," and "the crafty tricks of a very cunning messenger of the Jews."[40] It should be emphasized here that Thomas does not allege that Godwin explicitly accused the Jews of a crucifixion, striking though such an assertion would have been at the synod, and valuable as it would have been for Thomas's thesis. Instead, he puts some highly ambiguous words in Godwin's mouth that seem to concord with the lurid description of William's crucifixion that Thomas has already provided the reader. It hardly needs to be added that it is inconceivable that that highly unreformed priest, Godwin Sturt, had read the *Historia tripartita*.

Bishop Eborard replied to Godwin—and this is the only hint of doubt in book 1—that what he had alleged "is so far clearly uncertain to us."[41] Yet to ensure justice in this religious matter, Eborard thrice summoned the Jews to come and answer the charge. Obeying the sheriff, the Jews refused.

But once the synod was over, the bishop again summoned the sheriff and the Jews, who came this time, but departed without submitting to judgment. This dramatic event finally stirred up the inhabitants of Norwich, and for the first and only time the sheriff brought the Jews into the security of the castle. Thomas does not, however, mention any looting of houses.[42]

The excitement increased William's posthumous importance, which was first recognized by a visitor. Prior Aimar of the distant abbey of St. Pancras at Lewes had attended the synod for some unknown reason and stayed after. At some point he took a single priest aside (presumably Godwin) and got all the details of what had happened from him. He then declared publicly that he wanted to take the body back to St. Pancras, where he would make it famous and a precious treasure for his monastery. Bishop Eborard recognized the possibilities and refused. He ordered that William's body be exhumed on 24 April 1144 from Thorpe Wood—where it had now lain for a whole month in unconsecrated ground—and be buried, presumably as a potential relic, in the monks' cemetery. He did not treat it as the relic of an indubitable martyr by burying it in the cathedral.[43] When the body was brought to the priory, according to Thomas writing well after the event, the monks washed it and, examining it as a potential relic, discovered thorn wounds in the scalp and even "pieces of the actual thorns," together with evident signs of martyrdom in the hands, feet, and side and plain indications that the body "had been plunged into boiling water." They then buried it with psalms and praise.[44]

Despite the assured tone of book 1, book 2 reveals that many of the clergy attributed no sanctity to William in 1144 and for years after. Indeed, William's first translation did not even arouse much faith among the lay folk of Norwich, for hardly any miracles were reported. When Thomas sat down about 1154 to record the miracles that had occurred before the second translation in 1150, he could only assemble five stories.[45] Since three of these, including a long-blooming rose bush, are attributed to 1144, only two were reported in the five years from 1145 to April of 1150. The fourth of these

18

miracles occurred "some considerable time" after 1144, when Thomas was already present, and Thomas had to admit that before the fifth miracle, remembrance of William had almost died out.[46] It was the fifth miracle that revived interest, Thomas informs us. Since interest had certainly revived when William's body was translated for the second time to the chapter house on 12 April 1150, an event followed by many miracles, and since no miracles intervened between the fifth miracle and the translation, that fifth miracle was almost certainly reported in 1149 or early in 1150.

The miracle concerned a beautiful virgin from Dunwich who had been persistently pursued by an immodest but remarkably handsome incubus. She was saved by a vision in which Herbert of Losinga, carefully announcing himself as the bishop who had founded the church at Norwich, instructed her to bear candles to William's tomb. She came, told her troubles to Wicheman, Bishop William Turbe's deputy for confessions, took her candles to the grave in the cemetery, and was delivered.[47] Since we may doubt that young virgins of Dunwich were ecclesiastical historians, it would seem that Wicheman interpreted the virgin's vision for her and thereby revived interest in Norwich's potential relic. But that was by no means his only contribution.

In 1149, Aelward Ded, one of the richest citizens of Norwich, made his deathbed confession to Wicheman, who told Thomas of Monmouth about it. As Thomas reports it, Aelward had said that on Good Friday of 1144 he had encountered a prominent Jew named Eleazar (who was safely dead by 1149) and another nameless Jew on the outskirts of Thorpe Wood. Wondering for some reason what was in the sack one of them was carrying on his horse's neck, he approached, touched it, and recognized it to be a human body, whereupon the Jews fled into the wood. Aelward did nothing about them because he was distracted from his suspicions by devotional thoughts appropriate to the day. The Jews, however, fearing their crime had been discovered, dropped the body in the wood and hurried to—of all people—the sheriff. They took John of Chesney aside, bribed him with 100 marks to keep their great secret, and then told that Christian and prominent official—on Good Friday—what they had done. They persuaded him to summon Aelward and somehow compel that substantial citizen and Christian to swear not to tell anyone about his discovery.[48] And keep quiet Aelward Ded did, even after Godwin had publicly accused the Jews, even after the body had been translated to the monks' cemetery, even after John of Chesney died in 1146, and even for three more years until he himself was dying in 1149. Or so Wicheman alleged.

The story is superbly imaginative and unbelievable, but it provided "a lawful witness" to link Jews directly with the crime. We might try to explain it as the fantasy, based on some earlier encounter with Jews, of a senile old man on his deathbed, but it is far too coherent and too obviously serves a purpose for that. Not only does it link Jews solidly with the crime, but it explains away the uncomfortable fact that the sheriff, who should have investigated the accusation had there been any reasonable evidence, not only had not done so, but had also protected the Jews after Godwin had accused them. Together with the virgin of Dunwich's story, it must have contributed greatly to the revival of interest in William that resulted in his second translation the next year. But Wicheman was by no means solely responsible for William's new fame. Thomas of Monmouth was now at the priory.

The earliest date that Thomas provides for his presence is Lent of 1150, when he had the visions that were the immediate cause of the second translation, and he seems to have known the events of 1146 only by hearsay. He was present when the fourth miracle was reported [49] and when interest in William was almost dead before the fifth miracle, of about 1149. Given the strength of his obsession, which occasioned the translation, it is hard to believe that he could have been long at the priory without trying to enhance William's fame. It therefore seems probable that he arrived in or a little before 1149 and, inspired by Wicheman or in conjunction with him, worked to revive interest in William.

Between his arrival and the second translation, Thomas was busy interviewing people and gathering testimony to demonstrate Jewish guilt and thereby confirm William's sanctity. He doubtless first sought out the Sturts and was predictably rewarded. The glaring weakness in Godwin's case against the Jews had been that no evidence connected them with William's disappearance and demise. Godwin had only been able to adduce Leviva's dream of losing her leg, to ascribe the craftiness of the self-styled cook to the Jews, and to refer vaguely to circumstantial evidence. No wonder Bishop Eborard had been dubious. Leviva's dream of course proved nothing, although it does indicate, in a way that invites psychoanalytic examination, her unusual fear of losing her leg and of Jews even before William's disappearance. But by 1149, Leviva had more to offer. She could tell Thomas that when William and the "cook" had visited her on the Tuesday, she had—for no recorded reason—been suspicious and had told her little daughter to follow them. She did and saw them enter a Jew's house and close the door.[50] Since Godwin did not mention that important evidence in his original accusation, although it would have greatly strengthened his case, and since there would have been far more decisive action against Jews in 1144 had it been known that William was last seen entering a Jew's house, we can be sure that the story only surfaced later. Surprisingly, Thomas gives no name for the daughter, describing her only as a little girl; she may well have been dead by the time Thomas arrived. It is conceivable that as Leviva developed the family fantasy after 1144—and how many times she must have retold it—she drew in some story from her small child, who might sometime have seen William enter a Jew's house with someone. Since little attention would have been paid to so dubious an addition from so suspect a source, there is no way of telling when Leviva first told it. But just as Wicheman had produced the testimony of a lawful witness to connect Jews with the crime after the fact, so Leviva's story produced a link before the fact.

There was still a great gap, however. What had the Jews done to poor William between his disappearance and the disposal of his body? That could only be surmised by a free interpretation of his wounds. Thomas set out to fill the gap himself. After diligent inquiry, he discovered a Christian

21

woman who had worked in 1144 as a servant in the house of a prominent Jew, Eleazar, who had died about 1146. She took Thomas to the house and they discovered the marks of the crucifixion. The woman said that on that fateful Wednesday she had been told to bring boiling water from the kitchen and, with one eye through a chink in the door (another invitation to psychological analysis), she saw with horror a boy attached to a post. She had done nothing, however, because she was afraid she would lose her wages, and she feared the Jews would kill her since she was "the only Christian living among so many Jews."[51] Since there were relatively few Jews in Norwich, and they lived in leased houses, none of the houses can have been far from houses and streets with Christians, and she could easily have slipped out to find help. She could also have come forward as soon as Godwin had accused the Jews in the synod. But she did nothing—shades of Aelward Ded—and only told her story some time later, apparently after being questioned by Thomas of Monmouth. The story is completely unbelievable, and presumably she told it to excuse herself for having worked for Jews and to bask in William's reflected glory.

It was also Thomas himself who acquired the most famous testimony of all. He heard it "from the lips" of Theobald, who said he had been a Jew in Cambridge in 1144, had converted when he heard of the glorious display of miracles worked through William, and had become a monk. Where Thomas met Theobald we do not know. Had he become a monk at Norwich, known to all as Theobald, we would have expected Thomas to say so and thereby guarantee the authenticity of this striking evidence "uttered by one who was a converted enemy, and had also been privy to the secrets of our enemies."[52] But Thomas does not. Thomas may have met him elsewhere, or he may have visited William's shrine at Norwich and been warmly questioned by Thomas. We can be sure, however, that Theobald's revelation delighted Thomas.

Theobald told Thomas that the Jews of Spain assembled every year in Narbonne, where their royal seed and renown flourished, in order to arrange the annual sacrifice prescribed in the ancient writings of their fathers. To show contempt for Christ, to revenge themselves because Christ's death had made them slaves in exile, and to obtain their freedom and their return to their own land, they had to shed blood annually by sacrificing a Christian. Each year, the Jews of Narbonne cast lots to determine the country in which the sacrifice would take place that year, and the Jews of the metropolis of that country then similarly determined in which town of their country the sacrifice would be performed. The lot fell on Norwich in 1144, and all the synagogues in England knew and consented to the act, which was why Theobald had known about it in Cambridge.[53]

The falsity of the fable is manifest. Not only is it in contradiction with everything we know from massive evidence about classical, medieval, and modern Judaism, but something known, as Theobald claims, to every Jew in Europe would certainly have left many more traces. It is so obviously false that scholars have wondered whether Theobald is a product of Thomas's imagination. But as Joseph Jacobs pointed out in 1897, Theobald must have been a real person and said something like this because Thomas would not have known about the *nasi* of Narbonne.[54] Why Theobald said it is harder to answer. To express his hatred for the community he had left or from which he had been expelled? To prove the sincerity of his recent conversion? We shall never know. But what has not received attention is the fact that in this crowning testimony, even as reported by Thomas, there is no reference to a crucifixion, only a sacrifice. When a Christian thought about sacrifice, particularly in connection with Easter week, he or she would immediately think of a crucifixion.[55] But a former Jew who wished to defame the community he had left or to prove the sincerity of his conversion by revealing some evil Jewish habit would be more likely to distort something genuinely Jewish such as the sacrifices of the Old Testament. And it is noteworthy that the only essential of the sacrifice mentioned by Theobald is the shedding of blood, and that this is the only place in the whole *Life* where the shedding of blood is given a religious significance.

Thomas does not introduce Theobald and report his fable

until book 2, but there are allusions to him in the narrative in book 1. Just before the self-styled cook appears on the scene to lead William away, we are told that the Jews had been planning to kill some Christian, as Thomas had learnt "from certain Jews, who were afterwards converted to the Christian faith."[56] This can only refer to Theobald's revelation, even though he is made nameless and multiplied to sound more convincing. Another reference appears when the Jews are uncertain what to do with the body. They assemble the next morning and, "as we afterwards learnt from one of them," when they are still undecided after considerable discussion, one of them who had greater authority gives a speech, which Thomas presents in direct discourse, to warn of what will happen to Jews if such a horrible crime is discovered. He counsels that the body be disposed of far away, where it will not implicate Jews.[57] Thomas only refers to a single Jew here, and the construction of the sentence implies that it was a Jew present at the killing, but it is extremely unlikely that any Jew of Norwich would ever have said anything like that to Thomas. And if he had, Thomas would certainly have said more about him in book 2, where he assembles his proofs and tells us about Theobald and his fable, but never mentions any other Jewish informant. It is far more probable that when he was getting as much as he could out of Theobald, Thomas had asked Theobald to explain why the body had been found in Thorpe Wood on the other side of Norwich far from Jews and their synagogue. Then, when writing the nattative, Thomas molded Theobald's answer and put it in the mouth of a leading Jew of Norwich. Theobald did lasting damage to Jews, but he served Thomas's search for sanctity well.

By 1150, Wicheman and Thomas had collected new and apparently damning evidence of Jewish culpability and effectively revived interest in William's sanctity. And now Thomas becomes an even more important figure in the drama. He tells us he had three visions in Lent of 1150 in which Herbert of Losinga, duly identifying himself again as the church's founder (Wicheman's influence?), appeared and commanded Thomas to inform the bishop and prior that

24

William's body must be transferred to the security of the chapter house. Thomas did so, and though Prior Elias seems to have been skeptical, Bishop William Turbe commanded the second translation. On the Wednesday of Easter week, 12 April 1150, Thomas was one of the six monks designated to open the sarcophagus, an occasion from which he profited to steal two of William's teeth for his private relics.[58] Doubtless he felt he had a right. He had caused the translation, and thanks to his own devoted labors he could envisage William's martyrdom as no one else could unless he described it to them—as we can be sure he did when the rule of silence permitted.

Thomas had every reason to feel humbly proud. Indeed, he was so elevated that on Easter Sunday, four days after the translation, on the advice of some of his companions, he took a carpet from the church, placed it on William's tomb, and set a great candle at the head of the tomb without the authorization of the prior. Elias immediately ordered their removal, at which "the greater part of the convent was scandalized."[59] Three monks promptly reported two healing miracles and a vision in which the Virgin herself stood warranty for William.[60] To the monk who had the vision, one of the virgins accompanying the Virgin explained its meaning: "Behold, the queen of heaven and mother of the Lord has come to visit the patron so long assigned to this church, the martyr William, her truly beloved friend; she has crowned him and granted him the power of healing at his will."[61] The brethren paid more honor to the tomb, four more miracles were reported, and a monk had a vision in which William, referring to Thomas as his personal sacristan, appeared and commanded that candles be placed at his tomb.[62] Elias gave in; visitors to the tomb increased greatly; and on 22 October 1150, Elias died, perhaps from chagrin or, as Thomas suggests, as a punishment for his skepticism.[63] Prior Richard, Elias's successor, then personally took the carpet from the church and placed it again on the tomb.[64]

William had finally received the honors appropriate to a martyr, and to his tomb came a press of visitors, two-thirds from Norwich itself.[65] Their presence in the chapter house so disturbed the monks and so increased William's fame that the body was translated for a third time on 2 July 1151 to a place beside the high altar of the cathedral.[66] That signal honor brought further miracles, but after the peak in 1150–51 reports of miracles dropped sharply.[67] Although Thomas says that the fourth translation on Easter Monday, 5 April 1154, to the martyrs' chapel in the apse was done because the press of visitors was again inconveniencing the clergy,[68] it seems that miracles had been falling off, and the fourth translation may have been intended to revive William's fame and revenues.

William's fame was slow in coming; and although the story about him would ultimately spread throughout Europe, his miracle-working powers at Norwich soon diminished sharply. His alleged martyrdom had attracted very few believers in 1144 and was almost forgotten by 1149. He only attracted wide interest in Norwich itself in 1150–51 after Thomas's visions and the second translation, which inspired more miracles in one year than in the preceding six. But Thomas's contribution to William's sudden fame may have been much more substantial than those visions, for it is very probable that he wrote his narrative of the life and passion of William before the second translation and incorporated it later as book 1 of the larger work.

Although M. R. James believed that the whole work had been composed in 1172 or 1173, because the opening prologue and the last miracle story in book 7 were written then,[69] there are several indications that the work was not all written at one time. The last book, book 7, which was not completed until 1172–73, stands apart. It is the only book to have its own prologue, and Thomas there states that he had stopped writing about 1155, but the revival of miracles thereafter had impelled him to take up his pen again.[70] Book 6 must therefore have been completed by 1155; and since book 2 alludes to King Stephen as dead,[71] books 2–6 must have been written after 25 October 1154 and no later than 1155. They were written at Bishop Turbe's command to preserve the record of the miracles,[72] and they also describe the second, third, and fourth translations. They were probably written after the fourth translation in April of 1154 as part of the effort to restore interest in Norwich's saint.

Book 1 seems to have been written earlier. The only time that Thomas opens a new book by referring explicitly to a prior one is at the beginning of book 2, where he states that in the previous book he had presented William's childhood and death.[73] Later in book 2, Thomas argues against many people who were hard of heart and did not believe in William's sanctity even though they had seen his cruelly wounded body or read about his cruel death *in presentibus scriptis*,[74] in what Thomas had written, which indicates that the narrative of William's life of book 1 had circulated for some time before Thomas wrote book 2. And whereas in book 2, when he refers to the king, he feels it necessary to specify that he is referring to the dead King Stephen, not Henry II, in book 1 he refers three times to the king without specifying that he means Stephen.[75]

Book 1 also differs markedly in content and tone from all the other books. It is a self-contained saint's life which begins with William's conception and ends triumphantly with his burial in the monks' cemetery. In marked contrast to the other books, Thomas here hardly ever refers to himself, doing so only briefly in a few places where he notes that he had learned of certain events from later testimony. The narrative itself only deals with the events of 1144, and although there are passing allusions to later events such as Aelward Ded's death in 1149, there is no allusion to the second translation. Indeed, were it not for that mention of 1149, the reader might think that the narrative had been written shortly after the burial in the cemetery. Moreover, in striking contrast to book 2, where Thomas immediately departs from his stated purpose to launch a bitter attack on those who doubted William's sanctity, book 1 narrates his martyrdom as if no one could doubt its truth. Bishop Eborard's initial uncertainty is mentioned but soon seems canceled by his decision to order the first translation, and the book ends on a note of triumphant confidence.

Book 1 was just what those who wanted to promote William's reputation in 1149 would have wanted, whereas book

2, certainly written after October 1154, sounds very much like a defense of book 1 against those who had criticized it. And it is remarkable that the second translation occurred on the Wednesday of Easter week of 1150, precisely six liturgical years from that Wednesday of Easter week of 1144 which Thomas's reconstruction of the crime had established as the day of William's death. It is highly probable, therefore, that book 1 was written late in 1149 or early in 1150 to increase the new interest in William's powers and provide a compelling justification for his translation to a tomb more worthy of a martyr.

The dating of book 1 is important because it provides us with a *terminus ad quem* for the crucifixion accusation. We know that the accusation had been made and was known as Peterborough by 1155. If, as seems highly probable, book 1 was written about 1150, it had already been made by then. But when was it first voiced? And by whom? Where did Thomas get the idea and how did he "know" that William had been crucified? The only evidence he adduces that might seem to support the accusation is: the nature of the wounds; the servant's story of what she had seen in the Jew's house; the marks in the house; and Theobald's story. But none of these items explains the emergence of the accusation.

What Thomas says about the state of the body is highly suspicious. In the first place, the wooden gag or teazel—whose miraculous powers Godwin Sturt later made available for a price—and the knotted cord used to torture the victim have nothing to do with a crucifixion, nor does the boiling water.[76] If we then turn to examine the words about the wounds attributed to Godwin at the synod, we are struck by their vagueness. Apparently Thomas could not assert that Godwin had claimed in the synod that William had been crucified and had had to be content with paraphrasing Godwin's words about cruel wounds so that they seemed open to such an interpretation. Equally suspect is Thomas's description of what the monks who washed the body had found. The body must have been in remarkably poor shape by then. William had been killed, apparently cruelly, and left exposed to the elements and the animals for three days; his body had then been buried, dug up, and reburied in the following two days; and then it had lain buried in the wood for a month and been dug up again before being examined. Given the state of the body and the medical ignorance of the period,[77] nobody could have said accurately what had been done to the boy. Thomas, writing six years later, could impose his interpretation on the wounds without fear of contradiction.

Before Thomas arrived in Norwich, at least up to 1146, there had apparently been no crucifixion accusation. About that year, the squires of an indebted knight named Simon de Novers had murdered the Jew Eleazar. Thomas provides an avowedly fictitious speech that William Turbe, who became bishop in 1146, might have made to King Stephen in defense of Simon, his vassal. Thomas has Turbe argue that Christians ought not to reply to a Jewish accusation until the Jews had purged themselves of William's murder. But Turbe is not made to say that William had been crucified, though such an accusation would have greatly strengthened the defense. He is only depicted as saying that Eleazar and other Jews did, "as report says, miserably torment, kill, and hide in a wood a Christian boy."[78] Thomas apparently knew that Turbe would not have referred to such an accusation in 1146.

In fact, Thomas knew that the wounds had not manifestly indicated a crucifixion. When he discovered the servant and the house where the crime supposedly happened, the marks the woman showed him did not fit a proper iconographical crucifixion. In his narrative of the crime in book 1, he therefore states that the Jews nailed William's left hand and foot but tied his right hand and foot, so that if the body were discovered, its condition would not be recognized as evidence of a Jewish crime.[79] Since no one before 1144 thought that Jews crucified children, the motive alleged is ridiculous, but what Thomas unintentionally reveals is that no one could have known from the wounds that William had been crucified.

Interestingly enough, the only other evidence to support the accusation was obtained by Thomas himself in private conversations long after the crime. It was Thomas who discovered the Christian servant after he had made diligent inquiry, and she told him she had seen the boy attached to a post and pointed out some marks. But her story is completely implausible, and even Thomas does not claim that she spoke of a crucifixion. We should note, moreover, that Thomas only discovered precisely how the "crucifixion" had occurred after he had found the woman and looked at the marks on the posts. And although the marks contradicted the accepted conception of a crucifixion and, consequently, Thomas's conviction that a crucifixion could be detected from the wounds, he nonetheless persisted in his belief. Obviously, he was already convinced before he visited the house that William must have been crucified and was determined to maintain that conviction at all costs.

Finally, there was Theobald, Thomas's only and prized source of information about what Jews did in secret. But Theobald had not been in Norwich when the crime was committed. Moreover, there is no mention of crucifixion in Thomas's lengthy report of Theobald's revelation; and had Theobald told Thomas that Jews annually crucified a Christian, Thomas would have recorded it with delight to confirm William's martyrdom and confound his critics. It remains true, of course, that Theobald introduced the myth of ritually required annual murder, yet we may wonder whether even he would have invented that myth had not Thomas eagerly asked him to explain why Jews had killed William so cruelly. In any case, without Thomas, Theobald's fable would have had no influence, for it only came to be known to contemporaries and to us because Thomas reported it in the *Life*.

Who, then, first accused Jews of crucifying William? Although people in the twelfth century were accustomed to brutal homicides, particularly during the civil war that was raging in England in 1144, crucifixion was not a contemporary form of cruelty, and people would be most unlikely to think of it when confronted with a damaged corpse and no solid evidence of who committed the crime or why. Only after the accusation had been invented at Norwich would that possibility spring readily to some people's minds. The accusation had not apparently been made by 1146 and only seems to have emerged after Thomas's arrival. And it is striking that the testimonies that come closest to support-

ing it—the stories of the Christian servant and Theobald—
were Thomas's personal discovery. It is even more striking
that Thomas never has any of the people whose stories he
reports refer explicitly to a crucifixion. Instead, he attributes
ambiguous words to them that could be interpreted as referring either to great cruelty or, as Thomas wants the reader
to think, to a crucifixion. In fact, so far as the *Life* reveals,
the only person at Norwich up to 1150 who had explicitly
asserted that the Jews had crucified the boy was Thomas
himself.

It is conceivable that Wicheman or some other supporter
of William's sanctity suggested to Thomas that the Jews
might have crucified the boy. Once Godwin Sturt had made
his accusation of cruel murder, the association of Jews with
the cruel killing of an innocent in Easter week could easily
have brought that image to mind. But no one was more obsessed with William's sanctity and more likely to make that
connection than Thomas himself, especially since it made
William a Christ-like figure, thus elevating him above most
martyrs—as some of the miracle stories make explicit. Certainly no one devoted more energy to proving the accusation
than Thomas; and when his thesis was challenged, he defended it vehemently as if his pride had been injured. For it
was his own detective work that had revealed precisely where
and how William had died, thereby greatly augmenting his
fame. And certainly it was Thomas who did the most to pub-
licize the accusation. So far as we are ever likely to know,
Thomas created the accusation. Since he had not acquired
all the elements of his story until 1149, and had apparently
written book 1 by 1150, we may feel reasonably sure that the
fantasy that Jews ritually murdered Christians by crucifixion
was created and contributed to Western cuture by Thomas of
Monmouth about 1150.

So flushed with confidence was Thomas in 1150 by his
great discovery that he placed the carpet on William's new
tomb without Prior Elias's approval. But once the excitement of detection was over and the results published for all
to read, Thomas discovered, as many others have, that the
wider audience he sought included critics. Prior Elias was

only one of many. Five years later, when Thomas sat down to write book 2, he was very bitter. Although Elias had died in 1150, others in the priory still doubted. Thomas angrily tells us in book 2 that "many . . . mocked at the miracles when they were made public" and many "suggested that the blessed boy William was likely to be of no special merit after his death, who they had heard had been a poor and neglected lad in his life." And some "though they saw with their own eyes that he was cruelly murdered . . . yet say: 'We are indeed sure that he died somehow, but we are utterly uncertain as to who killed him and why and how; hence we dare not say he is a saint or martyr.'"[80] Despite the common desire for a precious relic, many who were far more familiar with the events at Norwich than we can ever be, and who had read Thomas's account, found his story unbelievable. The modern scholar who views Thomas's account with deep skepticism has good company from the allegedly credulous Middle Ages.

We should be grateful to those medieval skeptics, because their criticisms so angered Thomas that instead of simply recording the miracles and translations as he had announced he would, he spent most of book 2 in bolstering his argument for William's sanctity and setting out his proofs of Jewish guilt,[81] thereby enabling us to see more clearly how weak his case was. Only in book 2 do we learn that his detailed description of the murder depends primarily on the Christian servant's story, that the anonymous converted Jews of book 1 were only Theobald, and that Theobald told his fable to Thomas alone. Without book 2, we would not have known about the case of Simon de Novers and the words Thomas felt were appropriate to put in Bishop Turbe's mouth. Indeed, Thomas is so determined to prove his case that he gives us every proof he can think of, which reassures the modern investigator that Thomas's certainty does not depend on some information he forgot to include. He even proffers an early example of Jewish black humor as "a most effective proof," although he does not see the joke. Apparently some Jews later said to Christians, "You ought to have rendered us thanks, for we made a saint and martyr for you. . . . We did something for you that you couldn't do for yourselves."[82] And without book 2, we would have assumed that the first translation to the monks' cemetery had been followed by many miracles, instead of which we discover that there were amazingly few between 1144 and 1149, and that William was almost forgotten by the latter date. But above all, we would never have known that many people who had witnessed the events and read the results of Thomas's detection could not believe his story.

If those informed contemporaries were completely uncertain about who killed William or how, modern scholars, with only the data of Thomas's biased account to go on, will never know. The most likely candidate remains the self-styled archdeacon's cook who was never seen again, for he was the last person seen with William by witnesses whose testimony was available when the Jews were first accused in 1144. Nothing other than Godwin's suspicions connected the "cook" with Jews, and even Thomas recognizes that he cannot say whether he was a Christian or a Jew.[83] It is, moreover, impossible to believe that Elviva or Leviva would have let someone they suspected might be a Jew go off with William under false pretenses, or that Godwin would not have said in the synod that he was a Jew if he could have. Nothing connected Jews with the crime in 1144 except the Sturt family's fear and hate of them and the fact that William had been killed in Easter week. It also seems all but certain that no one accused Jews of crucifying William until Thomas of Monmouth did so about five years later and thereby ensured William's enduring fame.

Yet whatever the skepticism of many of Thomas's contemporaries at Norwich in the ten years after William's death, many began to believe in 1150 and to have miraculous cures. The news spread, and although interest in William declined at Norwich after 1151, more people came from a distance in search of a cure.[84] By 1155, the Peterborough chronicler knew of the crucifixion accusation and the miracles. By 1170, the rumor that Jews crucified Christians had crossed the Channel and was known at Cambrai.[85] Slightly later, the abbot of Mont-Saint-Michel recorded that the Jews had crucified, not only Saint William at Norwich, but also young Richard at Pontoise, a boy at Gloucester, and a boy at Blois.[86] And in 1255, England acquired its most famous mythical victim of ritual murder. Although no evidence linked Jews with the death of young Hugh of Lincoln, Jews were accused of crucifying him, which led to the execution of nineteen Jews by King Henry III and a new saint for Lincoln cathedral.[87] What evidence could not do, accusation had, thanks to the human capacity for wishful thinking, thanks to the desire to think evil of Jews and to find confirmation of Christian beliefs.

Thomas of Monmouth was an influential figure in the formation of Western culture. He did not alter the course of battles, politics, or the economy. He solved no philosophical or theological problems. He was not even noteworthy for the holiness of his life or promotion to monastic office. Yet with substantial help from an otherwise unknown converted Jew, he created a myth that affected Western mentality from the twelfth to the twentieth century and caused, directly or indirectly, far more deaths than William's murderer could ever have dreamt of committing. Those deadly consequences should not blind us, however, to the creative imagination with which Thomas manipulated religious symbols and his perception of events in his environment in order to reinforce his religious security, turn murder into a miraculous cure for disease, and mold the religiosity of others to support his own. For Thomas was more concerned to strengthen his own Christian cosmos than to destroy Jews.

Strange as it may seem, Thomas does not appear to have had any unusual animus against Jews compared with other Christians of his day. To be sure, he depicts them as impudent and avaricious and as cruel and blasphemous killers, but he only dwells on their alleged evil qualities when the exigencies of his proof of William's sanctity demand it. He betrays no overriding obsession with Jews. He does not interrupt his narrative with irrelevant outbursts against them, nor does he interject further abuse when reporting the miracles. The Sturts did hate Jews and first accused them of cruel murder; and Theobald, the converted Jew, introduced the idea of an annual sacrifice. But Thomas only used the material provided by the animosity of others to achieve his own objective: to ensure himself of a local supernatural protector and to gain prestige on earth by his successful labors to ensure recognition of William's sanctity. Thomas did, however, make his own fundamental contribution to the creation of what he believed to be the patron saint assigned by God to Norwich.

So long as William was only seen as a poor boy who might have been cruelly killed by some Jews out of religious animosity, he could be viewed as a passive victim but hardly as a saint; and in fact he attracted little attention. One small modification, however, could and did radically change the significance of his death. If an innocent boy of twelve was crucified by Jews during Passover and in Easter week for no other reason than that he was a Christian, that he was a symbol of Christ's truth; he would seem Christ in microcosm. He would also seem a representative of all those who felt defenseless as a child against the little-understood forces that menaced their existence, and who turned for comfort to their faith that Christ might intervene here and now or at least ensure them a better life hereafter. Only a little imagination was needed to make William a symbol of comfort and ultimate victory, and Thomas did not lack imagination. He crucified William and thereby made him a notable saint.

Thomas never described William's ultimate reward in his own words. Or he did so only in words he ascribed to others. He tells us about a very young virgin of Mulbarton, who was very religious for her tender age and had a vision of hell and heaven. Guided by a dove, she saw Christ in heaven with Mary at his right hand and, very close to him, a small boy of incomparable beauty whose robes were nearly identical with Christ's in all respects, in color, jewels, and gold, "as if the one garment had been cut from the other." The dove told her that this was William, the blessed martyr of Norwich, slain by the Jews. "Because he truly copied Christ in the passion of his death, Christ did not disdain to make him equal to himself by the honour of his purple robes."[88]

What Thomas of Monmouth heard about William after his

arrival in Norwich excited him to wishful thinking about earth and heaven; and William's image as reflected through Thomas has maintained its power to excite wishful thinking right down to the twentieth century. Modern scholars have been fascinated by the problem of who killed William and have exercised amazing ingenuity to provide a possible solution. But the evidence is so biased and inadequate that they had to rely heavily on assumptions, and they have produced strange and contradictory conjectures which tell us more about their authors than about William's death.[89] Yet if Thomas's *Life* of William will never reveal who killed poor little William, it is rich and rewarding evidence for something much more important, the creation of the crucifixion accusation, for the *Life* was written by the myth's creator.

Notes

1. *The Life and Miracles of St. William of Norwich*, edited with an introduction and translation by Augustus Jessopp and M. R. James (Cambridge, Eng., 1896), cited hereafter as *Life*. When I quote from the *Life*, I will sometimes follow the editors' translation and sometimes use my own. The title in my text is the only one indicated in the manuscript.

2. The dating of the writing of the *Life* is discussed below, pp. 26–28.

3. *The Anglo-Saxon Chronicle*, trans. Dorothy Whitelock (London, 1961), p. 200; and for the date, see p. xvi.

4. For the historiography on the Norwich incident, see my "Historiographic Crucifixion," in *Les Juifs au regard de l'histoire: Mélanges en l'honneur de Bernhard Blumenkranz*, ed. Gilbert Dahan (Paris: Picard, 1985), pp. 109–27, reprinted in Gavin I. Langmuir, *Toward A Definition of Antisemitism* (Berkeley: University of California Press, 1990), pp. 282–98. For a brief overview of the accusations of ritual murder through the centuries, see *Encyclopedia Judaica* (New York, 1971), 4:1120–31. And for an interpretation of the fundamental importance of such mythic charges in the formation of anti-Semitism, see my "Prolegomena to Any Present Analysis of Hostility against Jews," *Social Science Information* 15 (Paris, 1976): 689–727, and "Medieval Anti-Semitism," in *The Holo-*

caust: Ideology, Bureaucracy, and Genocide, ed. Henry Friedlander and Sybil Milton (Millwood, N.Y., 1980), pp. 27–36.

5. *Life*, pp. lxii–lxiv.

6. Menahem Stern, ed., *Greek and Latin Authors on Jews and Judaism*, 2 vols. (Jerusalem, 1974–80): 1:141.

7. Victor Tcherikover, *Hellenistic Civilization and the Jews* (Philadelphia, 1959), pp. 366–67. Tcherikover considers the charge a literary phenomenon, as do E. Mary Smallwood, *The Jews under Roman Rule* (Leiden, 1976), p. 224, and J. N. Sevenster, *The Roots of Pagan Anti-Semitism in the Ancient World* (Leiden, 1975), pp. 140–42.

8. Stern, *Greek and Latin Authors* 1:152–55, 530–31.

9. Ibid. 1:410–12.

10. Heinz Schreckenberg, *Rezeptionsgeschichtliche und textkritische Untersuchungen zu Flavius Josephus* (Leiden, 1977), p. 157.

11. Heinz Schreckenberg, *Die Flavius-Josephus-Tradition in Antike und Mittelalter* (Leiden, 1972), pp. 79–88, 201–3.

12. Schreckenberg, *Rezeptionsgeschichtliche Untersuchungen*, p. 157.

13. Franz Blatt, *The Latin Josephus* (Copenhagen, 1958), 1:26–94, nos. 3, 4, 6, 7, 16–18, 23, 31, 32, 96, 108, 109, 111, 128, 135, 143.

14. Carolus Boysen, *Flavii Iosephi opera ex versione Latina antiqua*, pt. 6, bk. 2, Corpus scriptorum ecclesiasticorum Latinorum 37 (Vienna, 1898; repr. New York, 1964), pp. ii–x, nos. 8, 12, 15, 23, 26.

15. Schreckenberg, *Josephus-Tradition*, pp. 147–49.

16. Ibid., pp. 201–3.

17. Blatt, *Latin Josephus*, p. 90, no. 161.

18. Ibid., pp. 87–94.

19. Boysen, *Flavii Iosephi opera*, p. vii, no. 20; Blatt, *Latin Josephus*, p. 28, no. 4.

20. Boysen, *Flavii Iosephi opera*, pp. viii–viiii, no. 24; Blatt, *Latin Josephus*, p. 29, no. 6.

21. Norman Cohn, *Europe's Inner Demons* (New York, 1975), pp. 19–31.

22. Marcel Simon, *Verus Israel*, 2d ed. (Paris, 1964), p. 160.

23. James Parkes, *The Conflict of the Church and the Synagogue* (New York, 1961), p. 234.

24. Ibid.; Simon, *Verus Israel*, p. 160.

25. Jean Juster, *Les Juifs dans l'Empire romain*, 2 vols. (Paris, 1914), 2:204.

26. Cecil Roth, "The Feast of Purim and the Origins of the Blood

Accusation," *Speculum* 8 (1933): 522; Bernhard Blumenkranz, *Les auteurs chrétiens latins du moyen âge* (Paris, 1963), p. 58.

27. *Historia ecclesiastica tripartita,* ed. Walter Jacob and Rudolph Hanslik, Corpus scriptorum ecclesiasticorum Latinorum 81 (Vienna, 1952), pp. 644–45; Walter Jacob, *Die handschriftliche Überlieferung der sogenannten Historia tripartita des Epiphanius-Cassiodor* (Berlin, 1954), pp. 8–54, esp. nos. 104, 124.

28. *Chronica Sigeberti Gemblacensis,* ed. D. L. C. Bethmann, MGH SS 4:304, 305.

29. *Historia tripartita,* pp. 645–46.

30. *Chronica Sigeberti,* p. 306; *Annales monastici,* ed. H. R. Luard, Rolls Series (London, 1864–69), 2:144.

31. Blumenkranz, *Les auteurs chrétiens.*

32. For background, see *Life,* pp. xix–xxv; M. D. Anderson, *A Saint at Stake: The Strange Death of William of Norwich, 1144* (London, 1964), pp. 25–53; V. D. Lipman, *The Jews of Medieval Norwich* (London, 1967), pp. 3–18.

33. H. A. Cronne, *The Reign of Stephen, 1135–1154* (London, 1970), pp. 149–50.

34. H. G. Richardson, *The English Jewry under Angevin Kings* (London, 1960), pp. 8–9.

35. The evidence for the accusation at Valreas in 1247 is also exceptionally rich.

36. *Life,* pp. 14–16.

37. *Life,* pp. 16–19.

38. *Life,* pp. 31–39. Thomas gives a very unlikely explanation of why Henry of Sprowston did not have the body buried in consecrated ground, but does not even attempt to explain why Godwin did not do it, reporting instead that Godwin, Robert, and Alexander "celebrated the obsequies" on the spot. Godwin later complained to the synod that William had not yet received a Christian burial, but Godwin himself did nothing about it until he decided to accuse Jews formally in public.

39. *Life,* pp. 40–42.

40. *Life,* pp. 43–45.

41. *Life,* p. 46.

42. *Life,* pp. 45–49. Although Thomas alleges (pp. 36–37) that people already suspected the Jews on the Easter weekend and were so angry that they would have attacked the Jews had they not feared the sheriff, the fact that the body was left unburied in the wood throughout the weekend and then buried there makes the assertion completely implausible.

43. *Life*, pp. 49–55.
44. *Life*, pp. 51–53.
45. *Life*, pp. 66–85.
46. *Life*, p. 84.
47. *Life*, pp. 79–85.
48. *Life*, pp. 27–30.
49. *Life*, p. 77.
50. *Life*, pp. 19, 89.
51. *Life*, pp. 89–91.
52. *Life*, p. 94.
53. *Life*, pp. 93–94.
54. "St. William of Norwich," *Jewish Quarterly Review*, o.s., 9 (1897): 752.
55. The fascination of some disturbed Christians with a reenactment of the crucifixion is evident in the case of the youth condemned at the council of Oxford in 1222 for piercing his own hands, feet, and side and giving himself out to be Christ: Ralph of Coggeshall, *Chronicon Anglicanum*, ed. W. Stubbs, Rolls Series (London, 1875), p. 190; see also *Die Exempla aus dem Sermones feriales des Jakub von Vitry*, ed. Joseph Greven (Heidelberg, 1914), no. 44.
56. *Life*, p. 15.
57. *Life*, pp. 23–26.
58. *Life*, pp. 125–26.
59. *Life*, p. 127.
60. *Life*, pp. 128–32.
61. *Life*, p. 131.
62. *Life*, pp. 132–45.
63. *Life*, pp. 165–66.
64. *Life*, pp. 172–74.
65. Ronald C. Finucane, *Miracles and Pilgrims: Popular Beliefs in Medieval England* (Totowa, N.J., 1977), p. 161.
66. *Life*, pp. 185–86.
67. Finucane, *Miracles and Pilgrims*, p. 162.
68. *Life*, pp. 220–22.
69. *Life*, p. liii.
70. *Life*, p. 262.
71. *Life*, pp. 92, 95.
72. *Life*, p. 65.
73. *Life*, p. 57.
74. *Life*, p. 85.
75. *Life*, pp. 46, 48, 49.
76. *Life*, pp. 20–22, 34, 90, 192.

77. Finucane, *Miracles and Pilgrims*, pp. 59–82.

78. *Life*, p. 107.

79. *Life*, pp. 22, 91.

80. *Life*, pp. 85–86.

81. *Life*, pp. 57–65, 85–112.

82. *Life*, p. 95.

83. *Life*, p. 16.

84. Finucane, *Miracles and Pilgrims*, pp. 161–62.

85. Lambert of Waterloo, *Annales Cameracenses*, ed. I. M. Lappenberg, MGH SS 16:536.

86. *The Chronicle of Robert de Torigny*, in *Chronicles of the Reigns of Stephen, Henry II, and Richard I*, ed. R. Howlett, Rolls Series (London, 1889), 4:250–51.

87. Gavin I. Langmuir, "The Knight's Tale of Young Hugh of Lincoln," *Speculum* 47 (1972): 459–82. For an overview of the spread of the accusation, see my "L'absence d'accusation de meurtre rituel à l'ouest du Rhône," *Juifs et judaisme de Languedoc*, ed. M.-H. Vicaire and Bernhard Blumenkranz, Cahiers de Fanjeaux 12 (Toulouse, 1977), pp. 235–49.

88. *Life*, p. 77.

89. See n. 4, above.

Little St. Hugh of Lincoln: Researches in History, Archaeology, and Legend

The case of William of Norwich in 1144 may well have been the first reported instance of ritual murder in England, or anywhere else for that matter, but surely the most famous alleged occurrence of Jewish ritual murder in England is that of Hugh of Lincoln in 1255. One reason for this is that the story was immortalized in ballad form. The ballad entitled "Sir Hugh, or, the Jew's Daughter" is number 155 in the standard canon of English and Scottish ballads compiled by Francis James Child (1825–96). The English and Scottish Popular Ballads *was published from 1882–98.*

The ballad is frequently used as a source for scholars interested in reconstructing the events surrounding the murder of little Hugh. Samples of that scholarship include Francisque Michel, Hugues de Lincoln: Recueil de Ballades Anglo-Normade et Ecossoises Relatives au Meurtre de cet enfant commis par les Juifs en MCCLV *(Paris: Silvestre, 1834); James Orchard Halliwell,* Ballads and Poems respecting Hugh of Lincoln, A Boy alleged to have been murdered by the Jews in the year MCCLV *(Brixton: for private circulation only, 1849), which relies heavily on Michel's 1834 work; Abraham Hume,* Sir Hugh of Lincoln or an Examination of a Curious Tradition respecting the Jews with a notice of the Popular Poetry connected with it *(London: John Russell Smith, 1849); Francis James Child,* The English and Scottish Popular Ballads, *vol. 3 (New York: Cooper Square*

Reprinted from Joseph Jacobs, *Jewish Ideals and Other Essays* (New York: Macmillan, 1896), pp. 192–224.

Publishers, 1962), pp. 233–54; and Gavin I. Langmuir, "The Knight's Tale of Young Hugh of Lincoln," Speculum 47 (1972): 459–82.

Joseph Jacobs (1854–1916) was an active folklorist in England in the last decade of the nineteenth century with a special interest in Jewish folklore. His essay on Little St. Hugh, written in that period, remains one of the most thorough studies of the incident. For more about Jacobs' contributions to folklore, see Brian E. Maidment, "Joseph Jacobs and English Folklore in the 1890s," in Studies in the Cultural Life of the Jews in England, *ed. Dov Noy and Issachar Ben-Ami, Folklore Research Center Studies 5 (Jerusalem: Magnes Press, 1975), pp. 185–96; and Gary Alan Fine, "Joseph Jacobs: A Sociological Folklorist,"* Folklore 98 (1987): *183–93. For a touching personal reminiscence of Jacobs by his daughter, see May Bradshaw Hays, "Memories of My Father, Joseph Jacobs,"* The Horn Book Magazine 28 (1952), *385–92. For other considerations of ritual murder by Jacobs, see "St. William of Norwich,"* Jewish Quarterly Review 9 *(1897): 748–55; and "The Damascus Affair of 1840 and the Jews of America,"* Publications of the American Jewish Historical Society 10 (1902): 119–28, *the latter essay written after he emigrated to the United States.*

> O yonge Hugh of Lincoln, sleyn also
> With cursed Iewes, as it is notable,
> For it nis but a litel whyle ago;
> Pray eek for vs, we sinful folk vnstable
> That of His mercy God so merciable
> On vs His grete mercy multiplye,
> For reuerence of His mooder Marye.
>   Amen.

Thus sings and prays Chaucer at the end of his Prioress's Tale, which is supposed to deal with the *cause célèbre* of Hugh of Lincoln.[1] This is not the fact, since he locates his tale "in Asie in the gret citee." But the invocation to the little Hugh at the end, marked as it is with signs of the most earnest and naïve piety, is even more significant of the general and thorough-going belief in the martyrdom of the little lad of Lincoln. And indeed we know from the widespread and popular ballads devoted to this subject that the case must have made a profound sensation in England, and remained as a standing example in the folk mind of Jewish cruelty and fanaticism. Such a case as this, therefore, well deserves the attention of the Jewish Historical Society of England. We may be tolerably confident at the start of our inquiry that we shall not be so easily convinced of any specific Jewish cruelty and fanaticism in the case. On the other hand, as Englishmen, we shall not be too ready to accuse the Englishmen of the thirteenth century of any deliberate falsification of evidence, or malversation of justice. They were thinking and acting under the prejudices of their time, and it will be part of our inquiry to consider the rise of the said prejudice. Mathematicians are accustomed to speak of "pretty problems" requiring special ingenuity or peculiarly elegant methods for their solution. The history and legend of Hugh of Lincoln presents in this sense to the historian and folklorist a specially "pretty problem." It might indeed be easily made into an object-lesson of the modern methods of research in history, archaeology, and legend.

1

Let us take the facts of the case first; and here we are especially fortunate in having them stated for us as they presented themselves to the mind of the time by Matthew Paris, the greatest historian of medieval England. We cannot start our inquiry better than by giving in English the contents of the Monk Matthew's by no means inelegant Latinity.[2]

OF THE BOY HUGH OF LINCOLN.

This year, about the feast of the apostles Peter and Paul [27 July], the Jews of Lincoln stole a boy called Hugh, who was about eight years old. After shutting him up in a secret cham-

43

ber, where they fed him on milk and other childish food, they
sent to almost all the cities of England in which there were
Jews, and summoned some of their sect from each city to be
present at a sacrifice to take place at Lincoln, in contumely
and insult of Jesus Christ. For, as they said, they had a boy con-
cealed for the purpose of being crucified; so a great number of
them assembled at Lincoln, and then they appointed a Jew of
Lincoln judge, to take the place of Pilate, by whose sentence,
and with the concurrence of all, the boy was subjected to various tortures. They scourged him till the blood flowed, they
crowned him with thorns, mocked him, and spat upon him;
each of them also pierced him with a knife, and they made
him drink gall, and scoffed at him with blasphemous insults,
and kept gnashing their teeth and calling him Jesus, the false
prophet. And after tormenting him in divers ways they crucified him, and pierced him to the heart with a spear. When
the boy was dead, they took the body down from the cross, and
for some reason disembowelled it; it is said for the purpose
of their magic arts. The boy's mother, when her son had been
missing several days, sought for him diligently, and the neighbours told her that they had last seen him playing with some
Jewish boys of his own age, and going into the house of a Jew.
So the mother entered the house suddenly and saw the boy's
body lying in a well; the bailiffs of the city were then cau-
tiously summoned, the body was found and drawn up. It was a
remarkable sight which then presented itself to the people;
the mother's cries and lamentations provoked all the citizens
assembled there to tears. There was present John of Lexington,
a man of learning, wise and prudent, who said, "We have heard
sometimes that Jews have dared to attempt such things in insult of our crucified Lord Jesus Christ"; and then addressing
the Jew whose house the boy had entered whilst at play, and
who, as being for that reason a greater object of suspicion, had
been arrested, "Wretched man, dost thou not know that a
speedy end awaits thee? All the gold in England would not suffice to ransom or save thee. Yet unworthy though thou art, I
will tell thee how thou canst save thy life and limb from destruction. Both of these will I save thee if, without fear or
falsehood, thou wilt expose unto me all that has been done in
this matter." Then the Jew, whose name was Copin, thinking
that he had found a way of escape, answered, "My lord John, if
thou wilt repay my words with deeds, I will show wondrous

things unto thee." Then when John zealously urged and encouraged him, the Jew continued: "What the Christians say is true. Almost every year the Jews crucify a boy in injury and insult to Jesus. But one is not found every year, for they do this privately and in remote and secret places. This boy, whom they call Hugh, our Jews crucified without mercy, and after he was dead, and they wished to hide his corpse, they could not bury or conceal it. (This they wished to do, as the body of an innocent boy was considered useless for augury, which was the reason for disembowelling it.) In the morning, when they thought it was hidden away, the earth vomited and cast it forth, and there it lay unburied on the ground to the horror of the Jews. At length they threw it into a well, but still they could not hide it, for the mother never wearied in her search, and finding the body, informed the bailiffs." The Jew was kept in chains, and the boy given to the canons of Lincoln, who had asked for it, and who, after displaying it to an immense number of people, buried it honourably in the church of Lincoln, as if it had been that of a precious martyr. The king, when he heard what had happened, was angry with John for having promised life and limb to such a wicked being, which he had no right to do; for a blasphemer and murderer such as that man, deserved to die many times over. Then the guilty man said, "My death is imminent, nor can John give me any assistance. I will tell the truth to you all. Nearly all the Jews in England agreed to the death of this boy, and from nearly every English city where Jews live some were chosen to be present at this sacrifice as a Paschal offering." Then he was tied to a horse's tail and dragged to the gallows, where he was delivered body and soul to the cacodoemens of the air. The other Jews who shared in the guilt, to the number of ninety-one, were taken to London, and imprisoned there; and if any Christians pitied them, they were only dry tears which their rivals the Caursines shed.

OF A CERTAIN SCANDAL WHICH AROSE IN LONDON AGAINST THE FRANCISCANS ALTHOUGH THEY WERE INNOCENT.

At the same time certain Jews notorious for the strange death of a boy crucified by them at Lincoln, having been condemned to imprisonment and death on the oaths of twenty-five knights, seventy-one of them were being kept in the Tower of London, and were about to be hanged. But they sent secret messengers to the Franciscans, as the rivals of these latter affirm, that they might intercede for them and rescue them from death and imprisonment, though they deserved a most dishonourable death. And they indeed did rescue those Jews by their prayers and intercessions from the imprisonment and death which they merited, being induced thereto by their money, as all the world believed, if the world can be believed in such a case, or rather, as I prefer to believe, led by a spirit of piety; since as long as any one is on earth because he has free will he can be saved and there is hope for him, but for the devil and the manifestly damned one must not either hope or pray because there is no hope for them; for death and an unavoidable sentence has once for all irrevocably ensnared them. But the above scandal besmirched them although they were innocent. But the common people did not help them as before in their alms, but withheld their hand from them.

JEWS ARE SET FREE WHO WERE DETAINED IN THE TOWER OF LONDON.

The same year, on the Ides of May, ninety-one Jews were set free from the Tower of London who were kept there as criminals, bound hand and foot, for the crucifixion of St. Hugh, the boy of Lincoln. These Jews, I say, were guilty by the assertion of a Jew who had been hanged at Lincoln in the first instance.

In this account it will be seen that all turns on the evidence of Copin, Jew of Lincoln. It was his evidence that gave to the case the character of a ritual murder connived at by all the Jews of England. It is clear that his evidence was, in the first instance, extorted from him by the unveiled threats of John of Lexington. It was Sir John who first suggested that the little boy's body, found in the pit, had been murdered; for all the evidence we have before us the whole case might be one of accident. It was John of Lexington who started the idea that it was a case of mock crucifixion. It may be said at once, as a key to the whole history, that it was the confirmed and prejudiced belief of all England in the practice of mock crucifixion by the Jews that gave rise to the belief in the "martyrdom" of little St. Hugh. We must first trace this belief to its source before proceeding further. England, I regret to say, is the source and origin of the myth concerning the practice of ritual murder of young children by Jews in contempt and derision of crucifixion.[3]

The myth first arose in connection with the death or murder of the boy William of Norwich in 1144. It sprung fully armed from the vile imagination of an apostate Jew of Cambridge, named after his conversion Theobald.[4] He, for reasons which we are at present unable to penetrate, first suggested that Jews were in the habit of sacrificing little children to gratify their hatred of the Christian religion. He seems to have implicated the Jews of the whole world in the crime, since he suggested that lots were cast each year in Europe as to the place in which the next sacrifice should take place. Thus he asserted that the "martyrdom" of William at Norwich had been fixed upon at a council of Jews in Narbonne. Incalculable has been the mischief which Theobald's accused lies have inflicted upon the Jews. They were published and obtained credence throughout Europe just at the time of the second crusade, when men's religious passions were aroused to fanatical fury, and Jews fell martyrs all along the track of the Crusaders. Ever since his time, whenever a little child has been missing about the Passover, near a Jewish quarter in Europe, it has been but a chance if the terrible suspicion of ritual murder has not again been raised.

I have been surprised to find in conversation with Christian friends, who have not the slightest taint of anti-Semitism, how general is the impression that there must be something at the bottom of all these charges, and perhaps for their sakes it may be desirable to point out how impossible it is for Jews as Jews to use human blood or human sacrifices in any way as a part of their religious rites. In the first place, contact with a corpse renders a Jew impure from that moment, and incapable of performing any religious rite whatever till he has been purified. For eating any blood or anything compounded with blood there is the stringent Biblical prohibition (Lev. 17.14): "Ye shall eat the blood of no manner of flesh: for the life of all flesh is the blood thereof: whosoever eateth it shall be cut off." Besides this, human sacrifice has been unknown in Israel since at least the time of the Judges, and the Levitical legislation restricted sacrifices of any kind whatever to the Temple. Since the destruction of the Temple, therefore, no sacrifice has been performed by Jews, except by the Samaritans, who still keep up the Paschal sacrifice to the present day. With the fall of Jerusalem the Rabbis laid down the fine principle that Prayer has replaced Sacrifice. From all this it is obvious that no Jews who believe in the Bible or follow the precepts of the Rabbis would ever think of sacrificing even an animal as part of a ceremony which they could consider pleasing to God.

But, my friends rejoin, may it not be possible that some secret sect of Jews exist who disagree with the general opinions of their fellows, and believe in the efficacy of human sacrifice? It is impossible that such a sect should exist without having left some trace of their existence in the vast literature of the Jews. This has been searched by the bitterest enemies of the Jews in the hope of finding some such evidence, but in vain.[5] That some Jews may have been murderers of little children during the long course of Jewish history, no one for a moment would deny; but that they did so for any religious reason, there is absolutely not a vestige of evidence to show, except the "confessions" of Jews extracted under torture, and the original assertion of the renegade Theobald, with whom the whole story arises. There remained only the possibility of certain Jews having indulged in these crimes for magical purposes, but if they did so they must have learnt their magic elsewhere than from Judaism, and were equally bad Jews as they were cruel and wicked men. Similar charges have been brought against all peoples who have incurred the distrust or hatred of their fellow men. They were brought against the early Christians, against the Cavaliers, against the Templars, against the Franciscans. A writer named Daumer has written a book, *Geheimnisse des christlichen Alterthums* (Hamburg, 1847), to prove that the characteristic of the Christian religion, from its origin to the end of the Middle Ages, consisted in human sacrifice and cannibalism, and the use of human blood. When Thackeray came over from India, Napoleon was shown to him at St.

Helena; he was told: "That is Bonaparte; he eats three sheep every day and all the little children he can put his hands on." The moment a myth of that kind arises, who can tell to what length it will be carried?

At Gloucester, in 1168, the disappearance of the boy Harold was attributed to the guile of the Jews.[6] At Bury St. Edmunds, in 1181, the little boy Robert was made into a martyr by the same prejudice;[7] and these seeming confirmations of the myth must have deepened the conviction of England as to its truth. We can see in the case of Hugh how the very existence of the myth would lead to further complications of it. The moment the little lad's corpse is found, without any inquiry as to whether the death had not been the result of accident, the legend of ritual murder by the Jews immediately occurs to men's minds, and John of Lexington gives voice to the suspicion by recalling the myth to the memory of his hearers. Mark what he does next without any further inquiry. Trusting practically to the truth of the myth, the Jew in whose house, or probably courtyard, the boy had last been seen to enter is taken into custody and threatened that unless he tells the truth he will be torn to pieces. The "truth" he tells is filled with a mass of impossibilities. The body of the boy, according to his account, was supernaturally endowed with a capacity for escaping from concealment. Buried in the earth, it rises to its surface again. There is one further touch which connects the whole incident with another set of legends connecting this disappearance of children with practices of Jewish magic. Copin asserts that the entrails of the lad had been removed for purposes of "augury." This is again an English tradition, for in 1222 a deacon of the English Church was executed on the charge of having been converted to Judaism, and having been *particeps criminis* in the evisceration of a Christian lad for magical purposes.[8] It would seem as if the accusers of the Jews had a second string to their bow; if they could not prove them guilty of crucifixion, they would attempt to convict them upon an equally terrible charge of magic by evisceration.

How far the confirmation by Copin of these charges was the result of a mixture of leading questions and violent threats by John of Lexington we are unable to determine from Matthew Paris's rather confused account. Nor does he tell us from what source was derived the further piece of evidence, that the Jews had kept and tortured Hugh ten days before his crucifixion. As to the later evidence of Copin, implicating the whole of the Jews of England in the charge, even Matthew Paris calls this his ravings ("deliramenta"). I fancy there was more method in Copin's madness than might at first sight appear. It was his last frantic effort to get his doom postponed. If he could implicate the whole of the Jews in his guilt, or in the charge with himself, he might hope to be kept alive as the chief witness while a long and protracted inquiry into the matter was being made. The whole of the Jewish influence would also be enlisted on his side by his perfidious trick. Perhaps I am doing poor Copin an injustice, and his motives were less profound and sinister than I have suggested. He may have been literally driven mad by fear. Both his original charge and his final reiteration of it have been but the delirious ravings of a lunatic. Indeed, Matthew Paris, by calling them "deliramenta," seems to favor this interpretation of Copin's action.

There can be little doubt, however, that some confession of some kind must have been extorted, for it is referred to in another contemporary account in the annals of the abbey of Burton-on-Trent.[9] This differs in several respects from Matthew Paris's account, and on the whole must be regarded as the superior authority. The boy is kept alive for twenty-six, instead of ten, days, with nothing to eat, instead of being pampered on milk food. His death is decreed by a council of Jews, who cut off his nose and crucified him. Suspicion is aroused against the Jews by the large number who had assembled at Lincoln under pretext of attending a grand wedding. The mother starts off to Scotland to petition the king for an inquisition, and the Jews then throw the body into a well. When it is drawn out a blind woman touches it with her hands, and says, "Sweet little Hugh, alas! that so it happened," and rubbed her eyes with the moisture of the body. By this means she recovered her sight. Thereupon the corpse is carried to the Minister, notwithstanding the protests of the parish priest, who would have liked to obtain the great prize of a boy martyr for his own church. The king then arrives at Lincoln and investigates the charges, and orders the Jews to be arrested. Thereupon a riot occurs, and the houses of the Jews are stormed. As in Matthew Paris, John of Lexington promises life to Copin, "the head of the Jews, and their priest," if he confesses—which he does, but fails to save his life. Eighteen more were hanged at London, though the Dominicans (not the Franciscans) tried to save them. Seventy-one others, the richest Jews of the land, were saved by Richard of Cornwall.

2

So far we have treated the subject entirely from the point of view of the materials offered us by the historians. The science of history has nowadays more means at its command for arriving at the truth than its artistic presentment as given by contemporary historians. In England especially we have almost from the earliest times contemporary records of the Kings' Courts and Chancery with regard to such charges as these. When I first commenced my inquiries into this subject, I was hoping that among the mass of records preserved in Fetter Lane we should be able to come across the official account of the trial of the Jews for the murder of Hugh of Lincoln. For days and days I have searched the records with this hope. I have found much bearing upon the externalities of the trial, but I regret to say have failed to find the record of the trial itself. The records of the king's jurisdiction in Henry III are still preserved in tolerable fulness. The trial at Lincoln, if there was a trial, must have occurred somewhere about September 1255, in the thirty-ninth year of the king's reign, as we have just heard from the historian, and shall find confirmed by the records I have discovered. A further trial seems to have taken place in London, at the Tower, in November of the same year—i.e., in the fortieth year of the reign. I have, therefore, looked through the Assize Rolls of the Justices Errant in Lincoln, 39 Hen. III, and for

51

the Tower Assize Rolls for 40 Hen. III; but unfortunately neither of these contain any reference to the *cause célèbre* of the year. I imagine that the record of the Lincoln trial must have been sent up to London for use in the trial at the Tower, and that both that and the record of the London trial and verdict were kept together in a special Roll which has disappeared.

We must, therefore, be content with a few items which occur in the various classes of Rolls. Thus we can trace the journey of the Jews from Lincoln to London by three entries on the Close Roll of 39 Hen. III. The first of these orders the Constable of Lincoln Castle to deliver the Jews accused of the crucifixion to the Sheriff of Lincoln, in order that he may bring them to Westminster.[10] The others give orders to the Sheriffs of Huntingdon and Hertford to assist him of Lincoln on his way through their counties. These are dated 14 October.[11] We then learn from the legal annals of London that on the Feast of St. Cecilia—i.e., 22 November—the Jews, then imprisoned in the Tower, had been brought to the number of ninety-two before the king at Westminster, and eighteen of them had refused to submit themselves to the verdict of a Christian jury unless there were Jews upon it.[12] These eighteen were indicted before the king, and condemned and executed before the close of the day. Doubtless this condemnation and execution were legal according to the law of the time, which regarded refusal to plead as a confession of guilt. But it was obviously unfair to press this on the present occasion without at least change of venue, and especially when the charge was practically one of conspiracy, notoriously one of the most difficult to prove. This was a severe lesson for the remaining seventy-four, who, as we shall see, were prepared to submit their case to a Lincoln jury, notwithstanding the obvious prejudices which existed against them in the county. On 7 January 1256 the king sends a royal letter to the Sheriff of Lincoln stating that a certain number of Jews had thrown themselves upon the county to take their trial for the alleged murder of Hugh, son of Beatrice.[13] To my mind this is conclusive evidence against their guilt. We have no record of the proceedings taken at

Lincoln; but two months afterwards, on 12 March, they were released from the Tower, as we learn from Matthew Paris, who attributes their release to the Franciscans, while the Annals of Burton credit the Dominicans with having brought about this act of mercy or of justice.[14] Whether they were all released on that date is somewhat doubtful; for even two years later I find on the Close Rolls an entry commanding the Constable of the Tower and other officials to release all the Jews in their custody, and on the same occasion Haggin and Cresse, Jews of Lincoln, are commanded to make no distress on the Jews till further orders.[15] But to go back to our records for the year 1256, we now come upon several that begin to throw some light on the action of the king in this matter. At the end of May of that year the king orders an inquisition to be made into the value of the houses of the Jews who had been hanged for the crucifixion of Hugh.[16] He had previously ordered the chest of the cyrographers of the Jews of Lincoln to be sent up to Westminster, obviously for the purpose of ascertaining what debts had been due to the condemned Jews, and claiming them for his own.[17] About the same time there is also a significant entry as to a local inquiry to be made as to what Jews were "of the school of Peitevin the Great, who fled for the death of the aforesaid boy."[18] We shall meet with this Peitevin again, but meanwhile I would draw attention to the evidence here given of the existence of a regular school at Lincoln at this date. As it is obviously implied that the scholars might possibly be implicated in the death of Hugh, it would seem that this school was grown-up people, and was a sort of Jews' College, or Beth Hamidrash, of the period.

But to return to the king's plunder. As the result of the inquisition of May, the king ordered the houses of Lincoln Jews in London and elsewhere to be sold on 20 August,[19] while he made his profit even out of those that were not sold by claiming fines from those renting the houses. By this means we learn, from entries in the Fine Rolls, the names of five Jews who had been the victims of the terrible prejudices of the times. These are: Elyas fil. Jacob, Isaac fil. Jude de Ballio, Deulacres de Bedford, Samuel gener Leonis, and Sampson Levy.[20] A son of the last-named is mentioned in the *Shetaroth* published by Mr. M. D. Davis.[21]

To understand what all this means we must go back a little. The king had been fleecing his Jews so unmercifully that only fifteen months before the alleged martyrdom Elyas of London, the Arch-Presbyter of the Jews of all England, had in an indignant speech asked permission for them to leave England and find a dwelling with some prince who had bowels of compassion.[22] Next year, in February 1255, they repeated their request in more pressing and indignant terms.[23] This the king refused, but at that date sold all his rights to his brother Richard in consideration of a sum of five thousand marks.[24] In other words, just at the time when the accusation is raised at Lincoln against the Jews the king, by his agreement with his brother Richard, had no right to extract any money from them except by escheat from condemned criminals. We can now understand his annoyance with John of Lexington for letting his prey out of his hands, and the reasons for his taking up the case again after it had been dropped by the local courts. Henry, like most weak princes, was cruel to the Jews; his conduct towards them aroused the compassion of even Matthew. Even his very religiousness would predispose to believe aught of ill from the murderers of Christ. There is no doubt that he approached the case prejudiced doubly by personal interest and religious prejudice, even if both motives were unconscious.

You begin to see how vitally important it would be for the king to make out of the disappearance of the boy Hugh a concerted plan of all the Jews, and especially of all the richest Jews of England, to commit a vile and sacrilegious felony. If it had been merely a case of a murder by a single Jew, the king's interest would be confined to the estate of a single individual; but if by any means it could be shown that it was a conspiracy of all the Jews, the king would once more get a terrible hold of them and their purses. His plan was perfectly successful; not alone did he obtain the estates of the eighteen Jews who were hanged, but there can be little doubt that he received ample compensation for the pardon of the rest. I deduce this from the fact that while the Franciscans and Dominicans, who could only appeal to his conscience or his mercy, were unsuccessful in obtaining "pardon" for the Jews, this was granted them at the request of Earl Richard, who had the control of the purse of the whole Jewry. Thus a close scrutiny of the historical records, if it does not altogether clear up the mystery of little Hugh's death or disappearance, at least enables us to penetrate to the motives which raised it into a martyrdom, and implicated all the Jews of England in the alleged sacrilegious crime.

It is worthwhile inquiring at this point what foundation there was for the statement that most of the Jews of England had collected together at Lincoln at this time under the pretext of celebrating a marriage. It was this fact, combined with Copin's confession, which lent color to the supposition that the death of little Hugh partook of the character of a ritual murder. I think I can suggest an appropriate occasion for such a gathering at such time. Sixteen years later, in 1271, we find a deed—perhaps the most interesting one in Mr. Davis's book [25]—in which Belleassez, daughter of the Rav Berachyah ben Rav Moshe, betroths her daughter, Judith, to a young man in Lincoln, the marriage to take place in four years' time, showing that little Judith was not yet of marriageable age, and that her mother, Belleassez, was still a comparatively young woman. I suggest that it was to attend Belleassez' marriage that the chief Jews of England were in Lincoln at the end of August 1255.

For her father, Rav Berachyah, was by far the greatest Jewish scholar living in England at the time of the tragedy. He is frequently mentioned in the tosaphists and halachic works [26] with great respect as Berachyah of Nicoll or Lincoln. He was in some way connected with the trial, for there is in Rymer's *Foedera* a document dated 7 January 1256, releasing Magister Benedict fil. Mosse de Londres from the Tower, and declaring his innocence of the alleged crucifixion. [27] If he could account for the festivities in his house as the accompaniment of his daughter's marriage, the suspicion which might attach to the rest who had traveled to attend the marriage did not apply to him, and he was accordingly released two months before the rest.

I think, too, I can suggest where the marriage of Belleassez took place. The Jews' House in Lincoln, at the bottom of the steep hill, is associated with the name of Bellaset of Walling-ford, and it has already been suggested by Canon Venables of Lincoln[28] that she is identical with Belleassez, daughter of Rav Berachyah. It was probably Berachyah's house at the time, and became part of Belleassez's dower, or was left to her at her father's death. It would accordingly be at this house—the finest private residence of its period still extant in England[29]—that the chief Jews of England assembled to do honor to their greatest scholar, and their rejoicings were turned to tragic dismay by the discovery of little Hugh's remains.

So much for what history has to say or conjecture as to the fate of Hugh of Lincoln, and the still worse fate of the Jews accused of his death. Let us, if we can, obtain any further light from that handmaid to history, archaeology, which deals with the physical remains of man's activity upon the earth. Can we, for example, find any signs of the existence of Hugh? For it by no means follows that in a medieval case of this kind, when a Jew was accused of murder, there should necessarily exist anybody who had been murdered. The late M. Isidore Loeb, whose loss for Jewish history is almost irre-parable, studied carefully a Spanish case very analogous to that of Hugh of Lincoln.[30] When I was at Toledo I was struck with a fresco on the cathedral walls, which I was informed dealt with the fate of El Niño de la Guardia. The picture rep-resented a little lad transfixed on a cross, and around him a crowd of scoffing Jews. Well, M. Loeb went carefully into this case, of which the records are very voluminous and de-tailed, giving an account of the torment and punishment of several open and secret Jews who were implicated in the so-called crime. He came to the conclusion, for which he gives well-founded reasons, that the little lad of la Guardia never existed at all, and that the Jews were accused and punished for the murder of a nonexistent corpse.[31] Can this possibly have been the case with Hugh of Lincoln? and can English justice in the thirteenth century have been so hasty and un-

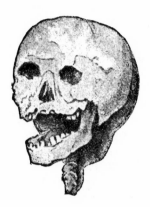

Stone coffin and skeleton, apparently of St. Hugh

just as to punish for crimes without any evidence of a *corpus delicti*? Here archaeology comes to our aid, and enables us after a lapse of 650 years to state that little Hugh of Lincoln was a lad of about four feet two inches high, and therefore well grown for his age of eight; that his face was round rather than long; and that if any violence was done to him, at least none of his bones were broken. You may perhaps wonder by what magic archaeology can use a time telescope of this description. The answer is very simple. In 1791 some repairs were being made at Lincoln Cathedral, and beneath a shrine

57

which had always been traditionally connected with the boy Hugh was found a stone coffin containing a skeleton which was obviously that of a lad, and which, there was no reason for doubting, was actually that of St. Hugh.[32] When these bones were thus exhumed, there happened to be visiting in Lincoln an artist named Grimm, who took very thorough and accurate drawings of the stone coffin and its contents for Bishop Kaye, who then held the see of Lincoln. Kaye's topographical collections ultimately came into possession of the British Museum, which attracts such things to itself like the magnetic mountain of Sindbad.[33]

During my researches in connection with the Anglo-Jewish Historical Exhibition of 1887 I came across these drawings, and thus found that we are practically able to see with our own eyes the actual bones of the little martyr. But dead men tell no tales, and dry bones cannot speak. Though this find of mine is of interest, even if the interest be perhaps a somewhat gruesome one, it still fails to solve the question of the guilt or otherwise of the Jews.

It was indeed stated at the time of their discovery that no dust was found in the coffin, therefore the story of the evisceration of the little lad was thereby confirmed. But this is a somewhat imaginative inference from the facts of the case. The bones, at any rate, were intact. No very extreme violence could have been used to the boy; but whether he died by accident or by malice, by cruelty or by chance, archaeology telleth not.

There is one part of archaeology which is nowadays being more and more utilised for the purposes of historic elucidation. The study of topography is more and more resorted to in order to throw light on problems like that presented by the disappearance of little St. Hugh. In his case, as we shall see, a study of the Lincoln Jewry is absolutely necessary for solution of the problem presented by his death. The following plan of the neighborhood of the Steep Hill of Lincoln, near which the Jews most did congregate in early days, will place the reader in a position to realize the locality of Hugh's death.

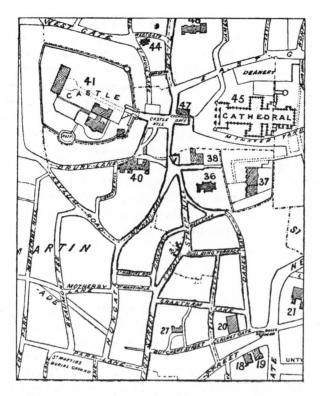

The Jewish Quarter, Lincoln. Numbered locations include the following:
1) Aaron of Lincoln's house   36) St. Michael's
2) Jopin's house   37) Bishop's palace
3) Bellaset's house   40) Bishop's hostel

The ancient Jewry of Lincoln ranged from Aaron of Lincoln's House at the top of the Steep Hill to the end of the Straight, just where it enters High Street; in earlier days there was a gate here known as St. Dunstan's Lock, but previously as Dernestall's Lock: it was through this lock, tradition states, that little Hugh went on to his doom. As you may see from the plan, he had not far to go. Midway up the Straight, on the left-hand side, are the three houses which local tradition associates with the early Jews of Lincoln.

The open space at the junction of the Straight and the Steep Hill was, there can be little doubt, the scene of the tragedy. Nearly opposite Bull Ring Terrace, so named from the bull-baiting that used to take place in the open space at the end of it, is the Jews' House associated with the name of Bellaset of Wallingford. This is on the left-hand side of the Steep Hill, going up; next door to this, higher up, is a house which, Mr. Haes informs me, is said by popular tradition to have been the old Jewish Synagogue. By this is a lane still called Jews' Court, and the next house is still pointed to as the place where little Hugh met his fate: in this house there still exists a pit or well which was pointed out to Mr. Haes as the very spot where the boy's remains were cast. Here archaeology passes over into tradition.

3

Where history, the written record, and archaeology, the physical remains of man's activity, fail to give a clue, legend, the oral tradition of men's memories from age to age and generation to generation, may possibly come to our aid. I have already pointed out that the legend of William of Norwich and the superstition as to the use of human entrails for the purposes of augury by Jews have exercised a shaping influence on the story of St. Hugh from the day his remains were discovered. Besides this, in the case of our little martyr, we are somewhat amply provided with remains of popular tradition of the so-called "martyrdom." There is one French and there are several English and Scotch ballads devoted to the subject. Let us see what contribution they can make to the elucidation of the problem.

The French ballad was published in 1834 by M. Francisque Michel,[34] from a manuscript in the Bibliothèque Nationale. From its diction and meter it was clearly written within a very few years of the martyrdom. It tells how in Nicole, that rich city, the boy Huchon was inveigled away by Peitevin, the Jew, on the eve of the gules of August. His mother sought in vain for him throughout the whole Jewry, and then betook herself to Henry the King, to call for justice on the wicked Jews. This he promises her, but threatens vengeance if her accusation prove untrue. Meanwhile, the richest Jews of England collected together, and the boy was brought before them, bound by a cord, by Jopin, the Jew, who offers him for thirty deniers. Agim, the Jew, buys him for that price from the new Judas, and the boy is then crucified. And when he expires, after being pierced by the knife of Agim, "the dear soul of this infant was borne at once by angels in heaven, chanting together before God all-powerful." The body is buried, but next morning is found again by the Jews upon the surface of the earth, and wherever they attempt to conceal it, it persists in rising to the surface—a fine imaginative touch of the folk artist who wrote the ballad. They then determine to take it outside Lincoln and place it near a fountain in the neighborhood. A woman finds it next day and raises the alarm. The body is borne back to Dernestal, the quarter where his mother lived. Then a convert comes along, and seeing the body all besmudged with mire and ordure, suggests that it should be washed with warm water: "I trow that thus we'll find how the child came to his death." Then became evident the treason of the Jews. The body is borne to the cathedral, and the Jews captured, who say, "We have been betrayed by Falsim." Then comes Jopin, the Jew, who tells again in ballad fashion the same story, with the addition that all the Jews of England knew of the crucifixion, and had decided upon it in common council. For all reward for his confession, Jopin is condemned to be torn to pieces by horses. And they hung him at Canewick, a mile south of Lincoln town.

In this ballad we get in very vivid form the popular account of the martyrdom which has much in common with that represented by Matthew Paris, though Copin here becomes Jopin. We get two other names of Jews concerned in the misdeed, Peitevin and Agim, which is obviously the English form of Chayim. You may remember that I have shown some years ago that Huggin Lane, in the City of London, derives its name from a London Jew of the same prenomen.[35] I think I can identify from Hebrew records both these new personages. In an undated deed, published by Mr. Davis in his volume of *Shetaroth,* no. 167, page 309, the Jewish creditor of the abbey of Bardeney signs himself Peitevin ben Beneit; and as the deed is also signed by Benedict fil. Mosse, who, as we have seen above, was implicated in the martyrdom, and declared innocent by the king, the deed must be about the date of the martyrdom, and the signatory can therefore be identified with the Peitevin mentioned in the French ballad. So, too, in another deed, published by Mr. Davis, no. 155, the signature occurs of Chayim de Nicole, who is equally obviously the original of the Agim of the French ballad.[36] Who Falsim, the convert who betrayed the Jews, was, cannot be at present ascertained.

It is, at any rate, a curious incident that among the Jews imprisoned in the Tower for this crime there was a convert named John, who was pardoned for his share in it, as we learn from Rymer's *Foedera.*[37] Here, again, we find the sinister presence of a renegade from the faith, always a sign of ill omen in cases of this kind.

Besides this contemporary French ballad there are, as you are doubtless aware, a number of English and Scotch ballads dealing with the legend of St. Hugh. Here the scene is altogether changed, and the historic background fades into the far distance as we can well understand from the late date in which the ballads were collected, none of them being earlier than the last century. Professor Child, in his magnificent work on the English and Scotch ballads,[38] has collected together no less than eighteen versions of it, but decides for the priority of that collected by Jamieson. In this there is no question of conspiracy of the Jews of England; the tragic interest is deepened by making the crime the work of a female hand.[39] The Jew's daughter entices little Hugh from his game of football with the allurement of an apple, and leads him through nine dark doors, lays him on a dressing-table, and sticks him like a swine.[40] She then rolls him in lead and casts him into our Lady's draw well, fifty fathoms deep. We then follow the fortunes of the poor little lad's mother.

When the bells were rung, and mass was sung,
  And a' the bairns came hame,
When every lady gat hame her son,
  The Lady Maisry gat nane.

She searches for him at the Jews' castell, at the Jews' Garden, and at last at the deep draw well; and at each place she cries—

"Gin ye be there, my sweet Sir Hugh,
  I pray you to me speak."
"Gae hame, gae hame, my mither dear,
  Prepare my winding sheet;
And, at the back o' merry Lincoln,
  The morn I will you meet."
Now Lady Maisry is gane hame—
  Made him a winding sheet;
And at the back o' merry Lincoln,
  The dead corpse did her meet.
And a' the bells o' merry Lincoln,
  Without men's hands were rung;
And a' the books o' merry Lincoln,
  Were read without man's tongue;
And ne'er was such a burial
  Sin Adam's days begun.

That fine touch of the supernatural ringing of the church bells is only found in Jamieson's version. But fine as it is, the ballad has little instruction to give us on the death of little Hugh, and might celebrate any murder of any child by any wicked woman. Indeed, Mr. Newell, an American folklorist, found in the streets of New York a version crooned by a little negress in which the tale is told of Harry Hughes and the Duke's daughter.[41] Thus the prejudices of the Middle Ages have begun to die away even in the memory of the folk. In Lincoln itself, however, the myth is still alive, and inhabitants of that city pointed out to Mr. Haes, after the lapse of 650 years, the very well adjoining Jews' Court into which poor little Hugh was thrown. Other traditions, however, identify it with Grantham's well, outside the old walls of Lincoln.

4

We have now before us all the materials which history, archaeology, and tradition can afford us with regard to the death of the poor little Lincoln lad of the thirteenth century. Do they enable us to arrive at the exact truth of the matter? I fancy they do, and would put forth the following hypothetical account—imaginative, I grant, but I trust not altogether imaginary—of what happened at Lincoln during the month of August 1255. On the eve of first day of that month,[42] a Saturday afternoon, a little boy Hugh, son of a widow named Beatrice,[43] aged eight years,[44] while running after a ball at play[45] fell by accident into a gong or cesspool[46] attached to the house of a Jew named Jopin,[47] or Joscefin,[48] two doors off the Jews House at Lincoln.[49] His body remained in this gong for some twenty-six days[50] subject to the disintegrating forces of its nauseous contents. Meanwhile there had assembled at Lincoln a number of the most important Jews of England[51] in order to attend the wedding[52] of Belleassez, daughter of the Rav, or Chief Rabbi of the town,[53] known to his Christian fellow citizens as Magister Benedict fil. Mosse de Londres,[54] and to his Jewish flock as Rav Berachyah ben Moses,[55] known also in Jewish literature as Berachyah de Nicole, an important tosaphist.[56] He was the greatest Jewish scholar of his time in England,[57] and to do honor to him most of the chief Jews of England attended the wedding. In the midst of their festivities their joy was turned to horror and dismay by the discovery on Thursday, 26 August,[58] probably the day after the wedding,[59] of the disfigured body of little Hugh, distended by the gases of corruption, which had risen to the surface of the gong.[60] We can imagine the horror of the party when Joscefin, the father-in-law of the bride,[61] broke in upon the company assembled two doors off[62] with the news of the ghastly discovery. The corruption of the body burst the walls of the stomach as soon as an attempt was made to remove it,[63] and the entrails were dissevered from the body.[64] Instead of announcing the discovery to the proper officials, the Jews, on the advice of Peitevin,[65] the Dayan[66] and Hagin,[67] committed the fatal error[68] of attempting to conceal the body, or, at any rate, of removing it from the neighborhood of the Jewry.[69] They cast it into Grantham's well,[70] where it was discovered after three days, on Sunday, 29 August,[71] by a woman passing by.[72] Among the crowd attracted by the discovery was one John of Lexington,[73] who was familiar, from tradition and his reading,[74] with the myth about the ritual murder of boys by Jews. As one of the canons of the Minster[75] he saw the desirability of claiming the body as a further attraction for the cathedral,[76] and his plan was assisted by the seeming miracle by which a woman in the crowd removed some obstruction to her eyesight[77] by wiping them with some of the moisture exuding from Hugh's body.[78] The parish priest attempted to compete with him for the possession of the precious charge, but the superior authority of Lexington overcame his protests.[79] In a grand procession, grander than Lincoln ever yet had seen,[80] the remains of little Hugh were transferred to a stone coffin in the South Aisle Choir,[81] in which they remain undisturbed for over five hundred years.[82]

Meanwhile Lexington had, by combined threats and promises,[83] induced Jopin to make such a confession[84] of the complicity of the Jews as could be twisted into evidence for making the boy a martyr of the faith.[85] Here he was content to rest,[86] having obtained for his cathedral an equal attraction to those of Norwich and Gloucester and the abbey of Edmondsbury.[87] But Beatrice, the mother of the poor little lad, was not content with this,[88] and hearing that the king was approaching Lincoln on his way from Scotland,[89] went out to meet him, and laid the case before him.

Henry III hated the Jews, while making use of them as sponges to replete his treasury. He had but six months before[90] lost his power over them by selling them to his brother Richard. Here he saw his chance of both gratifying his hatred and replenishing his treasury. He hurried to Lincoln, seized all the Jews he could find there,[91] and silenced the only witness who could declare the truth by hanging Jopin, after having caused him to be dragged round the city tied to the tail of a wild horse.[92] He brought the rest of the Jews up to London,[93] hanged those who refused to trust themselves to the tender mercies of a Christian jury,[94] holding its sitting in Lincoln, now all aflame with infuriated passions,[95] and only released the remainder after they had been imprisoned six months,[96] when the term of his agreement with Earl Richard was over and he had them again at his mercy.[97] The Franciscans, who constituted the noblest element in English life at the time, were on the side of the Jews—significant testimony to their innocence—but pleaded for them in vain.[98] The protracted nature of the inquiry, the severest punishment of the victim, the wide publicity given to the accusation, caused the martyrdom of Hugh and the cruelty of the Jews to become a fixed element of belief in the popular mind of England, which has retained the memory of the boy martyr down to the present day. It was a tale above all others likely to touch the tender human soul of Chaucer, and caused him to give utterance to the prayer with which I commenced this paper, in which I have endeavored to put together, for the first time, into a consistent narrative, all the scattered evidence which history, archaeology, and tradition give as to the fate of little St. Hugh of Lincoln, boy and martyr.

Notes

1. The boy martyr is called little St. Hugh to distinguish him from great St. Hugh of Lincoln, the bishop of that see, who died in 1200, and was curiously enough a friend of the Jews (see Joseph Jacobs, *The Jews of Angevin England* [London: D. Nutt, 1893] p. 207).

2. Matthew Paris, *Historia Major*, ed. Luard (Rolls Series), 5: 516–18, 522, 543 (?). [In an earlier version of his paper, Jacobs included an appendix which contained many of the original documents upon which his research was based, e.g., Matthew Paris's account in Latin. See "Little St. Hugh of Lincoln," *Transactions of the Jewish Historical Society of England* 1 (1893–94): 89–135. The appendices appear on pp. 115–135.—Ed.]

3. I speak here, of course, of the "blood accusation" in its modern form. There was no popular belief in it till after the case of William of Norwich. It is referred to as "fama communis" in 1236

(Strack, *Der Blutaberglaube*, p. 154; see n. 5, below). It is necessary to emphasize this, as the *Athenœum*, in reviewing an earlier form of this paper, referred to the murder of a child by some drunken Jews, mentioned by Socrates, the ecclesiastic historian, as the origin of the myth. But a myth must live in the minds of men, and there is no evidence of such a belief till after the case of William of Norwich.

4. We are still awaiting the full account of the martyrdom of William of Norwich by Thomas of Monmouth. Short abstracts are given in Jacobs, *The Jews of Angevin England*, pp. 256–58, and Augustus Jessopp, *The Nineteenth Century* (May 1893).

5. On the whole subject see the admirable monograph of Professor Strack, Protestant Professor of Theology at the University of Berlin, and the leading Conversionist of Germany, *Der Blutaberglaube*, 4th ed. (Munich, 1892).

6. Jacobs, *The Jews of Angevin England*, pp. 45–47.

7. Ibid., p. 75.

8. Paris, *Historia Major* 3:71.

9. *Annales Monastici*, ed. Luard (Roll Series), 1:340, *seq.* There is another and shorter account in the "Annals of Waverley," ibid., 2:346. This adds the trait that the body was thrown into a drinking-well.

10. Close Roll, 39 Hen. III, m. 2.

11. Ibid., m. 2.

12. *Liber de Antiquis Legibus* (Cam. Soc.), p. 23.

13. Shirley, "Royal Letters of Henry III" (Rolls Series), 2:46.

14. Paris, *Historia Major* 5:552.

15. Close Roll, 42 Hen. III, m. 6 d.

16. Ibid., 40 Hen. III, m. 11 d.

17. Ibid., m. 16 d.

18. Tovey, *Anglia Judaica.*

19. Patent Roll, 40 Hen. III, m. 2.

20. *Rotuli Finium.*, ed. Roberts (Rec. com.), 2:240. Other names, Aaron fil. Peytevin and Hacce (*sic*), are given in the *Athenaeum* review of Hume's monograph on Hugh of Lincoln (1849), p. 1271; I know not on what authority.

21. M. D. Davis, *Shetaroth*, no. 160, p. 304.

22. Paris, *Historia Major* 5:441.

23. Ibid., 5:487. This was the striking passage quoted twice in "Papers of the Anglo-Jewish Historical Exhibition," pp. 50, 266.

24. Paris, *Historia Major* 5:488. Patent Roll, 39 Henry III, m. 13.

25. *Shetaroth*, no. 156, p. 298.

26. Zunz, *Zur Geschichte* (Minchat Jehuda f, 89*b*., Mordecai Berachot, 124, Shilte, Aboda Sara, c. 2.); Neubauer-Renan, *Histoire littéraire de la France,* p. 441.

27. Rymer, *Foedera* (1816 ed.), 1:346; Patent Roll, 40; Hen. III, m. 19, at top.

28. E. Venables, "Walks through the Streets of Lincoln," p. 25.

29. It has been figured several times, e.g., Turner, "Domestic Architecture," 1:40; Gardiner, "School History of England." Details in Pugin, "Specimens of Gothic Architecture," pl. 2.

30. I. Loeb, *Le Saint Enfant de la Guardia in Revue des Etudes juives,* tome 15.

31. Ibid., p. 32 of tirage apart.

32. S. Pegge, "Life of Robert Grosseteste" (1793), p. 2.

33. The British Museum reference is Kaye, 2:363.

34. F. Michel, *Hugues de Lincoln: Recueil de ballades Anglo-Normandes et Ecossoises relatives au meurtre de cet enfant commis par les Juifs en MCCLV* (Paris, 1834), pp. ix–64. It was reprinted in 1849, with a pseudo-archaic English version by A. Hume. "Sir Hugh of Lincoln; or, An Examination of a curious Tradition respecting the Jews, with a Notice of the Popular Poetry connected with it" (8vo, 54 pp.).

35. "Papers of the Anglo-Jewish Historical Exhibition," p. 49.

36. The French form Agim is nearer to the Hebrew Chayim than the Hagin of the English records.

37. 1816 ed., 1:333.

38. Cambridge (Mass.), 1882, *seq.,* pt. 5. Professor Child has an elaborate and instructive introduction to the ballads, which brings together in a convenient form all that has been hitherto known of the subject from history and tradition.

39. May we not see here, as Mr. York Powell has suggested to me, some reminiscence of Belleassez?

40. Reference to the mysterious evisceration mentioned by Matthew Paris?

41. "Games and Songs of American Children" (Boston, 1883). I drew attention to Mr. Newell's interesting version in the *Jewish Chronicle.*

42. Gules of August (French ballad), a popular name for the first day of August, also called Lammas. This used to be a popular holiday. "Gules" occurs transcribed in Hebrew characters in Mr. Davis's *Shetaroth,* no. 103, p. 232. The *Acta Sanctorum* gives the date of Hugh's martyrdom as 27 July (33:494); and Matthew Paris favors

that date. The king's itinerary, as given in Rymer and the Patent Rolls, rather favors the date of the ballad.

43. Shirley, "Royal Letters," 2:110.

44. Paris, *Historia Major.*

45. English ballads. Owing to their late date little confidence can be placed on this point, but it seems antecedently probable.

46. The French ballad declares that the body was covered with ordure.

47. French ballad; Matthew Paris calls him Copin. Either name might be derived from Jacopin, diminutive of Jacob.

48. There was a Josephin living at Lincoln at the time whose son, Chayim, married Bellaset. Davis, *Shetaroth*, nos. 154, 156.

49. Local tradition reported by Mr. Haes.

50. "Annals of Burton." Matthew Paris says ten days, but this is quite discordant with his own date of the martyrdom.

51. Paris, *Historia Major;* "Annals of Burton"; French ballad.

52. "Annals of Burton."

53. Conjecture derived from date of Shetar; Davis, *Shetaroth*, no. 156.

54. Rymer, *Foedera.*

55. Davis, *Shetaroth.*

56. Zunz, *Zur Geschichte;* Neubauer-Renan, *Histoire littéraire.*

57. Meir of Norwich, poet, is the other chief name known from this period.

58. "Annals of Burton." French ballad allows for a considerable period to have elapsed between the disappearance of Hugh and the "summoning" of the Jews to Lincoln.

59. Wednesday has always been a favorite day for weddings among Jews, and but little time can have elapsed or the assembly would have dispersed to their homes elsewhere.

60. Conjecture to account for the appearance of the body just after the wedding.

61. Conjecture (see n. 48, above).

62. Local tradition.

63. Conjecture to account for the disemboweling of the body; Paris, *Historia Major.*

64. Or, as Mr. York Powell suggests, the entrails were removed by some Jewish physician when it was decided to remove the body.

65. French ballad. His flight, as recorded by Tovey, seems to argue the consciousness of complicity.

66. Deduced from reference in Tovey to his school.

67. French ballad.

68. Copin's confession cannot be explained without assuming some connection of the Jews with the matter.

69. Tradition reports two places in which the body was found, in Jopin's house and in Grantham's well. The suggestion here made reconciles the two statements, and at the same time allows for a certain amount of complicity, or at least injudicious concealment, on the part of the Jews.

70. Oulton, "Traveller's Guide" (1805) 2:54.

71. "Annals of Burton."

72. Ibid. According to Matthew Paris it was the boy's mother who discovered the corpse; this disagrees with the "Annals of Burton" and with the French ballad.

73. Paris, *Historia Major.*

74. Ibid.

75. "Annals of Burton."

76. Conjecture from his remark on discovering the body.

77. "Annals of Waverley," French ballad.

78. "Annals of Burton."

79. Ibid.

80. French ballad, Scotch ballad (Jamieson). Here is a point which remained in the folk memory for over five hundred years.

81. E. Venables, "A Walk through Lincoln Minster," p. 41.

82. Pegge, "Life of Robert Grosseteste"; Michel, *Hugues de Lincoln,* p. 63.

83. Paris, *Historia Major;* "Annals of Burton."

84. Paris, *Historia Major;* "Annals of Burton"; French ballad.

85. Without a confession implicating all the Jews, little Hugh could not be raised to the position of a martyr. As a matter of fact, his name was never formally received into the Roman martyrology. See Michel, *Hugues de Lincoln,* p. 51, n. 23.

86. Deduced from the fact that Jopin was not even tried till the king arrived at Lincoln.

87. See Jacobs, *Jews of Angevin England,* pp. 45, 75, 256.

88. French ballad.

89. This would be in October 1255 (see itinerary of Henry III; as given in *Foedera,* the king was at Alnwick 23 September, at Westminster 18 October).

90. 24 February 1255 (Patent Roll, 39 Henry III, m. 13).

91. Paris, *Historia Major.*

92. Paris, *Historia Major;* "Annals of Waverley"; "Annals of Burton."

93. Close Roll, 39 Henry III.

94. *Liber de Antiquis Legibus* (Cam. Soc.), p. 23.

95. "Annals of Burton."

96. Paris, *Historia Major* 5 : 552, 12 March 1256.

97. See n. 3, above.

98. Paris, *Historia Major* 5 : 546; Annals of Burton attribute the intervention to the Dominicans.

BRIAN BEBBINGTON

Little Sir Hugh:
An Analysis

The ballad of Little Sir Hugh (Child 155) might be said to have a life of its own, independent of any historical events which may have given rise to it. It is very widely known throughout the English-speaking world, in part because of its early appearance in prominent folksong collections. Bishop Thomas Percy (1729–1811) included it as the third ballad in the first book of his celebrated Reliques of Ancient English Poetry, *published in 1765. Percy's* Reliques *is generally considered to be one of the landmark publications that sparked the beginning of the serious study of folklore. Percy's text, which came from a manuscript sent to him from Scotland, was introduced by a headnote in which Percy remarked that the ballad "is founded upon the supposed practice of the Jews in crucifying or otherwise murthering Christian children, out of hatred to the religion of their parents: a practice, which hath been always alledged in excuse for the cruelties exercised upon that wretched people, but which probably never happened in a single instance." Percy continues, ". . . we may reasonably conclude the whole charge to be groundless and malicious."*

Percy's Scottish text was translated into German by Johann Gottfried von Herder (1744–1803) so as to be included in Herder's 1778 anthology Volkslieder, *another important folksong collection which influenced the development of international interest in the genre. It is Herder, one must remember, who is usually credited with first coining the term* Volkslied, *"folksong."*

Reprinted from *UNISA English Studies* (Journal of the Department of English, University of South Africa) 9, no. 3 (September 1971): 30–36.

72

Some of the highlights of the nineteenth-century scholarship devoted to the ballad are: Francisque Michel, "Ballade Anglo-Normande sur le meurtre commis par les Juifs sur un enfant de Lincoln," Mémoires de la Société Royale des Antiquaires de France *10 (1834): 358–92; Abraham Hume,* Sir Hugh of Lincoln; or, an Examination of a Curious Tradition respecting the Jews, with a notice of the Popular Poetry connected with it *(London: John Russell Smith, 1849); and Francis James Child,* The English and Scottish Popular Ballads *(New York: Cooper Square Publishers, 1962), 3:233–54 (first published in 1889). Twentieth-century studies include: James R. Woodall, "'Sir Hugh': A Study in Balladry,"* Southern Folklore Quarterly *19 (1955): 77–84; Faith Hippensteel, "'Sir Hugh': The Hoosier Contribution to the Ballad,"* Indiana Folklore *2, no. 2 (1969): 75–140; and Neil C. Hultin, "'The Cruel Jew's Wife': An Anglo-Irish Ballad of the Early Nineteenth Century,"* Folklore *99 (1988): 189–203. For a substantial sampling of some 66 texts and tunes of the ballad, see Bertrand Harris Bronson,* The Traditional Tunes of the Child Ballads *(Princeton: Princeton University Press, 1966), 3:72–104.*

There have also been some striking literary citations of the ballad. One of the most noteworthy is James Joyce's inclusion of a text as well as a melody of the ballad in a critical scene in Ulysses. *His character Stephen, a Gentile, sings the anti-Semitic ballad just at the point in the novel when he has been invited to stay the night at the home of the Jew Bloom, who has a marriageable daughter. See James Joyce,* Ulysses *(New York: Modern Library, 1934), pp. 674–76. Earlier in the novel, Joyce refers explicitly to ritual murder: "It's the blood sinking in the earth gives new life. Same idea those jews they said killed the christian boy" (p. 107). For further discussion of Joyce's use of the ballad, see Louis J. Edmundson, "Theme and Countertheme: The Function of Child Ballad 155, 'Sir Hugh, or the Jew's Daughter,' in James Joyce's* Ulysses*" (Ph.D. diss., Middle Tennessee State University, 1975).*

For the Percy text, see Thomas Percy, Reliques of Ancient

English Poetry *(London: J. Dodsley, 1765), 1:32–35; for Herder's translation, see J. G. von Herder,* Volkslieder *(Leipzig: Weygandschen Buchhandlung, 1778), 1:120–23.*

The following literary analysis of the ballad uses a synoptic or composite text as a point of departure (rather than concentrating upon a single individual version), and for that reason the author is able to illuminate many of the varying motifs and details of the ballad, especially from a symbolic perspective.

"Sir Hugh, or, the Jew's daughter" is an anti-Semitic English ballad about the ritual murder of a Christian boy by Jews. This essay will attempt an analysis of the symbols and legend of the ballad.

Briefly the ballad-story is this: a group of schoolboys playing football are joined by Sir Hugh, who kicks the ball either over the Jew's garden wall or through his castle window. Sir Hugh sees the daughter of the castle looking out of the window and asks her to return the ball to him which she refuses to do. She tells him to fetch it himself, but he is afraid to do so for various reasons. After offering him several enticements to come to her, he finally accepts and follows her into the castle to a table on which he is laid and stabbed to death. The daughter encloses his body in lead and throws it into a well. That evening his mother searches for him, going to the castle, the garden and the well, and asking her son each time to speak to her. At last he answers from the well, and tells her to return home to make his winding sheet and that he will meet her the next morning outside Lincoln. They meet and bells ring and books read of their own accord.

The ballad is allegedly based on fact. The four accounts given by Child[1] are more or less contemporaneous and agree on the main points of the story.

Of the religious references in the ballad, the most obvious concern Hugh's desire to be buried with objects which are familiar Christian symbols:

"Put the Bible at my head," he says.
"And a Testament at my feet"[a]

She laid the Bible at his head,
The prayer-book at his feet.[abcf]

His requests vary; at times they involve his right side or simply "the side of me," or even having the prayer book placed at his head and the Bible at his feet. One version stipulates the Catechise book in his own heart's blood, and another a songbook at his feet and a Bible at his head. A further version contains the lines

"And lay my Prayer-Book at my head,
And my grammer at my feet."[ae]

This reference to "my grammer" is significant because *grammar* has often been associated with witchcraft and black magic (Bishop Percy says the word is a corruption of *Grimoir*, a conjuring book),[2] and Hugh's body may have been used for rites of witchcraft and black magic.

The desire to be buried with the Bible, Testament or prayer book, is to ensure that "Christ and I shall meet."[a] A "seven foot Bible at my head and feet"[a] is probably a stronger assurance of Hugh's afterlife (since seven is a good-luck number and is the number of angels before God's throne), something of which he speaks with confidence to his mother when she finds him:

"And at the back of merry Lincoln
The morn I will meet you."[ae]

Child also records the following message from Hugh to his mother:

"Tell her I'm at heaven's gate
Where her and I shall meet."

But Hugh also goes on to say that before he meets Christ "the earth and worms shall be my bed."[a] This aspect of mortality was one of God's punishments for Adam. By accepting the apple (the Norse symbol of immortality) with which Hugh is tempted and afterwards being thrown into a well (a Christian symbol of salvation), his prospect of a life hereafter is guaranteed. And, of course, the account of Hugh could also embody a literal interpretation of Jesus' words: "unless ye come as little children . . . ," and "suffer little children to come unto me."

In most versions of the ballad the well into which Hugh's body is thrown is simply a draw well. However, we also find versions where the daughter throws him into "Our Lady's draw well"[a] or "St Mary's well."[a] These could be understood as oblique references to Hugh's mother having assumed some of the aspects of the Virgin. Like the Virgin Mary, she is the mother of a martyr and also goes to seek her son who has been killed by the Jews. The time of her assignation with her son ("tomorrow morning before it is day" or "before eight o'clock") is similar to the time of day when Mary visited Jesus' tomb. In addition to this, Hugh's mother "tuk with her a little rod in her hand"[a] or under her apron, and this becomes a (magic[a]) wand or "sally" (i.e., willow) rod—willow being traditionally symbolic of sorrow and mourning. The rod is sometimes of birch, the wood from which Hugh's coffin is to be made. The birch is associated with ghosts in Scotland. Hazel wood, also mentioned in connection with Hugh's coffin, is the wood used for divination, while the mention of broom suggests a spell against misfortune, witches, and death.

Reeves gives a curious line—a line which may hint at an unhealthy, possibly incestuous, relationship between mother and son. Addressing his mother, Hugh says that he is dead "so long with you I can't sleep."[f] Although this theory of incest may appear absurd at first sight, two of Sharp's versions make it seem more probable and worthy of consideration. In one of these versions Hugh's mother replies to his request to be taken out of the well:

> "Sink o sink, my little son Hugh,
> Sink o sink," said she.

> "Sink o sink and don't you swim,
> You are injury to me and my kin."[d]

In the other version her reply to him is:

> "Sink oh sink, my little son 'Ugh-ey,
> And don't you never swim.
> If you do it'll be a scandal
> To me and all my kin."[d]

A similar, though less clear, verse is

> "Lie there, lie there, little Harry," she cried,
> "And God forbid you to swim,
> If you be a disgrace to me,
> Or any of my friends."[a]

In these three extracts we can sense the emergence of a feeling of guilt.

Hugh is seduced by the daughter in exactly the same way as Adam (who was as naïve as is the young Sir Hugh) was seduced by Eve: with an apple—golden, like those of Hippomenes and the Hesperides—the traditional Christian forbidden fruit, and a fig, its Jewish counterpart. The fig symbolizes the female breast, and the apple can also be seen as a phallic symbol. Hugh is also tempted with a rose and a cherry, both symbolic of the vagina.

Allusions to color are very important in the ballad and occur often. The color of the apple is green, red and white, red and green, or red as is the cherry. The red anticipates the common ballad preoccupation with blood. The kerchief, with which he is also tempted, is as white as snow. The football with which he plays is tossed "among some blades of snow,"[b] and the rose, sometimes referred to, is either "lily-white" or a "red, red rose." After his death Hugh says:

> "She wrapped me up in a red mantle
> Instead of a milk-white sheet."[f]

This is reminiscent of Christ's robe which could be "either white, the symbol of a purified soul, or red, as washed in the blood of Christ";[3] the Holy Grail appears covered in red or white cloth. In addition to this, Hugh is usually taken by the "milk-white hand" or the "lily-white hand." The latter allusion has emotional connotations similar to the willow, since the lily traditionally sprang from Eve's tears after she had been expelled from Eden. White, too, has the additional significance of being the Roman color of mourning. The many references to the color red in various versions of "Little Sir Hugh" prepare the listener for Hugh's brutal murder: at the back of one's mind they evoke a vague sense of horror which is brought to the fore during the account of Hugh's murder. This "preparation" increases the pity the listener feels for Hugh. The references to color are most striking in the combination of red and white, which at first sight may seem to be strange colors for an apple. However, white (or innocence) could here be contrasted with the defilement of red (blood). Again, the association of red and green could reflect an intuitive response in which the color of life is stained with a hue associated with violence. The latter combination of red and green is transferred in one version to the daughter's dress which later becomes green, a suit of green, or apple-green, which suggests that the girl took on the role of a wood nymph and tempted the mortal Hugh herself. In some versions she invites him to dine with her—which in terms of fairy lore would be fatal to him—and the place where Hugh is murdered is where she is wont to dine, or where she often or sometimes dined, or is simply a table and a reminder of an ogress' dreadful meal. As her final temptation she comes out of her castle and insolently and seductively "leaned her back against the wall,"[a] calling to him "Come here to me, Sir Hugh."[a] For succumbing to her wiles, like Adam, Hugh sorely rued the day. In Jewish folklore Adam's blood was made of red dust, his bones of white and his skin of green.

The substitution of the daughter or, in some versions, a Jewish lady for the murderess—who in the Chronicles is the archetypal *ewige Jude* and who only appears in one version of the ballad—removes the tale to a land of fantasy but leaves its message untouched: here it almost becomes a morality lesson. Sir John of Lexington[4] and the king (who is mentioned only briefly) are both personifications of divine justice, and are left out of the ballad story; thus the daughter's reward for the murder is not mentioned, although in one version Hugh does say:

> "My soul is high up in Heaven above,
> While hers is low down in hell."[d]

But we can guess what will probably happen to her: whatever ultimately happened to Eve. However, the daughter

> . . . took him by the lily white hand,
> And led him thro the kitchen;
> And there he saw his own dear maid
> A roasting of a chicken.[a]

A nice touch this, as it creates an image of roasting, and it does not take too much imagination to substitute the woman herself for the chicken. In other versions Hugh's nurse is seen "a picking of a chicken,"[ab] and again the substitution is not difficult: the image this time suggests the woman being flayed. In these versions Hugh asks his nurse to help him which she refuses to do. In a further version, when in the kitchen, Hugh says:

> "And there I saw my own dear sister,
> A picking of a chicken."[a]

Could this be related to the earlier "scandal to me and my kin" to which Hugh's mother-murderess refers? Whatever the case may be, divine wrath seems now to be implicit.

But the daughter repents:

> She's tane her mantle about her head,
> Her pike-staff in her hand,
> And prayed to heaven to be her guide,
> Unto some uncouth land.[a]

Judas also repented; his uncouth land was Aceldama.

In the Chronicles, Hugh is avenged by Sir John of Lexington, who had heard before of the Jews doing such deeds.

This memory is recalled in the ballad itself. In reply to the daughter's invitation to enter the castle, Hugh says:

> "How will I come up? How can I come up?
> How can I come to thee?
> For as ye did to my auld father,
> The same ye'll do to me,"[a]

and

> "I won't come in, I shan't come in,
> I've heard of you before,
> For those who goes in the Jew's gardin,
> Don't never come out no more."[b]

In other versions the consequences for Hugh's merely being *found* at the Jew's house are equally sinister:

> "For if my mother should be at the door
> She would cause my poor heart to rue."[e]

> "My mother would beat me, my father would kill me,
> And cause my blood to pour."[a] *and*

> "For if my parents knew
> It would make my blood to run."[d]

But the most popular lines in this regard seem to be:

> "For if my mother should chance to know
> She'd cause my blood to fall."[ad]

After the daughter herself, the mother would seem to be the most likely murderess. This returns us to the relationship between mother and son which I have mentioned before, and which could contain a germ of the idea of incest.

The mention of a garden as the place in which Hugh is seduced seems to indicate that Eden is the locale. For instance, of the daughter we read:

> She's gane till her father's garden
> And pu'd an apple red and green[a]

or into the Jew's garden "where the grass grew long and green."[a] On the other hand, we hear of the mother who has

> . . . doen her to the Jew's garden,
> Thought he had been gathering fruit[a]

which is another hint at Hugh's seduction; or

> 'Twas up and down the garden there
> This little boy's mammie did run[f]

in search of her son. Also, in another version, his body was found by a schoolboy who was walking in the garden. Further possible evidence of an Eden locality may be seen in a number of references to flowers or their attributes, as in:

> Four and twenty bonny boys
> War playing at the ba;
> Then up and started sweet Sir Hew,
> The flower amang them a,'[a]

or where Hugh asks to be buried in the green churchyard "where the flowers are blooming fair,"[a] or where the ball is tossed into the Jew's garden "where the flowers blow."[a] The ball was also tossed

> And amongst the Jew's cattle,
> And amongst the Jews below.[a]

Christian tradition has it that Christ was born in a stable or cowshed. The reference to "the Jews below" may suggest that the Jews were in hell where they were "sitting a row."[a] The Jews, then, would have been rewarded for their part in the murder.

The place of Hugh's death, "a green gardeen," could also be an oblique reference to Gethsemane or a parallel to the garden in which Jesus was betrayed. A number of versions have Hugh murdered in a variety of rooms of which the "cellar" or the "stone chamber" most closely resemble Christ's tomb. In every case Hugh is taken to where none can hear his call.

Because he is brutally murdered—and by a non-Christian—Hugh naturally becomes a martyr. And, because of this, his place of death is important. Also his being given a title—he is *Sir* Hugh in most versions—may derive from the fact that, as a martyr, he is worthy of esteem. This titular aspect of Hugh may have been taken from John of Lexington, or it may simply be a matter of conforming to a traditional ballad convention. Whatever the case may be, we are meant to pity Hugh all the more now that he has been raised from the level of a mere football-playing schoolboy. For similar reasons Hugh's mother becomes "Lady Maisry," "Maisy," or "Lady Helen." Even the murderess is sometimes dressed in silk with its connotations of luxury and extravagance.

More than becoming a martyr, Hugh becomes a hero. As befits him, he is shown a "gay gold ring" or a "diamond ring" by the Jew's daughter which can be seen as an acknowledgment of his authority. Moreover, she sat him in a golden chair, or at least,

> She sat herself on a golden chair,
> Him on another close by.[a]

Some versions give it as a silver chair, which can be seen as a chair of state. It is also at times a "gilty chair."[e] In addition to this, Hugh's blood is caught in vessels of gold or silver (or a basin, specially cleaned for the purpose by Hugh's nurse![b]). And the football game was played with "a sweet silver ball,"[f] which could symbolize a lunar authority over birth and death. Another version gives the ball as "silken." Hugh is fed on sugar and "sweet"; and the apple for his temptation was hung on a "golden chain." However, as proof of Hugh's earthliness, he is also put into "a little chair," and his blood is also caught in a "pan" or a "washbasin."

These symbols of Hugh's authority—the golden chair and golden or silver vessels—have strong associations with ritual sacrifice. This becomes most striking when Hugh's chair is equated with an altar. Also the catching of his blood recalls the verse from *Cock Robin:*

> Who caught his blood-o
> I said the fish
> With my little silver dish
> It was I o it was I.[5]

Here it is worth noting that the story from which the ballad descends concerns a murder in contempt of Christ and does not mention the catching of the boy's blood. This is an exterior and possibly later motif related to another anti-Semitic charge: that of עלילת–דם or the use of Christian blood in the making of Jewish ceremonial food. The receptacle used to catch Hugh's blood has its parallel in the Holy Grail: the chalice at the Last Supper in which Christ's blood was caught after His Crucifixion. Moreover, the Grail appears in legend under the same circumstances as those for Hugh's body: at the bottom of a well.

A further indication of Hugh's elevation in rank is the daughter's placing him on a chair which is close to and like her own. This act recalls the custom of choosing a mate for a divine queen, a ιερος γαμος, who for a brief while rules as her equal before being sacrificed. Hugh's death is brought about by the daughter herself who, in this context, could be a reembodiment of a primordial queen-priestess. She lays him down on a dressing board, a dressing table, or a golden chest of drawers, and dresses and stabs him as a sacrificer would a pig or sheep. The significance here is that the pig is traditionally the Jewish "unclean animal" and the sheep the traditional Christian sacrificial animal. Like Christ, Hugh is flogged and mocked before his martyrdom.

Blood, an agent for the remission of sins, is naturally very prominent in this ballad. We hear that, after Hugh is stabbed,

> First came out the thick, thick blood,
> And syne came out the thin,
> And syne came out the bonny heart's blood,
> There was nae mair within.[a]

83

Since the heart has always been regarded as the seat of life, it is not surprising that after Hugh's heart's blood left his body he should die because "thair was nae life left"[a] in his heart, for that was "where"[a] "the life lay in."[a] (Here a comical note intrudes in one version where, even though he is dead, he still talks to his mother and tells her to "cheer up."[d]) In this version Hugh says of his bleeding that "the stream do run so strong," so recalling the legend of the soldier who pierced Christ's side after He had died and saw blood and water still issuing from His body. Closely allied to this are medieval poetic records of a profusely bleeding Christ.

The implications of weather are significant in the ballad. In general the most usual time for Hugh's murder in the ballad's many versions is during rain, which is a time of joy (as it ensures the growth of crops, for which our primeval queen's temporary escort has died). Rain also suggests a time of sadness—for rain and tears are almost synonymous—and so this allusion would prepare us for pitying Hugh. Besides the mention of rain, however, many of the ballad's versions expand and elaborate on the atmospheric conditions at the time of the murder: "the wind doth wither and blow."[f] This suggests winter, the time of the death of plants and of great hardship. Another allusion, to rains and mists,[b] suggests the mysterious and unknown, which is taken further in "it sprinkles all over the plain."[c] With a stretch of the imagination this could involve the mystery of life itself; life-giving rain covering everything like a mist.

In contrast to the winter we find also "twas on a summer's morning,"[a] "the middle o the midsummer tyme,"[a] or even on a May, on a midsummer's day.[a] May is the time associated with the rebirth of life, and midsummer is the time when the sun, the giver of that life, is most powerful. The date of Hugh's death is also given as Easter day—the time of Jesus' resurrection—or as a holiday or "Hallowday" (for holy day). The time can also be a high holiday, and both the Easter day and the Hallowday are, above all, days of the year in the Church calendar. Although the murder takes place on a holiday, some drops of rain did fall.[d] Sometimes the reference changes to some drops of dew. These drops of dew suggest the heralding of morning, the rebirth of day. But the holiday is sometimes a "low and a low and a low holiday,"[d] a dark and holiday,[d] or a "dark and dark some drizzling day."[d] This could be a reminder to us that even though life must die in winter to be reborn in spring, this death is a time of sorrow. (In a village in southern England women and girls used to carry peeled willow wands on May Day as a reminder of life's winter death and subsequent rebirth.) Hugh's death also takes place in a dark hollow, where the dewdrops never fall.[d] Thus the importance of the weather to the ballad-story is similar to the importance of spring and winter in medieval poetry.

The number of children who play football in the ballad vary: four and twenty, two, or three. The number of friends who must accompany Hugh into the castle range from nine to two or three. Other references to numbers occur in the ballad:

> She led him in through the dark door,
> And sae has she through nine.[a]

This can be seen as a parallel to the "thrice threefold the gates" of "Hell,"[6] and occurs less obviously in:

> She led him on through one chamber
> And so did she through nine.[a]

The three divisions of Hades can be inferred in:

> She wyl'd him into ae chamber,
> She wyl'd him into twa,
> She wyl'd him into her ain chamber,
> The fairest of them a.[a]

Also the number of objects used to tempt Hugh is usually three, and there are also three kinds of blood in his body. His mother "ran thryse about"[a] at the castle, the garden and the well and asks a total of three questions. The ballad-story itself revolves around a trinity. In the Chronicles the Jews try three times to dispose of Hugh's body. In the ballads, after the daughter murders Hugh,

> She wound him up in a lily-white sheet,
> Three or four times four.[d]

Three is the divine and four the earthly number. Twelve is the number of Apostles and also of the Olympic gods, and sixteen is the Pythagorean lucky number and the Cabalistic number for the path of victory for the righteous. The association of these numbers with Hugh is obvious. Twelve people carry Hugh's body to the well. The well can be eighteen (the Christian number of great reward and the numerical value of the letters in the word חיים, 'life'), fifty (number of the Holy Ghost and the Christian sign for the remission of sins), and fifty-five feet or fathoms deep. Fifty-five is the Cabalistic number for piousness. The well can also be forty cubits deep, and this is a number symbolic of probation.

Hugh is dead and it is therefore essential that he be given a proper burial if his soul is to rest. His desire for this rest prompts his asking for the Bible and other religious books, to be met with a winding sheet, and to be taken out of the well and buried in a churchyard. His burial clothes are various: a cake of lead, a quire of tin, a red mantle, a kerchief, a winding sheet and a lily-white sheet. Tin was the metal of Jupiter in alchemy,

> And the leed, withouten faile,
> Is, lo, the metal of Saturne.
> (Chaucer, *The Hous of Fame*, bk. 3, l.1448)

Saturn was the bringer of mourning and presider over death. Lead is also the Asian proof against demons and would thus protect Hugh's soul. For the rest, the red mantle, the milk-white sheet, and the linen kerchief, all are unadorned and could thus symbolize Hugh's relinquishing earthly worries. This symbolism is still found in Jewish custom. Adam was buried in linen; and of Hugh's funeral

> . . . neer was such a burial
> Sin Adam's days begun.[a]

Adam was the first man born and by command of God the first to be buried peacefully and attended by the angels. A further point about Hugh's unnatural burial is his recurring phrase "the penknife sticks so close to my heart"[adf] or in his throat. As long as the murder weapon is in his body his soul would not be able to rest. Perhaps this is the meaning of "long with you I can't sleep" (i.e., in heaven). If the murderess was his mother, what more unnatural death could Hugh have suffered? This also suggests he could perhaps have been an illegitimate child. The importance of a Christian burial to the English peasantry is illustrated by Thomas Hardy.

Miracle-laden as the story is, the ballad only contains three supernatural happenings. The most popular is the mother's conversation with her dead son (the ability to talk after death would be bestowed on Hugh if he ate the apple, as this is the food of the oracular dead), and their meeting the following morning.

> And a' the bells o merry Lincoln
> Without men's hands were rung,
> And a' the books o merry Lincoln
> Were read without man's tongue[a]

is the third supernatural occurrence. Books are symbols of wisdom; they are also Christian symbols of the writings of the Church. In this context it is interesting to note that Hugh wishes to be buried with a pen and ink at every side.[a] Bells are ancient proof against witches and evil spirits, and are rung on *Walpurgisnacht*. Bells also protect crops from bad weather. The phenomenon of bells ringing of their own accord occurs in the Icelandic version of the story of the rapist who inadvertently kills his own sister,[7] and also in the Moravian version of the biblical woman at the well.[8] Bells symbolize the preacher and his message—and is not the ballad itself didactic?

The ballad-story would appear to contain a great deal of fiction and imagination. Some of this, like

> Whan bells was rung, and mass was sung,
> And a' man bound for bed,[a]

(meaning that the day passed by and night came on[a]) is purely a ballad convention. But in some degree the story is based on fact. In the mid-thirteenth century, the time of Hugh's murder, Lincoln had a thriving Jewish community living in what is still called Steep Street; Hugh lived at the lower end of this street, a place now called St. Dunstan's lock. Here a barrier was erected after his death to confine the Jews to their quarter after sunset. The remains of Hugh's tomb are still to be seen in Lincoln Cathedral on the south aisle of St. Hugh's Choir.

Notes

1. F. J. Child, ed., *The English and Scottish Popular Ballads* 3:233–54; 4:497–98; 5:241. Child gives 22 versions of the ballad; these I shall refer to collectively by *a*. A similar method of reference will be used for:
  b. A. K. Davis, ed., *More Traditional Ballads of Virginia*, pp. 229–39;
  c. M. O. Eddy, ed., *Ballads and Songs from Ohio*, pp. 66–67;
  d. C. J. Sharp, ed., *English Folk Songs from the Southern Appalachian Mountains* 1:222–29;
  e. C. J. Sharp, ed., *English Folk Songs* (selected edition);
  f. J. Reeves, ed., *The Everlasting Circle. English Traditional Verse from the Mss of S. Baring-Gould*, p. 244.
  g. A. Lomax, ed., *The Folksongs of North America in the English Language*, p. 511.
2. Child, *English and Scottish Popular Ballads* 1:340.
3. F. E. Hulme, *The History, Principles and Practice of Symbolism in Christian Art*, p. 22.
4. See below. [For further discussion of the possible role of Sir John of Lexington or John de Lexinton in the creation of the blood libel

legend, see Gavin I. Langmuir, "The Knight's Tale of Young Hugh of Lincoln," *Speculum* 47 (1972): 459–82 (see esp. pp. 469–82). —Ed.]

5. Lomax, *Folksongs of North America*, p. 181.

6. Milton, *Paradise Lost*, bk. 2, l.645.

7. Child, *English and Scottish Popular Ballads* 1:173.

8. Ibid., 1:231.

Bibliography

Ausubel, N. *A Treasury of Jewish Folklore, Stories, Traditions, Legends, Humour, Wisdom and Folksongs of the Jewish People.* New York: Crown Publishers, 1948.

Bebbington, B. T. *On Current Sexual Symbolism.* MS Library of the South African Folk Music Association, 1970.

Brayer, M. B. "Psychosomatics, Hermetic Medicine and Dream Interpretation in the Qumran Literature." *Jewish Quarterly Review* 60 (1970).

Bulfinch, T. *Bulfinch's Mythology* (1855–63). Feltham, Eng.: Spring Books, 1968.

Child, F. J. *The English and Scottish Popular Ballads* (1882–98). 5 vols. New York: Dover, 1965.

Davis, A. K. *More Traditional Ballads of Virginia.* University of North Carolina, 1960.

Eddy, M. O. *Ballads and Songs from Ohio.* Hatboro, Pa.: Folklore Associates, 1964.

Frazer, J. G. *The Golden Bough.* 12 vols. London: Macmillan, 1932.

Freud, S. *A General Introduction to Psychoanalysis.* English translation. Garden City, 1953.

Freud, S. *The Interpretation of Dreams.* English translation. London: Allen & Unwin, 1948.

Ginzburg, L. *The Legends of the Jews.* English translation. 4 vols. Philadelphia: Jewish Publication Society of America, 1909.

Hardy, T. *Tess of the d'Urbervilles.* Macmillan Papermac, 1967.

Hulme, F. E. *The History, Principles and Practice of Symbolism in Christian Art.* London: Swan Sonnenschein, 1892.

The Jewish Encyclopaedia. 12 vols. New York: Funk & Wagnalls, 1907.

Jobes, G. *Dictionary of Mythology, Folklore and Symbols.* New York: Scarecrow Press, 1962.

Lomax, A. *The Folksongs of North America in the English Language.* London: Cassel, 1960.

Mee, A. *Lincolnshire.* London: Hodder & Stoughton, 1949.

The New Testament. Authorized version.

Reeves, J. *The Everlasting Circle: English Traditional Verse from the MSS of S. Baring-Gould, H. E. D. Hammond and George B. Gardiner.* London: Heinemann, 1960.

Sharp, C. J.: *English Folk Songs from the Southern Appalachian Mountains.* 1932. Reprint. London: Oxford University Press, 1952.

Sharp, C. J. *English Folk Songs.* Selected edition. 1921. Reprint. London: Novello, 1959.

Spence, L. *An Introduction to Mythology.* London: Harrap, 1931.

Spence, L. *The Outlines of Mythology.* New York: Fawcett, 1961.

Squire, C. *Celtic Myth and Legend, Poetry and Romance.* London: Gresham, n.d.

Stone, B. *Mediaeval English Lyrics.* Penguin, 1964.

Treharne, R. F. *The Glastonbury Legends.* London: Cresset Press, 1967.

"Vitae Adae et Evae" and "The Debate of the Body and the Soul." In *A Middle English Reader*, ed. O. F. Emerson. London: Macmillan, 1923.

The Prioress's Tale

There seems little doubt that the most famous literary articulation of Jewish ritual murder is Chaucer's Prioress's Tale. It involves ritual murder rather than the blood libel, strictly speaking, since the murdered boy's blood is not mentioned at all in the narrative. Inasmuch as Geoffrey Chaucer (1340?–1400) is one of the acknowledged giants of English literature and his masterpiece is generally conceded to be his Canterbury Tales, *of which the Prioress's Tale is one, Chaucer's version of the story is very much part of the history and dissemination of this anti-Semitic plot.*

Chaucer, to be sure, did not invent the story. Indeed, a great many of the Canterbury Tales *have been shown to have derived from original folk narrative traditions. For a convenient overview of the folktale and legendary sources of the* Canterbury Tales, *see Francis Lee Utley, "Some Implications of Chaucer's Folktales,"* IV. International Congress for Folk-Narrative Research in Athens, Laographia *22 (1965): 588–99. For the possible sources of the Prioress's Tale in particular, see Carleton Brown, "Chaucer's Prioress' Tale and Its Analogues,"* Publications of the Modern Language Association *21 (1906): 485–518, and the same author's* A Study of the Miracle of Our Lady Told by Chaucer's Prioress *(London: Kegan Paul, Trench, Trübner & Co., 1910), pp. 51–141. See also Margaret H. Statler, "The Analogues of Chaucer's Prioress' Tale: The Relation of Group C to Group A,"* Publications of the Modern Language Association *65 (1950): 896–910, as well as other references in Lynn King*

Morris, Chaucer Source and Analogue Criticism: A Cross-Referenced Guide *(New York: Garland, 1985), pp. 168–70, and Beverly Boyd, ed.,* A Variorum Edition of the Works of Geoffrey Chaucer, *vol. 2,* The Canterbury Tales, *pt. 20,* The Prioress's Tale *(Norman: University of Oklahoma Press, 1987), pp. 4–26.*

At least the reader does not have to wonder if Chaucer knew about the story of Hugh of Lincoln when he wrote the Prioress's Tale ca. 1387. Chaucer makes a direct reference to the alleged murder in 1255 and although he pretends to set his story in Asia, the details rather suggest Europe or even England.

One of the issues debated in the scholarship devoted to the Prioress's Tale is whether or not Chaucer himself was anti-Semitic. One view is that he was very much a product of his own fourteenth-century time and that it was natural enough for him to have shared anti-Semitic sentiments. The opposing view is that Chaucer was indulging in satire in the tale and that he put the anti-Semitic tale in the mouth of a pious Christian prioress precisely to demonstrate the hypocrisy of Christians who preach brotherly love and tolerance at the same time as they advocate the murder of Jews. For samples of the debate, see Albert B. Friedman, "The Prioress's Tale *and Chaucer's Anti-Semitism,"* Chaucer Review *9 (1974): 118–29; J. Archer, "The Structure of Anti-Semitism in the 'Prioress' Tale,'"* Chaucer Review *19 (1984): 46–54; Richard Rex, "Chaucer and the Jews,"* Modern Language Quarterly *45 (1984): 107–22; and the* Variorum Edition *of the Prioress's Tale cited above, pp. 43–50.*

Rather than force the reader to wrestle with Chaucer's original Middle English language, I have elected to select a modern English rendering of the tale by the late Chaucer scholar Nevill Coghill, who was Merton Professor of English Literature at Oxford from 1957 to 1966.

In Asia once there was a Christian town
In which, long since, a Ghetto used to be
Where there were Jews, supported by the Crown
For the foul lucre of their usury,
Hateful to Christ and all his company.
And through this Ghetto one might walk or ride
For it was free and open, either side.

A little school stood for the Christian flock
Down at the further end, and it was here
A heap of children come of Christian stock
Received their early schooling year by year
And the instruction suited to their ear,
That is to say in singing and in reading
—The simple things of childhood and good breeding.

Among these children was a widow's son,
A little chorister of seven years old,
And day by day to school he used to run
And had the custom (for he had been told
To do so) should be happen to behold
An image of Christ's mother, to kneel and say
Hail Mary as he went upon his way.

Thus had this widow taught her little boy
To reverence the mother of Christ, our dear
And blissful lady, and it was his joy;
A happy child will always learn and hear.
When I remember this, the ever-near
Saint Nicholas stands in my presence, he
Who did Christ reverence in infancy.

This little child, while he was studying
His little primer, which he undertook,
Sitting at school, heard other children sing
O Alma Redemptoris from their book.
Close as he dared he drew himself to look,
And listened carefully to work and part
Until he knew the opening verse by heart.

He had no notion what this Latin meant
Being so young, so tender too, so green;
But in the end, one morning there, he went
And asked a comrade what the song might mean
And why it was in use. He was so keen
To know it that he went upon his knees
Begging the boy explain it if he please.

His schoolfellow—an older boy than he—
Answered him thus: "This song, I have heard say,
Is to salute Our Blessed Lady; she
Will hear us when we turn to her and pray
For help and comfort on our dying day.
I can explain no more—that's all I know;
I can learn singing, but my grammar's slow."

"And is this anthem made to reverence
Christ's mother?" said this innocent. "If I may,
I certainly will show my diligence
To learn it off by heart for Christmas Day.
Though they should scold me when I cannot say
My primer, though they beat me thrice an hour,
I'll learn it in her honour, to my power."

So every day his comrade secretly
As they went homewards taught it him by rote;
He sang it with a childlike clarity
And boldly, word by word and note by note;
And twice a day it filled his little throat,
Going to school and coming back again,
Praising Christ's mother with all his might and main.

As I have said, this child would go along
The Jewish street and, of his own accord,
Daily and merrily he sang his song
O Alma Redemptoris; as it soared,
The sweetness of the mother of our Lord
Would pierce his heart, he could not choose but pray
And sing as, to and fro, he went his way.

First of our foes, the Serpent Satan shook
Those Jewish hearts that are his waspish nest,
Swelled up and said. "O Hebrew people look!
Is this not something that should be redressed?
Is such a boy to roam as he thinks best
Singing to spite you, canticles and saws
Against the reverence of your holy laws?"

From that time forward all these Jews conspired
To chase this innocent child from the earth's face.
Down a dark alley-way they found and hired
A murderer who owned that secret place;
And as the boy passed at his happy pace
This cursed Jew grabbed him and held him, slit
His little throat and cast him in a pit.

Cast him, I say, into a privy-drain,
Where they were wont to void their excrement.
O cursed folk of Herod come again,
Of what avail your villainous intent?
Murder will out, and nothing can prevent
God's honour spreading, even from such seed;
The blood cries out upon your cursed deed.

"O martyr wedded to virginity,
Now mayest thou sing and follow, on and on,
The white, celestial Lamb of Heaven," said she,
"Of whom the great evangelist, St John,
In Patmos wrote, who says that there they don
White robes before that Lamb, and sing afresh
That never have known woman in the flesh."

This wretched widow waited all that night,
She waited for her child, but all for nought;
And very early in the morning light,
All pale with sleepless dread and busy thought,
She searched his school, then up and down she sought
Elsewhere, and finally she got the news
That he was last seen in the street of Jews.

Within her breast her mother's pity closed,
She went about as one half out of mind
To every place in which, as she supposed,
There was some likelihood for her to find
Her child, and to Christ's mother, meek and kind,
She cried in heart, and in the end was brought
Among the accursed Jews, and there she sought.

She made enquiry with a piteous cry
Of every Jew inhabiting that place,
Asking if they had seen her child go by,
And they said, "No." But Jesus of His grace
Put in her thought, after a little space,
To come upon that alley as she cried,
Where, in a pit, he had been cast aside.

Great God, that to perform Thy praise hast called
The innocent of mouth, how great Thy might!
This gem of chastity, this emerald,
This jewel of martyrdom and ruby bright,
Lying with carven throat and out of sight,
Began to sing *O Alma* from the ground
Till all the place was ringing with the sound.

The Christian people going through the street
Came crowding up astonished at the thing,
And sent to fetch the Provost to entreat
His presence, and he came and heard him sing.
The Provost, praising Christ our heavenly king
And His dear mother, honour of mankind,
Bade all the Jews be fettered and confined.

They took the child with piteous lamentation
And he was brought, still singing out his song,
In high solemnity and celebration
Towards the nearest abbey by the throng.
His mother, swooning as they went along
Beside the bier, could not be reconciled,
A second Rachel, weeping for her child.

The Provost then did judgement on the men
Who did the murder, and he bid them serve
A shameful death in torment there and then
On all those guilty Jews; he did not swerve.
"Evils shall meet the evils they deserve."
And he condemned them to be drawn apart
By horses. Then he hanged them from a cart.

Still lay this innocent child upon his bier
At the high altar while a Mass was said.
The abbot and his convent then drew near
To hasten on his burial, and spread
A rain of holy water on his head;
And as they let the holy water spill
He sang *O Alma Redemptoris* still.

This abbot then, who was a holy man
As abbots are, or else they ought to be,
In invocation of the boy began
To say aloud, "Dear child, I conjure thee
By virtue of the Holy Trinity
To say how singing is permitted thee
Although thy throat is cut, or seems to be."

"Through to the bone my neck is cut, I know,"
Answered the child; "and had I been confined
By natural law I should, and long ago,
Have died. But Christ, whose glory you may find
In books, wills it be also kept in mind.
So for the honour of his mother dear
I still may sing *O Alma* loud and clear.

"That well of mercy, sweetest mother of Christ,
I long have loved with all that I could bring;
This at the hour of my death sufficed
To draw her down to me. She bade me sing
This anthem till my time of burying
As you have heard; and when my song was sung
She seemed to lay a grain upon my tongue.

"And so I sing as I must sing again
For love of her, the blissful and the free,
Till from my tongue you take away the grain.
For after that, the Virgin said to me,
'My little child, behold I come for thee
When from thy tongue this grain of seed is taken.
And have no fear; thou shalt not be forsaken.'"

This holy monk, this abbot, even he,
Touched the child's tongue and took away the grain;
And he gave up the ghost so peacefully,
So softly, and the marvel was so plain,
Salt fell the abbot's tears in trickling rain,
And down he fell, prostrate upon the ground,
And lay as still as one who had been bound.

And all the weeping convent also bent
To earth and praised Christ's mother with many a tear,
And after that they rose, and forth they went
Taking this little martyr from his bier,
And in a sepulchre of marble clear
Enclosed his little body, fair and sweet.
Where he now is, God grant we all may meet!

O Hugh of Lincoln, likewise murdered so
By cursed Jews, as is notorious
(For it was but a little time ago),
Pray mercy on our faltering steps, that thus
Merciful God may multiply on us
His mercy, though we be unstable and vary,
In love and reverence of His mother Mary.

Amen.

The Ritual Murder Accusation in Britain

From the preceding essays and selections, one might well gain the false impression that ritual murder and blood libel were strictly medieval superstition and that they had no place in the modern world. Such unfortunately is not the case. They have had a significant role in the resurgence of anti-Semitism in the nineteenth and twentieth centuries.

The following survey by Colin Holmes, Professor of History at the University of Sheffield demonstrates the continuation of the ritual murder and blood libel legends in England. The reader may also wish to consult Holmes's book-length work, Anti-Semitism in British Society, 1876–1939 *(London: Edward Arnold, 1979), for further details concerning twentieth-century British anti-Semitism.*

Expressions of anti-Semitic hostility possess considerable tenacity. If there are those who doubt this, they have only to consider the history of the ritual murder accusation to be disabused of their opinions. The charge, which flourished in medieval times, was significantly revived in the late nineteenth and early twentieth centuries, and indeed it still continues to be heard. In the present discussion, in order to provide a detailed account of this particular strand of anti-Semitism, attention is focused upon opinion in Britain, with special reference to the years between 1880 and 1939. But before engaging in a historical analysis of this kind, it is necessary to discuss and define the nature of the charge.

In effect the accusation covers a number of different claims, which have been grouped together under the term *ritual*

Reprinted from *Ethnic and Racial Studies* 4 (1981): 265–88.

murder. The origins of the charge would seem to stem from the years of Antiochus Epiphanes, ruler of Syria between 175 and 164 B.C., who desecrated the Temple in 170 B.C. Following this his supporters initiated a campaign of vilification against the Jewish community to justify the action, and in his defense Apion later claimed that it was the custom of Jews to kidnap a Greek foreigner, fatten him up for a year, and then convey him to a wood where he was slain. His killers, it was alleged, then proceeded to sacrifice his body in ritual fashion, eat his flesh, and swear an oath of hostility towards the Greeks. In this particular allegation there were three important components: ritual murder involved an expression of hostility towards an enemy people, the specifically ritual element was of secondary importance, and the blood motif, present in later accusations, was absent from the picture.[1] Later, in the twelfth century, the charge assumed other characteristics. For instance, it came to be alleged that Jews were required to crucify Christian children, usually during Passion week, to reenact the crucifixion of Jesus and mock the Christian faith. None of this made reference to the extraction of blood. In fact, it was not until the thirteenth century that the emphasis on the ritual use of the victim's blood seeped into the story. It was first mentioned in 1235, when it was suggested that Jews needed Christian blood for a Jewish celebration of Easter. Gradually, however, from the first half of the thirteenth century, although the connection with Easter did not lapse completely, this association was superseded by one which linked ritual murder with the Passover rites. And from the fourteenth century the idea originated that Jews used Christian blood in the preparation of "bread" for Passover and also mixed it with the wine used in the Seder service. However, at all times since the blood aspect was introduced into the myth, references have been made simply to the extraction of blood, without necessarily connecting this with Easter, Passover, or any kind of ritual.[2] In brief, the charge, known generically as the blood libel or the ritual murder accusation, contains a number of different nuances.

The medieval charges began in England at Norwich in 1144, after which they proceeded to spread over a great deal of Europe. In Norwich on Holy Saturday, 25 March 1144, a boy's corpse showing signs of a violent death was found in Thorpe Wood, and it was from such circumstances that the charge of ritual murder arose. Thomas of Monmouth, the author of a contemporary account, has described how the boy William was in the habit of frequenting the houses of Jews and was forbidden by his friends to have any more contact with them. On Monday of Holy Week 1144, it was claimed, he was lured away from his mother by a messenger with the offer of a place in the archdeacon's kitchen. Next day the messenger and William were seen to enter a Jew's house and from that time William was never again seen alive. On the Wednesday, so the legend runs, after a service in the synagogue, the Jews lacerated his head with thorns, crucified him, and pierced his side.[3] In making this accusation use was made of a claim by Theobald, a converted Jew, who told Thomas of Monmouth that "in the ancient writings of his Fathers it was written that the Jews, without the shedding of human blood could neither obtain their freedom, nor could they ever return to their fatherland. Hence it was laid down by them in ancient times that every year they must sacrifice a Christian in some part of the world"; in 1144 it fell to the Jews of Norwich to participate in such a sacrifice.[4] This fabrication provided the ground for the emergence of the charge of ritual murder, and it was an accusation which was almost certainly exploited by the monks of Norwich, who realized that the story was likely to swell the number of visitors to the cathedral.[5] At the time, however, such motivation was not readily apparent and the cult of the Norwich martyr grew. Furthermore, it was soon joined by other accusations of Jewish ritual murder.

In 1168 the charge was heard in Gloucester.[6] In 1181 it echoed in Bury St. Edmunds, and in Bristol in 1183.[7] In 1192—and again in 1225 and 1235—it was the turn of Winchester.[8] Then, in 1255, came the accusations relating to little Saint Hugh of Lincoln, a case which ranks first in importance in

England with that of William of Norwich, and which has passed into common circulation on account of its place in the Prioress's Tale, heard by Chaucer's band of pilgrims on their way to Canterbury.[9] In outline this particular accusation ran as follows. A body, allegedly bearing the marks of crucifixion, was found at the bottom of a well belonging to a Jew named Copin. Following this, Hugh, the son of a poor Lincoln woman, was said to have been crucified by the Jews. Copin was accused of having enticed Hugh into his house, where a number of Jews were reported to have tortured the child, scourged him, crowned him with thorns, and crucified him. Consequent upon this, Copin was accused of murder and confessed to the crime when he was threatened with death. In a testimony extracted under such circumstances Copin allegedly stated that it was a Jewish custom to crucify a boy once a year. The upshot of such developments was that Copin was put to a cruel death, eighteen Jews were hanged at Lincoln, and about ninety were imprisoned in London. These last mentioned were condemned to death but were released on the payment of a large fine. As for Hugh, miracles were supposedly wrought at his tomb and his body was brought from his parish into the cathedral. There seems little doubt that the accusation was related to the financial benefits which were almost certain to accrue to the cathedral in Lincoln.[10]

Up to this point these ritual murder charges were part of a general rash of such allegations in European society. They were heard, for instance, in France (Blois in 1171, Paris in 1180, and Valréas in 1247) and also in Germany (Erfurt in 1199, Wolfsheim in 1235, and Fulda in the same year).[11] But after the Lincoln case, while accusations continued to be made on the Continent, England never again heard claims of any fresh case.[12] However, this did not mean that charges alleging ritual murder were not referred to or discussed. John Foxe and William Prynne continued to put forward the charge, and in the eighteenth century William Romaine, a pamphleteer, could refer to Jews "frequently crucifying Christian children on Good Friday in Contempt and Mockery of Christ's Crucifixion" and claim that there were "the most glaring proofs" of this.[13] But it was the late nineteenth century which witnessed the significant modern recrudescence of the charge.[14]

Between 1880 and 1939 a major wave of anti-Semitism swept over most of Europe and America,[15] and it was in the course of this that the charge of ritual murder reappeared. Furthermore, a number of these incidents attracted particular attention in Britain. First of all, in 1881, a report in the *Globe* newspaper from its Cairo correspondent referred to the revival of the ritual murder charge in Alexandria, in which it was alleged that the Jews had kidnapped and killed a Greek child with the intention of securing his blood for the Feast of the Passover. The Cairo correspondent attempted to give background to his report by drawing attention, in garbled form, to the earlier well-known case in Damascus in 1840 and came to the conclusion that ". . . the position taken up by the Greeks is not on the face of it so absurd, untenable and prejudiced as the European colony would have us believe. If the voice of the vast majority be the voice of the people, and if it be true that *vox populi vox Dei*, then one should surely pause before exonerating the Jews of Alexandria of every suspicion of guilt."[16] Such comment stirred the delegate Chief Rabbi, Dr Hermann Adler, to write to the *Globe*, asking it to rebut the suggestions contained in the report. No action was forthcoming and it was in such circumstances that the Board of Deputies took up the issue and prevailed upon the editor to apologize for any slur which might have been cast on the Jewish community.[17] Later in the same year the board was once again in action, this time in defense of those Jews who were accused of ritual murder in Corfu.[18]

In 1882 attention switched from the Mediterranean to Hungary when the charge of ritual murder was heard at Tisza-Eszlar.[19] When this particular incident was discussed in the *Spectator*, the journal did not defend the accusation which was leveled against the Jews at Tisza-Eszlar; indeed, it referred to it as an "absurd libel."[20] But in the course of its discussion it tried to account for the charge and in doing so it ran into trouble. The offending passage ran as follows:

> The ancient and extraordinary charge against the Jews of sacrificing human beings in their Passover rites has been revived in Hungary. . . . The charge looks prima facie ridiculous, and derives its whole importance from its recurrence from time to time in widely separated countries and in nearly every century. We have read much apologetic Jewish literature but have never seen a reasonable explanation either of the charge, or of what is much more wonderful, the persistent popular belief in it. If that has any foundation, which is most improbable, there must exist embedded in Judaism a cabalistic sect which has preserved through ages some dark tradition of the efficacy in extreme cases of human sacrifice. Such a sect it is almost certain, is embedded in Hindooism, though the teachers of that faith repudiate it with unaffected horror.[21]

Such a suggestion—that there might be a sect within Judaism which engaged in ritual murder, and that this would account for the origins and persistence of the accusation—met with hostility from the Jewish community, with the *Jewish Chronicle* suggesting that the paper had displayed a "philosophic dislike" towards Jews.[22] This was denied by the *Spectator* and, in spite of Jewish protests, the journal persisted in the wake of Tisza-Eszlar with its attempts to explain the charge.[23]

In 1892, almost ten years after the allegation in Hungary, the Board of Deputies was in contact with the Foreign Office concerning an accusation which was heard in Malta in 1892–93.[24] But such matters retreated into relative insignificance with the onset of the Beilis affair in Russia in 1911, which over the next two years remained an issue of major importance for world Jewry.

Mendel Beilis, the superintendent of a Kiev brickworks, was charged with the ritual murder of Andrei Yushinsky, and it was only after two weary years that the charge against him was dismissed. Even then it was declared by the court that a ritual murder had taken place.[25] Such a gross campaign against Beilis drew the indignation of most liberal circles inside and outside Russia, to which protests the Jewish community in Britain, as elsewhere, made its own distinctive contribution.[26] In Britain there was, in fact, an almost complete condemnation of the action of the Russian authorities.[27]

A similar reaction was apparent twenty or so years later when, on 1 May 1934, as part of the Nazi campaign against the Jews, Julius Streicher published his charge of ritual murder in *Der Stürmer*.[28]

This survey of ritual murder cases has been concerned to make the point that, while such events occurred far from Britain, the anxiety of the Jewish community for its coreligionists and the hostility of sections of influential opinion towards the charge meant that accusations of ritual murder were discussed and commented upon within Britain itself. Against this background there were also home-grown developments which need to be considered. Comment in the *Globe* in 1881 and the *Spectator* in 1882 indicates that, below the surface where the charge was rejected, suspicions about the activity of Jews might be present. And, in fact, as we shall now discover, it was alleged in some quarters that Jews, or sections of Jews, engaged in ritual murder or, at some point in time, had indulged in the practice. It is a consideration of these allegations which forms the core of the present discussion.

Our survey of the major examples of this might begin in 1898, when Richard Burton's posthumous work *The Jew, the Gypsy and El Islam* was published. This episode has already received some attention and only the salient feature of it need be retold.[29] Burton collected his material when he was consul in Damascus between 1867 and 1871.[30] He began work on a book soon afterwards, but was advised against publishing it by certain friends who believed that it might hinder his advancement within the civil service. In view of this, his wife persuaded him to postpone publication until after he retired. However, Burton died in 1890, before his retirement, and the manuscript was still not ready for publication when his wife, who had taken over responsibility for the work, died in 1896. Consequently, the task of preparing it for publication fell to W. H. Wilkins, who had already displayed his hostility towards Jews in the course of the debate which was taking place in Britain over alien immigration.[31] There can be little doubt that Wilkins welcomed the opportunity for a further assault on the Jews.

In its published form in 1898, chapter 4 of the book contained a recital of what Burton considered to be the cruel and vindictive teaching of Judaism, which was followed by a catalogue of alleged Jewish crimes. In the course of this Burton made it clear that in his view Jews had engaged in ritual murder.[32] What is not apparent from the book is that a battle had been taking place behind the scenes involving Wilkins and the Board of Deputies, which restricted the published version of Burton's claims. The only hint of this appeared in the preface, where Wilkins wrote: "In the exercise of the discretion given to me, I have thought it better to hold over for the present the Appendix on the alleged rite of Human Sacrifice among the Sephardim and the murder of Padre Tomaso."[33] Wilkins had no doubt that, as it stood, Burton's book was anti-Semitic, and he was sure that English Jews would shrink with "abhorrence and repudiation before ritual murder," but in his view this did not mean that the charge was without foundation when directed against "their less fortunate Eastern brethren."[34]

The damage which could result from the publication of Burton's manuscript was quickly recognized by the Board of Deputies, and the published version was a concession to pressure from the board in 1897–98 rather than a voluntary abridgement by Wilkins. Even then the matter did not go away. In 1908 a member of the National Vigilance Society informed the Board that the publication of the omitted section was under consideration. In such circumstances the Board of Deputies moved quickly, and in February 1909 it was reported that arrangements had been finalized for the purchase of the manuscript. In March 1909 this was assigned to the President of the Board and an agreement was realized with the solicitors of the Burton family that the manuscript should not be published.[35] Action to defend the board's interest in the work was necessary in 1911 but since then no major problem on this score has arisen.[36] Even so, Burton's allegations were not forgotten. For instance, a version of his work circulated at the Beilis trial in Kiev in 1912, and in Britain the defensive activity of the board came to be cited in some quarters as an example of the way in which "Jew-power" could stifle and silence critics of the Jewish community.[37]

The next occasion when the claim of ritual murder was put forward in Britain did not attract the same amount of attention. The charge was referred to in the *Catholic Bulletin and Book Review* in 1916. Although the Beilis trial in Russia had passed, the incident was revived in this particular publication in a number of articles by Thomas Burbage. In essence they amounted to an account of the "Beylis" (*sic*) affair and suggested that a ritual murder by Jews might have taken place. It was noticed that six of the twelve jurors held Beilis guilty of the charge against him and that nowhere in the verdict was there any suggestion that, even if Beilis were innocent, a ritual murder had not been committed.[38]

There are four comments which might be made about Burbage's work. First of all, it must be noted that it came from a Catholic source. In this respect, even if it is dangerous to write about a tradition of hatred, it follows on at long distance from the charges in Norwich and Lincoln.

Secondly, the charge was put forward in particularly interesting fashion. The article opened with the question: "Does ritual murder exist among the Jews?" In reply it was stated: "This is one of those puzzling questions that is still awaiting a satisfactory answer."[39] But from that point Burbage went on:

> If Jews were content to hold that there was nothing in the beliefs and usages of the general body of their sect to justify the charge of ritual murder being made against their entire community, while admitting, at the same time, the possibility of a fanatical and superstitious body existing among their members whose actions might possibly warrant such a charge, their position would be reasonable enough. . . . But for reasons which it is hard to discover, they are not satisfied to act in this way. . . . If there is no real danger of the entire sect being involved in the ritual crime, there can be no reason for the uni-

107

versal panic that even a reference to it occasions among them, and if there were no foundation in fact for the charge, it should be possible to prove that without having recourse to unscrupulous trickery and lies. Yet . . . these are the weapons in which for the most part they put their trust.[40]

Then, turning to a specific case, the Kiev incident, Burbage asked: "If this act was not a ritual murder, what was the motive of the crime? The expert says it was a ritual murder. Has the ordinary reader a better explanation to offer?"[41] In short, Burbage presented his readers with an argument which blended implication and question to maximum effect.

In addition, a third point of interest arose when Burbage discussed those who defended the Jews against the charge of ritual murder. In the course of this he was particularly critical of the statement by Cardinal Ganganelli, later Clement XIV, a source which was widely quoted in the Jewish defence.[42] In opposition to Ganganelli's conclusions, Burbage vaunted evidence from the *Revue internationale des sociétés secrètes*, which since it was founded in 1909 had been obsessed with the idea of a Judeo-Masonic conspiracy. According to Burbage, the discussion of the Beilis affair in this journal was "most informative and impartial"—a remark which reveals a good deal about Burbage's own ideological position.[43]

Finally, and significantly, Burbage wove the charge of ritual murder into a more recent development within the ideology of anti-Semitism. That so little was known about the blood libel, he claimed, was due in part to Jewish pressure. "By means of the press they control" and "their great wealth" they were able to prevent any "impartial investigation."[44] Here we are moving into the world which feeds off its perception and fear of Jewish power, which can refer to the superior power of Jewry, which can hold out the prospect of the Jewish domination of society and which can proclaim that the tentacles of Jews already manipulate the world. In short, a world which finds its ultimate self-rationalization in *The Protocols of the Elders of Zion*. Such thought patterns were contained in Richard Burton's work and they were also clearly present in Burbage.[45]

The appearance of the articles was noticed in the *Jewish Chronicle*, where they were condemned as "nothing less than a deplorably wicked rehash of the disgraceful charges and exploded theories with which the civilization of the world has long been nauseated and which it is grievous beyond measure to see served up again in these islands."[46] What made the matter particularly regrettable to the *Chronicle* was that the work came from the pen of a priest, that it was published by H. H. Gill, a reputable firm in Dublin, and that Burbage's work had been advertised by posters which carried the caption "Murder among the Jews." This was regarded by the *Chronicle* as particularly dangerous at a time when Ireland was torn apart by civil strife and minorities could be easily exposed.[47] However, the articles would seem to have had no effect in stirring up a wave of Irish hostility towards Jews.

The next major discussion of ritual murder did not occur for another sixteen years, and once again we are pulled in the direction of a Catholic source. On this occasion the question arose with the publication of William Thomas Walsh's book *Isabella of Spain*. This particular work contained a chapter headed "Ritual Murder," in which, after stating that there was no evidence "that murder or any other iniquity" had ever been part of the "official ceremony of the Jewish religion," it was written:

> It does not follow by any means, however, that Jewish individuals or groups never committed bloody and disgusting crimes, even crimes motivated by hatred of Christ and of the Catholic Church; and the historian, far from being obliged to make wholesale vindication of all Jews accused of murder, is free, and in fact bound, to consider each individual case upon its merits. . . . One must admit that acts committed by Jews sometimes furnished the original provocation.[48]

With such opinions we are reminded of Burbage's earlier work in the *Catholic Bulletin and Book Review*.[49] For his part, and in line with his assumption that some Jews engaged in ritual murder, Walsh proceeded to quote specific incidents in support of his claim. These were the events of Sepulveda in 1468, and the well-known case of El Santo Niño de la Guardia, which was used as the immediate pretext for the expulsion of Jews from Spain in 1492.[50]

The attack on Walsh's writing came from Cecil Roth,[51] who took up the issue in the pages of the *Dublin Review*.[52] Faced with this challenge Walsh maintained his position and continued to assert that there were occasions when ritual murder had taken place.[53] The debate was fierce and uncompromising, and this was also reflected in the private correspondence which passed between the participants.[54] As for the public controversy, opinion in the *Review* shifted against Walsh with the publication of letters which deplored his attempt to "inflame unworthy passion."[55] Such sentiments were clearly welcomed by the editor[56] and with their appearance the skirmish in the *Review* came to a close, although it continued to echo elsewhere in Catholic circles.[57]

The last major charge of ritual murder which we have to consider carries us in a different direction. Arnold Spencer Leese[58] was one of the early recruits to fascism in Britain, and by mid-1928 he had formed his own political organization, the Imperial Fascist League. Before long, in his newspaper, the *Fascist*, and a large number of other publications, Leese began to express publicly the anti-Semitism which remained with him until his death in 1956.

According to Leese, Jews had inherent sadistic tendencies which led them to engage in ritual murder. Such behavior, he argued, was rooted in their biological constitution. It should be said at this point that an interest in ritual murder was not the central element of Leese's anti-Semitism: he was concerned essentially with Jewish power and domination and was more affected by the message he derived from *The Protocols of the Elders of Zion*. Nevertheless, he was prepared to charge Jews with ritual murder and with using their influence to cover up such activity.[59]

In line with this, in June 1934, shortly after Julius Streicher had published the special ritual murder edition of *Der*

Stürmer, and in the wake of the opposition which this aroused, Leese proclaimed: "It is an established fact that Ritual Murder is practised by Jews and that there are scores of recorded cases." On this occasion Leese chose to concentrate on the Damascus affair of 1840.[60] Shortly afterwards, while the protests over the *Stürmer* accusation were still very much alive, Leese drew attention to recently published German sources which, he claimed, underlined the participation of Jews in the practice. "Instead of making wholesale denials of ritual murder," he wrote, "the Jews would be well advised to admit that within their ranks is a superlatively unpleasant sect which at times is prone to this revolting rite."[61] Following this, the claim that Jews engaged in ritual murder appeared in the July issue of the *Fascist*, which was published on 30 June 1936.[62] Shortly afterwards, on 10 July, the *Jewish Chronicle* reproduced a paragraph from the publication, and urged the need for action.[63] Questions were asked in the Commons,[64] and on 31 July 1936 two summonses were served, one on Leese and the other on the printer, Walter Whitehead, who printed a great deal of fascist literature in the interwar years.[65] Altogether six charges were involved. There was a major one of seditious libel and among the lesser charges were those of conspiring to effect a public mischief and of effecting a public mischief.

The hearing took place at the Old Bailey on 18 and 21 September 1936 before Mr. Justice Greaves Lord.[66] Leese conducted his own defense and, with the degree of latitude which he was allowed, succeeded in securing his acquittal on the major charge of seditious libel. Whitehead, who was also unrepresented, based his defense on the question "What can a poor printer do?" In his business he could not afford to discriminate. Orders were orders. And, he said, there was no evidence that any disturbance had resulted from what he had printed.[67] In the event Leese and Whitehead were both found guilty of the two lesser charges. As a consequence Leese was sent to prison for six months in default of accepting the penalty of a fine and Whitehead was fined £20.[68] It was a verdict which George Webber, who worked in Neville Laski's chambers and provided the Board of Deputies with comments on the case, viewed with misgivings. A stiff sentence, he believed, would have been a better result for the Jewish community.[69] As it was, Webber claimed, Leese had been able to stand in court, proclaim himself a scientist and engage in political propaganda. In the course of this he was able to insinuate that the charge of ritual murder—which, effectively, had led to the prosecution—was true.[70]

But while sources close to the Jewish community could suggest that Leese was allowed to get away with too much at his trial, in Leese's own opinion he had not been able to go far enough. Consequently, when he turned his attention to the matter two years later, he entitled his reflections *My Irrelevant Defence,* and proceeded to publish information which the trial judge had considered irrelevant to the case. In the book, which constitutes Leese's fullest views on the subject, the charge of ritual murder was repeated. It was impossible to convince him to the contrary.[71]

We have now discussed the major charges relating to ritual murder which were heard in Britain between 1880 and 1939. In addition, some reference is necessary to the fainter echoes of the accusation which were present during these years. Consequently, we might now move from a major to a minor key.

We have noticed that in late-nineteenth-century Britain the first major allegation occurred in 1898 and that Richard Burton's manuscript afforded an opportunity for W. H. Wilkins, who had taken part in the opposition to alien immigration, to broaden the basis of his hostility towards Jews.[72] Around the same time the charge was in fact heard directly in the course of the immigration debate. In the *East London Observer,* for instance, in 1902 a letter from "England for the English," proclaimed:

> We in East London know only too well what bloodsuckers the Jews are. Here they drive the worker from his home through their rapacity; they verily suck the life blood of the nation. In Austria they use Christian blood for their abominable ritual. And not only in Austria but the same terrible system of using our blood widely obtains in European countries. It makes

one's blood boil to think that such things are tolerated. If the Jews are capable of such vile practices they are capable of anything and I for one would gladly assist a fund to stir up a great anti-semitic movement so that not one of the foreigners dare stay in England.[73]

In addition to such direct references, Jews could be referred to in blood-associated imagery, so that at the time of the 1904 Aliens Bill, the *Eastern Post* could ask: "Are our people . . . still to have his fangs fastened in their throats? Is the life-blood of the nation to be sucked by the human vampires?"[74] Such writing projected its own vivid impression of the Jews which was closely related to some expressions of the blood libel charge.

The major debate over Jewish immigration during these years did in fact arise from developments in the East End of London, but the question of Jewish newcomers echoed further afield than this. Although it remained small, the Jewish community in Ireland increased as a result of immigration, and in Limerick in 1904 Father Creagh, a Redemptorist priest, succeeded in raising the memory of ritual murder in the minds of his flock, although he suggested that in their own day a crueler martyrdom based on economic exploitation was cast upon them. Following this, in the wake of Creagh's remarks and with his encouragement, the Jewish community in Limerick experienced two years of almost unremitting persecution.[75]

Through his power over his congregation Creagh was instrumental in converting thought into action. Most accusations which we are concerned with in the present discussion, however, exercised no such apparent influence. We are involved essentially with the expression of attitudes hostile to Jews, and in line with this we might leave Ireland, and bring James Blyth, a prolific and popular novelist, whose work has now passed unrescued into oblivion, into our discussion. In 1910, when the debate over Jewish immigration was still alive, Blyth wrote *Ichabod*, which had the undermining of British society by aliens as its major theme. As befits a popular work, it was full of crude stereotypes, and presented a canvas on which good and evil appeared in stark opposing contrast. In this setting the Jew was a personification of evil. And in discussing the disappearance of one of the characters, the possibility of ritual murder was introduced into the story.[76] It is true that it was introduced only to be questioned. But this technique of extracting the best of both worlds, by attacking Jews and simultaneously saying enough to cover one's position, was a well-worn feature of anti-Jewish hostility at this time, and in this respect Blyth's novel, which was stuffed with such sentiment, fitted into a recognizable tradition.[77]

The world in which such discussion occurred witnessed a considerable public debate over Jews,[78] and this did not die in the war which soon followed. Indeed, as we have noticed, it was in the midst of hostilities that Thomas Burbage, writing about the Beilis case, once more thrust the charge of ritual murder into prominence.[79] And in reviving interest in the accusation at this time Burbage was not alone. If it was his analysis which captured attention, it should not be overlooked that in 1914–15 Stephen Graham of *The Times*, who had a particular interest in Russian affairs, cast anti-Jewish shadows over the picture when he too discussed the Beilis affair. No direct claim was made that Jews had committed a ritual murder, but it was emphasized that the victim had been killed in a way which had a "mystic significance" and, Graham proceeded to write, "Someone was guilty, a madman or a Jew; and indeed the probability is that a Jew did actually commit the crime. Whether it was for ritual purposes or not, is another matter." Unlike Burbage's offering, however, Graham's comments attracted little attention.[80]

We have now reached a point when, in considering the minor echoes of the ritual murder accusation in Britain between 1880 and 1939, we can move into the last chronological stage of the discussion and turn our attention to the interwar years. Here, there are a number of publications which ought to be mentioned. First of all, the charge was presented, without refutation, and as if it were authentic, in Montague Summers' *The History of Witchcraft and Demonology*, which appeared in 1926.[81] Then six years later, the *Hibbert Journal* found itself in an embarrassing situation on account of an article by Ray Knight, which at one point claimed: "The charge of ritual murder persistently brought against the Jews and always dismissed as a malignant calumny is proved up to the hilt by their own scriptures."[82] In the next issue this statement was withdrawn and the journal also published a note from F. J. Foakes-Jackson (whose work on Josephus had been quoted by Knight) emphasizing that he personally had never countenanced the charge.[83] While noting all this, the *Jewish Chronicle* nevertheless expressed regret that there was no editorial apology and no personal retraction of his beliefs by the author, and, coming as it did around the same time as Walsh's allegations in the *Dublin Review*, the *Chronicle* believed that there were grounds for the expression of some concern.[84] However, no significant anti-Semitic trend grew out of such comments.

Even so, the allegation continued to be made in scattered fashion. In 1933, for example, the Britons Publishing Society produced a one-leaf sheet for distribution in the United States, with the title *Jewish Ritual Murder in San Diego*, in which it was claimed that two Jewish ritual murders had been committed in San Diego in the previous three years.[85] In support of the general charge, reference was made to the work of August Rohling, and American readers were informed that several cases of blood accusation had recently been before the European courts, notably the Xanter (*sic*) case in Germany in 1897 and the Beilis case in Kiev in 1911.[86] This was one of the rare occasions when anti-Semitic material was made for export from Britain, and it led to correspondence between B'nai B'rith in Cincinnati and the Board of Deputies. As a consequence, the board established contact with the printers, who agreed to give the board notice if other orders were received. In fact, however, no further developments seem to have occurred.[87]

If at this point we consider reactions to the charge,[88] we might notice first of all that there have been expressions of righteous anger that such an accusation could be contemplated, let alone made. For instance, in the dark days of the Beilis affair, the *Jewish Chronicle* referred to it as "that heritage of mediaeval barbarism, a lie and a libel of the darkest of dark ages,"[89] and later, at the time of the *Dublin Review* controversy, the *Chronicle* could write about an atmosphere of "mediaeval darkness" in which "poisonous calumnies" such as "the immortal lie" could be put forward.[90] Finally, to Cecil Roth, at the heart of the latter controversy, the charge was fiercely attacked as "the foul accusation."[91]

Such comment was an immediate, emotional reaction. But there were more measured responses. For example, it was stressed that the charge was contrary to the principles of Judaism. At the time of the report in the *Globe* concerning the alleged ritual murder in Alexandria, Hermann Adler wrote to the newspaper, defending the community as follows:

> Is it to be believed that a religion which enjoins "whoso shed-deth man's blood by man shall his blood be shed: for in the image of God made He man" would sanction the slaughtering of a fellow being for the purposes of a religious rite? Is it to be credited that the professors of a faith which forcibly and re-peatedly commands to abstain even from the blood of animals would commit the iniquity of mixing the sacred Passover bread with human blood?[92]

Similar arguments were put forward shortly afterwards by the Catholic writer Herbert Thurston, when he claimed that there was "absolutely no trace of any such rite in the Talmud or any Hebrew ritual or Hebrew religious book of ac-knowledged authority."[93] This was also part of Roth's defense in the *Dublin Review* controversy.[94] Where admissions of a Jewish involvement in such practices did exist, it was suggested that they had been extracted under interrogation and torture and were therefore unreliable.[95]

This reference to torture brings to mind particularly the charges which were laid against Jews in Spain, which lay at the heart of the controversy between Roth and Walsh. In the course of his counterattack Roth drew upon the work of H. C. Lea, "that superb historical craftsman," and inclined towards Lea's judgment that torture had been used to extract confessions in the La Guardia case.[96] In other words, the charge of ritual murder was also rejected by reference to some alternative acknowledged authority and Herbert Thurston's reliance on H. L. Strack's *Der Blutaberglaube*, which later, in 1909, appeared in English translation as *The Jew and Human Sacrifice*, was a further indication of this.[97]

Interestingly enough, in view of the charges of ritual murder which emanated from Catholic sources, the accusation was also countered on occasions by an appeal to the teaching and position of the Catholic Church.[98] In this connection a number of major statements were used to defend Jews against the charges directed against them. Herbert Thurston, for instance, could refer to "the often quoted letters of Innocent IV, Gregory X and Martin V which fully exonerate the Jews from the charge of ritual murder."[99] And at the time of the Beilis affair similar evidence was sought for by Lord Rothschild when he wrote to Cardinal Merry del Val at the Vatican, seeking an assurance that an authentic condemnation of the blood libel had been made by Pope Innocent IV and that Cardinal Lorenzo Ganganelli had drawn up a report in 1758 which absolved the Jews of the alleged crime.[100] It is readily apparent, in fact, that in Britain as elsewhere Ganganelli's report assumed considerable importance in Jewish quarters in the defense of the community against the blood libel.[101] At other times, even if specific sources were not quoted, it was not uncommon to find general reference being made to the condemnation which had emerged from the highest authorities of the Church.[102] In addition Thurston in particular, arguing from within the Roman Church, was concerned to emphasize that *apparent* official approval of the charge by the Roman Church, as evidenced by the beatification of two alleged victims, Andrew of Rinn and Simon of Trent, did not involve the Church in formal beatifications and in neither case was it authoritatively claimed that a ritual murder had occurred, but rather that the Jews' victims had been killed *in odium fidei*. Such a distinction, however, was not easily grasped by all Catholics.[103]

In addition to these appeals to various authorities, the Jewish community engaged in positive practical action to counteract the accusation. It was to this end that the Board of Deputies contacted the printers of the pamphlet *Jewish*

Ritual Murder in San Diego and enlisted their cooperation in alerting the board about any similar orders.[104] Furthermore, it was with a similar aim that in 1936 Neville Laski, on behalf of the Board of Deputies, furnished material to the Director of Public Prosecutions which, it was hoped, could be used in the charges against Arnold Leese.[105]

So much for the major allegations of Jewish ritual murder which were heard in Britain between 1880 and 1939 and the attempts to protect Jews against these. Why, it might now be asked, did the charge arise?

There are those who would have nothing to do with any explanation: for them righteous anger is the only possible response.[106] But, if we do try to come to grips with the charge, it is advisable to start at an outer limit and then proceed towards the center. If we follow this path the charge needs to be set first of all within the general context of severe accusations directed towards minority groups. In the Roman world, for example, the early Christian minority was accused of engaging in human sacrifice, and in the nineteenth century allegations were made in China that Christian missionaries were intent upon devouring children. It was a claim of this kind which led to disturbances in Tientsin in 1871. And twenty years later Christian missionaries in Madagascar were accused of the same crime.[107] In similar fashion Catholics in nineteenth-century England were accused of building oubliettes in which to murder enemies of the faith[108] and of killing children in convents and making tea from their bones.[109] If we continue the catalogue, in medieval and more particularly in early modern times witches were also accused of sacrificial practices, and in some instances Christians accused heretical sects of similar abominable rites.[110] In other words, the ritual murder allegation should be considered as part of a tendency to attribute sanguinary and revolting practices to any cult or out-group which holds cryptic, unfamiliar, heretical, or minority beliefs. Its function is to render them antihuman and to categorize them as implacable enemies of society.[111]

This almost certainly accounts for the claims heard in the ancient world, but it is important to come in from this general outer limit and concentrate on the nature of the specific charges which have been heard against Jews since medieval times, in spite of the fact that, as a group, they are not known to have committed any such crime.[112]

As it developed in medieval society it was a charge which could be connected with Jews because of their association with magic and medicine. There was a stress on the need and value of human bodies in the practice of both. But the charge also contained a specific religious dimension: in this respect it was a perpetuation in simple, immediate form of the view that Jews killed Christ, for which act Jews were held responsible by the Roman Catholic Church until 1965. The alleged ritual murder of later Christians, representatives of Christ, served as a constant reminder of this. The accusation also provided a useful source of revenue for the Church, as a result of pilgrims' visits to pay homage to the martyrs of ritual murder, and a cynical awareness of this, against the wider background we have just been discussing, was another factor helping to generate some of the charges. It has also been contended—although the suggestion is speculative and requires further investigation—that those allegations which referred specifically to the extraction of blood involved an important transference of beliefs and practices from Christians to Jews. In other words the accusation additionally reflected the Christian obsession with blood projected onto a rival religious group. But why should an accusation of this kind have been significantly revived in the late nineteenth century? In considering this it is necessary to remark first of all on the general expansion of anti-Semitic activity at this time. It was in tandem with this that the ritual murder charge received a new lease of life. So far we have been concerned with British opinion, but the revival assumed a European dimension. We might notice, first of all, the publication in 1866 of Konstantin Pawlikowsky's *Der Talmud in der Theorie und Praxis,* which listed seventy-five alleged cases of human sacrifice by Jews. In addition, at the time of the Tisza-Eszlar trial, August Rohling claimed he could substantiate on oath the ritual murder accusation, and a few years later, in 1889, Henri Desportes, in *Le mystère du sang chez les juifs de tous les temps,* asserted that dangerous passages justifying ritual murder which were omitted from the Talmud were nevertheless passed on to Jews through an oral tradition. Then in 1892 a Milan newspaper, *Osservatore Cattolico,* published a series of articles on the practice of ritual murder by Jews. In 1934 such offerings were supplemented by the special issue of *Der Stürmer,* and throughout these years there was a string of specific incidents in which it was alleged that ritual murder had taken place. To reiterate: the rash of ritual murder charges needs to be set within the framework of a revival of anti-Semitism between 1880 and 1939 which in Britain occurred mainly at the time of Jewish immigration and in the 1930s. It was in such circumstances that old forms of anti-Semitism were reactivated, to exist alongside and reinforce more recent expressions of conspiratorial hostility towards Jews.[113]

Within this context three specific influences were instrumental in reviving the charge in Britain. First of all, as elsewhere in Europe, account has to be taken of a Catholic involvement. The early charges in the medieval world were associated with the Church, and while there were important denunciations of ritual murder by Innocent IV and Cardinal Ganganelli, the cases of Andrew of Rinn (1462) and Simon of Trent (1475), which were held to be murders of Christians by Jews *in odium fidei,* helped to create suspicion among some Catholics.[114] And, as direct evidence of Catholic links in Britain with the ritual murder accusation, we might note that Lord Acton believed in it,[115] that Creagh, who made the accusation in Limerick, was a Catholic priest, and so was Burbage, whose work appeared in the *Catholic Bulletin and Book Review.* Walsh was also a Catholic writing in the *Dublin Review* and he was defended in the *Catholic Times.* Finally, we might note that Montague Summers shared the same faith. In other words, against the background of an international revival of anti-Semitism, this Catholic influence, the continuation of an old religious animosity towards Jews, was a powerful force in Britain—and other countries—in the expression of ritual murder charges.[116]

But it did not act alone. In comparison with most of Europe, anti-Semitism in Britain existed at a subdued level, and those who did embrace it sometimes turned to Europe for evidence which might then be used in a British context. Consequently, although it can be overstressed, a European influence can be detected in anti-Semitic developments in Britain, and with specific reference to ritual murder two incidents assumed some significance. These were the Beilis trial and the publication of the special ritual murder issue of *Der Stürmer*. T. H. Burbage was clearly influenced in the *Catholic Bulletin and Book Review* by events in Russia, and it is possible that in part Leese was encouraged to emphasize the ritual murder theme by the publication of Streicher's special issue of *Der Stürmer*. This is not to suggest, however, that the traffic in ideas was in one direction only. At the time of the Beilis trial we have noticed that a version of Richard Burton's work circulated in Kiev, and the Russian authorities also used the work of the anthropologist J. G. Frazer to strengthen their flimsy case.[117]

There were, in short, specific social influences which need to be acknowledged if we are to understand why the ritual murder myth was manifested in Britain between 1880 and 1939. But it is also important to come even further inwards and refer to individual circumstances.[118] This is not to suggest that society and the individual remain separate entities, but rather that a rounded explanation would need to take account of the interaction of the individual and the wider society and that in some instances individual personality structures are such that they need to receive a special emphasis. We simply do not have the kind of information which historians need to construct a significant argument about the motivations of individuals such as Burbage and Walsh, but in other cases more work has been done and it is almost certain that the anti-Semitism of Burton[119] and Leese[120] needs to be significantly related to drives within their own personalities. In their case the acceptance of the ritual murder charge was only one element in a constellation of ideas of which they had a fundamental need.

On such a note, having moved from an outer to an inner limit of explanation, we might conclude this survey of the ritual murder accusation in Britain between 1880 and 1939. A belief in the charge had an amorphous existence in British society, but its most tenacious home was in committed anti-Semitic groups whose ideology never exercised a wide appeal.[121] Consequently, the main interest of the charge for historians lies elsewhere: it is a firm reminder of the proposition advanced at the beginning of the discussion, that anti-Semitic images possess considerable durability. And lest we are tempted to take refuge in a later enlightenment and celebrate the vanquishing of the past, we should do well to remind ourselves that Arnold Leese continued his attacks upon Jews for ritual murder until his death in 1956, constantly scouring the press and historical sources for details which, to his mind, would support the charge.[122] And, since Leese has exerted an ideological influence upon the National Front,[123] it is not surprising that it is this organization which is most prominently involved in perpetuating in our own times that most resilient element of anti-Semitism, the dark myth of Jewish sadism and Jewish ritual murder.[124]

Notes

I gratefully acknowledge the support of the Twenty-Seven Foundation in the preparation of this paper. I am also grateful to C. C. Aronsfeld and Robert Singerman, who provided me with a number of references, and to R. I. Moore and L. P. Gartner, who commented on my first draft. None of them is responsible for the arguments and views which I present.

1. S. W. Baron, *A Social and Religious History of Jews*, 2d ed., revised and enlarged (New York, 1958), 1:192–93. See also J. Trachtenberg, *The Devil and the Jews* (New York, 1966), p. 126, and M. Stern, *Greek and Latin Authors on Jews and Judaism* (Jerusalem, 1976), 1:530–31, for additional comment on the early references to ritual murder. More generally, see the *Universal Jewish Encyclopaedia* (New York, 1948), 2:407–10, and the *Encyclopaedia Judaica* (Jerusalem, 1971), 4:1120–32. Trachtenberg, *The Devil*

and the Jews, pp. 127–28, is critical of Cecil Roth's argument in "The Feast of Purim and the Origins of the Blood Accusation," *Speculum* 8 (1933): 520–26, which relates the charges to acts at the Feast of Purim. [See pp. 261–72 of this volume.–Ed.]

2. Trachtenberg, *The Devil and the Jews,* chaps. 9 and 10, refers to such developments. H. Strack, *The Jew and Human Sacrifice* (London, 1909), chaps. 2–10, has a valuable discussion on blood myths. See also E. O. James, *Sacrifice and Sacrament* (London, 1962), chap. 3.

3. Detail from the *Catholic Encyclopaedia* (London, 1912), 15:635.

4. Ibid.

5. See M. D. Anderson, *A Saint at Stake* (London, 1964), pp. 198–99. Chap. 9 of the book discusses the various theories relating to William's death. A valuable earlier discussion is A. Jessop and M. R. James, *The Life and Miracles of St William of Norwich* (Cambridge, 1896), which between pages lxxvii and lxxviii also clears Jews of the charge of ritual murder.

6. *Universal Jewish Encyclopaedia* 7:624.

7. On Bristol, see ibid. 14:1378, and on Bury, see ibid. 14:1535.

8. Ibid. 16:536.

9. See any edition of Chaucer's *Canterbury Tales.* See also the *Times,* 15 October 1959, for the removal of a notice on the incident from Lincoln cathedral and the plan to install a new plaque which cast doubt on ritual murder stories.

10. *Catholic Encyclopaedia* (London, 1910), 7:515, notes the financial aspect behind medieval allegations of ritual murder. L. O. Pike, *A History of Crime in England* (London, 1873), 1:195, dismisses the charge against the Jews. For a later discussion, see J. W. F. Hill, *Medieval Lincoln* (Cambridge, 1948), pp. 224–32.

11. *Universal Jewish Encyclopaedia* 2:409.

12. Ibid., pp. 409–10, gives a list of cases down to 1940. H. D. Traill, ed., *Social England* (London, 1893), 1:407, notes the extent of ritual murder charges and comments: "It is difficult to refuse all credit to stories so circumstantial and so frequent; but on the other hand it may be said that the tales are too many for them all to be true, and most of them may be dismissed as wholly fictions." This comment was seized upon by Arnold Leese, *My Irrelevant Defence* (London, 1938), p. 15, to argue unequivocally in favor of a Jewish involvement in ritual murder.

13. William Romaine, *An Answer to a Pamphlet* (London, 1753), p. 23; for earlier comment see John Fox, *Acts and Monuments*

(London, 1583 ed.), p. 327, and William Prynne, *A Short Demurrer to the Jews* (London, 1656), pp. 67–69 (there is a particularly vicious remark on p. 69).

14. A major case which occurred just outside the time limits of the present study was the 1840 Damascus affair, which created considerable interest in Britain. On this, see S. Baring Gould, *Historic Oddities and Strange Events*, 2d ser. (London, 1891), pp. 86–106. Later comment appears in A. M. Hyamson, "The Damascus Affair—1840," *Transactions of the Jewish Historical Society of England* (henceforth *TJHSE*), 16 (1945–51): 47–71, and *Encyclopaedia Judaica* 5 : 1249–52. For an anti-Semitic account, see Leese, *My Irrelevant Defence*, pp. 24–28. See above pp. 105 and 111 for the longer-term repercussions and interest in the incident.

15. See John Higham, "Anti-Semitism in the Gilded Age," *Mississippi Valley Historical Review* (henceforth *MVHR*), vol. 43 (1956–57): 570–71, for reference to the importance of the years between the 1880s and the 1930s in the history of anti-Semitism.

16. *Globe*, 18 April 1881.

17. Board of Deputies Minute Book 12 April 1878–February 1889, meeting of 25 May 1881, provides details. See also *Jewish Chronicle*, 13 May 1881.

18. See the correspondence from the Board to the Foreign Secretary, Earl Granville, on this matter in File B2/9/16 in the Board archives. In 1913 the attention of the Board of Deputies was drawn to a Greek novel, Stephanos Xenos, *The Devil in Turkey*, 3 vols., (London, 1851), which in 2 : 30, 40, had suggested a Jewish involvement in ritual murder. See the letter in File E3/148.

19. *Universal Jewish Encyclopaedia* 15 : 1155–56.

20. *Spectator*, 7 July 1883. For another opinion see C. H. H. Wright, "The Jews and the Malicious Charge of Human Sacrifice," *Nineteenth Century* 14 (1883): 753–78.

21. *Spectator*, 23 June 1883.

22. *Jewish Chronicle*, 29 June 1883, in the course of a leader on the blood accusation which takes up points made by the *Spectator* on 23 June.

23. *Spectator*, 7 July 1883.

24. See the correspondence in the archives of the Board of Deputies in File B2/9/16.

25. The incident is fully covered in two books: A. S. Tager, *The Decay of Czarism: The Beiliss Trial* (Philadelphia, 1935), and M. Samuel, *Blood Accusation: The Strange History of the Beilis Case* (London, 1967).

26. Zosa Szajkowski, "The Impact of the Beilis Case on Central and Western Europe," *Proceedings of the American Academy for Jewish Research* 31 (1963): 202–6, gives some indication of the issues which were raised and the protests which were forthcoming outside Russia. For more general comment, see Tager, *Decay of Czarism,* and Samuel, *Blood Accusation,* Material at the Board of Deputies relating to the Board's response is contained in File B2/9/16.

27. However, Leese, *My Irrelevant Defence,* pp. 32–33, spoke out later against the Liberal condemnation of the Russians. At the time the Russian government made use of J. G. Frazer's work to justify the charge against Beilis. This drew a sharp retort from Frazer in the *Times,* 11 November 1913. See Add MS b 35[1] in the Frazer collection at Trinity College, Cambridge, for a letter from I. Abrahams, dated 11 November 1913, congratulating Frazer on his "manly letter" to the *Times.* Frazer 3[121] consists of an undated letter from Wickham Steed of the *Times* alerting Frazer to the report from Kiev, informing him that in some editions the *Times* had mounted a defense based on comment in *The Golden Bough* and urging him to write in himself if he wished to add anything. It has to be said, however, that Frazer's position on the matter was not crystal clear. See *The Golden Bough: A Study in Magic and Religion,* 6, *The Scapegoat* (London, 1919; this edition was first published in 1913), pp. 394–96. For comment on Frazer's position, see S. G. Bayme, "Jewish Leadership and Anti-Semitism in Britain 1898–1918" (Ph.D. thesis, Columbia University, 1977), p. 158. For brief details on Frazer (1854–1941), see the *Concise Dictionary of National Biography* (Oxford, 1961), 2: 156–57.

28. See the comment in the *Jewish Chronicle,* 11 May 1934. For additional detail, see Cecil Roth, *The Ritual Murder Libel and the Jew* (London, 1935), pp. 106–9.

29. For a full discussion, see chap. 4 of my book, Colin Holmes, *Anti-Semitism in British Society, 1876–1939* (London, 1979).

30. For a general account of Burton's career, see Fawn Brodie, *The Devil Drives* (Harmondsworth, 1971).

31. On Wilkins' publications on such matters, see Holmes, *Anti-Semitism,* pp. 249–50, n. 63.

32. Sir Richard F. Burton, *The Jew, the Gypsy and El Islam,* edited with a preface and brief notes by W. H. Wilkins (London, 1898), p. 128.

33. Ibid., p. v.

34. Ibid., p. xi.

35. Holmes, *Anti-Semitism*, pp. 51–54, provides details. The manuscript is still at the Board of Deputies.

36. Ibid., pp. 53–54, discusses the 1911 action. A reprint of the 1898 version of the book is currently being offered by the Sons of Liberty of Metairie, Louisiana. It is one of their many reprints of anti-Semitica.

37. See, for instance, the writings of F. H. O'Donnell in the *New Witness* discussed by Holmes, *Anti-Semitism*, p. 59. For much later comment in anti-Semitic sources, see *Plain English*, 9, 23, and 30 April 1921; Leese, *My Irrelevant Defence*, pp. 5, 28; *Free Press*, December 1936.

38. Thomas H. Burbage, "Ritual Murder among the Jews," *Catholic Bulletin and Book Review* 6 (1916): 309, 441.

39. Ibid., p. 309.

40. Ibid., p. 439.

41. Ibid., p. 441.

42. See ibid., p. 435 *et seq.*, for his attack upon the "time-worn weapon" of drawing the Catholic Church into a defense of Jews against blood libel charges.

43. Ibid., p. 310. On the *Revue*, which had strong Catholic connections, see Norman Cohn, *Warrant for Genocide* (Harmondsworth, 1970), p. 182.

44. Burbage, "Ritual Murder," p. 309.

45. See Holmes, *Anti-Semitism*, chap. 4, for a discussion of such trends in Burton's thought.

46. *Jewish Chronicle*, 9 June 1916. The appearance of Burbage's work was also noticed in ibid., 30 June, 21 July, and 18 August 1916.

47. Ibid., 9 June 1916.

48. W. T. Walsh, *Isabella of Spain* (London, 1931), p. 400. Apart from this work Walsh wrote *Scientific Spiritual Healing* (1926), a novel called *A Murder Makes a Man* (1935) and a biography of Philip II (1938).

49. See above, pp. 107–9, for Burbage's views.

50. See Walsh, *Isabella of Spain*, pp. 125–26 and 440–67. See the *Jewish Encyclopaedia* (New York and London, 1905), 11:200, for reference to Sepulveda; on the other case, see H. C. Lea, "Santo Niño de la Guardia," *English Historical Review* 4 (1889): pp. 229–50.

51. On Roth (1899–1970), see the *Universal Jewish Encyclopaedia* 14:326–28, and Chaim Raphael's essay in *Commentary* 50, no. 3 (September 1970): 75–81.

52. See Cecil Roth, "Jews, Conversos, and the Blood-Accusation in Fifteenth-Century Spain," *Dublin Review* 191 (1932): 219–31.

53. W. T. Walsh, "Reply to Dr. Cecil Roth," in ibid., pp. 232–52. Walsh was later defended by the fascist Arnold Leese. See Leese, *My Irrelevant Defence*, pp. 20–21.

54. See the correspondence in E3/148 in the Board of Deputies, particularly Roth's letter to Walsh of 16 November 1932.

55. See the letter from Bede Jarrett, O.P. and Herbert Loewe from Blackfriars, Oxford, and that from C. Lattey, S.J., at Heythrop College in *Dublin Review* 192 (1933): 128. The *Jewish Chronicle*, 26 January 1933, welcomed these repudiations of "the foul insult to our people."

56. *Dublin Review* 192 (1933): 129.

57. See the letter of "Firenne" in the *Catholic Times*, 8 February 1935. This arose out of correspondence in ibid., 9 November 1934, in which it was alleged that there was historical evidence to support the charge of ritual murder against Jews. "The Jews and the Masons do not like the truth being told about the murder of Arbues. They like it to be hidden away with the story of the Holy Child of La Guardia and the murder of Father Thomas of Damascus." (On the two latter cases, see above, nn. 50 and 14 respectively. Pedro de Arbues, the Inquisitor of Saragossa, was killed on 14 September 1485 before the high altar in the cathedral. This led to an intensification of the persecution against converted Jews. See the *Encyclopaedia Judaica* 1:300.) This letter was followed by one from Cecil Roth on 1 February 1935 denying the charges. It was at this point that "Firenne" entered the correspondence, in which he supported Walsh against Roth.

58. On Leese, see J. E. Morell, "The Life and Opinions of A. S. Leese: A Study in Extreme Anti-Semitism" (M.A. thesis, University of Sheffield, 1975), and R. M. Gorman, "Swastika over England: The Life and Thought of Arnold Spencer Leese," (M.A. thesis, Milledgeville, Georgia). See also Leese's autobiography, *Out of Step* (Guildford, 1947).

59. See Holmes, *Anti-Semitism*, chap. 10, or further details of Leese's general anti-Semitic outlook.

60. *Fascist*, June 1934. See above, n. 14, for reference to the Damascus affair.

61. *Fascist*, February 1935. Leese was making reference in this comment to the Chassidim. See Holmes, *Anti-Semitism*, p. 165.

62. *Fascist*, July 1936. This was not an isolated reference by Leese to Jewish ritual murder. See ibid., November 1932, June 1934, August 1934 (a discussion of the Damascus case, which referred to the "instinctive sadism of the 'Hither Asiatic'"), February

1935, March 1935 (a reference to Beilis), April 1935, January 1936 (an alleged case in Afghanistan), February 1936 (an account of the Lindbergh baby case), June 1938, April 1938, January 1939, August 1939 (a discussion of the Torso Murder in Leeds, which, it is clear from his private papers, Leese was anxious to regard as a ritual murder). After the war Leese still continued to assert that the Jews were guilty of ritual murder. See *Gothic Ripples*, no. 40 (June 1948): 4; no. 63 (April 1950): 3; no. 72 (February 1951): 4; no. 101 (May 1953): 3; no. 105 (September 1953): 4; no. 106 (October 1953): 1; no. 107 (November 1953): 1; no. 109 (January 1954): 2; no. 127 (May 1955): 3.

63. *Jewish Chronicle*, 10 July 1936.

64. *Parliamentary Debates*, Commons, vol. 314 (1935–36), col. 1570. D. N. Pritt referred to the charge as "that old, that brutal, that cruel accusation."

65. A sheet, headed British Aryan Defence Fund, in the archives of the Board of Deputies (File E1/16) provides details of developments.

66. There is a manuscript in the archives of the Board of Deputies (File E1/16), entitled "Observations upon the case of R v Lease (*sic*) and Whitehead, September 18 and 21, 1936," by George Webber, which provides considerable detail on the trial. Hereafter referred to as "Observations MS." The case was also reported in the *Times*, 19 and 22 September 1936.

67. "Observations MS," pp. 6 and 8.

68. See another manuscript, "To the American Jewish Committee on the trial of Arnold Spencer Leese and Walter Whitehead at the Old Bailey on 18 and 21 September 1936 before Mr Justice Greaves-Lord," p. 38 (File C 13/4/3/ in the Board of Deputies). Hereafter "Memorandum MS."

69. "Observations MS," pp. 10–11. For additional comment, from differing perspectives, see the *Jewish Chronicle*, 25 September 1936, and the *Fascist*, September and October 1936.

70. "Memorandum MS," p. 29.

71. Leese, *My Irrelevant Defence*, passim.

72. See above, p. 106.

73. *East London Observer*, 12 April 1902. See the support from "Union Jack" in ibid., 19 April 1902. The reference to practices in Austria may have derived from the report by the Vienna correspondent of *The Times* who, at the time of the Ripper murders, filed a report on the alleged ritual murder of a woman near Cracow. This created tension in the East End and it may have passed into folk

memory. See the *Times*, 2 October 1888, for the report. For surrounding comment, see Chaim Bermant, *Point of Arrival: A Study of London's East End* (London, 1975), pp. 111–21.

74. *Eastern Post and City Chronicle*, 2 July 1904.

75. For early comment on Limerick, see the *Jewish Encyclopaedia* (New York and London, 1910), 8:89. For a later discussion, see L. Hyman, *The Jews of Ireland* (London and Jerusalem, 1972), p. 212. See also Holmes, *Anti-Semitism*, pp. 97–99. In 1903, the year before the onset of the troubles in Limerick, a servant girl in Pontypridd claimed she was abducted, wrapped in cloth, and taken to the synagogue, where she was insulted and spat upon. From this the story grew that she had been taken for ritual purposes, and for a few days the Jewish community lived in a state of tension. See *Jewish Chronicle*, 25 September 1903 and 2 October 1903, for accounts of the incident.

76. James Blyth, *Ichabod* (London, 1910), pp. 129–30. Beatrice Baskerville, *Passover: A Novel* (London, 1920), another popular book, set in Poland and influenced by the Beilis case, attributes a belief in the ritual murder charge to certain of its characters.

77. Holmes, *Anti-Semitism*, p. 315, n. 106.

78. See J. A. Garrard, *The English and Immigration, 1880–1910* (London, 1971); B. Gainer, *The Alien Invasion* (London, 1972); and Holmes, *Anti-Semitism*, chaps. 2–7, on such matters.

79. See above, pp. 107–9.

80. Stephen Graham, "Russia and the Jews," *English Review* 19 (1914–15): 325. On Graham (1884–1975), see the obituary in *The Times*, 20 March 1975.

81. Montague Summers, *The History of Witchcraft and Demonology* (London, 1973 ed.), pp. 195–96. N. Cohn, *Europe's Inner Demons* (London, 1975), p. 120, describes Summers as "a religious fanatic: a Roman Catholic of a kind now almost extinct."

82. Ray Knight, "Biblical Mistranslation," *Hibbert Journal* 30, no. 4 (July 1932): 596.

83. F. J. Foakes-Jackson, *Hibbert Journal* 31 , no. 1 (October 1932): 141.

84. *Jewish Chronicle*, 20 January 1933. The ambiguous withdrawal runs as follows: "In view of the Editor's judgment that the statement regarding ritual murder among the Jews on p. 596 of the *Hibbert Journal* for July 1932 is not justified by the evidence, I hereby withdraw the note (signed) Ray Knight." *Hibbert Journal* 31, no. 1 (October 1932), 141. See above, pp. 109–10, for reference to the issue involving the *Dublin Review*.

85. On the Britons, see Holmes, *Anti-Semitism*, chap. 9, and Gisela C. Lebzelter, *Political Anti-Semitism in England, 1918–1939* (London, 1978), chap. 3, and her chapter on the Britons in Kenneth Lunn and Richard C. Thurlow, eds. *British Fascism* (London, 1980), pp. 41–56. For the British market the Britons produced *Jews' Ritual Slaughter* (London, n.d.). The first part dealt with the slaughter of animals, the second with ritual murder (mainly the 1840 Damascus case).

86. *Jewish Ritual Murder in San Diego* (London, 1933). On the Xanten case, see *Encyclopaedia Judaica* 16:685–86. The Beiliss case is discussed above, p. 104. On Rohling (1839–1931) and the ritual murder accusation, see Strack, *Jew and Human Sacrifice*, pp. 155–68, and J. Kopp, *Zur Judenfrage nach den Akten des Prozesses Rohling-Bloch* (Leipzig, 1886).

87. See the two letters in File E3/148 in the Board of Deputies.

88. It should not be assumed, however, that the charge alleging Jewish ritual murder has been absent from Britain since the aftermath of the Leese case. We have already noticed Leese's continuing interest (see above, n. 62). In addition, it is present in recent fascist writings. In 1963 Martin Webster wrote that not only did the medieval Jew "suck Britain dry of gold, he had to drain away the blood of the nation's children." See the *National Socialist* 1, no. 5 (August 1963):6. For examples of vampire imagery, similar to that present in the East End at the time of the great immigration, see the comments from the National Front's *Spearhead* publication, quoted in M. Billig, *Fascists: A Social Psychological View of the National Front* (London, 1979), pp. 181–82. See n. 124 below for further references to the National Front on related matters.

89. *Jewish Chronicle*, 10 October 1913.

90. Ibid., 30 January 1933.

91. *Dublin Review* 191 (1932):225.

92. *Globe*, 22 April 1881. This kind of argument did not impress Arnold Leese. In his view it was tantamount to saying "John Smith cannot be guilty of theft from William Brown because the Eighth Commandment says 'Thou shalt not steal.'" See Leese, *My Irrelevant Defence*, p. 35.

93. Herbert Thurston, "Anti-Semitism and the Charge of Ritual Murder," *Month* 91 (January–June 1898):568.

94. *Dublin Review* 191 (1932):226.

95. Herbert Thurston, "The Ritual Murder Trial at Kieff," *Month* 122 (November 1913):503. For a much earlier reference to the use of torture, see *Jewish Chronicle*, 18 October 1861. See also Roth's

reference in *Dublin Review* 191 (1932): 229, and the article by Yehuda Slutsky in the *Universal Jewish Encyclopaedia* 2 : 407.

96. *Dublin Review* 191 (1932): 229–30.

97. *Month* 91 (January–June 1898): 568, for reference to "Professor Strack's admirable pamphlet." Leese, *My Irrelevant Defence,* p. 38, as might be expected, is jaundiced about Strack's work and notes his connections with the Jewish community. Strack's analysis forms an important element in the discussion of the blood accusation charge in the *Universal Jewish Encyclopaedia.*

98. This was well recognized by those who accused Jews of ritual murder. See *Catholic Bulletin and Book Review* 6 (1916): 434–39. Leese, *My Irrelevant Defence,* pp. 43–45 (basing himself in part on Burbage), also engages in critical comment.

99. *Month* 91 (January–June 1898): 568. See also p. 569. In turn Thurston was used by C. Lattey, S.J., in *Dublin Review* 192 (1933): 128, and by the editor in ibid., p. 129.

100. Letter from Rothschild to Merry del Val, 7 October 1913, in File E3/148 in the archives of the Board of Deputies. See S. Rapaport, *The Blood Accusation and Its Refutation* (London, 1902), pp. 5–6, for an earlier reliance by a Jewish source on papal authority.

101. See the letter from Lionel D. Barnett to N. Laski, 29 October 1933, urging an edition of Ganganelli's report edited by Cecil Roth. Barnett was led to comment: "It would do an enormous amount of good. There are thousands of Catholics, especially of the black Irish breed, like Walsh, who still hold fast to the old lie and parade it, their mouths would be stopped and their faces blackened by the publication of Ganganelli's letter." File E3/148 in the archives of the Board of Deputies. The outcome of this was Cecil Roth's *Ritual Murder Libel and the Jew,* which provides further evidence of the importance which was attached to Ganganelli's views by the Jewish community.

102. See, for instance, *Jewish Chronicle,* 9 June 1916; ibid., 20 January 1933; and *Dublin Review* 192 (1933): 128, the letter by Jarrett and Loewe.

103. *Month* 91 (January–June 1898): 569. See below, p. 120, for further reference to these cases.

104. See n. 87 for the source of this statement.

105. File E1/16 in Board of Deputies, letter of Neville Laski to the Director of Public Prosecutions, 26 April 1936.

106. *Spectator,* 23 June, 30 June, and 7 July 1883 for arguments in favor of an investigation and the Chief Rabbi's hostility to this suggestion. Frazer, *Golden Bough,* pt. 6, p. 395, was led to com-

ment that considerable discussion had taken place concerning the charge, "with a heat which, however natural, has tended to inflame the passions of the disputants than to elicit the truth."

107. For Roman charges against Christians, see Rapaport, *Blood Accusation*, pp. 3–4. See also J. Rendel Harris, "The Blood Accusation against the Jews in Southern Russia," *Expository Times* 25 (1913–14): 199. For later comment, see *Universal Jewish Encyclopaedia* 2:408. The accusations in China and Madagascar are discussed in S. Reinach, "L'accusation du meurtre rituel," *Revue des études juives* (1892): 166. For further comment on the exploitation of the charge of human sacrifice, see the letter by Peter Hulme in *The Times Literary Supplement*, 29 February 1980, stimulated by the publication and review of W. Arens, *Man-eating Myth* (New York, 1979).

108. Cardinal Newman, *Eight Lectures on the Position of Catholics in England* (London, 1890), lecture 3, pp. 28–33.

109. General Sir Robert Phayre, *Monasticism Unveiled*, pt. 2 (London, n.d.), pp. 15 and 28.

110. On the alleged activity of witches, see N. Cohn, *Europe's Inner Demons* (London, 1975), pp. 100–102. See Reinach, "L'accusation du meurtre rituel," p. 150, for reference to the accusations against Christian heretics.

111. Thurston, *Month* 122 (November 1913): 510. See also Cohn, *Europe's Inner Demons*, p. 12.

112. For scriptural references which tell against the practice of ritual murder, see Leviticus 17:10, 12, 14, and Deuteronomy 12: 16. Reinach, "L'accusation de meurtre rituel," p. 179, writes: "En résumé il est possible, il est même certain, que plus d'une fois, depuis quinze siècles, un Chrétien a été tué par un Juif: mais il n'est moins certain que jamais, à aucune époque, dans aucun pays, un Chrétien, jeune ou vieux, n'a été immolé par un Juif pour servir à l'accomplissement de rites secrets." In spite of claims that there might be a secret Jewish sect which engaged in such practices, no evidence has been adduced to support this charge, which is more insidious in its essence than an accusation directed against all Jews. See Joseph Jacobs, "Little St. Hugh of Lincoln: Researches in History, Archaeology and Legend," *TJHSE* (1893–94): 94, for an awareness of the charge against a section of Jews. See pp. 104, 107, 110, and 111 of the present article for suggestions by the *Spectator*, Burbage, Walsh, and Leese which moved in this direction.

113. Trachtenberg, *The Devil and the Jews*, pp. 126–54, refers to the more historically remote origins of the charge and the connec-

tion with magic and medicine. See above, pp. 101–2 for the financial aspects of the charges. Higham, *MVHR*, p. 570, discusses the revival of anti-Semitism in the late nineteenth century. See Jacobs, "Little St. Hugh," p. 93, for reference to the awareness in late nineteenth-century Britain of earlier forms of anti-Semitism. See *Universal Jewish Encyclopaedia* 2:410, and S. Maccoby, "Ritual Murder, the Growth of an anti-Jewish Legend," *Jewish Chronicle* (supplement), April 1936, for comment on the incidence of ritual murder charges in the nineteenth and twentieth centuries. Finally, Cohn, *Warrant for Genocide*, p. 12, comments on the link between old and new forms of anti-Semitism.

114. Strack, *Jew and Human Sacrifice*, p. 259, discusses the charges. The *Encyclopaedia Judaica* 4:1124, notes that it was not until 1965 that the beatification of Simon of Trent and the celebrations in his honor were canceled.

115. Acton Add MS 5751, p. 57 (Cambridge University Library). This consists of notes made by Acton in Rome on 23 May 1857.

116. See above pp. 113, 107–8, 109–10, and 114 for additional information on these individuals. In addition, Anderson, *Saint at Stake*, p. 201, notes the opposition apparent in certain Catholic circles to Strack's book, *The Jew and Human Sacrifice*. However, the *Jewish Chronicle*, 7 November 1913, noticed that the Catholic journal the *Tablet* had condemned the accusations against Beiliss. Furthermore, Thurston, whose work has been frequently cited, was a Jesuit. For additional, mainly passing references to Catholic attitudes towards Jews, see Holmes, *Anti-Semitism*, esp. chaps. 2 and 5, pp. 212–13, which are mainly concerned with Chesterbelloc hostility towards Jews.

117. On Burbage and the Beiliss affair, see Burbage, "Ritual Murder," pp. 310, 360, 436–43. See Leese's comments in the *Fascist* (June 1934), on the important role of Streicher in exposing "the abominations of Jewry"—a role for which Leese also saw himself as specially fitted. See also ibid., February 1935. For additional comment on the European influence on anti-Semitism in Britain, see Holmes, *Anti-Semitism*, pp. 233–34. For the use of Burton's and Frazer's works in Kiev, see ibid., p. 250, and n. 27 above.

118. L. Loeb, "Un mémoire de Laurent Ganganelli sur la calomnie du meurtre rituel." *Revue des études juives* (1889), p. 184, refers to the importance of psychological factors in creating the accusation. For more recent comment, see Cohn, *Europe's Inner Demons*, pp. 260–63, and his earlier references in *The Pursuit of the Millennium* (London, 1962 ed.), pp. 69–74.

119. See Holmes, *Anti-Semitism*, chap. 4, for a discussion of such matters.

120. See ibid., chap. 10, for a full account of Leese's thought and for references to his psyche.

121. However, this did not prevent Heinrich Himmler from believing that propaganda value could be extracted from it. In a letter to Kaltenbrunner on 19 May 1943 he suggested that the Security Police should be put to work on court records and descriptions of missing children "so that we can repeat in our radio broadcasts to England that in the town of XY a child is missing and that it is probably another case of ritual murder." Quoted in R. Hilberg, *The Destruction of the European Jews* (Chicago, 1961), pp. 656–57. These thoughts came to Himmler consequent upon the publication of Helmut Schramm's *Der jüdische Ritualmord—Eine historische Untersuchung* (Berlin, 1943).

122. See n. 62, above.

123. Billig, *Fascists*, p. 182.

124. See n. 88, above. It comes as no surprise that sources which have supported the ritual murder myth have also referred to what they regard as other evidence of Jewish sadism. See the comment in the *Guardian*, 4 January 1974, on National Front interest in blood sports and animal slaughter, and the article in *Spearhead*, no. 75 (May 1974), p. 5, on "Alien Cruelty to British Animals," which amounted to an attack on Muslim and Jewish practices. Throughout his life Arnold Leese was also diametrically opposed to *shechita*. See his *Legalised Cruelty of Shechita* (Guildford, 1940). In addition to his knowledge of animals, derived from his veterinary practice, Leese was influenced in his views by the *Report of the Committee appointed by the Admiralty to consider the Humane Slaughtering of Animals* (1904), Cd. 2050; see also *Jews' Ritual Slaughter* (n. 85, above). The charge of ritual murder also has links with other strands of anti-Semitic thought. The image of the Jews drawing blood (the life source) from a body is similar not only to that of the Jews as a vampire (see p. 113, above) but also to the categorization of the Jew as a parasite who battens himself upon the body of the nation, reducing its will and finally overpowering it. See L. Lowenthal and N. Guterman, *Prophets of Deceit* (Palo Alto, 1970 ed.), pp. 55–58, for a discussion of anti-Semitic imagery, including that of the parasitological variety.

The Hilsner Affair

Nowhere were there more famous or infamous cases of blood libel than those which occurred in Eastern Europe. Among the better known of these instances were the ones reported in Tisza-Eszlar, Hungary, in 1882, in Polna, Czechoslovakia, in 1899, and in Kiev in 1911. In the following essay by František Červinka, Lecturer at the Faculty of Philosophy, Charles University, Prague, the incident at Polna is examined with special attention to its continuing effect on Czech political consciousness. One reason for the case's ongoing role stems from the fact that the accused Leopold Hilsner was defended ultimately by none other than Thomas G. Masaryk, who was later to become the first president of the Czech Republic. For further details of the trial and of Masaryk's courageous role in the case, see Ernst Rychnovsky, "The Struggle against the Ritual Murder Superstition," in Thomas G. Masaryk and the Jews: A Collection of Essays *(New York: B. Pollak, 1949), pp. 154–243. See also Arthur Nussbaum, "The 'Ritual-Murder' Trial of Polna,"* Historia Judaica *9 (1947): 57–74, and Steven Beller, "The Hilsner Affair: Nationalism, Anti-Semitism and the Individual in the Hapsburg Monarchy at the Turn of the Century," in* T. G. Masaryk *(1850–1937), vol. 2,* Thinker and Critic, *ed. Robert B. Pynsent, (London: Macmillan, 1989), pp. 52–76.*

Some of the earlier monographs devoted to the Tisza-Eszlar case were ably surveyed by Charles H. H. Wright in "The Jews and the Malicious Charge of Human Sacrifice," Nineteenth Century *14 (1883): 753–78, itself a near-contemporary account of the trial. The second portion of*

Reprinted from *Year Book XIII* of the Leo Baeck Institute, London, 1968, pp. 142–57, by courtesy of the Editor, Dr. Arnold Paucker.

Wright's essay recounts the efforts of "expert" witnesses who sought to influence the trial's outcome through their testimony. In particular, the astonishing machinations of August Rohling (1839–1931), a Roman Catholic theologian and professor at the University of Prague, are reviewed. Rohling claimed he could prove that ritual murder by Jews was part of their secretly held doctrine. The purported aspect of secrecy was intended to explain why there were no overt textual references to the practice. Rohling volunteered to swear to all this under oath at the trial.

Fortunately, Rohling's absurd and unsubstantiated contentions did not go unchallenged. Hermann L. Strack (1848–1922), a distinguished Protestant theologian at Berlin University, refuted Rohling and even devoted a chapter of his important book The Jew and Human Sacrifice [Human Blood and Jewish Ritual], to "the Austrian Professor and Canon Aug. Rohling." In the fourth edition of his book (1892), Strack wrote: "I publicly accuse herewith the Imperial Royal Austrian Professor and Canon August Rohling of Perjury and Gross Forgeries." Rohling never responded.

Jewish scholars also leaped into the fray to attack Rohling's blatantly anti-Semitic "evidence," most of which was plagiarized from Johann Andreas Eisenmenger (1654–1704), a professor of Oriental languages at Heidelberg who wrote a vicious tract, Entdecktes Judenthum [Judaism Discovered], in 1700. One of the most notable was Josef Samuel Bloch (1850–1923), who painstakingly disputed Rohling's statements one by one. Bloch accused Rohling of fabricating data and cast serious doubts as to Rohling's self-proclaimed competence in Hebrew. Rohling, stung by Bloch's allegations, brought suit against Bloch for libel. However, at the very last minute, Rohling withdrew his libel accusation thereby tacitly admitting the truth of Bloch's charges. For Bloch's own account of the struggle, see his Israel and the Nations (Berlin-Vienna, 1927) and especially his book My Reminiscences (Vienna and Berlin, 1923; rpt., Arno, 1973). For Strack's discussion, see The Jew and Human Sacrifice (New York: Bloch Publishing, 1909), pp. 155–67. It is interesting that although Strack's clear purpose in this *classic book was to call into question the alleged historicity of the blood libel legend, a reviewer in the prestigious* Zeitschrift für Volkskunde, *Germany's leading folklore journal, began his review: "The fact that annually around Easter time Jews are reproached for seeking Christian blood for their ritual purposes . . . ," and later stated baldly, "We have no fondness for Jews especially for those profit-seeking and arrogant ones who . . . dance around the golden calf," a gratuitous anti-Semitic remark which led folklorist Friedrich S. Krauss in Vienna to write a letter of protest to the editor of the journal (see* Zeitschrift für Volkskunde 5 *[1895]:223–25, 353). For a more objective scholarly folkloristic evaluation of Strack's work, see E[ugene] M[onseur]'s review in* Bulletin de Folklore 3 *(1898–1909):229–49.*

For samples of the abundant literature devoted to the case in Kiev, see George Kennan, "The 'Ritual Murder' Case in Kiev," Outlook 105 *(Nov. 8, 1913):529–35; Herbert Thurston, "The Ritual Murder Trial at Kieff," Month 122 (1913), 502–13; Alexander B. Tager's comprehensive study* The Decay of Czarism: The Beiliss Trial *(Philadelphia: Jewish Publication Society of America, 1935); Zosa Szajkowski, "The Impact of the Beilis Case on Central and Western Europe,"* Proceedings of the American Academy for Jewish Research 31 *(1963):197–218; Hans Rogger, "The Beilis Case: Anti-Semitism and Politics in the Reign of Nicholas II,"* Slavic Review 25 *(1966):615–29; and Isiah Berlin, "The Beiliss Case: Prelude to Revolution,"* Midstream 13 *(February 1967):66–72.*

A wave of anti-Semitism broke over Vienna in the 1880s when the pan-German nationalist and the Christian-socialist movements began their activities. The first was led by Georg Schönerer, the second by Karl Lueger who in 1895 was elected mayor of Vienna. The Emperor Franz Joseph, who called him "the cheap-jack," twice refused to confirm the validity of his election, but voters, turned into fanatics by Lueger's motto: "for the common man," finally succeeded in placing their candidate in the mayoral chair in 1897. To Lueger, a soap-box orator and a capable communal politician, anti-Semitism was good propaganda to use against the liberal establishment which at that time dominated Vienna.

There were many Jews among the Austrian industrialists and bankers, and the House of Rothschild had connections with French banks. Lueger's propaganda against "Jewish capital" was therefore also welcomed by pro-German circles in their fight against French competition. As Jews were also strongly represented in the middle classes, among lawyers, doctors, merchants, and craftsmen, their ability and mutual solidarity provoked a feeling of rivalry in the "common man."

Lueger's slogan quickly spread to the industrialized regions of Austria and to the Czech territories where the national struggle between Czechs and Germans was also developing. Lueger felt no enmity towards the Slav nations. Nor was he a racialist. He cultivated the acquaintance of all those who might be of use to him, including individual Jews, and his speeches also gave encouragement to the Christian socialists who were mobilizing their forces in Bohemia and Moravia at that time. Following Lueger's example, the Christian socialists used anti-Semitic propaganda in Bohemia and Moravia in their fight against the growing influence of social democracy. This does not mean that anti-Semitism in the Czech territories was merely an echo of the clerical-chauvinist trends in Austria. It had a "tradition" of its own. Certain historical elements of Czech anti-Semitism were derived from the struggle between the Czechs and the Germans for linguistic and cultural equality. In this case, too, it was mainly a tool of demagogy intended to influence the backward masses of the population and to win their votes for the new-type Czech nationalist politicians. These politicians tried to suppress the traditional and, in Bohemia, accepted philosophy of František Palacký and later of Professor Dr. T. G. Masaryk who had stressed the humanitarian character of the Czech nation and its tolerance in religious and national affairs.

In 1898 the so-called Czech national socialists formed a

political party led by Václav Klofáč (who, still faithful to his
ideas of long ago, was to declare in 1937, on his death-bed:
"We must not only catch up with Germany and its national
socialism, we must overtake it"). In 1898, the Czech national socialists declared that their main concern was the
struggle against international social democracy, against foreign pioneers of the German-Jewish culture, and naturally
also against such politicians as T. G. Masaryk and his supporters, who were referred to as "realists." At that time, in
the late nineties, the leaders of the right wing of the "progressive" students' movement also tried to establish a new
nationalist trend headed by Dr. Karel Baxa, who sought popularity with everyone and at any price.

The reference above to the relatively large participation of
Jews in trade, industry and finance in the Austro-Hungarian
Empire must be qualified by pointing out the existence of a
large indigent Jewish population both in the western and in
the Slavonic parts of the Empire. The ideologists who identified the Jewish population with capital, usury, and speculation were ignorant sociologists since poverty among the
Jews was one of the most burning social problems of that period. This fact was also stressed at a Zionist Congress, which
aroused great interest, worth recalling, among Czech intellectuals. The fifth Zionist Congress, which met in Basle in
1901, had pleaded for a thorough analysis of the anthropo-
logical, economic, biological and intellectual structure of
Jewish communities and demanded remedies for its needs.
Apart from Jewish workers and craftsmen there were many
"gasping for breath," living from day to day and hopelessly
waiting "at street corners and at the entrances to alehouses"
for an opportunity to earn an honest or dishonest penny. An
inadequate industrial tradition, a heritage from the time of
the ghetto, and the disproportionately large number of Jewish
craftsmen in shoemaking, tailoring, and hat-making were
weighty but only secondary causes of the economic plight of
the Jews, who were judged solely according to their useful-
ness or uselessness to the ruling classes. The Congress could
see no solution to the problem as long as a large part of
the Jewish community remained outlawed and "persecuted,

hated, and surrounded by lack of sympathy."[1] Neither the
meeting of Austrian Zionists at Olomouc (24–25 March
1901) nor the stormy sixth Zionist Congress in 1903 were
able to find an effective remedy to the problem of the Jewish
poor. Both events revealed differences of opinion regarding
the territory where Jews could be settled, free from indirect
and artificially maintained servitude.

In the Czech orbit, as elsewhere, two conceptions of a
solution of the Jewish problem were recommended. One
favored the idea of assimilation, or at least coexistence of
Czechs, Jews, and Germans. Assimilation found strong support in the so-called Czech-Jewish movement, and also with
the majority of German-speaking Jews. The second conception, Zionism, regarded the idea of assimilation as utopian.
As early as 1898 the political writers of *Naše doba* (Our
Time), under the leadership of Masaryk, tried to clarify the
perspectives of the Jewish problem in the Czech territories.
The "realists" represented by this periodical dissociated
themselves from the then current socialist criticism of
Zionism.

The Czech socialists criticized Theodor Herzl for linking
bourgeois interests with democratic and socialist ideas. They
disliked his intention of winning entrepreneurs by offering them profits, and simultaneously promising the workers
housing and employment in return for three years of "decent
behavior." To the socialists Herzl's "Truck-system"[2] seemed
to be a narrow-minded concept intended to conceal the antagonism between capitalism and labor. Against this, the
political writers of *Naše doba* posed the fundamental question: Is Zionism of importance for the Jews or not? Their
reply was unambiguous: "It is. Zionism is needed to raise
Jewish morale. The life of the poor Jews is like a desert, but
now a breath of idealism has begun to blow—be it a mere
fiction—and it is chasing the evil spirits away; we welcome
it particularly because it has democratic progressive tendencies."[3] Regardless of whether the original plans of Zionism
were to prove imaginary, the political writers of *Naše doba*
sought a realistic approach to the Jewish problem. They
regarded every exaggeration of nationalism as harmful to

democracy. In particular they were strongly biased against primitive anti-Semitism which was an attribute of all nationalist manifestations, whether Czech or German. Even before 1899 these views had placed nationalists like Karel Baxa and Václav Klofáč in opposition to Masaryk and the social democrats, regardless of whether they were in favor of Austro-Marxism or of national reform.

In this political climate an event occurred in the little Czech town of Polna in 1899 which resulted in a nationwide conflict between two camps. As far as the rural population was concerned, it was a struggle between the past and the future, between superstition and reason, and between bestiality and humanity. It seemed that fate favored the most primitive form of clerical anti-Semitism. The affair started when a crime was committed in a quarter inhabited by poor Jews. The bestial murder of a young girl at Polna not only aroused the passions of believers in superstition, but also inflamed unscrupulous and hypocritical agitation against the Jews. In an atmosphere as hostile as that described above, opposition to this agitation required a great deal of civic courage. This courage was displayed above all by one man: Thomas G. Masaryk, professor of sociology, philosopher, and politician. He led the fight against superstition and primitive anti-Semitism. He was drawn into the whirl of events almost unwittingly, a fact to which he himself drew attention.[4] Nevertheless, one has to admire Masaryk's political insight and sense of justice. He was aware of the fact that the attitude taken towards the Jewish problem in the civilized world was becoming the criterion of progressive thinking and of enlightened politics. Under the impact of the Dreyfus affair in France, Masaryk understood, at the right moment, that even though the trial of Leopold Hilsner, accused of the murder at Polna, seemed to be of a nonpolitical character, it was actually designed to serve the nationalists in their iniquitous play with the soul of the people.[5]

Let us first of all recapitulate the facts as briefly as possible. On 1 April 1899, the dead body of the nineteen-year-old Anežka Hrůzová, a dressmaker who used to walk every day from her native village of Malá Věžnice to the town of Polna, was found at Brežina near Polna. She had been employed by the dressmaker Prchalová who lived on the outskirts of the Jewish town. A detailed description of Anežka Hrůzová's daily walk in the environs of Brežina forest and the circumstances in which her body was found, were recorded in the indictment against the person suspected of the murder—Leopold Hilsner.[6] The indictment stated that "under the body there was an insignificant pool of blood, no bigger than a hand." This statement was meant to suggest that the motive for the murder was neither robbery nor sexual perversion, but a desire to obtain blood from the body of an innocent Christian virgin. "In the light of the problem with which we are confronted we declare that we found no signs of indecent assault on the body and on the basis of an external and internal examination we can state with certainty that the body of Anežka Hrůzová had been completely bled and that the traces of blood found under the body did not correspond to the amount of blood one would expect to find near the body after a murder of this kind."[7] The details and the statements of a number of witnesses were given in a seemingly objective tone, yet suggestively directed towards the unproved act that the murder was committed by a local Jew, Hilsner, and two unknown Jewish accomplices. A one-sided preliminary inquiry manifested the effort to prove, with the aid of several witnesses, Hilsner's presence at the scene of the crime and the existence of a long knife with which a lengthy incision was said to have been made in Hrůzová's throat.

The preparation of the indictment was obviously influenced by public opinion. Leopold Hilsner personified the poor Jew of Polna with no fixed trade or income. Not one of those who disputed the strange procedure of the court did so in order to defend Hilsner as an individual. Hilsner was rightly described to the court as a man of low morals, an idler and vagabond who allowed himself to be maintained by his mother, a poor widow who herself depended on alms from other Jews. He had already received a twenty-four-hour sentence for once concealing his real name from a policeman. Witnesses described him as a man capable of all vices, who sought the company of "girls and women," and who, as a shoemaker's assistant, "never wanted to work and never remained with a master for more than four weeks."[8]

Reading the records one cannot fail to realize the cheerless existence of the poverty-stricken Jews of Polna, frequently unemployed and consistently insulted by their fellowmen. The little town of Polna was situated in the "German-speaking island of the Jihlava [Iglau] region on the border between Bohemia and Moravia. It had approximately 5,000 inhabitants, 212 of whom were Jews. Their number was steadily decreasing; at the time of Hilsner's trial anti-Semitism had reached such heights that many Jews sought shelter elsewhere. (Those who remained were exterminated by the Nazis during the German occupation; today there is not a single Jew in Polna.)

At the time in question Hilsner's mother lived in the Jewish quarter of Polna, near the house in which B. Prchalová, the dressmaker, had her workshop. The house, in which Mrs. Hilsnerova occupied the lower floor, belonged to the local Jewish community. On the first floor there was a Jewish German School which, according to the anti-Semitic press, was attended at the time by no more than seven local pupils and six who did not live in Polna. One such press report stressed that the attendance at the school had not attained the standard number "for six years."[9] The Jews of Polna, living in a condition of linguistic confusion, spoke partly German, partly Czech. They were anxious that their Czech neighbors should not accuse them of cooperating with the "Germanizers." Hilsner's mother was allowed to remain in her basement flat free of charge and in return was obliged to offer shelter to "traveling Israelites." This explains why Hilsner told the court that "during the Easter holidays many Jews were accommodated [there]." It was in that flat, which was more like a "medieval cellar,"[10] that the prosecution looked for Hilsner's unknown accomplices. The crime was made to appear even more dreadful in that it had been preceded by a similar murder of a certain Marie Klímová in 1898. The court persistently pursued the one line of inquiry and even rejected the proposal of Hilsner's defending counsel, Dr. Zdeněk Auředníček, to summon to court the murderer F. Wehr, who had been arrested earlier and taken to court at Warnsdorf. It appears likely that Wehr had been living in the vicinity of the scene of the Polna murder. From the beginning of the trial the indictment was based, in counsel's words, "solely on the fact that Hilsner had been seen at, or on the way to, the scene of the murder at the time. Nothing is said of him but that he is an idler, and the same is said in testimony against an unknown man who was seen the day before the murder." The counsel had his own ideas about the description of this man tallying with that of Wehr. When he insisted on a more rigorous and thorough inquiry, he was confronted with the strongest public opposition; he immediately lost his local clientele.

At the trial the judge spoke objectively to the jury and the witnesses. The Public Prosecutor addressed the members of the jury as follows:

"A certain Czech newspaper has referred to the Polna murder as the Austrian Dreyfus affair. It is true that the press printed daily reports several columns long, during the Dreyfus trial, and in the same way the Polna murder has filled both home and foreign newspapers. Two parties opposed to each other have chosen this case in order to clash on the battlefield of the press. Everyone knows them, it is not necessary to name them. Immediately after the discovery of the body of the unfortunate Anežka Hrůzová the papers of both sides published long articles, raising first of all the question what might be the motive of this mysterious case. Esteemed gentlemen, do not let this controversy confuse you. Even if one or the other of the parties publishes long articles, this must not influence your verdict. You must only consider the evidence and decide whether it is to the advantage or to the detriment of the accused. The motive is of secondary importance."[11]

In spite of this instruction, it was in fact the question of "motive" that pervaded the whole inquiry. The superstitions about ritual murder permeated the case; the whole trial took place within their shameful shadow. Dr. Karel Baxa, a nationalist politician, later to become Mayor of Prague, influenced the whole jury in this direction. As a lawyer, he behaved prudently. But he frequently exceeded his powers as legal representative of the murdered girl's mother and thus contributed, as Dr. Auředníček put it, "to turning the whole town of Polna into a state of intoxication and to putting the idea that Hilsner was a ritual murderer in the minds of the witnesses." Baxa pleaded with the members of the jury: ". . . Kindly pay attention to the motive behind Anežka Hrůzová's murder. The murderers were not concerned simply with her life; everything depends on the method of the murder, which is still unknown to us." Finally, in his view, it was "proved" that the perpetrators of the crime had murdered a Christian person, an innocent girl, in order to obtain her blood. "All pretexts are of no avail. This motive for the murder really existed. The world has been made aware of the fact that there are people who try to kill their neighbors in order to get hold of their blood. That is ghastly and terrible."[12] The "ghastly and terrible" reports from Polna spread to the outside world indeed.

Counsel for the defense at the trial stood up against these insinuations. Dr. Auředníček said:

> "My task here is difficult. The judge and the jury are prejudiced because the charge has been made that the accused committed the deed out of religious fanaticism. This had been done by the anti-Semitic press which from 1 April onward began to blaze out to the world that this was a case of ritual murder. In a criminal way they published reports full of lies in order to incite public opinion against the accused. . . . Pamphlets on ritual murder were circulated and some even tried to impair the objectivity of the judges by swamping them with pamphlets and with distorted news. It is very sad that at the end of the nineteenth century racial hatred could go to such lengths. . . . Dr. Baxa has raised a charge not only against Hilsner, but against a whole nation. He claims that as a member of the Jewish nation Hilsner murdered for religious purposes, and that this is a case of ritual murder."[13]

145

Against this, Counsel quoted many warning and expert statements, such as from the Pope and from learned rabbis, about the absurdity of such superstitions; he also emphasized the unreliability of certain witnesses. But all this was in vain.

Hilsner was found guilty of participating in the murder and was sentenced to death by hanging. His trial, before a jury at Kutná Hora, necessarily became the concern of world Jewry as it was the Jews as a whole who were being accused of practicing ritual murder. The case had to be investigated by scientific experts. The very fact that the charge was seriously discussed by scientists at all indicates the growth of chauvinism and racialism at the end of the last and the beginning of this century, which reached its climax in the outrageous crimes against the Jews in the mid-twentieth century.

At that time, however, the Czech nation was able to provide an antidote against a slanderous and odious charge that exploited the ignorance of the people to the advantage of political careerists and self-seeking businessmen.

The Kutná Hora trial naturally caused a great sensation,and it was studied by lawyers and doctors. Among them was the Prague physician Dr. J. A. Bulova who pointed out a number of basic errors in the inquiry and in the execution of the postmortem examination. Having hurried to the scene of the crime and to the court and having obtained permission to inspect the exhibits, he urged a thorough investigation as to whether the indications for a murder with a sexual motive were not overwhelming. On 18 September 1899, he examined the court records in detail.[14] In 1900 he published a brochure which contained devastating criticism of both Hilsner's first and second trial (at the town of Písek).[15] Urgent demands were raised, both at that time and later, for the re-hearing of the case. Among the challengers of the verdict was the *Österreichisch-Israelitische Union* in Vienna whose supplementary reports and materials dating from the years 1905, 1909, and 1913 drew the attention of the court, though not throughout convincingly, to other possible perpetrators of the crime.[16] Apart from various newspaper comments, however, the sharpest attack on the miscarriage of justice came from Professor Thomas G. Masaryk.

Already in 1899, Masaryk had visited the scene of the crime and in the same year, in periodicals and, in 1900, in a book, he argued in favor of the *Notwendigkeit der Revision des Processes Hilsners.*[17] Later he summarized his chief finding concerning the false premises of the accusation and exposed the real significance and meaning of the ritual superstition, in a circumstantial treatise which was published in 1900 in the periodical *Naše doba.*[18]

Some of the points which Marsaryk made in his articles are worth quoting because of their fundamental way of tackling the central issue. At the time they attracted the attention of the educated public all over the world. Masaryk started by saying:

In view of the significance which the anti-Semitic superstition of a ritual murder is acquiring in our country I have compiled the main available reports and facts on this subject. From these facts readers can gain more detailed and thorough knowledge of the problem. Before doing so I tried to find an expert able to present the subject in an authoritative way, but as I did not find one in Bohemia I was obliged to fill the gap myself. I am, of course, hampered by my lack of knowledge of oriental languages and therefore have to rely on my judgment. Yet I set about my task and tried to establish a reliable and authentic assessment. However, although our anti-Semites also lack the necessary knowledge of languages, the mass of Czech readers does not inquire about their sources and data, but blindly believes anything that incriminates the Jews.

It was in this vein that Masaryk approached his objective. In his determined fight against anti-Semitism he emphasized the growing danger of "spiritual and physical" violence against the Jewish people.[19] It was his voice which warned the Czech nation in good time against participation in such terrible crimes as were to be committed almost half a century later. It was also Masaryk's enlightened and humanistic philosophy that impelled him to stand up against the dangerous spread of absurd superstition in the Polna case.

The political and moral importance of his articles was obvious from the very beginning. In order to clarify his views, Masaryk commented on statements made by one of the leading anti-Semitic Christian-Socialist deputies, Ernst Schneider, in the *Reichsrath* (parliament) in Vienna on 10 November 1899.[20] Masaryk declined to regard Schneider as "any kind of authority," he referred to him only to uncover the dubious ideology on which "Viennese anti-Semitism and thus also its Prague twin" were based. Schneider had endeavored to defend the superstition of ritual murder, relying on authors such as Dr. August Rohling,[21] whose fraudulent and unreliable character Masaryk described very convincingly. He dealt in a similar way with other contemporary "specialists" in anti-Semitism. Masaryk expressly denied any feelings of personal sympathy for Hilsner as a person. Rascals, he said, could be found everywhere, "among the Jews, too, there are blackguards, arsonists, and imposters"; but, contrary to liars and tricksters like Rohling, Masaryk declared that "religious rules forbid Jews to bear false witness or to swear a false oath." He accompanied his evidence of the absurdity of the slanderous lies against the Jews with the comment: "After all, you yourselves know that it is not the case! Why throw sand in the eyes of the public?" Masaryk did not pretend to be the first to reveal the falsity of authors like Rohling; he was concerned with something else: "And now let us imagine our radicals, led by Dr. Baxa, who, as late as 1899 was still repeating, parrot-fashion, Canon Rohling's lies! In his statement to the Jury at Kutná Hora, Dr. Baxa relied on lies which had been disproved ages ago!" On such occasions Masaryk abandoned his otherwise sober and factual way of pleading:

> Dr. Baxa cannot offer the excuse that he is not an expert. I am not, either, as I do not know Hebrew, but that is not necessary since all controversial points have long since been publicly clarified so that they are accessible to anyone who wishes to know about them. Before suggesting the existence of ritual superstition it was Dr. Baxa's duty to brief himself on the

facts. . . . People who pretend to save the Czech nation actually poison it with base, incongruent lies and ignorance. . . . Shame!

Masaryk also discussed the possibility of whether individual crimes could be interpreted as ritual murders. He explained how "shameless anti-Semites" looked upon every murder committed by a Jew as a "ritual" murder while the main concern should be an investigation of the real motive of a crime. Answering the suggestion that there may be individual Jews here or there who believe in superstitions or that there might even be some unorthodox sect with such beliefs, Masaryk retorted that there was not the slightest evidence for their existence. Reactionary circles described the "Polna case" as "a typical case of ritual murder," but in 1899 Masaryk was able to write that "all data, particularly the expert medical data on bleeding to death" confirm that the assumptions on which the Kutná Hora trial was based were unjustifiable. Although condemning superstition of any kind, Masaryk admitted that simple and good people could fall victims to it. He recalled that the Roman Emperor Marcus Aurelius was a philosophically enlightened man and yet he persecuted the Christians because he considered them to be sorcerers. Similarly, "many a thinking and good man suffers under the terror of anti-Semitic superstition, not realizing that he is bringing himself and his nation to destruction."

Nevertheless, not even at the time of the Hilsner affair did in Bohemia any such violence of a pogrom character occur as happened in similar circumstances in Russia and elsewhere. Assaults, demonstrations, window-breaking, boycotting of shops, affronts, and psychological tyranny were, however, daily occurrences. On the other hand, one has also to record the reaction of the Czech social democrats and of the student population.

The Czech social democrats were opposed to both Czech and German nationalists and anti-Semites. This did not evoke opposition from the ranks of the working classes or bring about a decrease in the number of their supporters.

The leaders of the Czech social democratic party were workers and intellectuals most of whom were not of Jewish origin. At the time of the Hilsner affair they proved to be more
democratic than their French and German comrades who a
year earlier had dogmatically believed that the Dreyfus affair
was only a row between two factions of the French "bourgeo-
sie." In the fight against Czech chauvinism the Czech social
democrats laid emphasis on a program of democratization
of the whole of Austria. In the slogan "Czech home-rule,"
which stood for state autonomy for the Kingdom of Bohemia
within Austria, they had as little confidence as had Masaryk. When they issued the "anti-home-rule declaration" in
the *Reichsrath* in 1897, the Czech nationalists affronted
them by calling them agents of German-Jewish capital. At
the time of the Hilsner affair such insults were also directed
against Masaryk, whereupon the social democrats declared:
"What is now happening to Masaryk happened to us social
democrats for our anti-home-rule declaration."[22] The social
democrats saw an ominous "sign of the time" in the way
in which the Czech public accepted the original sentence
of death passed on Hilsner. They regarded the applause and
cheering of the crowd as mean and undignified. Yes, they
said, here "manifested itself that intelligence, that culture,
that modernity, that progress, that civilization, so readily
talked about on all sides and bragged about by our rulers, the
manipulators of this public opinion. One short moment has
opened our eyes to their true character." In a sharp attack on
those who "put such low instincts in the minds of the crowd
and want to build their own personal business, political interests on this social pathology,"[23] the social democrats declared they were aware that they "had to go into the fight
with their fists clenched until sparks began to fly."[24] They
refused to flatter the people and supported Masaryk's fight
against apathy, "passionate narrow-mindedness and by now
downright inhumanity almost approaching cruelty."[25] The
thing that brought together Masaryk and the social democrats at that time was not only their common aversion
against clericalism, but also against the extreme national-

ists. The cause of the fact that Austro-Hungary was neither preserved nor democratized as Masaryk and the social democrats had once desired must be sought mainly in the blind and preposterous policy of Hapsburg Austria. This was admitted by most shrewd observers at the time, as reflected in the words of Max Brod: "If, however, Austria destroyed itself, if it brought itself on the rocks through its own mad policy, how was it possible to have faith in its path, how else could the beginning of the end be regarded but with hopeless sorrow?"[26] Therefore one has to evaluate highly all active participants in the fight against reactionary nationalism and racialism in the Czech Lands. In the struggles of this kind before the First World War it was a question of strengthening the vitality of those democratic traditions which have shown themselves again and again in modern Czech history.

It still remains, however, to describe the situation prevailing among the young Czech intelligentsia at the time of the Hilsner affair and also the way in which it manifested itself directly within the Charles University in Prague. Nothing caused such a disturbance among the ranks of the Czech students at the time as the Hilsner affair. It shook the reigning theories on nationalism and the political impartiality of students. As soon as Masaryk raised scientifically sober arguments against rough chauvinism, discussions on nationalism, Zionism, and Jewish problems began to abound among the students. The demonstrations staged against Masaryk by right-wing students became a major political issue. The attitude of all parties and factions to these demonstrations reflected the division of the nation into "right-wingers" and "left-wingers." In the middle of November 1899 both camps measured their strength in the Klementinum lecture-hall at the philosophical faculty of the Charles University. "The students were divided into two camps of relatively equal strength. While one wing demonstrated in favor of Masaryk, forming a strong wall round him and manifesting its sympathy towards him through stormy applause and waving hats, the other raged like mad, banging on the stove and the windows, whistling and waving sticks in the air."[27] An important force in the progressive students' camp was not only Masaryk's own ideological supporters, but also the young socialists grouped around "The Students' Magazine" edited by a student named Bohumír Šmeral. The whole of the November 1899 issue of this magazine was devoted to the fight against the chauvinist right-wingers. A provocative personal declaration was published jointly therein by several socialists (V. Houser, L. Sacha, V. Vacek, F. Tomášek, F. Soukup, and T. Bartošek) and so-called individualists and realists (L. K. Hofman, Z. Tobolka, F. Papírník, and J. Náhlovský).[28]

The social democratic and pro-Masaryk press took a prominent part in the struggle.[29] This was also a recognition of the political importance of the student population. The democratic students appealed to "the ranks of ignorant students from the countryside with no knowledge of the situation" who allowed themselves "to be exploited for the purpose of this dirty business and who lifted a stick against the man whose hand they should kiss for his cultural work among the Czech nation."[30] The defense of Masaryk became the defense of free personal belief and also of academic freedom at the universities. When the timid bureaucrats decided to cancel Masaryk's lectures on "practical philosophy" these students requested the academic board to recall him from his "enforced leave" and to allow him to continue his teaching.

> We, the undersigned students of Professor Dr. T. G. Masaryk, who has been sent on leave until the end of the winter term, respectfully request the distinguished academic board to cancel Professor Dr. T. G. Masaryk's leave and allow him to deliver his lectures again. . . . To the undersigned ninety-nine students Professor Dr. T. G. Masaryk's enforced leave represents the yielding of scientific authority to the unthinking behavior of one part of the student population and is a degradation of university authority, making it the servant of vulgar opinion. This offends all serious elements of student population regardless of whether they are political followers of Masaryk or not. . . . This enforced leave could give rise to new conflicts and quarrels among the student population and the possibility is not excluded that party passions could be re-

kindled which could also have serious consequences for the university itself.[31]

Discussions on Masaryk's theories, and particularly on the Jewish problem, occupied the minds of the Czech intelligentsia for a long time. They were linked with the fight against feudalism, clericalism, and medieval superstitions. The resonance was felt in the whole of Central Europe. Racialism was gradually pushed into the background.

The Czechs were reminded of the anti-Semitic atmosphere of the Polna affair at a time of great tragedy for the whole nation. In March 1939 when the Nazi army of occupation marched on to Czech territory, a book entitled *Hilsneriáda a TGM* (The Hilsner Affair and TGM) was published whose author was allegedly the "leader of the Czech fascist movement"—Jan Rys. This "movement"—known as the "Vlajka Movement"—was formed of small groups of despicable Czech fascists, loathed even by the State President of the Nazi "Protectorate of Bohemia and Moravia," Dr. Emil Hácha. These people offered their services as informers to the Nazis. Jan Rys's book was dedicated to the memory of the man who had fostered the ritual murder superstition, August Rohling, and to the fight against the "Jewish influence" of T. G. Masaryk in the Czech Lands. Kowtowing before the swastika of the invaders the author wrote: "The purpose of this work is not merely to defend the truth about the ritual murders committed at Polna, but also to draw the attention of Aryans to the terrible fact that there are Jews among us who murder Christians in order to obtain their blood."[32] The intention was to revive the old superstitions just at the very time when the Czech nation was being robbed of its independence and when masses, adorned with the Czech tricolour and with so-called "Masaryk caps," were staging demonstrations in the streets of Prague against the Nazi occupiers. Yet it was just this period that brought about the total collapse of anti-Semitism in the Czech nation. Even the national right-wingers among the students scorned the Czech fascists. During the six years of occupation anti-Semitism was the domain of collaborators. After the liberation of the Republic in 1945 it was sharply condemned by all political parties and trends.

This does not mean, however, that the memory of the Hilsner affair and anti-Semitism were completely wiped out in Bohemia. The fact that the identity of the perpetrator of the murder at Polna has never been satisfactorily established gave rein to various surmises and rumors. True, it would be difficult to find a person in Czechoslovakia today who still believes in ritual murder. Yet it cannot be denied that some people fail to realize the full importance of the fight against racialism and the general character of the Hilsner trials. This phenomenon is not, however, in any way connected with the recent doctrinal and political discussions on Masaryk's theories. It is no secret that in the fifties Czech and Slovak communists sharply criticized so-called "Masarykism" and, in a milder form, they do it still. But even Masaryk's radical communist opponents have always acknowledged his merits in the fight against nationalism, medieval anachronism, ritual superstitions, and anti-Semitism.

The still unsolved mystery surrounding Hilsner's guilt and the understandable endeavors to discover a possible perpetrator of the murder among other people suspected at the time, gave cause not only to lasting hidden prejudices, but also to myths. Certain descendants of those who testified before the Kutná Hora and Písek juries are unable to believe or understand even today that their ancestors could have been used, be it even indirectly, as instruments for ulterior purposes. They believe in the integrity of the administration of the law of those days and naturally in the authenticity of the witnesses. Any attempt at finding another possible murderer was often regarded only as a "Jewish intrigue."

The present writer could not reconstruct the story of the murder and the Kutná Hora inquiry in this article and, anyway, he does not wish to support any unproved conjecture. Among those suspected of having committed the crime was the brother of the victim, Jan Hrůza, who, on his sister's death, became the sole inheritor of his mother's cottage. The inquiry against him was stopped in 1899 and since that time there have been no known reasons for its renewal. Other persons were also suspected, but all inquiries failed to bring results. The title of murderer stuck to Hilsner. Nevertheless various conjectures and beliefs were and still are rife among the people.

Certain Jews who were exposed to insult and direct persecution in 1899 were even at that time not willing to believe that Hilsner had committed the murder. On the other hand, Czech anti-Semites and certain descendants of the witnesses obstinately defended the verdicts of the Kutná Hora and Písek juries; it is not surprising that even before 1939 fascist agents and provocateurs became interested in these people. Without relying on guesswork we want to mention a recent literary controversy which shows the continuing topicality of the Hilsner affair.

The name of Petr Pešák, the crown witness, appeared in the press again after more than sixty years. At Kutná Hora Pešák had testified that on the day of the murder he had gone to the scene of the crime and had apparently seen about six hundred paces away a figure whom from the way he was moving, he recognized as Hilsner. When asked why he had offered this important testimony only after a charge had been made against Hilsner, he replied: "I worked for the Israelites. Any kind of money is good enough for me. And so I thought I couldn't bring the dead back to life and I'd lose my wages. And since then every Israelite has really avoided me and looked at me sadly." In his concluding speech the public prosecutor, Dr. Schneider-Svoboda, stated: "Pešák's statement is a basic source. Here we have the proof that the accused took that direction."[33]

In his booklet on the necessity of a revision of the Polna trial Masaryk expressed his doubts about this "decisive source" and pointed to dubious spots in Pešák's testimony.

In 1964 a modern Czech writer, Bohumil Hrabal, who considers it his artistic right to "lightly deform" the reports of folk narrators, mentioned in an ironic and humorous way Pešák's testimony and the rumors about Jan Hrůza's guilt, in the first edition of his work entitled *Taneční hodiny pro starší a pokročilé* (Dancing Lessons for the Elderly and the Advanced). The son of Pešák, who still lives at Polna, sent a letter to "*Československý spiovatel*" ("Czechoslovak Writer"—an organization of writers): "Your member Mr. Bohumil Hrabal . . . crudely attacked the memory of my dead father by describing him as a fool; he ridiculed him by saying that he held a bicycle in one hand and passed water with the other, etc."[34] The writer of the letter considered this

> a slander against a worker who had been entirely blameless right up to the time of his death and enjoyed great respect and esteem in his place of residence and in the widest surroundings due to his not having allowed himself to be frightened by anything in the mentioned trial in spite of all possible threats (an attempt was made to deprive him of his sight and instead of him someone else was murdered by mistake, a worker who resembled him in looks), or let himself be bribed by what at that time were large sums to recall his testimony. The family of the murdered Anežka Hrůzová is also grossly insulted in this fantastic book, in particular by the false and fictitious assertion that Anežka's brother Jan, who died at Ždírec as a law-abiding citizen, is supposed to have confessed that he murdered her himself for money!!![35]

The letter of protest written by Pešák junior aroused my suspicion. After all, the Czech Nazi agent and collaborator Jan Rys "conversed" in 1933 with "the witness who had sealed Hilsner's fate," namely Petr Pešák. He had visited him in order "to pry out of him some data which were not made public." He wrote: "My action was successful. I am placing at the disposal of the wider public those data, hitherto unknown, just as they were told to me in a steady voice, interrupted in places by the coughing of that old man with kind eyes and a gentle, resigned appearance."[36] And then there followed, in the order already known from the letter written by Pešák's son, those atrocious stories, according to which Pešák was to have been blinded and murdered. The fact that, in the words of the fascist Jan Rys these "hitherto unknown reports" were not published in the contemporary chauvinist press and that the "leader" of the so-called Vlajka

Movement himself made them known in 1939, and Pešák's son in 1965, suggests not only their improbability; it is also a pointer to the doubtful reliability of the "crown witness" himself.

After this exchange of letters Bohumil Hrabal omitted in the following editions of his work the passage allegedly impinging on the honor and reputation of Petr Pešák, or the relations of Anežka Hrůzová.

Since 1899 the mysterious murder at Polna has served the aims of anti-Semitism. Its legal treatment, on the other hand, has given rise to skepticism among intelligent and liberal people. After World War II all historical facts touching on the prehistory of fascism gained in importance. Racialist beliefs were not the invention of the fascists. Fascism employed them to the widest extremes for justification of the crime of genocide. The Polna murder revealed the ignorance and fanatical superstition of at least part of the people of a country whose democratic traditions have otherwise proved themselves throughout the long course of their history.

Notes

1. *Naše doba* (Our Time) 9 (1902):327, article entitled "V. Sionisticky Kongres v Basileji" (The 5th Zionist Congress in Basle).

2. In his original pamphlet *Der Judenstaat* (1896), Herzl suggested that it might be advisable to pay immigrant workers' wages in kind instead of money because of the particular circumstances during the first stages of settlement.

3. *Naše doba* 5 (1898):439, article entitled "Zionism," signed F.B.

4. An excellent description of the events which took place at Polna and the intervention of T. G. Masaryk was written by Ernst Rychnowsky; see "Im Kampf gegen den Ritualmord-Aberglauben," in *Masaryk und das Judentum* (Prague, 1931), pp. 166–273.

5. "So seltsam und fast kitschig-romantisch ist manchmal der Gang der Geschichte, und das tschechische Volk konnte wohl zu der Zeit, als es Professor Masaryk, der sich des Juden Hilsner annahm, in überwältigender Majorität verunglimpfte, nicht ahnen, dass gerade dieser Kampf seines späteren Präsidenten gegen den Ritual-

mord und sein Eintreten für den verkommenen jüdischen Hausierer Hilsner ein nicht unwichtiges Glied der Kette werden würde, die einst das tschechische Volk erlösen sollte." (Felix Weltsch, "Masaryk und der Zionismus," in *Masaryk und das Judentum* (Prague 1931).

6. Přelíčení's Hilsnerem před porotou v Kutné Hoře pro vraždu v Polné (Hilsner's trial before a Jury at Kutná Hora for the Polna Murder). Verbatim copy of stenographic records, Prague 1899. Archive material relating to the Hilsner affair is deposited at the Central Archives in Prague under the reference *Státní zastupitelství Kutná Hora* (State Representation Kutná Hora) 572/99, box 1; *Státní zastupitelství Písek* (State Representation Písek) 530/00, box 2; *Státní zastupitelsví Praha* (State Representation Prague) no. 9, box 3. Quoted here as *Přelíčení*.

7. The medical certificate bore the signature of the physicians who carried out the postmortem examination: MUDr Válav Michálek, forensic physician at Polna; MUDr Alois Prokeš, forensic physician at Polna; Doc. Dr. Slavík, forensic physician in Prague. The twelve members of the jury consisted of local peasants, millers, and factory-owners. Thirty-two witnesses were called before the court, most of whom were from Polna, Malá Věžnice, Velké Meziříčí, and Bližnov. The legal representative of the mother of the murdered girl was Dr. Karel Baxa. The counsel for the defense of the accused was Dr. Zdeněk Auředníček. The names of all the court officials are given in *Přelíčení*, p. 5.

8. *Přelíčení*, p. 394.

9. *Radikální* Listy (Radical Paper) of 3 June 1899, article entitled "Ku vraždě v Polné" (The Murder at Polna).

10. *Přelíčení*, p. 378.

11. Ibid., p. 375.

12. Ibid., p. 401.

13. Ibid., p. 409.

14. Central State Archives, *Státní zastupitelství Písek* (State Representation Písek) 530/1900, box 2.

15. Dr. J. Ad. Bulowa, *Zum Polnaer Ritualmordprocess im Stadium vor dem Zweiten Urteile. Ein Brief an die Herren Professoren der gerichtlichen Medicin, Juristen und an alle ehrlichen Menschen überhaupt* (Berlin, 1900).

16. These materials are deposited at the Central State Archives, *Státní zastupitelství Písek* 500/1900, box 2.

17. Masaryk's brochure *Die Notwendigkeit der Revision des Polnaer Processes* was sent to print before the verdict of the Kutná

Hora jury acquired legal validity and was consequently confiscated on 6 November 1899. On 9 November 1899 a successful interpellation was raised in the House of Deputies for permission for the brochure to be printed. The interpellation was signed by a number of deputies, in particular Austrian, Polish, and Czech social democrats. In the brochure Masaryk drew attention to a number of conflicts at the Kutná Hora trial. A new trial was later held at the regional court at Písek, the proceedings commencing on 25 October 1900. Hilsner's counsel for the defense was once again Dr. Z. Auředníček and the legal representative of the murdered girl's mother Dr. Karel Baxa. The Písek trial did not throw any new light on the case and Hilsner was again convicted of participation in the murder. During the trial the jury refused to consider the idea of a sexual motive behind the murder as well as all questions of necrophilism and fetishism, simultaneously, avoiding more circumspectly direct suggestions of ritual murder. As proofs of Hilsner's guilt were lacking once again, the Emperor granted Hilsner grace by having the death sentence changed to life imprisonment. In 1918 he was pardoned and lived once more as a poor pedlar under the name of Heller, sometimes in Prague and sometimes in Vienna. He died in 1928 at the age of 59.

18. *Naše doba* 7 (1900):321, 481, 579; T. G. Masaryk, *O pověře rituální* (Ritual Superstition).

19. On pp. 481ff. of the mentioned study T. G. Masaryk listed a bibliography of the contemporary anti-Semitic and scientific literature with which he had dealt.

20. Ernst Schneider had been the addressee of a letter written in April 1899 (a few days after anti-Jewish excesses at Polna of 4 April 1899 after which the investigating Judge Reichenbach had issued a writ to arrest Hilsner "because of public opinion") by Jaromir Husek, editor of a small anti-Semitic paper who had been sentenced already in 1893 for spreading false rumors about ritual murder. Husek appealed to the influential member of the Viennese parliament to support the accusation against Hilsner and the Jews —which Schneider gladly did. See Maximilian Paul-Schiff, *Der Prozess Hilsner* (Vienna, 1908), p. 2.

21. August Rohling, professor of theology at the German University in Prague, published his anti-Semitic pamphlet *Der Talmudjude* in 1870. He was publicly challenged by Dr. J. S. Bloch (editor of *Dr. Blochs Österreichische Wochenschrift*) and had to sue him for libel, but under the impact of evidence that exposed Rohling as an ignoramus unable to read a single Hebrew sentence, he had

to back down and to withdraw his writ. Nevertheless, Rohling's pseudo-scholarly arguments were freely quoted in later cases. See *Zur Judenfrage nach den Akten des Prozesses Rohling-Bloch von Dr. Josef Kopp, Abgeordneter des österreichischen Reichsraths* (Leipzig 1886).

22. *Právo Lidu* (The People's Right) 8, no. 318, of 17 November 1899, article by František Soukup, entitled "Klerikální reakce na obzoru" (Clerical Reaction on the Horizon).

23. *Právo Lidu* 7, no. 259, of 19 September 1899, article entitled "Znamení doby" (A Sign of the Times).

24. *Právo Lidu* 8, no. 275, of 5 September 1899, article by F. Soukup entitled "V aféře Hilsnerově" (The Hilsner Affair).

25. *Právo Lidu* 8, no. 318, of 17 November 1899, article entitled "Demonstrace na filosofické fakultě" (The Demonstrations at the Philosophical Faculty).

26. Max Brod, *Streitbares Leben* (Czech trans., 1966), p. 82.

27. See n. 25, above.

28. *Studentsky Sborník* (The Students' Magazine) 4, no. 3 (1899–1900):38–40, article entitled "K posledním událostem ve studentstvu" (The Latest Events among the Student Population).

29. I have dealt in greater detail with Masaryk's influence on the student population and anti-Semitism at the universities in my book *Boje a směry českého studenstva na sklonku minulého a na počátku našého stoleti.* (The Struggles and Trends of Czech Students at the End of the Last and the Beginning of Our Century) (Prague 1962).

30. See n. 25, above.

31. *Právo Lidu* 8, no. 13, of 14 January 1900, article entitled "Dovolená prof. Masaryka a česká universita" (Professor Masaryk's Leave and the Czech University).

32. Jan Rys, *Hilsneriáda a TGM* (The Hilsner Affair and TGM) (Prague 1939), p. 2.

33. *Přelíčení*, p. 388.

34. In Bohumil Hrabal's version the sentence—referring to folk narrations—originally read: . . . "our people imagined that Hilsner had done it and still another good fellow came forward with the statement that he had seen that Hilsner standing in Březina forest, the crown witness holding a bicycle with one hand and passing water with the other, so that Hilsner was sent to prison and the Jews had to leave Polna . . . and then . . . on his death bed Anežka's brother confessed that he had done it for money which at that time ruled the world." B. Hrabal: *Taneční hodiny pro starší a pokročilé*

(Dancing Lessons for the Elderly and the Advanced) (Prague 1964). The passage is also fully printed in the German translation of the book: *Tanzstunden für Erwachsene und Fortgeschrittene* (Verlag Suhrkamp Frankfurt, 1967), p. 64.

35. Bohumil Hrabal "Morytát o zavraždění Anežky Hrůzové" (Death Ballad on the Murder of Anežka Hrůzová), Magazine Impuls (Impulse) 1 (1966), no. 12.

36. Rys, *Hilsneriáda a TGM*, p. 255.

SANFORD SHEPARD

The Present State
of the Ritual Crime in Spain

*The blood libel legend seems to have flourished in Catholic
Europe. For this reason, it should come as no surprise to
learn that ritual murder accusations were reported quite
early in Spain. One of the most famous or infamous cases
was that which was alleged to have occurred in the town of
La Guardia ca. 1488 with a trial in 1490 and 1491. Some
scholars believe that this supposed murder of a Christian
infant in La Guardia and the ensuing trial was a contributing cause of the expulsion of Jews from Spain in 1492.*

*The following survey of the blood libel legend in Spain
was made by Sanford Shepard, Professor of Spanish and
Chairperson of the Humanities Program at Oberlin College.
For representative discussions of the La Guardia case, see
Isidore Loeb, "Le Saint Enfant de la Guardia,"* Revue des
études juives *15 (1887): 203–32; Henry Charles Lea, "El
Santo Niño de la Guardia,"* English Historical Review *4
(1889): 229–50; and Yitzhak Baer,* A History of the Jews in
Christian Spain *(Philadelphia: Jewish Publication Society
of America, 1966), 2: 398–423. Noteworthy in particular are
the conclusions arrived at by Isidore Loeb in his praiseworthy essay: (1) The testimony of the witnesses obtained by
torture or the threat of torture are full of contradictions, un-
truths, and impossible "facts." (2) The judges did not make
a single inquiry to discover the truth. (3) They were not able
to fix the date of the crime nor were they able to discover
either the body or the remains of any Christian infant. The
conclusion: The infant of La Guardia never existed!*

Reprinted from *Judaism* 17 (1968): 68–78.

Throughout the Middle Ages, Christianity nourished the half-hidden hope that the Jews secretly believed in Jesus. Not only the ignorant masses but also scholars and ecclesiastics were obsessed by the notion, to which they clung with a fierce, irrational passion, that the Jews placed credence in the supernatural character of consecrated wafers, the efficacy of black masses, and mock crucifixions. The accusation leveled against the Jews, that they were mocking Christian sacraments, was not based on rancor alone, but rather on what was held to be their skillful, malevolent manipulation steeped in belief. One might be persuaded to think that Christians doubted the articles of their own faith and sought confirmation of Christian miracles in Jewish sorcery.

The allegation that the Jews kidnapped Christian children for the purpose of ritual murder, which recapitulated the crucifixion of Jesus, is widespread in the literature of the Middle Ages and, perhaps, best known to English readers from the Prioress's Tale in Chaucer's *Canterbury Tales*. Much material could be extracted from European literature to illustrate the nature of the accusation and its consequences to the accused. But readers familiar with the Beiliss case from Maurice Samuel's *Blood Accusation* or Bernard Malamud's *The Fixer* can supply their own details. A ramification of the blood libel was the accusation repeatedly leveled at Jews that they obtained consecrated hosts and performed acts of desecration on these objects which, according to Christian theology, were equivalent to the person of Jesus. Thus, such an act of desecration was, like the murder of a Christian child, a reenactment of the deicide attributed to the Jews.

It seems reasonable in the mid-twentieth century to attribute the accusation of the blood libel to the credulity and superstition of the medieval mind or to find some psychological explanation in the remote regions of the human unconscious. But in Spain today the ritual crime still continues to hold a special place from which it will not be dislodged by the light of reason.

The poet García Lorca once remarked that a dead man in Spain is more alive as a dead man than anywhere else in the world. The same can be said of certain events of Spanish history. The myth of a unified Roman Catholic Spain continues to be perpetrated, reinterpreted, and accepted by the conservative Spanish intellectuals of today, whose voices are the only ones tolerated by the church-state. Those events of Spanish history which can serve Roman Catholic unity and Roman Catholic ideals are carefully resurrected, cultivated, and disseminated, while other events are distorted or consigned to a dead and unproductive past. Official Spanish history is populated with the dead of five hundred years ago who are made to serve a modern purpose satisfying an old longing for a Christian past that Spain can only partially claim.

From the time of the Islamic invasion of Spain in 711 to the Conquest of Granada in 1492 Spain was a land of three cultures. The Moslem invaders brought to Spain the civilization they had acquired in the Orient after the conquest of Persia, Syria, and Egypt, along with their new monotheistic religion. These conquerors put Jews (who had survived the persecution of the priest-ridden Visigothic state) into the affairs of government and financial administration. It was in this new environment that Maimonides, Yehuda Halevi, and Ibn Gabirol lived. As the Christian kingdoms slowly pushed southward, conquering the lands held by the Hispano Moslems, they, too, made use of Jews in the administration of their affairs. By the twelfth century Spain was recognized at home and abroad as a land of three religions. The "King of the Three Religions," as the Spanish ruler called himself, employed his Jewish courtiers and finance ministers to such a degree that the functions of government were for centuries a Jewish monopoly as was the profession of medicine. Intellectual activities in Spain were cultivated for so many centuries by so many Jews that during the period of the Inquisition the mere ability to read and write brought suspicion of Judaizing. The coexistence of the three cultures of Spain was ended in 1492 by Ferdinand and Isabella with the edict expelling the Jews and with the overthrow of Granada, the last Moorish stronghold in the Iberian peninsula. The events of 1492, which included the founding of the Spanish overseas empire, produced a "New Society" that turned its back on the political and social conditions of the Middle Ages and attempted to forge a new beginning.

The two principal kingdoms of Spain, Castile and Aragon, had been united by the marriage of Ferdinand and Isabella in 1469. From their union came the plan for a political and religious union of the new dual monarchy. Despite the fact that both the court of the Queen of Castile and that of her husband, the King of Aragon, were managed almost entirely by public Jews, crypto-Jews, and recent converts from Judaism, the "Catholic Monarchs," as they are called in Spain, chose to ignore the eight hundred years that had intervened between the Arabic invasion and the union of Castile and Aragon. The first act in the interest of political and religious unity was the establishment of the Inquisition in 1478. The main function of this body was to ferret out converts to Christianity who had returned to Judaism. It was assumed by the inquisitors that the chief impediment to sincere conversion was the large number of public Jews who were constantly seducing the converts back to their original religion. As an illustration of the activities of the public Jews the inquisitional priests invented the most celebrated case of blood libel in Spain—the La Guardia affair.

1

La Guardia is a small town in the province of Toledo, a province that was throughout the three hundred years of inquisitional activity a crypto-Jewish enclave. In June 1490 a certain *converso*, Benito García, was brought before the Inquisition and under torture admitted taking part in the crucifixion of a Christian child on the Jewish Passover. His testimony implicated another *converso*, Juan de Ocaña, who had tried to lead García back to Judaism, and a public Jew of a nearby village named Jusé Franco, a shoemaker. Also involved was a *converso*, Alonso Franco, apparently unrelated to his Jewish namesake. The converts Benito García and Alonso Franco

165

had for some years been drifting back into Judaism after having become disillusioned with Christianity. On a visit to La Guardia the Jewish Franco had become acquainted with the convert of the same name. Their common rejection of Christianity became the source, according to the allegation, of a plan that proposed nothing less than the destruction of Christendom through magic. Jusé's brother Moses and their father Zag, a man in his eighties, were brought into the conspiracy. The end of the Christian order was to be effected by a spell involving a consecrated host and the heart of a crucified Christian child. A Jewish doctor, deceased at the time of the trial, Juza Tazarte, was in charge of the sorcery. The child and host were procured and the crucifixion carried out in a cave near La Guardia.

Torquemada, the Inquisitor General, interested himself personally in the case and had the trial transferred from the jurisdiction of Toledo to Segovia and later to Avila. He appointed, as well, a special tribunal of fanatical anti-Semites to sit in judgment. The testimonies of the accused persons are replete with contradictions of detail; yet no attempt was made to locate the grave of the child allegedly murdered. No investigation was conducted to discover whether a child had even been reported missing in Toledo where the kidnapping was supposed to have taken place. The trial was intended to create the impression of a Jewish plot against Christianity. For this purpose a group of ignorant working-class Jews and *conversos* was chosen. From their inconsistent testimonies taken under coercion—as each of the defendants tried to throw blame on the others at the prompting of the inquisitors—the elements of an overall Jewish conspiracy were formulated.

The removal of the trial from the province of Toledo to the more bigoted city of Avila and the appointment of special inquisitors by Torquemada himself were political maneuvers. The imagination of the pious queen Isabella was stirred by the trial and execution of the alleged crucifiers. Only four months later she signed the Edict of Expulsion. The inquisitor, Luis de Páramo, stated that the La Guardia affair was one of the factors that moved Ferdinand and Isabella to sign it.[1] During the trial and at the time of the *auto-da-fé* in which the convicted murderers of the La Guardia child were executed, the populace of Avila was brought to such a pitch of excitement that the Jews of that city asked for special protection against the mobs that demanded a massacre.

The blood libel of La Guardia found a ready place within the *Realpolitik* of Ferdinand and Isabella. The geographical unity of Spain was assured by the conquest of the Moorish kingdom of Granada, while the Edict of Expulsion supplied the religious unity that had only recently become an overriding ideal in the Iberian Peninsula. The confiscation of Jewish property offered a means of replenishing the exhausted treasury after the cost of the Moorish war. Furthermore, neither Ferdinand nor Isabella could resist the propaganda value of the murder their inquisitors had invented.

Over one hundred years after the Edict of Expulsion Lope de Vega, the most celebrated dramatist of classical Spanish literature, made use of the La Guardia case in a propaganda piece intended to defend the Inquisition. The Holy Office had worked diligently since its inception to eradicate the Jewish heresy. Yet Judaism persisted throughout Spain. Lope de Vega's drama, *El Niño Inocente de La Guardia,* was intended to recall the crime that was supposed to have sealed the fate of the Spanish Jews. In 1605, about the time the play was written, a general pardon was granted in Portugal (then a part of the Spanish Empire) to prisoners of the Inquisition held for Judaizing. The Edict of Pardon, which removed the pressure of investigations by the Holy Office, was purchased by crypto-Jewish merchants and bankers who were for the most part of Spanish origin. The economic conditions of Spain were so strained by mismanagement and ineptitude that the government welcomed the bribe. The pardon was rescinded in 1610, but during the five years it was operative Spain was exposed to a heavy migration of secret Jews who hoped to fade into a new and larger environment aided by Portuguese passports that made no mention of their inquisitional antecedents. These emigrants sought wider areas for their talents in such fields as medicine, diplomacy, and commerce—professions for which their medieval Spanish ancestors were famous and which they hoped to resume under the protection of their newly acquired status as "Portuguese Christians." "Portuguese" soon became a slang expression for "Jew" and is so used in the Spanish novel of the period.

Lope de Vega's play was written during the period of the pardon or immediately thereafter. It is not merely an excursion in martyrology but a timely attack against Judaism and a defense of the Inquisition by one of its familiars. It is based on an allegation of brutal Jewish criminality—a theme commonly manipulated by writers and artists of this period with the intent of producing a minor variety of religious experience. The ritual crime implies that a solid phalanx, controlled by a predatory cabal, lies in wait to overwhelm the world order. An emotional relationship is assumed that links all Christians together against the unique forces of aggression which propose the destruction of civilization. The acceptance of the legend of the death of the child of La Guardia is also the acceptance of the New Society established by Ferdinand and Isabella and their inquisitors. Lope de Vega was the poet of the new dogma that wished to see in the Inquisition and in the Expulsion of the Jews a purification of Spanish Catholicism and the establishment of spiritual links with the Gothic Empire that had passed away almost nine hundred years earlier. Thus the socioreligious phenomenon of the crypto-Jews and insincere converts was opposed by a modern mythology. Isabella, the "Queen of the Goths," as she is called in the play, reestablishes contact with the source that was intended to nourish Spanish nationalism. The title "Queen of the Goths" is not merely a poetic figure—it is, rather, a denial of the historic and enlightened past in favor of a mythological national origin.

2

From the fifteenth century to the present Spain has held Queen Isabella in special reverence. The cult that has grown up about her has culminated in a recent (but not the first) proposal for her canonization. In Granada, where she and Ferdinand are buried and where she signed the Edict of Expulsion, a bell still rings daily from a tower of the Moorish Alhambra on the hour the city fell to the arms of Castile. In the center of the Plaza of Isabel la Católica is a fountain dominated by a figure of the queen being entreated by Columbus. Above a building in the center of town another enormous statue of Isabella broods over Granada from a height more lofty than the towers of the cathedral she built.[2]

For the present Spanish regime "Isabella the Catholic" has become a symbol of orthodoxy in both politics and religion. Propagandists are quick to point out that the return to Christianity and the unity that the reign of Isabella and her husband brought about is similar to the purification of Spain effected by General Franco. Spanish historians and the official spokesmen of the present régime, for both political and personal reasons, feel an obligation to explain the history of Spain from a Roman Catholic point of view—a perspective that makes it necessary to suppress important facts of history, to perpetuate legends, and to resurrect attitudes long dead. The points of view expressed below by modern Spanish authors are not buried in obscure corners of libraries but available on any moderately stocked bookshelf in Spain.

Spanish historians are rarely willing to treat the "Catholic Monarchs" other than as the saviors of Spain and their artifact, the Inquisition, as the principal instrument of Spain's salvation. A famous Spanish historian, Angel González Palencia, writes:

> In order to watch over the faith menaced by the activities of the converts and in order to investigate the customs of the secret Jews. Ferdinand and Isabella petitioned and obtained from Rome the establishment of the Inquisition, an institution not invented by the Catholic monarchs and not even of Spanish origin but a tribunal of faith that existed in various European states during the Middle Ages, a tribunal eminently popular and received with general applause by the entire Spanish people. . . . Several months after the Conquest of Granada

on March 31, 1492, the Edict of Expulsion was issued. The problem of the Jews was, thus, resolved then and forever.[3]

It is curious to note that the statement about the existence of inquisitional tribunals in other European countries repeats one made by Lope de Vega in the La Guardia play. By both Lope de Vega and González Palencia, despite the four hundred years separating them, the Inquisition is regarded as the traditional Christian procedure for maintaining purity of faith—but not specifically of Spanish origin. Theirs is thus a rejection of responsibility that spans centuries.

According to Claudio Sánchez Albornoz, a historian much admired in Spain for his "accuracy," the Inquisition was ". . . a Satanic invention of the Hispano Jews that reflects the sinister and mysterious processes of the Jewish courts . . . but Spanish tradition rose up against the dark atmosphere of denunciation and duress."[4] Another curious reminiscence from the days of the Inquisition is found in the three-volume work on the Spanish Jews by Julio Caro Baroja, the most famous of Spanish sociologists and the nephew of Pio Baroja, an eminent Spanish novelist of the "Generation of 1898," a friend of Ernest Hemingway, and a notable anti-Semite. According to Caro Baroja the unification of Spain by Ferdinand and Isabella was a harking back to the Visigothic nationality of seven hundred years before,[5] a thought he, too, shares with Lope de Vega and the "Queen of the Goths." Pinta Llorente, a well-known Spanish historian, states that "as a modern intellectual" he finds the Inquisition inexcusable. Nevertheless, he fervently defends the right of a country to protect its orthodoxy. He regards the Jews as weakening the virtue of any people among whom they live because of the Jews' supposed internationalism and inclination toward free thought. "The extermination of the Jews and the Inquisition are not the fruits of the intolerance of the Spanish kings but a great chapter in the tenacious defense of the spirit of the Spanish people."[6]

The Inquisition established by Ferdinand and Isabella is thus made to represent the will of the Christian population who, like its Queen, is determined to combat a great moral evil. In comradeship and orthodox zeal, the common man (the descendant of the Old Goth in the myth of the New Society of Ferdinand and Isabella) and the royal pair share the same idealism and religious experience.

The case of the alleged ritual crime at La Guardia is inextricably connected with the foundation of the Inquisition and the reign of Ferdinand and Isabella. So reverently is Isabella regarded in Spain that it is essential to clear her of the barbarous act of having permitted the condemnation, torture, and public execution of the converts and Jews involved in the La Guardia affair. She must also be relieved of having fallen victim to her own credulity in having believed in the ritual crime in the first place. It is not sufficient to call on the customs or practices of the age in which the "Catholic Queen" lived to explain her complicity in the blood libel. Nothing like fanatical religious zeal can be accepted as an explanation. Furthermore, finding some reasonable but honorable explanation of the ritual murder accusation is important to save the good names of those ecclesiastics involved in bringing the supposed criminals to justice. It is especially important to save the reputation of Isabella's confessor, the Inquisitor General Tomas de Torquemada, who still enjoys a high esteem in Spain: according to W. T. Walsh, the modern defender of the Inquisition whose books are among the few on the Inquisition easily available to the Spanish public, "when his [Torquemada's] tomb was opened in order to transfer his remains elsewhere, those who were present related that they noticed an especially sweet and pleasing odor. They began to pray. Nevertheless, he has not yet been canonized."[7]

The *Diccionario de Historia de España,* a historical dictionary found in many Spanish homes and in all libraries and published by the enlightened Revista de Occidente (the publishers of Ortega y Gassett and the liberal Julian Marías), discusses the La Guardia case under the article "Jews." This affair, says the historical dictionary, "provoked a general indignation coupled with the recollection of a similar case which took place in Saragossa centuries before."[8] However, such crimes are not sponsored by Jews as a whole but by a few fanatics. "These fanatics," continues the article, "have so embarrassed Jewish historians that they have tried to deny the authenticity of these ritual murders."[9]

The sociologist, Caro Baroja, whose volumes on the Jews in Spain were intended to be the final word on the subject, speaks as follows of the authenticity of the blood libel of La Guardia: "Certain Jews and *conversos* might well have practiced certain murders along with other acts for purposes of magic and enchantment. But these acts cannot be attributed to the Jewish people as a whole and much less to the teachings of the synagogue."[10] With this statement both Isabella and the Jews are apparently exonerated.

Another modern writer on inquisitional matters, Nicolas López Martínez, accepts the ritual crime as authentic,[11] as did the greatest of Spanish scholars, the universally admired and respected Menéndez Pelayo.[12] W. T. Walsh, the contemporary apologist of the Inquisition, brings "reason" to bear on the condemnation of the accused murderers of La Guardia: "It is difficult for us to believe that the three Dominican inquisitors, well instructed in the philosophy, science, and theology of their age, and the other twelve gentlemen, all with Catholic educations, conspired with one mind to burn eight innocent Jews."[13]

The above confessions of faith become a fact of history in the prestigious seventy-volume *Espasa-Calpe* encyclopedia. This encyclopedia is a standard reference work equivalent in Spain to the *Encyclopedia Britannica* in the English-speaking world.

> The blessed child of La Guardia was sacrificed by the Jews in imitation of the passion of Christ. The Jews cut out his heart in order to mix it with a consecrated host supplied by the Judaizer, Juan Gómez, a sacristan of the parish who was under the impression that the Jews intended to work a spell that would destroy the power of the inquisitors. But in reality they planned to deliver the heart and host to the synagogue of Zamora. A Judaizer, Benito Mesuras, was chosen to deliver the object. Passing through Avila he stopped to visit the cathedral. While he was pretending to be praying from a prayerbook in which he carried the consecrated host it was observed that a splendor of radiance came from the book of prayers. The Holy Office of

the Inquisition was informed. The religious authorities came to Mesura's house and demanded the book. When they saw the Jew's confusion they searched his luggage and discovered a human heart preserved in salt and some letters for the Jews of Zamora. . . . the sacrifice of Christians by Jews was relatively frequent and completely authenticated in that period of history.[14]

Had the above article been written during the period of the Inquisition, one might believe that the author was attempting to prove his own sincere Christianity in order to avoid being considered a Judaizer.

In the publication of the University of Granada dedicated to Semitic studies, *Miscelánea de Estudios Arabes y Hebraicos*, there appeared in the issue of 1963–64 an article by the literary historian Pasqual Recuero entitled "Jews in the Works of Quevedo." The satirist Francisco Quevedo is one of the principal figures of Spanish letters in the seventeenth century and an anti-Semite. In the course of his article Dr. Recuero writes the following: "The Expulsion [of the Jews] was not, according to popular belief, the work of the priests. The Expulsion was made possible by the accusation of deicide and the recollection of certain crimes committed by the Jews throughout the Spanish Middle Ages, which legend was careful to perpetuate."[15]

One of the most famous of these "crimes" allegedly took place in the city of Segovia in the year 1410 and involves Mayer al Guadex, the physician and advisor of King Henry III of Castile. It was Mayer al Guadex who sponsored his kinsman Solomon HaLevi at court. This Solomon HaLevi later became Chief Rabbi of Castile and, after conversion to Christianity, was Bishop of Burgos under the name of Pablo de Santamaría, perhaps the most famous Jewish apostate of Spanish history. It might be instructive to remark here that, according to Spanish historians, Rabbi Solomon was baptized on 21 July 1390. This date relieves the rabbi of having converted under the compulsion of the mobs that devastated the Jewish communities of Spain in the spring and summer of 1391, forcing baptism on great multitudes of Jews. The pious wish to place the bishop beyond the reach of coercion is an attempt to ignore the real circumstances of his apostasy, which, according to contemporary documentation, took place after the duress of 1391. He had probably ceased to believe in traditional Judaism before the pogroms for reasons that could not have induced him to accept Roman Catholicism except under threat of violence. The bishop's relative, Mayer al Guadex, was involved in the following alleged affair. The Jews of Segovia purchased a consecrated host from an indigent sacristan for the purpose of working black magic with the sacred object. It was to Mayer that the host was delivered. While the Jews were working their spell the authorities became miraculously aware of the sacrilege, rushed to the scene of the crime, confiscated the synagogue of Segovia, dedicated it as a church, and arrested Mayer al Guadex. Under torture he admitted his crimes, among them the poisoning of the king.

3

The synagogue in which the host was desecrated still stands today in Segovia under the name of Corpus Christi. A large painting depicting the Jews working their sacrilege on the host hangs at the entrance of this church, and visitors are informed of the blasphemy and miracle by the caretaker. In 1967, for one peseta a seven-page pamphlet could be obtained in Corpus Christi explaining the happenings which took place in this former synagogue—a replica of the older of the two synagogues which still stand in Toledo. After describing the manner in which Don Mayer obtained the consecrated host, the text of this pamphlet reads:

> The Jew [Mayer] was delighted and secretly called the other Jews. When they were assembled, he told them he had in his possession the host which the Christians venerate as God. And he instructed them to deliberate on how to employ the holy wafer. After holding council, they took the body of Our Savior and Redeemer in their filthy hands [*sucias manos*] and scornfully carried it into the synagogue, where they made a

great fire on which they placed the cauldron filled with resin. When it came to a boil they determined to cast in the body of Our Savior Jesus. But behold, the very great miracle of the sacred host! As they were about to cast it into the cauldron it went flying through the air. The criminals pursued it thinking to catch it, but suddenly the synagogue began to tremble. . . .[16]

The narrative painfully continues to relate the dedication of the church of Corpus Christi and the execution of Mayer al Guadex.

In spite of the obvious burden to the credulity of the above account, its acceptance is not limited to the naïvely devout. The very possession of the former synagogue by the Roman Catholic Church must either be justified by the legend or remain an embarrassment to the defenders of the Spanish church-state. For at the time of the dedication of Corpus Christi as a church, Judaism was still a legal religion in Spain. But now even the educated Spaniard can defend the dedication of the synagogue at Segovia as a church by referring to the assertions by Caro Baroja and other enlightened scholars that certain Jews might well have carried on the practices of black magic involving holy waters. The more orthodox can turn to W. T. Walsh's pious explanation, others to the opinion of the great Spanish polygraph Menéndez Pelayo or to the massive seventy-volume *Espasa-Calpe* encyclopedia.

In 1960, a much publicized convention was held between leaders of the Jewish community of Madrid and officials of the Spanish church. More recently, other meetings have been organized to further understanding between Christians and Jews, such as one between Jewish leaders and the Dominicans in Avila. On 21 July 1967, a law purporting to grant freedom of religion went into effect in Spain—a law that attempts a liberal gesture without real legal commitment. The new Spanish legislation does not guarantee religious freedom as a fundamental human right. The Spanish state retains the privilege of establishing the type of status each religion will have before the law and to deny recognition of non–Roman Catholic religions as it deems fit. The government may or may not grant the right to practice any non–Roman Catholic religion. If legal recognition is not given or if it is not solicited by the non–Roman Catholic religious body, public worship is illegal. The state, therefore, does not protect the freedom of non–Roman Catholic religions.

For liberal Spaniards Vatican Council II held out hope for some changes in the traditional and medieval structure of their church-state. But even in Rome, where some Spaniards looked for liberalization, there were historical and psychological problems that could not be easily eradicated. During its entire history the Roman Catholic Church has taught as a dogma of faith that the Jews were guilty of deicide and that their guilt is hereditary.

The fourth chapter of *The Declaration on the Relation of the Church to Non-Christian Religions* issued by Vatican II was intended to repudiate the anti-Semitism that has been inseparable from the growth and development of Christianity for two thousand years. The Church so deeply cherished its hatred of Jews that many representatives of the Council feared a serious rupture of Church cohesion if any modification of the traditional attitude concerning Jews were made. Bishop Luigi Carli wrote in the February 1965 issue of his diocesan magazine that the Jews of Jesus' time and their descendants down to the present were collectively guilty of the crucifixion. At an outdoor mass in Rome in 1965 Pope Paul spoke of the heavy role of the Jews in the death of Jesus. In regard to the Pope's statement Elio Toalf, the Chief Rabbi of Rome, made the following shrewd psychological comment: "In even the most qualified Catholic personalities, the imminence of Easter causes prejudices to reemerge." Cardinal Augustin Bea, a German Jesuit and one of the leading figures of Vatican II, apologized for the Pope's sermon with the following justification: "Keep in mind that the Pope was speaking to ordinary and simple faithful people—not before a learned body." The connection between faith and anti-Semitism could not be more closely drawn. Even the learned body of Vatican II could not overcome their own simple faith and deepest historical roots. After four years of soul searching the Council approved on 28 October 1965 a weak and vacillating statement that apparently represented the zenith of Roman Catholic liberalism and the depths of its understanding and good will.

> Although the Jewish authorities and those who followed their lead pressed for the death of Christ, nevertheless what happened to Christ in His passion cannot be attributed to all Jews, without distinction, then alive, nor to the Jews of today. Although the Church is the new people of God, the Jews should not be presented as rejected by God or accursed, as if this follows from the Holy Scriptures. May all see to it, then, that in catechetical work or in preaching the word of God they do not teach anything that is inconsistent with the truth of the Gospel and with the spirit of Christ.
>
> Moreover, the Church, which rejects every persecution against any man, mindful of the common patrimony with the Jews and moved not by political reasons but by the Gospel's spiritual love, deplores hatred, persecutions, displays of anti-Semitism, directed against Jews at any time of by anyone.

The mentality which lengthily debated and finally approved that declaration is, comparatively speaking, much elevated over the permanent condition of the Spanish-speaking world. As the theologians of the Vatican Council gave themselves over to medieval notions, so the Spanish historians surrender to that traditional attitude that has made Spain the favorite daughter of the Church. The after-image of the Inquisition and the reign of Ferdinand and Isabella continue to haunt the textbooks and the interpretations of those historians who cannot abide the Inquisition as an institution of Spanish origin and yet cannot condemn its work. The blood libel and the ritual crime, so inextricably connected with the exile of the Jews from Spain and the politics of the "Queen of the Goths," are shadow figures from the past that weigh heavily on Spain's present.

Notes

1. Luis Páramo, *Origine et Progressu Officii Sanctae Inquisitiones* (1598), p. 166.

2. St. Louis, Missouri, apparently will soon possess a monument to Queen Isabella. Mayor Cervantes of that city, with the help of his full-time assistant and brother, Fr. Cervantes, S.J., has recently arranged for the acquisition of the Spanish Pavilion of the New York World's Fair at a cost of $6 million along with a statue of Queen Isabella and a cornerstone from her tomb to be built into the Pavilion. The statue in question is a duplicate of the one that stood before the Pavilion in New York. (The present Spanish régime has closely collaborated on this entire scheme.) Mayor Cervantes might conceivably arrange for the erection of a monument to his illustrious namesake, Miguel de Cervantes, whose relationship to the Inquisition was that of potential victim. To commemorate Isabella is to honor the accomplished facts of Spanish barbarism and the inquisitional mind.

3. Angel González Palencia, *La España del Siglo de Oro* (Madrid, 1940), p. 6.

4. Claudio Sánchez Albornoz, *España, un enigma histórico* (Buenos Aires, 1956), 2:288.

5. Julio Caro Baroja, *Los judíos en la España Moderna y Contemperánea* (Madrid: Ediciones Arion, 1961), 1:159.

6. Pinta Llorente, *Procesos inquisitoriales contra la familia judía de Juan Luis Vives* (Madrid: Instituto Arias Montano, 1964).

7. William Thomas Walsh, *Personajes de la Inquisición* (Madrid: Espasa-Calpe, 1963), p. 209.

8. The "similar case which took place in Saragossa centuries before" is dealt with in a résumé of Spanish history used to instruct Spanish children who are being prepared for their first communion. This vicious little textbook, entitled *Yo soy español,* by Agustin Serrano de Haro and published by Editorial Escuela Española, Hijos de Ezequiel Solana, Calle Mayor 4, Madrid, had gone through twenty-five editions by 1961. In one chapter entitled "Moors and Christians" the children are instructed to write and memorize the following statement, printed in blood-faced type: "The Moors took over Spain because they were aided by the Jews and other traitors." The Saragossa case is described as follows: "In those days there were many Jews in Spain. And some Jews hated the Christians, and they were furious that the children believed in the Virgin and the Lord. For this reason they killed Saint Domingo de Val. Little Domingo lived in Saragossa and wanted to be a Captain. He was charitable and used to give his food to hungry children. He was brave. He used to protect the children who were weak and helpless. He was pious and used to go through the city with his friends, singing

songs in praise of the Virgin. This was the thing that irritated the evil Jews most. Because of this they planned to kill him. One quiet afternoon, as he was passing a Jewish house, a Jew threw a blanket over him and dragged him in. At midnight many evil men gathered together; they took Domingo's crucifix away from him and ordered him to tramp on it. But he answered valiantly (although he was only seven years old), 'This I will never do, for it is my God.' 'Then you will die like your God,' the Jews told him. They placed a crown of thorns on his head and nailed him to a cross and pierced him with a lance. Little Domingo was crucified like the Lord." This text is accompanied by illustrations showing the kidnapping and the crucifixion. In the crucifixion scene four Jews are shown attired in Moorish dress. Two are nailing the child to a wall while their companions catch his blood in wineglasses.

9. *Diccionario de Historia de España*, vol. 2 (Madrid: Revista de Occidente, 1952), article "Judíos."

10. Caro Baroja, *Los judíos*, p. 171.

11. Nicolás López Martínez, *Los judaizantes castellanos* (Burgos, 1954), pp. 191–99.

12. Menéndez Pelayo, *Historia de los heterodoxos españoles* (Madrid, 1880–81), 1:636.

13. Walsh, *Personajes de la Inquisición*, p. 206.

14. *Enciclopedia Espasa-Calpe*, article "Tribunal."

15. *Miscelánea de Estudios Arabes y Hebraicos* (University of Granada, 1963–64), "Los judíos en las obras de Quevedo" by Pascual Recuero.

16. *Copia de la explicación del Cuadro del Milagro* (Segovia).

Damascus to Kiev:
Civiltà Cattolica on Ritual Murder

The fact that ritual murder or blood libel accusations seem to have originated or at any rate flourished in Catholic Europe did not escape the notice of the Catholic hierarchy. Some courageous popes even issued official statements denouncing the legend. The investigative report of 1759 by then Cardinal Lorenzo Ganganelli (1705–74), who later became Pope Clement XIV (1769–74), resulted in a major documentary refutation of the blood libel.

The above efforts notwithstanding, it is also true that some Catholic priests and theologians took an active part in promoting the blood libel legend. One striking example is that of Johann Eck (1486–1543), a German Catholic theologian known for his opposition to Martin Luther. In 1541, Eck published Ains Judenbüchlins Verlegung *(Refutation of a Jew-Booklet), which was intended to be a rebuttal of an anonymously published booklet originally written in 1529 but not published until 1540. The booklet's title in English translation: "Whether It is True and believable that Jews secretly kill Christian children and use their blood: A splendid text presented for everyone's Judgment." It was written by a Protestant Lutheran preacher from Nuremberg, one Andreas Osiander (1498–1552) in response to an inquiry about the credibility of ritual murder charges (in connection with a 1529 Poesing ritual murder trial in Hungary). The booklet was later published without Osiander's consent to help defend Jews accused of the blood libel in Sappenfeld in 1540. In any event, Eck claimed to have been himself an eyewitness to such a child murder in 1503, and he proceeded to "document" the existence of ritual murder*

Reprinted from *Wiener Library Bulletin* 27 (1974): 18–25.

occurrences. *One scholar has called Eck's* Refutation *"the most massive and systematic formulation of the blood libel . . . the summa of learned discourse on ritual murder." If so, it is not without importance that the author of such a work was a Catholic theologian. It should, however, be noted that Protestants could be just as anti-Semitic as Catholics.* Martin Luther's own On the Jews and Their Lies, *published in 1543 is a classic example.*

The present essay treats Catholic-inspired anti-Semitism of the modern period, specifically that sponsored by a periodical, the Civiltà Cattolica, *published under the auspices of the Vatican. Although not officially a formal outlet for Vatican views, it is a nonetheless influential one. The evidence presented by Charlotte Klein, speaks for itself. See also her book* Anti-Judaism in Christian Theology *(Philadelphia: Fortress Press, 1978).*

For further details concerning the works of Eck and Osiander, see Steven Rowan, "Luther, Bucer and Eck on the Jews," Sixteenth Century Journal *16 (1985): 79–90, and especially R. Po-chia Hsia,* The Myth of Ritual Murder: Jews and Magic in Reformation Germany *(New Haven: Yale University Press, 1988), pp. 124–31, 136–43 (for the scholarly assessment of Eck's* Refutation, *see p. 126). For the papal statements on blood libel, see* Die Päpstlichen Bullen über die Blutbeschuldigung *(Munich: August Schupp, 1900). For the Ganganelli report of 1759, see Isidore Loeb, "Un Mémoire de Laurent Ganganelli sur La Calomnie du Meurtre Rituel,"* Revue des études juives *18 (1889): 179–211; and Cecil Roth,* The Ritual Murder Libel and the Jew: The Report by Cardinal Lorenzo Ganganelli (Pope Clement XIV) *(London: Woburn Press, 1934). For a discussion of the anti-Semitic context of another Catholic periodical,* La Croix, *see Pierre Sorlin,* La Croix et les Juifs (1880–1899) *(Paris: Éditions Bernard Grasset, 1967). For an English Catholic critique of French Catholic bigotry, see Herbert Thurston, "Anti-Semitism and the Charge of Ritual Murder,"* Month *91 (1898) 561–74.*

Christian-Jewish relations will never become normalized until Christians as well as Jews have examined the prejudices and horrors of their common history. The two-thousand-year-old past has to be analyzed to discover what lies buried in those centuries through which they lived, though separated by more or less wilful misunderstandings and persecutions inflicted on the minority. It is the duty of the historian to lift the veil which blinded the eyes of many otherwise humane and committed Christians who showed themselves singularly loveless and insensitive where Jews were concerned. The semiofficial Vatican periodical, the *Civiltà Cattolica*, and its contributors are a case in point; they remained, up to World War II and after, unconscious of the fact that they encouraged the "teaching of contempt" among countless readers who regarded this periodical as the official source and fountainhead of papal thinking.

Though many articles derogatory to Judaism had appeared in the *Civiltà* between 1850, when it first appeared, and 1881, it was in this latter year that ritual murder was first casually mentioned as a well-known Jewish practice. The authority quoted was Rabbi David Drach, the early nineteenth-century French convert, who was archivist in Rome from 1832 to 1842. He was the author of *Lettres d'un rabbin converti* and a number of other books and pamphlets aiming at the conversion of Jews and describing their religious beliefs. In April 1881, the *Civiltà* quotes from his *De l'Harmonie entre l'Église et la Synagogue* (1844), the assertion that the Jews of Damascus had been responsible in 1840 for the ritual murder of the Capuchin Fr. Thomas and that their guilt had been established beyond doubt. The powerful influence of international Jewry had, however, obtained their release. The evidence was, in the *Civiltà's* view, all the more convincing, since Drach must have found it particularly distasteful to incriminate members of his own race. But, according to the *Civiltà*, the ritual murder was a fact: almost every year Jews murdered Christian children for their Passover in order to fulfil a talmudic law. The custom, the paper noted, was especially observed in Poland.

It is not immediately clear why the years 1881–82 should have seen the detailed exposition, with "irrefutable proof," of the ritual murder allegations of the past. The Damascus affair was forty years old, while the Tisza-Eszlar, Xanten, Polna, and Kiev trials were still to come; the reason must therefore lie elsewhere. At that time, the general climate of opinion was particularly receptive to "investigations" into this "most detestable of Jewish crimes." Russia, Germany, and France experienced during this period an upsurge of anti-Semitism, fanned by men like Drumont and Stoecker and a wave of pogroms in Eastern Europe.

The *Civiltà* took great care to forestall any reproach of contradicting a famous Papal Bull of 1247 by Innocent IV, which stated explicitly that Jews do not kill Christian children and eat their hearts. In the eighteenth century, Cardinal Ganganelli, later Pope Clement XIV, also investigated the blood libel and pronounced it pure fiction. The authors of the *Civiltà* had examined Innocent IV's Bull and considered it to be both true and mistaken: Jews do not eat the child's heart but they did need its blood. The pope had not known this, but it could now be proved. From then on the *Civiltà* began to provide evidence of the Jewish need for Christian blood.

The absence of any Jewish law concerning the use of Christian blood in their better-known religious writings was, for the *Civiltà*, easily explicable: the law was secret and had nothing to do with the original religion of Israel but was rooted in the talmudic tradition. It was only observed according to the Talmud where Jews lived in Eastern Europe and in oriental countries. That was also the reason why most converted Jews, for instance the Ratisbonne brothers, ignored it, as they came from highly assimilated families. The evidence of ritual murder, however, was "irrefutable": partly because the crime had been committed in various countries repeatedly and throughout the centuries, as was proved in the ensuing trials, despite the secrecy in which it was shrouded; partly because the *Civiltà* had carefully investigated two of these cases which, although separated by about four hundred years, showed the same characteristics: the murder of Simon of Trent in 1475 and that of the Capuchin monk Fr. Thomas at Damascus in 1840. The evidence establishing Jewish responsibility for these crimes was to be submitted to the readers in subsequent issues (August 1881). Less publicized and not so fully investigated was the accusation brought by the Greeks of Alexandria in this very year, that the Jews had abducted and slaughtered one of their children—an accusation which, to the *Civiltà*, sounded plausible enough.

In October 1881, the "Chronicle of Contemporary Events" began a series of articles to prove how well-founded was the ritual murder accusation. Jews, it suggested, do not kill Christians simply out of hatred. These assassinations are, however, committed in obedience to one of the rabbinic-talmudic laws, and therefore inspired by piety, devotion, and a heinous religiosity, which obliges the Jew to use Christian blood for the celebration of his Passover (p. 227). The documents of the two trials, Trent and Damascus, were cited as proof of this. The authors had for the first time access to the authentic reports of the Trent trial, kept in the secret archives of the Vatican. The important discovery, reported the *Civiltà* in November 1881, was that the murders were committed because of a strict religious necessity: Christian blood *must* be mixed with the Passover wine and with the unleavened bread: the converted Jew John of Feltres (fifteenth century) relates that the Jews he knew did this habitually. If they could not kill a Christian child in any one particular year, they took care to import its blood from Germany: such blood was always conserved for several years for just such an emergency, since without it the Passover could not be celebrated. The countless reports, documents, and convictions of members of the Jewish communities were proof, according to the *Civiltà* authors, that the rite could not have been a pure invention but was solidly based on facts.

Apart from their lack of any critical faculty in analyzing these folkloristic tales, the writers showed little psychological insight into the reasons which could motivate a religious majority group to vent its resentment, due perhaps to various nonreligious causes, on a defenseless minority. Their infantile credulity, masked by a pseudo-scientific approach, can only be explained by the *Zeitgeist* and more particularly by the general situation of the Church, which throughout the nineteenth century had seen its influence constantly wane. Catholic Rome needed an explanation for the occupation of the Vatican state, a fact neither forgotten nor forgiven. The particular mentality of the authors prevented them from understanding that the growth of industrialization and of national feeling, as well as of a critical view towards the Church's alliance with the conservative and reactionary bourgeoisie of Western Europe, was fast leading to the alienation of whole sections of the liberal-minded population. The Church felt itself persecuted from without and in this siege situation all weapons seemed legitimate, especially against the Jew.

Nothing new was added in 1881, except the names of two more eighteenth-century witnesses, Paul Medici and Leon Modene. The latter, writing on Jewish rites and customs, added that Christian blood was also needed for mixing the *haroseth*—put on the Passover table as a symbol of the bricks made for Pharaoh by the Israelites in Egypt. It actually consists of a harmless mixture of finely ground nuts, apple, and a little wine. Throughout 1882, blood libel articles continued. They were a curious concoction of the "facts" from the Trent case and parallels from other, less spectacular, legends. There is the tale of a certain Jew, Orso of Saxony (fifteenth century), whose passport allowed him to travel freely and bring Christian blood to the Jewish communities who for the moment had no child to kill. The date of Trent, it was said, was special: it was a Jewish Jubilee year and on that occasion fresh blood had to be obtained, and hence the death of little Simon. In ordinary years even an adult Christian might serve and that was what had happened at Damascus. The blood obtained is "never used up completely," it is dried, powdered, and stored for further use.

Further "facts" were disclosed by the *Civiltà*. It asserted, for example, that the Jewish law concerning the need for Christian blood dated from the fifth century; it was formerly contained in the Talmud but, as this became too dangerous, the passage was deleted and the tradition handed on orally in certain chosen families; there was no reason to doubt that it was still observed. Gougenot des Mousseaux in his "excellent" *Le Juif, le Judaisme et la Judaisation des Peuples Chrétiens* (1869)—in fact an anti-Semitic tract treading the well-worn paths of accusation—had preserved an "important" eyewitness report by a Greek monk, a former rabbi, writing in Moldavia in 1803, who explicitly stated that Jews celebrated Passover with Christian blood, today as in the Middle Ages. He had given three good reasons for the necessity of this blood: the hatred of Christ, superstitious and magic practices, and the suspicion that after all Jesus might have been the Messiah and thus the blood of a baptized Christian would have the power to save the Jew too.

Further evidence for Jewish ritual murder was deduced from the circumcision ceremony in Judaism and the use of blood at the feast of Purim. At the time of the Purim festival in 1882, a Turkish child, it had indeed been alleged, was abducted by the Jews of Port Said, baptized, and then slaughtered. The killing itself must, the *Civiltà* stated, follow a traditional rite: it had to be performed in the most cruel and sanguinary manner, to resemble the passion and death of Jesus himself; the child lies bound on a table, as on an altar, several Jews pierce the body to allow the blood to flow freely. The point was made that the Jews themselves had recently given away the secret that the wine was mixed with blood: a French Jewish newspaper had carried an advertisement for a shop selling kosher wine and unleavened bread, certified as "ritual" by the Chief Rabbi himself. Kosher and ritual, says the author, mean that Christian blood, pulverized and preserved, is mixed with both and therefore fit for Passover. . . . The *Civiltà* quite seriously presented this as evidence of the contemporary use of Christian blood by Jews.

Readers were told that the Damascus murder of two adult Christians was not intended for Passover but for Purim; the rule for this feast was that every Jew had to get drunk and to kill one Christian in place of Haman; this was one of the main reasons why popes and bishops forbade all familiar intercourse between Jews and Christians. The *Civiltà* also claimed that the Jew Pfefferkorn (ca. 1500), a convert, had returned to Judaism on his deathbed and confessed to the murder of eight Christians. As a matter of historical fact, there was not the slightest evidence that Pfefferkorn ever returned to Judaism. Moreover, despite his numerous anti-Jewish pamphlets, he never presented the blood libel as truth. Another Jew, from Sienna, mentioned by the Bollandists (*Acta* no. 266), is said to have affirmed that as a physician he had murdered thousands of Christians. The papers of the ex-rabbi from Moldavia, "discovered" by Gougenot des Mousseaux but "no longer accessible," contained details of the Purim slaughters: they were without torture and women and children could assist; the blood was baked into the Purim cakes, in the shape of a triangle, as an additional insult to the Trinity. All these fantastic tales were reported by the *Civiltà* with the utmost seriousness as the result of genuine historical investigations.

In May 1882, the story of the Damascus case was finally told in a special *Civiltà* report: Fr. Thomas had been invited into a Jewish home, attacked, bound, and a certain Jew, Harari, had cut his throat, his blood being collected in a bottle. As it was impossible to find any evidence of his murder, the most prominent Jews of Damascus were imprisoned and tortured. The accusation was in fact strongly supported by the French Consul, Ratti-Menton, France having taken upon herself the protection of Middle Eastern Christians. Politics played some part in the affair, for France supported Mehemet Ali's annexation of Syria from Turkey and influenced the Egyptian governor to extort a confession from the Jews. The anti-Jewish reaction of the French press helped to justify the trial. Other countries, especially Austria and England, reacted differently. When the torture and death of several of the accused became known, the Jewish communities of Europe united to support their unfortunate brethren in Damascus. Several Chief Rabbis, whose reputation was above suspicion, took a solemn oath that there was not a word of truth in the blood libel. The *Civiltà's* comment was that Jews were allowed to commit perjury in a Christian court. Supported by Queen Victoria herself, the venerable Sir Moses Montefiore and the French lawyer (and later deputy) Isaac Adolphe Crémieux were delegated to undertake the journey to Cairo and Damascus. The embarrassed Mehemet Ali had to give in to the united pressure of all foreign consuls, the French always excepted. The Jews, as far as they had survived the torture of the governor Sherif Pasha, were released and completely exonerated. Contrary to a statement in the *Civiltà*, the words "killed by the Jews" were deleted from the tombstone of Fr. Thomas.

Neither the body of the Capuchin monk nor that of his servant were ever found. They were probably killed by a Moslem who, after a violent quarrel, had been heard to threaten the monk whose life, moreover, had been far from saintly. He had engaged in dealings as a kind of quack physician with all sorts of people and had made a number of enemies. But this was not, of course, the view of the *Civiltà;* according to them, Montefiore had succeeded in bribing Mehemet Ali with Rothschild's gold, so that the truth of the affair should not become known; the ritual murder of Fr. Thomas must have been a fact, because it followed the same pattern of other such killings of Christians by Jews throughout the centuries. What the *Civiltà* writers omitted to mention were the unspeakable tortures practiced on Jewish men, women, and even children, which were bound to force out a "confession" by at least one person. Under duress, one or two abjured their faith and accepted Christianity (or Islam), but when faced with death were "stiffnecked" enough to return to the faith of their ancestors.

The *Civiltà* prided itself on its exact information, the authors of the articles having access to several Hebrew books which allegedly taught that every Jew should at least once in his life inflict grievous bodily harm on a Christian—killing him if possible. The rite was obligatory for five different religious ceremonies: circumcision (a parody of baptism); weddings—the blood must be mixed with two eggs which both spouses have to eat; the ninth of July (Tisha b'ab), the fast day in memory of the destruction of the Temple; Purim; Passover. This was the greatest mystery of the iniquitous synagogue according to one writer (May 1882) and these are the deepest reasons for the ritual murders, repeated in every country and in every generation.

It is perhaps easier to understand the men of the Middle Ages for whom the Jews were weird, mysterious beings, since their religion, their customs, their resistance to the religious and cultural values of the majority, their life as a tightly knit group, seemed a threat to Christianity. But this was 1882, in the age of democracy, of the Industrial Revolution, cheap books, and the spread of education. Hebrew was no longer a secret language; the Jews had been emancipated and had adopted the speech, dress, and customs of the nations among whom they lived. Yet the reactionary Vatican milieu accepted and spread the most ignorant and infamous libels about men and women, many of whom were distinguished citizens and practicing in all the professions open to them. Is it possible to ascribe to these nineteenth-century Christians the same motive which was at least partly responsible for the Jew-hatred of medieval times—namely fear? Probably fear played some part, fear for the hierarchical Church which no longer enjoyed a dominant position in a Europe that had once been coterminous with Christendom. However irrational, this would seem a psychologically convincing answer. After all, a few years later, Edouard Drumont in *La Libre Parole* and the Catholic paper *La Croix*, as well as the same *Civiltà*, succeeded in convincing millions of Frenchmen that Dreyfus must be a traitor because he was a Jew.

Whatever its reasons, the *Civiltà* continued to analyze the Trent case of 1475 in nauseous detail. Their final triumphant argument was that "little Simon" was beatified and that many miracles had taken place at his shrine. They could not foresee that in 1965, at the end of the Second Vatican Council, the Bishop of Trent would forbid his cult, would order all his relics to be withdrawn from the church and that the whole hideous episode which had cost many Jews their lives would be declared one vast fraud.

But the *Civiltà* was not living wholly in the past: the present offered it new possibilities of justification: in Hungary, at Tisza-Eszlar, another ritual murder had just taken place, and at Constantinople a child had been saved only at the last minute. The guilt of the Jews at Tisza-Eszlar was "established beyond doubt," for there was a witness who had spied through the synagogue keyhole and watched the gruesome murder of the fourteen-year-old servant girl, Esther Solymosi. Well might the judges acquit the accused Jews—Rothschild's money had done it again, as at Damascus. This time all Hungary was threatened with financial disaster if the murderous Jews were condemned, yet in their hearts everyone "knew for certain" that the Jews had committed the crime. The witness, the boy Moritz Scharf, son of the accused janitor of the synagogue, had never altered his tale, according to the *Civiltà*, which continued to refer to the case between 1882 and 1884. One fact only needed further explanation: a girl had been chosen instead of the customary boy; this was unusual but not unprecedented, a similar case having occurred in Lithuania in 1574. Perhaps there were still more Jewish rites of which Christians were ignorant. Perhaps a girl's blood was good enough for Purim cakes.

The truth of the matter became evident during the trial. The twelve-year-old Moritz was the pet of the police, who by promises and threats, had persuaded him to accuse his own father together with other Jews. Altogether some eighty Jews were arrested and interrogated. Under torture some "confessed" but revoked their extorted confession later. Moritz entangled himself in a tissue of lies and contradictions. Moreover, some two months later the fully clothed body of a girl, identified as that of Esther, was found in the river. Now Jewish rivermen were accused of body-snatching; neither could this be proved, experts from the University of Budapest declaring that the explanation of body-snatching did not fit the facts. No container for the blood was ever found and all the Jews were acquitted although they continued to be suspected. The whole affair was a tragedy for the Hungarian Jews; their relationship with their Gentile neighbors deteriorated, and the parliamentary anti-Semitic faction increased markedly. Many Jews, including the Scharfs, left Tisza-Eszlar.

For the *Civiltà* the "absolute veracity" (February 1884, p. 491) of Moritz Scharf was nevertheless a fact. They feared for him; his family might easily kill him, for "perhaps nothing is forbidden to this race" (p. 493). The universal indignation of Jews everywhere was taken as additional proof of the religious significance of ritual murder: they were all waiting for the badly needed Christian blood. It was in similar cases that, from the earliest times onwards, all Jewish communities had been seen to unite to help the accused, said the *Civiltà*, quoting the medieval chronicler Matthew of Paris and his description of the murder of Blessed Hugh of Lincoln (1255). Ritual murder, it alleged, had occurred throughout the centuries in every country because of the desperate need for blood; as for the solemn oath by the Chief Rabbi of Hungary that Jews never used Christian blood, it was worthless: not only because perjury was permitted, but because the rabbi referred only to a written law. The *Civiltà* had "clarified the issue": the ritual murder obligation was kept secret and handed on orally. For further information, August Rohling's *Der Talmudjude* (1872) was highly recommended. As for the Jewish need for Christian blood, its ultimate rationale was the unavowed belief that the blood of Christ possessed redeeming qualities from which Jews wished to profit.

The authors of the *Civiltà* were unaware of the ludicrous tangle of contradictory statements into which they had stumbled. Jews need Christian blood for ritual purposes, yet Jews do not believe in Jesus; Jews hate Christ and Christians, yet they believe in the saving power of Christ's blood. The conflicting explanations were probably due to the deeply engrained anti-Judaism of the whole editorial group, afraid of the new times, of liberalism, of the waning power of the Church, and of the role some Jews played in the various anti-clerical parties in Europe. This had blinded them so far that any accusation against the Jews and their faith was welcomed, even if there was no logical coherence among the bewildering variety of charges.

In November 1891, the *Civiltà* was presented with a new

case in Corfu; the body of a Jewish girl had been discovered but the people, claiming it as a Christian child, had risen against the Jewish community, killing two of its members. Finally the governor intervened, but as in most such cases a vague belief in mysterious Jewish sacrifices remained. The author did not find this anti-Semitic outbreak such a "mystery," for he added that the people of Corfu hated the Jews as the most successful businessmen on the island.

Much simpler and more definite was the Xanten murder (March 1892). Many witnesses, it was alleged, had seen the Jewish butcher's wife on 29 June 1891 force a Christian child to enter the shop. The corpse, drained of blood, was found later. No doubt in the writer's mind that the butcher was guilty; both he and his wife had been arrested, set free, then rearrested after the inhabitants raised a storm of protest. The whole affair, with an exact description of the bloodless corpse, was reported in such a manner that no doubt could be left of the writer's firm belief in this ritual murder. Many reliable witnesses, he affirmed, saw little Hegmann enticed into the shop, yet the police neglected to search the premises until three months later: of course they found nothing. "The culprit was not discovered at Tisza-Eszlar, nor at Corfu, and similarly not at Xanten!" (p. 505). The *Civiltà* lamented the "injustice" in all these cases, each time blaming Jewish influence in the press, parliament, and the courts.

The *Civiltà* at least could proclaim itself objective and incorruptible. In January 1893, it published a list of authors who had written on the Jewish need for Christian blood; they ranged from the eleventh to the nineteenth century and places and dates were given; could it be that they were all mistaken? The *Anglo-Saxon Chronicle*, Chaucer's *Canterbury Tales*, Eisenmenger's *Entdecktes Judentum* (1699), the anonymous *La Question Juive* (1822), Toussenel's *Les Juifs, Rois de l'Époque* (1845), and finally Drumont's "excellent" *La France Juive* (1886)—all described ritual murder in verifiable detail. To make it easy for the reader, the *Civiltà* added a full list of some sixty ritual murder cases, from 1071 at Blois in France to 1891 at Xanten in Germany. This was indeed irrefutable evidence in their eyes—the historical facts must convince the most suspicious investigator. It was time therefore that the secular press stopped proclaiming that the *Civiltà* spread calumnies, for both history and local tradition were on their side. The perfidious Jews had fallen so low that not only did the Mosaic Law no longer exist for them, but they did not even observe the natural law. Talmudic religion had turned them into savages. They were a constant danger, a plague to the nations who had so generously offered them shelter, food, and liberty (pp. 281–86). Under the headline "Jewish Morality and the Blood Mystery," the same accusations were repeated ad nauseam for seventeen pages.

Why did the *Civiltà* so obviously press these charges? No doubt, confronted by the antagonism of the secular press, it sought to justify its attitude. It should be remembered that the Vatican, in its precarious situation, needed a scapegoat, and the Jew was ideal for this role. All that the Vatican most feared and disliked in the modern world which sought emancipation from the Church's authority was embodied in the Jew. That the credibility of the *Civiltà*, of the Church itself, was imperiled by this continued process of gratuitous libel was totally ignored.

Today we are struck by the fact that the ever-increasing knowledge of Judaism did not seem to have made any impact on the contributors to *Civiltà*. Their good faith must be called in question when, in 1900, after the murder of a Protestant student named Winter in Konitz (Prussia), they again evoked the likelihood of ritual murder. Anti-Jewish riots broke out, but in spite of a thorough investigation no trace of the murderer could be found. Again *Civiltà* ascribed this to Jewish machinations. More space was given to a slightly earlier event, the murder of two Christian girls in Polna, Bohemia (1899). The accused, a Jew named Hilsner, was at first condemned to death but "Jewish influence" meant that the penalty was commuted to life imprisonment. The half-witted Hilsner, for whom Masaryk, later the first president of Czechoslovakia, intervened personally, was not released until 1916. The *Civiltà* had no doubts: "The history of ritual murder, for those who know something about it, is rich in facts and details which recall the facts of the murder at Polna" (August 1901, p. 500).

The last case to be reported in full was the accusation, trial, and acquittal of Menaham Mendel Beilis of Kiev, 1911–13. The bare facts of the case are that Beilis was a watchman in the brickyard near which a Russian boy of thirteen, Andrei Justchinski, was seen for the last time on 19 March 1911. Later his mutilated body was discovered in a cave outside the town. Police investigation led to the strong suspicion that the boy had known too much about the activities of a gang connected with a certain notorious Vera Cheberiak. But the "Black Hundred," known for their reactionary anti-Semitic views, roused part of the population of Kiev against the Jews who, they alleged, had used Beilis as their instrument although he had neither instigated nor carried out the "ritual murder" of the Christian boy. The Minister of Justice took about two years to prepare the case, and it was only years later, when the archives became accessible, that evidence of a government plan for a pogrom came to light. From 1911 until the trial in 1913, the world press played its part; Russian and foreign experts, Jews and Christians, published their opinions, almost always favorable to Beilis; the case created a storm and the jury refused to condemn him. Beilis was released.

In the *Civiltà*, however, the story looked very different. Its version appeared in two lengthy articles, "Jewish Trickery and Papal Documents—Apropos of a Recent Trial" (11 and 25 April 1914). Medical opinion was quoted to the effect that death was brought about in three stages: the boy was stabbed in such a manner that all his blood could be collected, he was tortured, and finally his heart was pierced. These were all held to be signs of ritual murder, which only Jews could perpetrate, since it required long experience. One Catholic expert on Judaism, Professor Pranaitis, spoke of the existence of a "dogma of blood" (p. 210); the killing of Christians was a commandment, an act of highest religious heroism; each murder of a Christian hastened the coming of the Messiah, and was also a valid substitute for the Temple sacrifices. As for the prohibition of consuming blood, this, according to Professor Pranaitis's Talmud, did not apply to boiled blood, which, on the contrary, was necessary for the unleavened Passover bread.

Kiev, according to the *Civiltà*, was a civilized town with neutral magistrates and an unbiased police force; if the Jews were really so sure of Beilis's innocence, why did they raise a worldwide outcry against the trial? This was one more proof of their bad conscience. They lamented the fate of the imprisoned Beilis, but did anyone consider the poor victim of what was certainly a ritual murder?

The press was in the hands of the Jews, hence the agitation. True, the Cardinal of Westminster had sent a courteous letter to the British Chief Rabbi, stating that the Church had never believed in these atrocious crimes, but no other prominent churchman had joined him. The trial itself was so full of contradictory evidence that it was difficult to get at the truth, but the *Civiltà* pointed out one significant fact: the two children of Vera Cheberiak, Eugene and Valia, were found dead a few days after Beilis's arrest. A Jewish doctor in the Kiev hospital stated that their death was due to dysentery, but shortly afterwards it was confirmed that these two witnesses against Beilis had been poisoned with chocolates. The Jews maintained that this was the work of their own mother—she had been offered a bribe of forty thousand rubles—yet this only shows what store the Jews set by a mother's love. The *Civiltà* continued with many more details: the discovery of a secret synagogue near the brickyard where Andrei had been last seen, the disappearance of several Jews, the collaboration of the Kiev police with the Jews, the fact that the counsels for the defense were all known "champions for the cause of Judaism." Influenced by all these factors, the jury had finally been equally divided and Beilis had profited from their indecision.

Whatever part Beilis himself may have played in the murder of the child Andrei, the article continued, the unbiased reader of all the evidence would remain convinced that this crime showed all the marks of ritual murder, and resembled that of Tisza-Eszlar. The medical evidence of the manner of

195

his death, all the blood being extracted, proved to the *Civiltà* beyond doubt that the Jewish race must be guilty. It might be that many assimilated Jews knew nothing of the religious custom of ritual murder, but the fact remained that "there exist Jews who, because of superstitious beliefs founded on false doctrines, procure Christian blood for these rites" (end of article, 25 April 1914, p. 344).

This was the last time that the *Civiltà* mentioned ritual murder. But it was not unfortunately the last time that "ritual murder" was used to arouse anti-Semitism. The *Civiltà* carried a heavy responsibility for having "proved" the truth of the blood libel in the years when anti-Semitic movements were growing in strength on the Continent, when Hitler became a disciple of Lueger in Vienna, when the Dreyfus case shook France, when millions of wretched Jewish refugees, threatened by pogroms, had to leave Russia. The last sentence in the *Civiltà* article is not the last word on this fantastic accusation. In Germany, under Nazi rule, it was taken up again in a special issue of Julius Streicher's *Der Stürmer* (May 1934), under the title "The Greatest Secret of World Jewry," carrying on its first page a picture of the ritual murder of six children in Regensburg in 1476. From 1881 to 1914, the *Civiltà* had done its utmost to produce evidence of the truth of these events, yet never, not even in the thirties, had it been felt necessary to issue a retraction—although the ritual murder stories have long been recognized as a malicious anti-Jewish invention, motivated by a desire to persecute Jews who were hated for very different reasons. Might it not have been of comfort, even of help, to the Jews under Hitler, if the authoritative Vatican periodical had reexamined and restated its views? Instead it silently consented to be classed together with *Der Stürmer.*

JACOB M. LANDAU

Ritual Murder Accusations in Nineteenth-Century Egypt

The blood libel legend may have originated among Christians, but it has spread to the Arab world, where there is also a tradition of anti-Semitism. The following survey of late nineteenth-century instances of blood libel accusations in Egypt by Jacob M. Landau, Gersten Professor of Political Science at the Hebrew University of Jerusalem, shows how well entrenched the legend is in Egypt.

For a brief discussion of blood libel reports elsewhere in the Islamic sphere, see Bernard Lewis, The Jews of Islam *(Princeton: Princeton University Press, 1984), pp. 156–59. Lewis observes (p. 158) that even in the Islamic context, the blood libel rumors almost always originated among the Christian population, especially in the Greek press. However, more recently, in the twentieth century, the accusations did not always start in the Christian community, but were rather appropriated by certain Egyptian Muslim newspapers for anti-Semitic propaganda purposes (p. 159).*

Persecution of the Jews in Egypt during the last thirty years of the nineteenth century has not received much attention in historical studies of the Jews of Egypt[1] or in other books.[2] Perhaps the famous Damascus ritual murder accusation of 1840 overshadowed lesser—and equally baseless—ones in the East. From the beginning of the 1870s, the number of rit-

Reprinted from Jacob M. Landau, *Middle Eastern Themes: Papers in History and Politics* (London: Frank Cass, 1973, pp. 99–142. It was first published in *Sěfūnōt* (Jerusalem) 5 (1961): 417–60. Translated and published by permission of the Ben Zvi Institute, Jerusalem.

ual murder accusations increased in both European and Asiatic Turkey—in Izmir, Istanbul, Magnesia, Adalya, and other towns. From 1884 to 1901 they occurred also at Bayramiç (near the Dardanelles), in Istanbul, Salonika, and even as far south as Damascus and Beirut and as far west as Monastir and Kavala. In most of these cases, a Greek mob spread a rumor that a Christian child had been kidnapped and slaughtered—usually around Passover. In some cases, the authorities discovered that the plotters had hidden the child and they were arrested.[3]

Although it is difficult to connect the ritual murder accusations in Egypt with other such occurrences in the Ottoman Empire, it is reasonable to assume that they were caused by similar circumstances. Such accusations throughout the Ottoman Empire came to the knowledge of Jewish organizations in Western Europe and were reported in the Jewish and general press[4]—but this was not so with regard to the persecution of the Jews in Egypt. Consequently, it may be worthwhile to publish the documents concerning the ritual murder accusations which have been stored in various archives and to try to determine their place within the context of the period in which they took place.

The Documents and Their Significance

The fifteen documents printed below have been copied from the Foreign Ministries in London and Rome and they complement one another. They can be divided into six main groups, according to date and subject.[5]

The first category contains only one document: a letter in French from the committee of the Jewish Community in Alexandria to Colonel Stanton, British Consul General in Egypt, dated 23 May 1870 (Document I). An elderly Jew named Sason[6] had been arrested and the population of the city stressed the man's Jewishness, even claiming he was a rabbi. He was held for a month without being charged and the press exploited his imprisonment for incitement. Newspapers from Malta[7] and Alexandria hinted at the designs of this "rabbi" to kidnap a Christian child[8] in order to strangle him and use his blood for the baking of matzah for Passover—this despite the fact that it happened at the end of holiday. The Maltese in Alexandria plotted to attack the synagogue; some of the Jews of the city began to talk about retaliation; the committee of the Jewish community therefore appealed to the British Consul General to use his influence to secure the freedom of the prisoner and prevent riots in the city.[9]

The second grouping also consists of only one document (Document II). G. B. Machiavelli, the Italian Consul in Alexandria, informed the Italian Foreign Minister, Cairoli, on 1 April 1880, that the fact that a Greek boy had fallen from a balcony into the yard of the synagogue of Alexandria had given the Greeks an opportunity to accuse the Jews of a plot.[10] Four doctors[11] who examined the body testified that they had not found any external wounds. But the Greek mob nevertheless vilified the Jews and attacked them with local Arabs joining in the fray.[12] Machiavelli demanded that the police protect those Jews who were Italian subjects, a number of whom had been insulted or attacked. When a delegation of Jewish dignitaries appealed to him, he also asked the Italian Consul General in Cairo to intervene with the Egyptian authorities to send reinforcements to the tiny (four hundred strong) police force of Alexandria. Three days later Machiavelli again wrote to Cairoli that order had been restored and that everything had been done to prevent a recurrence of the attacks against the Jews with Italian citizenship in particular and Jews in general.[13]

The third and largest section consists of six documents relating to the ritual murder accusation of March 1881. The first (Document III) is a report by Charles A. Cookson, British Consul in Alexandria, to E. B. Malet, British Consul General in Cairo, dated 23 March 1881. Cookson tells of a ten-year-old Greek boy[14] who had disappeared from home. Rumors had spread that the Jews were using his blood for the baking of matzah. A delegation of Jewish dignitaries, British subjects, had come to his office and expressed its concern about what they feared might happen. Cookson appealed to the governor of Alexandria and was promised that everything possible would be done, but doubted whether the police—even with reinforcements they would number only fifteen hundred men—could enforce law and order. When he applied to the Greek Consul General in Alexandria, Rangabé, he was told that the child of a Greek family,[15] an Ottoman subject, had disappeared on his way to school. The Greek mob had threatened to attack and loot the Jewish quarter and only he had managed to calm the mob. Suspicion had fallen on the Baruch family [16] whose children the boy had frequently visited and played with. The family was arrested, but no proof was found to convict it except for the admission by one little girl that the Greek boy had eaten in their home soon before he disappeared. According to Cookson, Rangabé showed readiness to cooperate and even to ask the influential Greek Patriarch to soothe the Greeks. Cookson stressed the danger of riots breaking out, since the population of Alexandria was made up of the scum of Europe— Greeks and Italians of the lowest sort, who sought every opportunity to loot—and there was danger that the local police would not be able to stop them. In the meanwhile the boy's body was retrieved from the water. The governor of Alexandria asked that Cookson send a representative for the first examination. When the fear of new riots arose,[17] he again appealed to the Italian and French Consuls as well as to the governor of Alexandria, asking for their intervention. The governor announced that the boy's parents had agreed to the transfer of the body to the Greek hospital in town for autopsy and that military reinforcements had meanwhile arrived from Cairo. Three Jewish dignitaries later came to report attacks on Jews [18] and a British subject complained that a Greek had assaulted him because he was in the company of a Jew.

The second document (Document IV) is a report from Machiavelli to de Martino, Italian Consul General in Cairo, dated 24 March 1881. A few days earlier a nine-year-old boy of Cretan origin had disappeared. He had been accustomed to playing with Jewish children in their homes, and on the day of his disappearance he had visited a Jewish home. The Greek community in Alexandria demanded the return of the boy and the suspected Jewish family was arrested. Machiavelli feared that the thirteen hundred[19] policemen and soldiers would not be able to control the two hundred thousand residents of Alexandria. The boy's body was, in the meantime, retrieved from the sea, and no signs of violence were found on it. The family, however, refused an autopsy and thus the incitement against the Jews continued. The British and French Consuls, together with Machiavelli, called the city governor's attention to the attacks against the Jews. However, only after an autopsy had confirmed the preliminary medical findings,[20] and military units arrived from Cairo, did the riots subside. The Alexandrian authorities did not act firmly and some Jews were attacked—among them four Italian subjects, three of whom were lightly wounded. A Jew of French citizenship was badly hurt in the eye, and the number of Egyptian subjects injured was not known.

The third document in this group (Document V) is a report from the same Machiavelli to Foreign Minister Cairoli, dated 25 March 1881. In this report he states that the Jews were continuing to suffer, although the attacks had become somewhat milder. Even the most prestigious of the Greek families of Alexandria were participating in the riots against the Jews, and a Greek who had attacked a Jew and was detained, was "saved" with their aid from the police. The Greek Consul General refused to take legal steps against them. He even told Machiavelli that the bereaved family of the boy wanted to exploit its tragedy in order to obtain money and that he was collecting a fund for them.

Cookson's report to Malet, dated 26 March 1881 (Document VI), confirms and elaborates on these events. The autopsy showed that the boy's death was caused by drowning. Peace was restored. Machiavelli had told him, in the name of the governor of Alexandria, that a Greek who had been arrested by the police as a result of a complaint by a Jew (who was a German citizen) had been freed by upper-class Greeks armed with pistols. When he was arrested for a second time, and brought to the Greek consulate, he was freed without even being charged. By request of Machiavelli and Cookson, the Swedish Consul General, who was the doyen of the consular corps in Alexandria, went to the Greek consulate general to demand an explanation. The Greek Consul excused the matter and said that most of the Greek population was sorry about the incident. The arrival of additional troops in Alexandria put an end to the riots.

The fifth document (Document VII),[21] is a report from Machiavelli to Cairoli dated 28 March 1881. All the members of the consular corps in Alexandria had met with the Egyptian Minister of War who had arrived in the city with the army. The minister announced that he was thinking of issuing an order for dispersing gatherings even if it meant the use of force. On 27 March 1881 the Greek newspaper *Telegrapho* published an article of incitement aimed at igniting tempers; it was distributed free.[22] According to Machiavelli, quiet had been restored to Alexandria, but the incitement was beginning to spread to the countryside, Damanhur and Kafr al-Zayyat, where a Jew of French nationality had been killed. Machiavelli concluded by saying that he had reported these matters also to de Martino and that he had requested him to demand that the Egyptian government protect the Jews in the villages.

In the sixth document (Document VIII),[23] dated 31 March 1881, de Martino informed Cairoli of his visit to Alexandria (his seat was in Cairo) and of the promise he had received from the Greek Consul General—in his name and in the name of the Greek patriarchate—that in the near future this type of activity by Greeks against Jews would not recur. But since it was the local authorities who controlled the situation, he could not take upon himself the responsibility for the future conduct of the Greek colony in Egypt. De Martino pointed out with shock that it was the Egyptian intelligentsia and not only the Greek community, who were prejudiced against the Jews and believed that they used Christian blood for baking their matzah. The consular corps accepted the suggestion made by the Greek representative that the Egyptian government should be asked to appoint a special committee to deal with the security situation and devise ways of punishing offenders. After de Martino's appeal, the committee was appointed.

In the fourth group there are two documents (Documents IX and X), both from February 1882. De Boccard, Italian Vice Consul in Port Said, informed Machiavelli on 5 February 1882 of the disappearance of a girl a day earlier. According to him, a Muslim boy of sixteen had come to Port Said from Cairo; he was seen there buying sweets for the seven-year-old girl who disappeared. After a search, she was found dead in a house on the edge of the Arab quarter. A medical examination revealed no signs of rape but scissor wounds were found on her face and her carotid vein had been cut. The youth was arrested at a nearby café. In Port Said the rumor spread that the Jews had killed the child in order to use her blood for the baking of matzah. Immediately a mob gathered which rushed to the Arab quarter, but police patrols stopped them, arrested the youth and buried the girl. Even so a stone injured a Jew in the face and some damage was caused to the local synagogue. The Jews appealed to the French Consul who was at that time in a French cruiser in the port. The governor of Port Said asked the consuls to inform their nationals that the Muslim youth would be charged, and to warn them against rioting. Rumors spread that the youth had admitted that he carried out his crime at Jewish requests or that he himself was a Jew who needed Christian blood.

In the second document (Document X), dated 6 February 1882, Machiavelli reports his suspicions to Mancini, the new Italian Foreign Minister. He says that there was a danger that the disturbances which had occurred and recurred in Alexandria in 1880 and 1881 would erupt in Port Said with greater ferocity because of the political tension.[24] The authorities carried out an investigation and announced that the Muslim youth had confessed his crime;[25] only then did tempers cool and the danger pass.

There are three documents in the fifth group, all dated June 1890. The first (Document XI), dated 20 June 1890, is a letter of appeal from a Jew named David Ades of Cairo to Sir Evelyn Baring,[26] British Consul General in Egypt. Ades protested to

Baring about the incitement against the Jews published in the Arabic weekly *al-Maḥrūsa*, and its anti-Semitic accusations. He was particularly angry about the recurrent libel that the Jews were using blood for the baking of matzah.

The second document (Document XII) is a detailed report, dated 24 June 1890, sent to Baring by Raphael Borg, British Consul in Cairo. *Al-Maḥrūsa*, the mouthpiece of Syrian Christians—French citizens—was inciting against Egyptian Jews who had lent money with interest to the Syrians and had later pressed their debt. The paper had blown up an incident in which an Armenian Catholic boy of seven had disappeared in Damascus several weeks earlier[27] and charged the Jews with wanting to use his blood for the baking of matzah. The articles in the paper were strewn with imaginary details of the child's torture at the hands of the Jews of Damascus and of the bribe given to the Wali of Damascus so that he would stop investigation of the matter.[28] Another newspaper belonging to the same group repeated the accusations in French. Borg estimated that the number of Jews in Cairo was between 7,000 and 8,000—and that the entire Jewish population of Egypt numbered about 20,000. The Jews' anger grew at the accusation and they demanded that the detractors apologize. Borg was concerned lest the Greeks[29] join the Syrians in their denunciations and that riots would break out and the Muslims too would be dragged into the riots. The Syrians had been informing their children and thus keeping alive their belief that in the famous ritual murder accusation of Damascus in 1840 the Jews were indeed to blame. Borg pointed out the need for the government to warn the newspaper to stop the incitement and compensate the Jews.

The third document (Document XIII) is a report from Baring to Salisbury, British Foreign Minister, dated 25 June 1890. Baring encloses originals of Ades's letter and Borg's report and expresses the view that no harm would come to the Jews as long as the British garrison was in Egypt.

There are two documents in the sixth group. The first (Document XIV) is a report from Baring to Salisbury dated 19 March 1892. It is based on details received from the British Consul in Port Said. In that town, riots had broken out on 15 March 1892.[30] A Greek girl[31] had played in a Jewish home and the door had accidentally closed behind her. Immediately rumors spread that the child had been kidnapped by the Jews for human sacrifice. A Greek mob descended upon the house, found the child alive and well, but nevertheless beat up and frightened an elderly Jew who then died of shock. The police arrested some of the rioters and dispersed the crowd. On that and the following day, Greeks and Arabs gathered again and smashed windows in Jewish homes.

The second document (Document XV) is a signed copy of a petition drawn up in French by the Jews of Port Said who were citizens of various countries, and submitted to the ruler of Egypt, ʿAbbās Ḥilmī (ʿAbbās II) on 17 April 1892. The copy was delivered to Baring. The petition describes the same ritual murder accusation and riots mentioned in Document XIV in greater detail. The Greek child's mother did not wait to find out what had happened to her child but had immediately called to passers-by to rescue it. Among the crowd that gathered was also a Greek priest. The Jew who was killed was from the Carmona family.[32] He had been beaten and trampled under the feet of the mob, and his body[33] was dragged along the main road to the police station where a Greek struck it. The chief of police did not manage to detain the attacker. The old man's son who ran to his father's aid was beaten and wounded by the mob and nearly lost his life. The mob then attacked the Carmona family house, injuring the servant and a number of Jews, and forcing the son to flee for his life. The governor decided not to arrest the man accused of beating the old man in order not to arouse passions. The governor's decision was interpreted as a sign of weakness. Since then families (Jewish, it seems) had left Port Said, leaving their belongings and businesses; they were now without shelter and livelihood. The sixty-six signatories of the petition demanded the interference of ʿAbbās Ḥilmī so that they could return to their normal lives. Baring was requested to seek from the authorities assurances that those responsible would be punished and that the Jews would be secure from those plotting against them.

205

The Anti-Jewish Accusations,
Their Background and Causes

Why did blood libels occur in Egypt in 1870, reach their peak in 1880–82, and then recur in 1890 and 1892? In 1870 Pan-Islamic propaganda was on the increase;[34] the effects of gross extravagance in earlier years (particularly over the inauguration of the Suez Canal) were being felt by the treasury; the nationalist movement began to spread with the organization of various secret societies.[35] It is likely that the public tension caused by the rise in taxes, on the one hand, and the religious and nationalist awakening, on the other, prepared the ground for the blood libel of 1870. However, it is quite possible that the awakening at that time was only a chance occurrence and that the accusation could just as easily have occurred in another year. The fact that there was no real basis for the accusation caused it to blow over quickly. It is not for no reason that there is nothing on the matter in the sources. This is not the case, however, with respect to the ritual murder accusations which occurred and recurred during the three years 1880–82. Moreover, at that very time similar libels took place not only in Egypt: in 1880 there was one near Izmir and yet another in Costandil, near Salonika.[36]

However, ritual murder accusations in Egypt were more numerous and more frequent, and this was no mere coincidence. This was a period of great tension in Egypt, in the wake of the dismissal of Egypt's ruler, Ismāʿīl, by the Ottoman sultan (in 1879) and his succession by his weak-willed son Tawfīq. This change and the discontent of some Egyptians (especially in military circles) because of foreign interference in their country were exploited for the organization of a military revolt against Tawfīq. With the growing tension speeches were delivered and articles written attacking all foreigners. The atmosphere was such that all rumors were believed, including ritual murder accusations and other acts of abomination attributed to the Jews. In September 1880 the Jews were accused of attempting the rape of a Christian girl in Alexandria.[37] In February–March 1881, even before the ritual murder accusation of that year, there were incidents and clashes between Jews and Greeks, both the humblest and the wealthiest.[38] Around Passover 1882 the Greeks in Cairo accused the Jews of being involved in the murder of a girl,[39] and in Upper Egypt rumors were spread that the Jews had killed a Greek boy in order to use his blood.[40] Against this background mention should be made of the sporadic robbing of foreigners in Egyptian cities (July 1882), including attacks on Jews and their property.[41]

Why was it the Greeks who were the major inciters against the Jews and the instigators—with others joining in—not only of all the plots in Egypt, but also in other parts of the Ottoman Empire (except for one incident, on 29 May 1884, in which rumors were spread of the kidnapping of a Muslim boy in Constantinople)? Indeed, as early as 1864, the Greek Archbishop of Izmir—which was largely populated by Greeks—found it necessary to preach tolerance toward the Jews.[42] There is, indeed, no simple answer. It seems that the Greek mob exploited the weakness of the Ottoman government. It does not follow that some Greeks started the riots only because they were riffraff thrown out of their own country. The documents cited here indicate that sometimes even members of the most prominent Greek families of Alexandria took part in the riots. The two Greeks, who were members of the international commission of inquiry appointed by the foreign consuls to investigate the accusations against the Jews in the murder of the Furnaraki youth, refused to clear the Jews of all blame, and it is likely that both of them were among the distinguished Egyptian Greeks.[43] If not all the Greeks in Egyptian cities were involved in incitement and violence, it is true that a part of the Greek leadership was dragged in by the rioters and, by ignoring their crimes, encouraged them to continue their anti-Semitic activities. This statement is backed up by the attackers of the Baruch family and the murderers of Carmona in Port Said. In both cases, because of lack of action on the part of the Greek representatives, the perpetrators were not punished[44] (the local authorities could not try and punish foreign citizens, who were protected by the Capitulations).

Lord Cromer's praise of the Greeks' productive activities

in Egypt[45]—which he had observed during his twenty-four years as Consul General there—is probably based on their skill in commerce. However, it is precisely this activity which was likely to cause economic competition between the Greeks and Jews in the cities since they were involved in the same occupations.[46] It is likely that precisely for this reason the Greeks wanted the Jews to be their scapegoat for the mob's hatred of foreigners and thus save their own position. This was probably also the cause of the readiness of the Greek press in Alexandria to latch on to every libel against the Jews, even outside Alexandria—such as their incitement at the time of the Port Said ritual murder accusation in 1892.[47] The stage was set for it. The Greeks had legal immunity because of their status as foreign citizens; there was a tradition of hatred for the Jews; the Jews kept themselves separate from their neighbors in Egypt, preferring to maintain foreign citizenship, and built many synagogues[48] which were thorns in the sides of their enemies. The local Egyptian population's anti-Jewish feeling was marked in the cities, but it spread to the country, too.[49]

A new factor entered the arena of ritual murder accusations against Jews—the Syrian Christians whose numbers grew significantly in Egypt after the persecutions against them in their home country in 1860. Their hatred found expression mainly in the press, in which they incited against the Jews in 1890 (some excepted themselves from this incitement, however).[50] The reasons for their hatred of the Jews were generally identical with those of the Greeks: they were a foreign minority trying to transfer the animosity of the Muslim majority to the Jewish community, and there was economic competition which seemingly grew because they owed money to Jews. To this was added a tradition which, according to Consul Borg, the Syrians brought with them from Syria. The tools of incitement were also in their hands since in the last thirty years of the nineteenth century the Syrian Christians took over much of the Arabic press in Egypt, which developed greatly thanks to the energy and initiative invested. Moreover, during the British rule in Egypt, which prevented serious outbreaks of violence against the minorities, the press became a tool for incitement against the Jews, just as it became a mouthpiece for nationalist propaganda against British control of the country.

The places where the ritual murder accusations occurred (or at least began), according to the documents presented here, are also worthy of special mention: Alexandria in 1870, 1880, 1881; Port Said in 1882; Cairo in 1890; Port Said in 1892.

In Cairo the incitement was limited to the Syrian Christian press and directed at the country at large; this did not lead to any concrete acts. Cairo was the main seat of government and attempts to injure the Jews would meet with opposition on the part of the police and army authorities. Consequently, only one incident occurred in Cairo, while three of the others were in Alexandria and two in Port Said.

It is not difficult to understand the concentration of these events in Alexandria. This city was the major point of entry for Europeans. Most of the foreigners in Egypt were residing there and the nationalist and Muslim elements saw themselves as most threatened from the point of view of economics and administration as well as religion and ritual. In Alexandria the incitement against the foreigners was concentrated and first came to light in 1870; it developed most in the early 1880s. In addition, the police force in Alexandria was particularly small (even including local army personnel).[51] There was a large number of Greek criminals and unemployed people.[52] Indeed, it is surprising that there was no ritual murder accusation in Alexandria in 1882, too. After the beginning of the British occupation of Egypt (July 1882), the strong hand of British rule prevented any occurrence in Alexandria just as it did in Cairo.[53]

The ritual accusations in Port Said in 1882 and 1892 are equally interesting. The first, which occurred soon after those in Alexandria, is another link in the chain of incitements against foreigners which characterized the first years of the 1880s. The rioting of 1892 stands out sharply for its extreme severity and because it was practically the only such incident in Egypt during the British occupation (excluding the incitement in the Cairo press in 1890 and a number of plots which were hatched but foiled before they could be carried out). Its special significance is obvious from the documents cited here, that anti-Jewish feeling began to spread in Egypt at the end of the nineteenth century outside the large cities in which most of the Jewish community lived (Cairo and Alexandria). Besides the ritual murder accusation in Port Said in 1892 and a suspicion that the Jews of Cairo had murdered the Christian servant of a Jewish family, who had disappeared and was found strangled,[54] a rumor spread in Damanhur—a large rural center—that the Jews had kidnapped a Muslim child to use his blood,[55] a rumor which aroused a great deal of excitement there and quieted down only three days later when the child returned home.[56] This is another sign of the spread of anti-Jewish feeling among the Fallahin and others outside Cairo and Alexandria.[57]

The first census in Egypt which included the Jews took place in 1897 and it is reasonable to assume that its data can largely be applied to 1892. Among the 25,200 Jews in Egypt in 1897,[58] there were 8,819 in Cairo[59] and 9,831 in Alexandria[60]—a total of 18,650 for these two cities. After Tanta (883) and Mansura (508) the next largest concentration of Jews was in Port Said with 400.[61] In Port Said there were in 1892 some 5,000 Greeks,[62] who were potential competitors with the Jews, constituting 16 percent of the population of the town and 55 percent of the European population of 9,000.

It is interesting to compare these numbers with the general populations of the three cities in which blood accusations took place: Cairo, 589,573; Alexandria, 315,844; Port Said 42,972.[63] One can see from these statistics that the Jews were proportionally almost as prominent in Port Said as in Cairo and Alexandria—400 Jews in a total population of 42,972 is about 1 percent of the population of the city; in Cairo the Jews made up 1.5 percent and in Alexandria approximately 3 percent. If we consider the entire Egyptian population (excluding the British occupation forces) of 9,714,525,[64] the number of Jews in Egypt—25,200—averages 0.26 percent of the entire population. Because of their concentration in Alexandria, Cairo, and Port Said, their ratio in the population in other parts of Egypt was considerably lower.

The Jewish Reaction

It is difficult to find a definite pattern to Jewish reaction particularly because of the paucity of information. What we know is as follows: In 1870 the Jewish community council in Alexandria presented a petition to the British Consul General in that city. In 1880 a delegation of Jewish dignitaries appealed to the Italian Consul in Alexandria. In 1881 a delegation of Jewish dignitaries from Alexandria, who were British subjects, appealed to the British Consul. In 1882 the Jews of Port Said appealed to a French navy unit asking for its protection. In 1890 two Jews from Cairo appealed to Baring. In 1892, sixty-six Jews from Port Said submitted a petition to ʿAbbās Ḥilmī and sent a copy to Baring.

It is doubtful whether this information reflects all the reactions of the Jews. It is likely that there were additional requests for assistance (perhaps to the French Consul) and even meetings, conferences, appeals to Jewish organizations, and there are hints of such steps in the documents. There is a trend which indicates a development in the Jewish reaction to the ritual murder accusations in Egypt: the first three appeals—in 1870, 1880, and 1881—for intervention on their behalf were pleas for mercy, aid, and defense, as was usual in some Jewish communities in different periods. In 1882, with the deterioration of the internal situation in Egypt, the Jews of Port Said asked France to defend them with armed force. The two appeals of 1890 and 1892, the full text of which is published here, were different in their content and even more so in their style. Perusal of them and of Borg's report on the agitation of the Jews of Cairo, the firmness of their demands and the refutation of the accusations against them leaves the impression that the emphasis had passed from appeals and pleas for help and intervention to a clear—al-

211

though polite—demand for the restoration of the rule of order and the punishment of the inciters in the press and the rioters in the streets. A growing feeling of security among the Jews of Egypt came in the wake of the British rule which began in 1882. The improvement of the internal security situation in all aspects relating to life and property, together with Jewish insistence that the legal system be used to punish criminals, gave, it seems, the Egyptian Jews, during the first decade of the British occupation, the courage to demand redress for insults and attacks against them in a different manner than before the occupation.

The consolidation of the status of the Jews during the British occupation did not bring an absolute end to ritual murder accusations in Egypt; it moved them into the columns of the press. Even serious Arabic periodicals (bimonthlies such as *al-Hilāl* and *al-Muqataṭaf*) published entire articles on the subject between the last years of the nineteenth century and World War I.[65] Letters to the editor were published from such far-flung places as Fayyum, Port Said, Asyut, Alexandria, Worcester, and Natchez in the United States (where communities of Syrian and Lebanese immigrants lived). The questions testified to naïve beliefs in the "atrocities" perpetrated by the Jews on the bodies of Christian children for religious purposes. In most of their replies the editors repudiated the accusations and declared that there was no mention of them in the commandments of the Jewish religion or its holy books, although there was nothing to prevent individual Jews from committing such sins.

These questions and answers were only one expression of the increasing curiosity of the Egyptian public (especially in the cities). This public's questions and answers encompassed many aspects of Judaism—even Zionism.[66] It seems that most of the Egyptians continued to see the Jews as a foreign element (identifying Zionism with the European infiltration of the Middle East) and a strange one (the belief in the ritual murder accusations). This feeling of strangeness and estrangement was the reason for attacks on the Jews with the rise and outbreak in 1921 of nationalism[67] and even a renewal of the ritual murder accusation (when a Catholic priest taught his pupils about it in Alexandria in 1925).[68] And it was this, along with the self-willed isolation of the Jews in Egypt, which may have contributed to make it difficult for them to settle down as an integral element of the population in the following years.

The Documents

III: Cookson to Malet

Sir,[69]

Yesterday evening I sent you a telegram in cipher in which I had the honour to inform you that in consequence of the disappearance of a boy which was attributed by the Greeks to his having been taken away by the Jews for their passover, there was fear of a riot in this city. The military force being insufficient to repress it I asked you to point out to Government the need of sending fresh troops and I added that perhaps this opportunity might be taken to remove certain regiments from Cairo.

I have now the honour to report on the reasons why I made this communication.

Yesterday afternoon I was informed by Mr. Zananiri the Dragoman of this Consulate that he had seen a very large assemblage of Greeks in the neighbourhood of the Governor's Palace and that considerable excitement prevailed among them. The cause was stated to be that a Greek boy had disappeared from his home, and that this had given rise to the revival of the wicked and ignorant fable of the child having been kidnapped by the Jews for the purpose of mixing his blood with their paschal cake.

Later in the day I received a visit from several of the leading British members of the Israelite Community who represented that there was imminent danger of a repetition of the disgraceful scenes which have before occurred in this and other Oriental towns, when a lawless mob of Christians and Moslems have inflicted serious injuries on the persons and property of unoffending Jews. I at once went with two of the principal persons who had called upon me to visit the Governor of Alexandria and represented to him the grave responsibility which would be incurred if immediate steps were not taken to prevent disorder. His Excellency[70] replied that it was true that there was danger of riot but expressed some apprehension lest the force of his command should not prove sufficient to repress it. He said that even with the troops which he could call in from Osman Pasha the Military Commandant at Alexandria he could only command about 1,500 men, but that he was going immediately to see Osman Pacha[71] in order to concert with him and if necessary he would telegraph for reinforcements from Cairo. His Excellency added that he was taking every measure in his power to prevent any breach of the peace, but that the mob being Greek it was very desirable that the Greek authorities should exert their influence to quiet it and therefore he wished me to see the Greek Consul General and represent to him the state of affairs. His Excellency had already made the same request of my Italian Colleague, Mr. Machiavelli, whom I had found leaving the Governor on my arrival. We therefore at once went together to the house of Mr. Rangabe the Greek Agent and Consul General. He told us the history of the agitation which is shortly this. Some six days previous a boy ten years old, child of Greek parents belonging to Candia and therefore Ottoman subjects, had been missing from his home which he left to go to school. His parents made enquiries for him through the Greek Patriarchate which stands to Greek Rayahs in the position of their national authority; but no trace could be found of him. The fact of his disappearance having been reported among the Greek population, some of them took advantage of it to set up an agitation which Mr. Rangabe admitted to have assumed a formidable character. He told us that the crowd have threatened to sack the Jewish quarter unless the child were forthcoming that day; but that by a mixture of persuasion and threats he had calmed them for the moment. Their suspicions were directed especially against one Jewish family, neighbours of the missing boy—whose house he had been in the habit of frequenting, and whose children were his play-fellows. These people have been arrested and examined but as was to be expected nothing had been found to incriminate them—only one of their children a girl of the same age as the Greek boy had stated under examination that he had eaten at their house about the day of his disappearance. I suggested to Mr. Rangabe that the influence of the Greek Patriarch should be brought to bear upon his

214

compatriots, and he said he would speak to his Eminence on the subject. I need hardly add that Mr. Rangabe showed the greatest desire to render every assistance to the Local authorities in allaying the excitement among his compatriots.

On my return home I sent you the telegram suggesting that representations should be made of the insufficiency of the Military force in Alexandria in case of tumult or disorder. There is here a population composed in large proportion of the very dregs of society, to whom nothing could be so acceptable as the opportunity of pillage and the European element which mainly consists of Greeks and Italians of the lowest class, who are but very slightly under the control of the local police.

From the information and from the visits I myself made in the town I felt warranted in telegraphing to you subsequently at midnight that all was quiet.

This morning I heard that the missing boy had been found by some Italian fishermen drowned in the harbour. About ten o'clock a.m. the Governor called on me to request that I would send a medical delegate to assist at the examination of the body. But His Excellency said that the agitation still continued and that further military force was urgently required. I therefore telegraphed to you to this effect.

This afternoon Mr. Machiavelli again called to tell me that several Jews had been injured and insulted. I went with him to the French Consulate and held a short consultation with my two Collegues[72] at which I learnt that the body after a superficial examination by the Doctors had been removed to the house of the boy's parents which surrounded[73] by an excited crowd. I then made another visit to the Governor and afterwards to Mr. Rangabe. The latter told me that the parents had consented to have the body removed tomorrow to the Greek Hospital in order to undergo a regular autopsy, in the meantime the Governor told me that the house was being watched by soldiers. I learnt afterwards that a body of troops had been despatched from Cairo. While I have been writing this 8:30 p.m. I have received visits from three Jewish gentlemen who narrate numerous attacks on their co-religionists and expressed their apprehensions that there would be riotous proceedings during the night, and one[74] from a British Subject who was this afternoon assaulted dangerously by a Greek because he was in company with a Jew. The whole city is in considerable excitement and I fear this may not subside without further disturbance. There is in my opinion absolute necessity for a strong reinforcement of the military now at the disposal of the Police.

I have, etc.[75]

VI: Cookson to Malet

Sir,[76]

In continuation of my despatch No 6 of 23rd instant I have the honour to report that the post-mortem examination of the body of the boy Vangele Formarake[77] took place at the Greek Hospital on the 24th instant. I enclose a copy of the report (transmitted to me by His Excellency the Governor of Alexandria) of twenty-five Medical men who took part therein. Their unanimous conclusions are.

1. That the death was not owing to any external injury or violence.
2. That it was owing to drowning.
3. That from the condition of the corpse it must have been in the water from four to seven days and must have fallen in a short time after eating; the shell fish found in the stomach having been taken in shortly before its immersion.

During the post-mortem examination which lasted several hours the Hospital was guarded by troops. A reinforcement of 560 strong arrived at 11 a.m., and was immediately posted to relieve the force which had been on foot for more than fifteen consecutive hours. The body after the autopsy was taken straight to the Greek Church, where the funeral service was performed, and thence to the cemetery where it was interred. The crowd then dispersed and public tranquillity apparently was almost restored. During this day there were only isolated cases of attacks on Jews without any serious consequences. Yesterday the 25th March the Governor called on me about 11 a.m. and told me that the tumult had apparently passed over. But about 3 p.m. I received a visit from Mr. Machiavelli my Italian Colleague who informed me that an officer had just called on him on the part of the Governor to tell him that His Excellency felt paralysed in his efforts to preserve the peace by an incident which had occurred that afternoon. A Jewish gentleman of German nationality having been assaulted, and having complained to his Consulate, Local Police Officers were sent to arrest the accused a Greek servant; but the prisoner had been rescued from them in front of the bourse by Greek gentlemen of the highest standing armed with revolvers; and when subsequently arrested a second time and taken to the Greek Consulate he had been immediately released without any steps being taken against him. This was the story told to Mr. Machiavelli; and the Delegate added that the Governor believed the Greek Consul General was powerless against his own people; and His Excellency therefore requested the Consular body to take some concerted measures to support public order. I suggested to Mr. Machiavelli that before taking any other step in the matter we should give Mr. Rangabe an opportunity of offering explanations on the subject. For this purpose I proposed to call together on Mr. Bodtker Consul General of Sweden and Norway the Doyen of the Consular body in Alexandria and requested him to see Mr. Rangabe. This we did, and Mr. Bodtker at once agreed to this. Mr. Machiavelli and I then went to Mr. Dobignie the French Consul and asked him to meet us here. In a short time Mr. Bodtker returned from Mr. Rangabe's house and told us that the latter had given an entirely different version of the matter. Mr. Rangabe stated to Mr. Bodtker that the Greek servant had not been brought by the Police to the Greek Consulate, but after being released had come of his own accord to complain of his arrest; and that when the rescue was reported to him, Mr. Rangabe had made immediate enquiries into the matter, and summoned the persons accused—two young men of respectable position but not in any way prominent persons in the Greek colony—to give an explanation of their conduct. They denied entirely that any one had displayed any weapons, but said that all they had done had been to join with others in hustling the Policemen and that in the confusion the prisoner had escaped. This account was afterwards repeated to us by Mr. Rangabe himself who spontaneously joined our meeting. Mr. Rangabe assured us that the occurrence was regretted by all the members of the Greek colony whom he had seen, that such conduct was far from receiving their approval. In fact Mr. Rangabe assured us that it had no importance whatever as a proof of the sentiments of the better class of his countrymen. I asked Mr. Rangabe whether any steps had been taken to prosecute those who had been guilty of so serious an offence of rescuing a prisoner from the Police at a time of such public excitement, thereby giving the worst possible example to the more danger-

217

ous class who were keeping the city in terror. Mr. Rangabe
frankly told us that he could hardly answer for the consequences if this course were pursued, and that he thought it
would now be very undesirable for him to risk his influence
over the superior class of his countrymen by treating seriously
what was really only a boyish freak. This view seemed the
more prudent to the majority of those presents[78] and we
agreed that Mr. Machiavelli and Mr. Dobignie (to whom a
similar message had been sent) should reply to the Governor
that after considering the incident with some of their Colleagues, they did not think it of the gravity which His Excellency attributed to it. I learnt that night that everything in the
town seemed quiet.

This morning I heard that a fresh body of troops under the
command of the Minister of War had arrived from Cairo; and
at 10 a.m. I received the summons herewith enclosed. On our
arrival at the Governor's house we found that His Excellency
had prepared a document which he wished us to sign and allow to be published, the effect of which was to announce
1. That the police would prevent all assemblages in the streets
and if they did not disperse would employ force. 2. That the
police would enter houses in case of necessity for arrest of persons causing disorder; but that the Consulate should be informed of any arrest made.[79]

A discussion followed in which I on my part expressed my
willingness to consent to the proposed measures, if the Government thought them necessary for the public safety. The
first proposal I thought a declaration of an admitted right of
the Government as guardian of the public peace, and the second only a general exercise of the power which each Consul
possesses in any individual case of allowing the Local Police to
enter the house of one of his compatriots. But I stipulated that
these exceptional concessions should be understood to be only
temporary. The majority of those present concurred in this.
Some however objected to the publication of any document as
likely to revive the feeling of uneasiness which was already
disappearing. And the Governor and Minister of war themselves finally adopted this view, being satisfied with the verbal
permission which had indeed been given by some, and by the
Greek Consul General among the first—and which was now
accorded by nearly all of us—that the Police might for some
time, and in case of necessity, disperse crowds and enter houses

without previous applications to the Consulates. Those who did not feel themselves justified in going so far consented to put a janissary at the disposal of the Police in order that he might enter with them in the name of the Consular authority. With this understanding the meeting separated.

During the rest of this day I have heard of no disturbance whatever and I hope there will be no fresh outbreak.

Unfortunately there is an ineradicable belief in the minds of the Greek populace that there are certain horrible rites practiced at the Jewish passover, for the performance of which a christian child is necessary; and if a child disappears, as is only too probable, about that time the renewal of the lawless proceedings we have just witnessed is very much to be feared.

Next year it will in my opinion be absolutely necessary that the most vigorous measures should be taken at the very commencement. I very much fear that the agitation has been fostered, if not originally got up, by persons actuated by the worst motives; and any exceptional inquiry which may be demanded into the causes of the death of the child, which has been made the pretext for these disorders, should be extended, if possible, to the discovery of those who are guilty of this serious crime against society.[80]

I have, etc.

XI: Ades to Baring

David & Nissim Ades[81]
Caire, Égypte

Cairo, June 20th 1890
To Sir Evelyng[82] Baring, Bart.

Sir,

I beg sir to draw your attention to the violent articles which has[83] appeared in an arabic paper called (El-Mahroussa) in[84] which contained nothing but lies & false accusations against the Jews especially those of the 14th/17/&19 inst.

Nowe[85] Sir are we to have here an ante-semitic[86] party amidst fanaticism[87] Greeks Armenians etc? or is he[88] to be allowed to continue to poison the people's minde[89] with exaggeration & painted words? In an article he asserted that the Jewes[90] does use a christian blood for passover of course this has coursed[91] a deal of excitement. I hope sir something will be done to put a stop to it in time.

I am sir, etc.

XII: Borg to Baring

Sir,[92]

A campaign directed against persons of the Hebrew persuasion has been undertaken in Cairo which, unless checked in time, may lead to serious consequences; and I regret to say it is conducted by persons under the aegis of the French flag.

You are no doubt aware that in April last an Armenian catholic child, about 7 years old, disappeared at Damascus and after a search of about 10 days its body was discovered in a disused well belonging to a Christian; and as this happened to take place about Passover time the Jews were accused of the disappearance of the child.

In the early days of this month the local newspaper 'Al Mokattam' published the above fact, and soon afterwards a short answer appeared in the same paper referring to the correspondence that was lately exchanged between Rabbi Adler and Cardinal Manning on the subject of the use of Christian blood in the preparation of unleavened bread for Passover; and 'Al Mokattam' then dropped the subject.

Among other newspapers that appear in Cairo in the Arabic language is one by the title 'Al-Mahroussa', owned and edited, I am informed, by Raphael Zind and his son Azeez—Syrians— with whom are associated one Naggar, also a Syrian, one Marodeck (or Mérodack) and one Loison. These persons are French subjects or protégés. The printing establishment of the paper seems to be in the name of the three last-named persons. The Zind, father and son, being in need of money had recourse to a 'Shylock' who advanced a sum of £62½ at 2 per cent interest per month on a bill of exchange that arrived at maturity some time since, and they also owe to the same party a further sum of £60 payable by monthly instalments of £4. The creditor being unable to get his money obtained a sequester on the strength of the bill of exchange, and that sequester was executed upon the household furniture of the debtors.

The sequester roused the ire of the Syrian debtors and— whether from a thought of extortion or religious hatred I am unable to say—on June 14 appeared in 'Al-Mahroussa' an article narrating the tragedy of Damascus—the disappearance of the child—imaginary recitals of the tortures endured by him at the hands of his fiendish tormentors—his appeal to his Maker, to the Sultan, and to the fiends around him to spare his young life—the dropping of the blood into proper basins carefully removed and treasured as soon as filled—finally the death of the victim, the secreting of the body in a sack and its disposal by dropping it into a disused well, were all dealt upon and described in a vivid and pathetic style well calculated to impress the oriental reader, who was promised further information and comments at a later date. A second article resumed the thread of the narrative and stated that the Wali[93] of Damascus had proved unable to resist the powerful influence brought to bear upon him in the shape of 1,000 Liras and had ordered the matter to be hushed up. The paper gives certain initials as of the persons who paid the above amount to the Wali and another sum to other influential personages. Other two articles followed in succession, the last however seemingly trying to mitigate the charge of bribery made against the Wali of Damascus.

While this attack was made on the Jewish Community in 'Al-Mahroussa', another publication, issuing from the same printing establishment, and of which Mérodack claims the paternity, reproduced in the French language the alleged crime, under the title 'Les Juifs en Syrie (un crime horrible)'. ('Les Grimaces', N. 3, dated 22 June,[94] published the previous evening).

These attacks made upon a quiet and very patient community have had the effect of rousing them from their seeming natural lethargy, and last Saturday evening the matter was very gravely discussed at the Jewish Quarter where excitement and feeling both ran very high; but, ultimately, the advice of some cooler heads prevailed and a number of about 300 proceeded to the house of the representative of the community—M. Cattaui Bey—to demand and insist that satisfaction be given them for the grievous insults. The great tact displayed by that gentleman has enabled him temporarily to quiet his excited co-religionists in order to gain time. I say 'temporarily' because they are waiting earnestly and anxiously the issue of the steps he would or may take, firmly resolved at the same time, I have reason to think, not to allow the matter to drop; and I could not undertake to say what may not be the consequences if some satisfaction—even though more apparent than real—were not given! The need for some step is even more pressing because, I am informed and I have good reason to think correctly, another publication on the same subject will shortly appear in pamphlet form.

I am informed that some of the leading Jewish French Subjects at Alexandria will call the serious attention of the French Agent and Consul General to these publications, and urge upon him the necessity of putting a stop to the appearance of such productions; but it is difficult to foretell whether and to what extent the Minister of the Republic may be able to accede to the just request.

I beg to submit few[95] considerations which I think find their place here, and I trust you will pardon my encroaching so much upon your time.

The Jewish community in Cairo numbers about 7 to 8,000 persons, the majority belonging to the class of petty tradesmen, peddlars etc.; and the number in all Egypt of that persuasion is of about 20,000. By the tenets of their religion they look upon themselves as the elect of God, and they regard Egypt as the country wherein they hold a special status. Their standing in Egypt has been recognized from time immemorial, and to this day they enjoy the privilege, alternately with the Moslems and the Copts, of cutting the dike of the Khaleedj and letting the water of the Nile into town of Cairo. They are a race proud of their past history, patient, inoffensive and uncomplaining; but although ordinarily not showing much pluck their feelings are roused and excited to no small degree whenever their religion is attacked, as has been shown on Saturday. Were I concerned, however, with the Hebrews alone I might perhaps attach somewhat less importance to the matter: but two other elements exist, which I could not well lose sight of—I mean the Greek orthodox, and the Syrian communities.

The former seem to regard as an article of faith that the blood of Christians is indispensable in the preparation of unleavened bread for Passover; and I need only refer, in support of my assertion, to the scandal at Alexandria few years since—1880 or 1881—in connection with the disappearance of a young Greek boy, when but for the firm attitude of the Consuls and of the Local authorities, a serious disturbance of the peace would have occurred. That such a belief is deeply rooted in the masses is proved to me by the fact that on the occasion in question a Greek professional gentleman, in every respect worthy of esteem, tried to convince me that as a matter of fact the punctures made by fishes on the lips of the child and in other exposed parts of the body before it was recovered from the sea, had been for the purpose of drawing therefrom the blood of the victim—and I think I can safely say that the belief exists to this day. At all events there is reason to fear that the Greek Orthodox mob, of which we have not few representatives and those of a very dangerous class, would not be slow in joining any open movement against the Jews, even if the belief in the blood ceremony has ceased to exist.

With regard to the Syrian element I would observe that the disappearance, in 1840, of Father Thomas at Damascus, and his supposed martyrdom by the Jews has been religiously handed down and has served to imbue the Syrians with a deeply-set hatred of the Jews. These two elements stirred up by the excited recitals of 'Al Mahroussa' might at any moment break out, from religious hatred or from a desire of lust or pillage, and cause a serious disturbance of the peace.

But there is yet a third element, namely the Mohammedan Community which was the object a short while ago of attacks by the same newspaper 'Al Mahroussa'; and the Moslems might either espouse the cause of their Jewish brethren if order were[96] disturbed, or act indiscriminately against all non-Moslems.

Under the circumstances I beg to call your early and serious attention to the matter with a view that some steps should be taken to prevent a disturbance of the peace; and I venture to suggest that by way of, temporarily at least, appeasing the just resentment of the Jewish Community an 'Avertissement'[97] should be given by the Egyptian Government to 'Al Mahroussa'. This would strengthen the hands of the leaders of the Community as it would shew that satisfaction, slight though it be for the time, is being given and thus enable them to calm the excitement now prevailing among their co-religionists. I have had conversations with several of the leading men of the Community and strongly recommended them to use their influence in the maintenance of order, but while expressing their readiness and willingness to do all they can in that line, they feared lest the task should prove beyond their power if some satisfaction were not given.

As to the suggested 'Avertissement' I would observe that the Egyptian Government, if so minded, might properly give a warning to the paper for the accusation of bribery brought against a high official of the Sultan—the Wali of Damascus—and this even without dwelling upon the attacks made upon the Jews. 'Al Mahroussa', I understand, is published under permission of the Government and although owned and edited by French subjects or protégés, the French authorities could not, and perhaps would not, consider that the rights of citizens of the Republic are being infringed upon by an 'Avertissement'.

I have, etc.

XIII: Baring to Salisbury

My Lord,[98]

I have the honour to enclose a letter which I have received on the subject of some violent anti-semitic articles which have appeared in one of the local Arabic papers, and also a report drawn up by Mr. Consul Borg.[99] El-Mahroussa, the newspaper in question, has made use of an incident which happened in April at Damascus, connected with the disappearance of a Christian child, to revive an ancient fable that Christian sacrifices form part of the celebration of the Jewish Passover, and to wage a very fierce campaign against the Jewish nation. This paper is one which, as I informed your Lordship in my despatch No. 140 of the 25th April,[100] recently published some violent articles against the Mahommedans.

The Jewish Community in Egypt are naturally alarmed at the tendency of writings of this sort to stir up the fanatical and anti-semitic feelings which are to found among the more ignorant classes in this country. The Egyptian Government are powerless to help them in the matter, as the Mahroussa is conducted by French subjects. So long, however, as there is a British garrison in Egypt to ensure the maintenance of law and order, such attacks need give rise to no serious alarm, though the spirit of ignorance and prejudice which they indicate is greatly to be deplored.

I have, etc.

XIV: Baring to Salisbury

My Lord,[101]

Information having reached Cairo that an anti-Jewish riot of a somewhat serious nature had broken out at Port Said on the

15th instant I immediately telegraphed to Her Majesty's Consul at that place for particulars on the subject and asked him if it would be desirable to send a British ship there.

Mr. Gould now informs me that the accounts received at Cairo of the disturbances were much exaggerated. It would appear that on the afternoon of the 15th a Greek child strayed into the house of a Jewish Ottoman subject, not far from its own home, that the door of the house was immediately afterwards accidentally closed, that the child having in the meantime been missed, and having been last seen to go into this Jewish house, a cry was raised that it had been kidnapped by the Jews for human sacrifice, in accordance with a widespread belief among the more ignorant classes throughout the Levant, and that thereupon a mob of Greeks stormed the house, found the child, of course uninjured, and beat and frightened an aged Jew, who has since died, more however it would seem from the effects of the shock and fright, than from actually bodily injuries. The police then appeared and arrested some of the rioters, whereupon a Greek mob created a disturbance, which, however, was easily suppressed, round the police station. The disorders were renewed in the evening, and again in the following day, the 16th, when a crowd of Greeks and Arabs broke the windows of Jewish houses. On both occasions the Governor, Mahmoud Pasha Riaz, appeared on the scene of the disturbances, and was active in putting them down, and in causing the streets to be patrolled by police. Extra police, both English and Egyptian, have been sent from Cairo and there has been no renewal of the riots since the 16th. Five Jews, British subjects, have complained to Her Majesty's Consul of the breaking of their windows, and of their confinement to their houses from fear of the mob—but of no more serious injury.

I have, etc.

Notes

1. Such as M. Fargeon, *Les juifs en Egypte depuis les origines jusqu'à ce jour* (Cairo, 1938). B. Taragan, *Les communautés israélites d'Alexandrie: Aperçu historique depuis les temps des Ptolémées jusqu'à nos jours* (Alexandria, 1932). Even when a ritual murder accusation is mentioned, this is only incidentally and

225

briefly—see Noury Farhi, *La communauté juive d'Alexandrie de l'antiquité à nos jours* (Alexandria, 1946), p. 23.

2. Leven (see the following note) makes no mention. M. Franco, *Essai sur l'histoire des Israélites de l'empire ottoman* (Paris, 1897), pp. 220–33, omits Egypt from his discussion of ritual murder accusations in the Ottoman Empire.

3. N. Leven, *Cinquante ans d'histoire: L'alliance israélite universelle*, vol. 1 (Paris, 1911), pp. 233–36, 387–92.

4. The scattered, brief items are insufficient for the forming of a complete picture.

5. [Not all fifteen documents included in the original essay have been reproduced in this volume. The six written in English have been retained to give the reader the flavor of official reaction and action with respect to blood libel incidents. For the remaining documents, written in French and Italian, the reader is directed to the original source of this essay—Ed.]

6. *Jewish Chronicle* (London), 8 July 1870, p. 12. *Der Israelit* (Mainz) 11, no. 29 (supplement), 20 July 1870, p. 551.

7. According to the sources in the previous note, the child's father was a Maltese. This would explain the interest of the press in Malta.

8. Apparently, a four-year-old girl (not boy).

9. According to the two newspapers (n. 6 above), Sason was freed after thirty-two days in jail, thanks to Stanton's intervention. The petition, whose text we reproduce here, may have moved him to act. Stanton does not seem, however, to have considered the matter as important, as he failed to report it to London.

10. The accusation may have gained strength in that this happened on the second day of Passover, that the boy fell into the synagogue yard and that his body was stabbed. The latter detail, not mentioned by Machiavelli, is reported in *Der Israelit* 21, no. 16, 21 April 1880, p. 402.

11. One of whom was Greek, probably to lend credence to the committee's findings, Cf. *ha-Maggīd* (in Hebrew, Lyck) 24, no. 18, 5 May 1880, p. 148. *Jewish Chronicle*, 16 April 1880, p. 10.

12. It would appear that the mob attacked the synagogue, and a fight ensued, after which more than one hundred Greeks and about sixty Jews were arrested. See *Der Israelit* 21, no. 16, 21 April 1880, p. 402. Cf. *Jewish Chronicle*, 23 April 1880, p. 10.

13. Italian State Archives, Archivio Storico, Affari Esteri Roma (further: AER), Serie Politica, vol. 1299 (Egitto), Machiavelli's 53/1723 to Cairoli, dated Alexandria, 4 April 1880. See also *Jewish*

Chronicle, 16 April 1880, p. 10; ibid., 14 May 1880, p. 13. According to *Der Israelit* 21, no. 19, 12 May 1880, p. 478, the leaders of the Greek instigators were sent away from Egypt; these included the dead boy's family (who, an investigating legal committee decided, had stabbed his body after death, to throw the blame on the Jews). This development certainly did nothing to increase affection between Greeks and Jews in Egypt.

14. His name was rendered as Evangeli Fornaraki or Furnaraki, cf. *ha-Melīṣ* (Hebrew periodical) 17, 3 May 1881, p. 307. *Ha-Maggīd* 24, no. 18, 11 May 1881, p. 147. See also below. n. 77.

15. The family's name (of the dead boy's stepfather) was Argostaki (*ha-Melīṣ,* ibid.) or Arganastako (*ha-Maggīd,* ibid.).

16. Public Record Office (London), Foreign Office Series (further: FO), 141/149, Cookson's legal report no. 10 to Malet, dated Alexandria, 3 November 1881. This document is not reproduced in the present article.

17. The Greeks had armed themselves with sticks and forks. *Der Israelit* 22, no. 17 (supplement), 17 April 1881, pp. 403–4.

18. The Jews needed protection both at the entrance to the Jewish Quarter and in the city's streets. See *Der Israelit* 22, no. 14: 6 April 1881, p. 330. *Ha-Melīṣ,* 17, 31 March 1881, p. 266.

19. Cookson, in an earlier document, had mentioned fifteen hundred policemen. Either way, the police force was numerically insufficient to prevent riots.

20. The medical findings were published in the non-Arabic press in Egypt, see *Messaggiere Egiziano,* 26 March 1881.

21. Only the part of the document which does not duplicate what the others have reported is reproduced here.

22. A probable indication of organized activity. On the contrary, English and French newspapers, published in Egypt, defended the innocence of the Jews, particularly the *Courier Egyptien.* See *ha-Maggīd* 25, no. 18, 11 May 1881, p. 147.

23. Of this document, also, only a relevant portion is reproduced.

24. This referred to the revolt led by Aḥmad ʿUrābī. See also below.

25. The confession was printed in the official *Moniteur Egyptien,* 21 February 1882, according to the *Bulletin de l'Alliance Israëlite Universelle* (Paris), 2d semester of 1881 and 1st semester of 1882, p. 28. The local authorities ordered the publishers of Greek newspapers not to incite against Jews; see *ha-Maggīd* 26, 20 April 1882, p. 122.

26. Later called Lord Cromer. Baring had a decisive influence on

everything of importance in Egypt; his strength rested on the British occupation army.

27. On the Damascus 1890 ritual murder accusation, see Leven, *Cinquante aus d'histoire* 1:390–91, esp. n. 3.

28. Apparently, the newspapers accused the Jews of Damascus of bribing not only the Wali, but also the physicians who had examined the dead child's body. See report in the *Jewish Chronicle*, 4 July 1890, p. 15, and *Der Israelit* 31, no. 55 (supplement), 14 July 1890, p. 999.

29. The Greek newspapers had copied these accusations. Cf. *Jewish Chronicle*, 4 July 1890, p. 15.

30. According to a letter from Alexandria, dated 17 March 1892, printed in *Der Israelit* 33, no. 26 (supplement), 31 March 1892, p. 506, these events occurred on 16 March, not on 15 March, as reported by Baring. However, another letter, from Port Said, dated 29 March 1892, printed ibid., nos. 29–30, 11 April 1892, p. 569, cites the date of 15 March. Baring was right, after all.

31. Not a boy, as in Document XV, but "a three-year-old girl"?— as reported by *ha-Maggīd* 36, no. 14, 8 April 1892, p. 107, supposedly based on the Greek press. See also *Der Israelit* 33, no. 26 (supplement), 31 March 1892, p. 506, Alexandria letter dated 17 March 1892; and *Jewish Chronicle*, 8 April 1892, p. 3, Cairo letter dated 23 March 1892.

32. According to the *Jewish Chronicle*, 8 April 1892, Cairo letter, Carmona was the president of the Jewish community in Port Said. See also *Der Israelit* 33, no. 26 (supplement), 31 March 1892, p. 506, Alexandria letter, and ibid., nos. 29–30, 11 April 1892, p. 569, Port Said letter, where he is said to have been a merchant.

33. According to the *Jewish Chronicle*, ibid., he died the following day, in hospital. Contrast *Der Israelit* 33, nos. 29–30, 11 April 1892, p. 569.

34. See chap. 1 of Jacob M. Landau, *Middle Eastern Themes: Papers in History and Politics* (London: Frank Cass, 1973).

35. Details in J. M. Landau, *Parliaments and Parties in Egypt* (Tel Aviv, 1953), pt. 2, chaps. 1ff. For the limited share of the Jews in the nationalist movement in Egypt, see chap. 8 in J. M. Landau, *Middle Eastern Themes.*

36. *Bulletin de l'Alliance Israélite Universelle*, 1st semester for 1880, p. 41.

37. For details on these rumors and how they were quickly disproved, see ibid., 2nd semester for 1880, p. 21.

38. *Ha-Maggīd* 25, no. 16, 27 April 1881, p. 131, reported a gun-

fight in the Alexandria stock exchange between well-to-do Greek and Jewish businessmen.

39. *Ha-Mel̄iṣ* 18, 22 March 1882, p. 229. If this is not a reference to the Port Said alleged murder at the same time, this report would indicate yet another ritual murder accusation, not reported in other available sources.

40. Ibid. attributes this rumor, again, to the local Greeks.

41. See, e.g., A. Dayan's demand for compensation from the Egyptian authorities, dated 12 September 1882—in AER, Serie Politica, vol. 1300 (Egitto), enclosure in a letter from the Prefettura della Provincia di Livorno to the Italian Foreign Minister, no. 12450, dated 13 September 1882. Cf. FO 141/165, no. 460, Father Hugolinus's letter to Malet, dated Cairo, 27 October 1882. See also Edward Vizetelly, *From Cyprus to Zanzibar by the Egyptian Delta* (London, 1901), p. 117. E. Chaillé-Long, *My Life in Four Continents* (London, 1912), 1:248.

42. Leven, *Cinquante ans d'histoire* 1:150–51. Cf. ibid., pp. 233ff.

43. *Bulletin de l'Alliance Israélite Universelle*, 1st semester for 1881, pp. 66–67. It should be mentioned that, among the accused, the Baruch family were Greek subjects, later tried in Corfu and acquitted (ibid., pp. 67–68).

44. According to a letter from Port Said, printed ibid., 1st and 2d semesters for 1892, pp. 67–68.

45. Cromer, *Modern Egypt* (London, 1908), vol. 2, pp. 250–51.

46. Such as money changing; see G. Godio, *Cose d'Egitto* (Turin, 1882), p. 41.

47. *Der Israelit* 33, nos. 29–30 (supplement), 11 April 1892, p. 570. Ibid., no. 38 (supplement), 12 May 1892, p. 710.

48. Moritz Lüttke, *Aegyptens neue Zeit: Ein Beitrag zur Culturgeschichte des gegenwaertigen Jahrhunderts sowie zur Charakteristik des Orients und des Islam* (Leipzig, 1873), 1:97. A. Frhr. von Fircks, *Aegypten 1894: Staatsrechtliche Verhaeltnisse, wirtschaftlicher Zustand, Verwaltung* (Berlin, 1896), 2:85–86.

49. A description—not reproduced here—may be found in FO 78/4145, Baring's no. 138 to Salisbury, marked "secret," dated Cairo, 24 March 1888, enclosure, being a copy of Foster's report to Baring, dated Alexandria, 21 March 1888.

50. E.g., the journal *al-Muqtaṭaf* generally took a stand against such incitement, see e.g., 14, no. 10, 1 July 1890, pp. 688–89.

51. As reported by the British and Italian Consuls.

52. See Machiavelli's report, at the end of Document IV above.

53. Port Said, however, is at some distance from Egypt's two main cities.

54. Letter from Cairo, dated 23 March 1892, printed in the *Jewish Chronicle*, 8 April 1892, p. 13.

55. Letter to the editor, in the *Egyptian Gazette*, translated in *Der Israelit* 33, no. 40, 19 May 1892, p. 744. Cf. *Jewish Chronicle*, 13 May 1892, p. 19, which describes the attack on the synagogue in Damanhur and the desecration of the Torah scrolls.

56. According to the *Egyptian Gazette* of 23 April 1892, summed up by *Der Israelit* 33, no. 40, 19 May 1892, p. 744, the child had been abducted by a quack doctor.

57. For which see the preceding notes.

58. L. Mboria, *La population de l'Egypte* (Cairo, 1938), p. 125, table 39. E. A. Wallis Budge, *Cook's Handbook for Egypt and the Sudan*, 2nd ed. (London, 1906), p. 73. The estimate of 30,000, cited for 1892 by Theodor Neumann, *Das moderne Aegypten* (Leipzig, 1893) and by von Fircks, *Aegypten 1894*, vol. 1 (1895) seems somewhat exaggerated for those years.

59. According to the sources mentioned in the preceding note. This figure confirms the estimate of Consul R. Borg, in 1890, that Cairo's Jews numbered between 7,000 and 8,000 then. If the figures for the 1890s are correct, a rapid increase must have taken place among Cairo's Jews. In 1880, their number had been estimated at 3,000 by S. W. Samuel, *Jewish Life in the East* (London, 1881), p. 6, while at the end of the First World War it reached 15,000, approximately, according to Leven, *Cinquante ans d'histoire* 2:127.

60. This was on the increase, also, and reached about 14,000 at the end of the World War I, according to Leven, *Cinquante ans d'histoire* 2:131.

61. Fargeon, *Les juifs en Egypte*, p. 306. Actually, their number may have been slightly smaller, in 1892, if one accepts the report of the letter from Port Said, printed in *Der Israelit* 33, nos. 29–30, 11 April 1892, p. 569, that there were some fifteen Jewish families in this town.

62. According to unconfirmed figures, in *Der Israelit*, ibid., p. 570.

63. Jewish Agency for Palestine–Economic Research Institute, *Statistical Handbook of Middle Eastern Countries*, 1st ed. (Jerusalem, 1944), p. 54, table 3. The figures in Budge, *Cook's Handbook*, are almost identical. These authoritative data (copied from the official census for 1897), merely five years after 1892, cast doubt on the information in the letter from Port Said, printed in *Der Israelit*

(above, n. 61). The reports about the Greeks and their interests in Port Said appear more reliable, however.

64. Jewish Agency, *Statistical Handbook*, p. 55, table 4. Again, the figures in Budge, *Cook's Handbook*, are practically identical.

65. *Al-Hilāl* 4, 15 December 1895, pp. 299–301; 15 January 1896, pp. 374–76; 11, 15 April 1903, pp. 435–36. *Al-Muqtaṭaf* 28, 1 July 1903, p. 616. *Al-Hilāl* 13, 1 February 1905, pp. 303–5; 19, 1 October 1910, pp. 53–54.

66. See J. M. Landau, "Lo scritorre arabo Ḍōmeṭ e l'impresa sionistica di Erez Israel," *La Rassegna Mensile di Israel* (Rome) 22, no. 9: (September 1956), esp. pp. 398–99 and the footnotes ibid.

67. See the documents in the official British book, Cmd. 1527: *Egypt No. 3* (1921). *Minutes of proceedings and report of the military court of enquiry into the Alexandria riots*, esp. pp. 87–88, 102–3, 104, 111, 120–21, 186–87.

68. This was the priest Leonas, a teacher in St. Catherine, a French school in Alexandria; he was expelled from Egypt because of criminal incitement. See *Haménora: Organe Mensuel du Béné Bérith du District d'Orient No. XI* (Istanbul) 3, no. 6 (June 1925), p. 169; and *Archives Israélites* (Paris) 86, no. 23, 4 June 1925, pp. 89–90. The ritual murder accusation was renewed several times, in the twentieth century in Port Said—that is, far from the main centers of British rule. The police, however, generally intervened in time. See *Archives Israélites* 68, no. 15, 11 April 1907, p. 115. *American Jewish Yearbook* for 1903–4, pp. 217–18; ibid., for 1909–10, p. 138.

69. FO 141/148, Charles A. Cookson (British Consul in Alexandria) to E. B. Malet (British Consul General in Cairo), no. 6, dated Alexandria, 23 March 1881.

70. That is, the governor of Alexandria.

71. Cookson uses the British form "Pasha" and the French form "Pacha" indiscriminately.

72. Read: colleagues.

73. Read: was surrounded.

74. That is, "one visit."

75. Cookson's cables to Malet, referred to in this letter, may be found in FO 141/148, no. 69, dated 22 March 1881; and nos. 70, 72, and 73, all dated 23 March 1881.

76. FO 141/148, Cookson's letter to Malet, no. 7, dated Alexandria, 26 March 1881. There are two enclosures in this letter—the report of the physicians and the invitation to the Governor of the city.

77. The correct form is Furnarakis or Fornarakis, probably the former, and in Greek Εὐάγγεηος Φουρναράχης.

78. Read: present.

79. The approval of the Consuls was necessary since, according to the Capitulations, then in force throughout the Ottoman Empire (of which Egypt formed a part), the authorities could not enter the homes of most foreign citizens, nor arrest them, without the formal consent of their Consul.

80. The subsequent investigation cleared the Jewish Community and the Baruch family, but did not uncover the instigators. See FO 141/149, Cookson's legal report, no. 10, to Malet, dated Alexandria, 3 November 1881.

81. FO 78/4310, letter from David Ades to Baring, enc. 1 in Baring's letter no. 207, to Salisbury, dated Cairo, 25 June 1890.

82. Read: Evelyn. Ades's letter contains many errors.

83. Read: have.

84. Read: and.

85. Read: now.

86. Read: anti-Semitic.

87. Read: fanatics.

88. Read: it.

89. Read: minds.

90. Read: Jew.

91. Read: caused.

92. FO 78/4310, R. Borg's letter to Baring, dated Cairo, 24 June 1890, enc. in Baring's letter no. 207 to Salisbury, dated Cairo, 27 June 1890.

93. I.e., Governor.

94. 1890.

95. Read: a few.

96. Read: were.

97. That is, a warning.

98. FO 78/4310, Baring's letter no. 207 to Salisbury, dated Cairo, 25 June 1890.

99. This refers to Documents XI and XII, above.

100. 1890.

101. FO 78/4450, Baring's letter no. 207, to Salisbury, dated Cairo, 25 June 1890.

ABRAHAM G. DUKER

Twentieth-Century Blood Libels
in the United States

The instances of blood libel accusations in the United States
are admittedly much fewer in number and less serious in
terms of consequences than those occurring in Europe or
the Middle East. Still, it is of interest that the legend did
cross the Atlantic from Europe and that it has undoubtedly
contributed to the rise of anti-Semitism in the United
States.

This survey compiled by Professor Abraham G. Duker,
Chairman of Judaic Studies at Brooklyn College, does docu-
ment the presence of the legend in North America. Perhaps
the best-known case of blood libel in America, the events
reported in Massena, New York, in 1928, is not really dis-
cussed at length in this survey. For details, see Saul S. Fried-
man, The Incident at Massena: The Blood Libel in America
(New York: Stein and Day, 1978), and Samuel Jacobs, "The
Blood Libel Case at Massena—A Reminiscence and a Re-
view," Judaism *28 (1979): 465–74.*

The *'alilat dam,* blood libel or ritual murder accusation, i.e.
the false charge that Gentile blood (Christian or Moslem de-
pending on the environment) is necessary in the baking of
Passover matzah, became widespread in the Middle Ages.[1]
Although popes and many other high church dignitaries in-

Reprinted from Leo Landman, ed., *Rabbi Joseph H. Lookstein Memorial*
Volume (New York: KTAV Publishing House, 1980), pp. 85–109.

veighed against it, it was increasingly employed in the eighteenth and nineteenth centuries as an effective issue by anti-Semitic political parties and in economic warfare against Jews. The most notorious case in the twentieth century was the Mendel Beilis affair (1912, Kiev, Russian Ukraine).[2] The blood libel is still used effectively by anti-Semitic movements and leaders as well as by political demagogues. It was an influential instrument in Nazi propaganda. The Soviet press reported cases in Soviet Dagestan and Magalan (Uzbekistan) in 1961, in Tashkent (Uzbekistan's capital) and in Georgia (the Caucasus) in 1962; another case was reported seven weeks before Passover, 1963 in Vilnius (Vilna, Wilno), Soviet Lithuania's capital.[3]

What appears to be manifestly unreasonable and unbelievable to many (it is hoped, most) clergy and laypeople, nowadays, after the Vatican synods and the far-reaching changes in the Church's attitudes to Jews and Judaism and in the era of ecumenism, seemed reasonable, believable, and in accord with tradition earlier in the century even after Auschwitz. In fact, the ritual murder accusation of Kielce (Kelts), Poland, 4 July 1946, was well organized, precipitated mass killings, and stimulated a sizeable exodus of Jews from Poland.[4]

Of late, Arab states have been using the accusation in their agitation against Israel, the Jews, and Judaism. Such propaganda emanated from Egypt in 1967, 1971, and 1973 and appeared in Lebanon and Iraq in 1971.[5] The well-connected and popular Cairo monthly *Octobre* raised it as late as 1978.[6] The libel has also been prompted in democratic countries, including Canada[7] and, as we see, also the United States, in other democracies and in those under dictatorial rule.[8] It is likely to be used in the present Arab-Moslem global campaign against Israel and by other interested parties for the purpose of undermining democracy. This threat supplied the second stimulus for my interest in the history of blood libels in the United States.

The Pittsfield story has always fascinated me, and until the 22 September 1928, Massena case,[9] I viewed it as unique. However, while perusing the Gotthard Deutsch Clippings

Collection at the Hebrew Union College in Cincinnati in 1941, I came across a Yiddish newspaper clipping reporting a ritual murder accusation, but not in Pittsfield, about 1919. Regrettably, I mislaid my note on it. Although Professor Jacob R. Marcus was unsuccessful in his efforts to locate that clipping upon my request in 1976, fortunately, his searches produced Yiddish newspaper clippings on several such cases, including the Pittsfield libel.[10]

The Clayton, Pennsylvania, Incident, 1913

The first twentieth-century incident dates back to 1913, when a sixteen-year-old girl had the dreadful fear that she was the chosen victim of a planned murder in connection with a Jewish religious rite. Much fuss was made about it locally, but all turned out to be well when the girl reappeared the next morning.

The story appeared on the front page of the New York Yiddish socialist daily *Forverts* (Forward) of Wednesday, 5 February,[11] featuring the "terrible experience" in the household of one Jacob Miller, a happy father of a newborn boy, Saturday night before the *brit* (circumcision) ceremony and feast were to take place on the next day. A Mrs. Stein, in charge of the cooking and baking, asked the Millers' Christian servant girl Anna Hansel (of Slavic descent) to help her with the preparations. When Mrs. Stein began to sharpen her knife for carving the fowl, the girl became frightened. She thought that "the Jews wanted to offer her as a sacrifice." Her cries attracted neighbors and brought about turmoil and a false fire alarm. When Anna found shelter in the neighborhood, calls went out that "the Jews killed the Christian girl." On Sunday morning the would-be victim was found "hale and hearty" and the crowd calmed down.

The very occurrence of the incident is proof of the public's readiness to believe such allegations and of the ease with which mobs can be stirred up on such occasions. This pertains not only to "Slavs." However, the impact of the Beilis trial on peoples of Central and East European origin should be taken into account.

The New York City Incident, 1913

The second incident in the series was the murder on the eve of the Passover holiday of a janitor of a Lower East Side tenement house by his demented wife. She talked it into herself that her husband had sold their little son to the Jews for use in their alleged nefarious practices and that they murdered the boy, who was then at play and appeared soon after the murder. The *Forverts* reported the incident as the main front page story on 21 April. It treated it as a crank case, as did the general press.[12]

The next incidents reported occurred right after World War I in Fall River, Mass., Chicago, Ill., and Pittsfield, Mass. The accusations were not always connected with the Passover holiday, the traditional season of blood libels, but all three involved American Poles. A description of the cases follows in chronological sequence.

The Fall River, Massachusetts, Case, 1919

The first report of this case appeared in the local *Evening Herald* on Tuesday, 22 April. It related that a four-year-old boy was enticed by Jews into a cellar with an offer of money. There his tongue was slashed and his blood drawn.[13] However, the story was not that simple. Three weeks later, on 15 May, the New York Yiddish Orthodox daily, *Der Tageblat*, presented more details as well as an angle of an interethnic strife between Poles and Jews. A "special telegram" reported that when the boy came home with marks of blood, his mother complained to a local Polish priest that the stains were the proof of its extraction by Jews for their religious purposes. Local Poles immediately embarked upon an anti-Semitic campaign with an emphasis on an economic boycott against Jewish merchants. Intercessions by the Jewish community with the Catholic clergy and even the bishop seem to have been of no avail.[14]

The Chicago, Illinois, Case, 1919

The Chicago Case of July 1919 assumes additional importance because that city was the center of American Poles and the seat of their national organizations and representation of the newly restored Poland.

According to the local Yiddish daily, *Jidisher Courier*, Monday, 7 July, a rumor spread on the South Side that a Jewish businessman, H. Kohn, murdered a small Polish boy for ritual purposes. Led by an agitator, a mob was preparing to attack the Jews. The police interfered. Some of the rioters were arrested and brought before Judge William N. Gemmill. The fear of pogroms evidently spread among the Jews and Polish clergymen preached in the churches trying to calm their parishioners.[15] I regret my inability to trace the developments further. The lack of press materials on Chicago in New York City and the difficulties of securing documents and court records here forced me to leave the treatment of later developments for another occasion or to other researchers.[16]

The Pittsfield, Massachusetts, Case, 1919

Like its other 1919 predecessors, the Pittsfield case was symptomatic of the crisis in Polish-Jewish relations in Poland and abroad. It also illustrates the differences in the approaches of the older established Jewish settlers of German and German-periphery regions in origin and the more recent newcomers, mainly of "Litvak" (Lithuanian and White Russian) descent, as well as the involvement of at least one national Jewish organization, the B'nai B'rith Anti-Defamation League. The more intensive research on this case[17] taught

237

me useful lessons on the limits of oral history and memories. The failure of the immigrant generation to convey to its
offspring the important events in their own lives in the community, so reminiscent of their European background, is
painfully obvious. Location of the sources also strengthened
my views concerning the importance of local community
histories for a more realistic history of national events and
trends and on the need for a fuller use of the Yiddish and ethnic press in American Jewish history.

The simple version of the Pittsfield case as conveyed by
my father and local eyewitnesses during my many visits to
the city in the 1920s and 1930s, oral histories from sources
contemporary with the incident, agree that when the rumor
of the boy's disappearance began to spread, the local outstanding civic and Jewish communal leader, George A. Newman,[18] advised the chief of police that the "victim's" parents
be questioned separately in the police station. The parents
admitted that a priest was responsible for staging the affair
and that the lad would be found in a nearby farm. After the
police found him there, the boy was paraded in an open car
in the Polish neighborhood, thus calming the populace and
preventing the expected physical outburst against Jews. The
priest was transferred to another town.[19]

With the passage of time, the blood libel was well nigh forgotten, to judge by the results of my later inquiries and by
the fact that it is not even mentioned in the local Jewish history.[20] Interestingly, the incident occurred closer to Christmas than to Easter, as we have learned from two reports in
the *Berkshire Eagle,* the Pittsfield daily, of 30–31 October
1919.[21] However, a fuller version, indicating more involved
implications and tactics and the differing views on the significance of the case in its own days appeared in an anonymous correspondence in the liberal New York Yiddish daily,
Der Tog (The Day), of 15 November.[22]

I have already alluded to the Massena case of 1928. The
next case to my knowledge was that of Akron, Ohio, in 1971,
when the National Socialist White Peoples' Party, using
anti-Semitic, antiblack, and anti-Catholic recorded tele-

phone messages, charged the Jews with ritual murder of two little girls.[23] An article in a serious medical journal suggested in 1971 that William of Norwich, England, alleged "victim" of the 1144 blood libel, was a true martyr.[24]

The Clayton and New York City episodes were described as "incidents" in contrast to the "cases" of Fall River, Chicago, and Pittsfield, due to lack of political and economic uses and involvement of important personalities. Though rare and possibly unprecedented in American interethnic relations, similar cases may be discovered among other ethnic groups. To judge from its occurrences in many countries, including Canada and the United States, in certain circles the publicity around Beilis' trial buttressed the belief in the authenticity of the canard despite his exoneration.

While organized manifestations of Jew-hatred among American Poles go back to the nineteenth century,[25] resurrected Poland's anti-Jewish policy bears the responsibility for the interethnic tensions that led to the instigation of blood libels here. Soon after the 7 October 1918 declaration of independence, Poland became involved in armed clashes on all her as yet undetermined borders against Germany, Lithuania, Czechoslovakia, and in a most risky war against the Soviet Union that grew out of resistance to a Ukrainian coup in eastern Galicia. The battle against Bolshevism was viewed by many Poles not only as the continuity of the Polish-Lithuanian Commonwealth's historical mission of the *antemurale* defender of Roman Catholicism against schismatic Russia, Protestant Prussia, and the infidel Tatars and Turks. It was also widely interpreted as western civilization's stand against the alleged Jewish-Masonic-Bolshevik partnership in a plot to gain world rule and destroy Christianity, beginning with Poland. The Jews' struggle for minority rights under international protection was often interpreted as an effort to turn Catholic Poland into "Judeo-Polonia"—a Jewish state. *The Protocols of the Elders of Zion* added credibility to these ideas. With independence came nationalist self-assertion and opportunities to put anti-Jewish theory into practice with the backing of the state. Anti-Semitism

239

that had been growing particularly since the initiation of the nationalist anti-Jewish boycott in 1912 became a popular and a leading ideology in reborn Poland.

Consequently, in addition to murders, rapes, robberies, and mayhem that are common in unsettled times of war, there were pogroms, diplomatically termed "excesses," perpetrated even by army units, killings of Jewish individuals, court-martial trials, and speedy executions of groups of Jews falsely accused of aiding the Bolsheviks. In addition there were many cases of molestation of Jews, beatings, insults, robberies, forced barracks and street cleaning, ejections from moving trains, plucking or cutting off of beards to the extent that travel became unsafe. Such "pettier" and "recreational" (quotation marks mine—A. G. D.) acts were often committed by Polish volunteers from America. Neither the moderate leftist nor conservative successive governments cared or dared at all times to interfere with the military or contend against prevailing public opinion. Furthermore, the authorities demanded that the Jews in areas disputed with non-Polish ethnic majorities, such as eastern Galicia or Wilno region, declare themselves as members of the Polish nationality in order to strengthen Poland's territorial claims. The Jews, fearing reprisals and not wishing to interfere with the struggle of the contending nationalities declared their neutrality as a national minority, additional reasons for Polish distrust.[26]

Throughout the world, important individuals and organizations protested against the attacks and the acts of discrimination against Jews. In the United States, too, the Polish authorities were condemned by many prominent persons, churches, organizations, and legislative bodies, including the Senate and state legislatures. The protests continued as the news, eyewitness reports, and testimonies emanated form Poland, with constant mass meetings, street demonstrations, marches, and public relations efforts as well as pressures on Washington and other Allied capitals. American Jews, mainly immigrants from Eastern Europe, demanded protection for their relatives and friends there.

Poland's policy was to minimize the extent of the pogroms and incidents, to emphasize difficulties of controlling the situation, and to justify some as necessary wartime measures against Bolsheviks and other enemies. Generally, State Department officials and U.S. diplomats and relief personnel backed the Polish side. The Poles also feared the effects of the protests on Poland's public standing and on the Allies' decisions on her boundaries and on cultural, national, and religious rights for her many national minorities. The continuing disturbances in Poland and the protests abroad served as convincing arguments in favor of minority protection in the peace treaties. After many hesitations and many-sided pressures, most Allied leaders, including President Woodrow Wilson, a devoted friend of Poland, ultimately arrived at the decision calling for the insertion of such protective clauses in the treaties with the new and succession countries, not only Poland. Early in the fall of 1918, it would appear, the Polish Government asked the leaders of Polonia (Polish Americans) that they undertake a campaign to discredit the protest movement. The strategy called for labeling the American Jewish community as allies and promoters of Bolshevism. Many American Poles accepted the truth of these charges and viewed their campaign as a holy war in defense of the homeland and Christendom. There were also local psychological and economic factors such as the envy of the rise of the Jews and of their prominence in American life in contrast to their former low status in the homeland and of their economic competition with the emerging Polish middle and professional classes in Polish neighborhoods. The "war" was waged on many fronts, diplomacy, legislature, lobbying, and negotiations with anti-Zionist and antinationalist Jews. It involved bitter attacks in the press on both sides, counter protest meetings and marches, outright anti-Semitic propaganda, boycotts, and even physical encounters between Jews and Poles in certain neighborhoods in some cities. Even before Poland's attainment of independence, the established Jewish leadership, Zionist and non-Zionist, negotiated with representatives of the Poles abroad and in the United States.

241

Such negotiations continued throughout the period of confrontation without any visible results. Meetings were also held in a few cities between Polish and Jewish community leaders in attempts to bring peace.[27]

The Beilis affair coincided chronologically with the declaration and beginnings of the anti-Jewish boycott of 1912. Its instigators and promoters utilized the affair in their propaganda. Occurrences of blood libels during the initial years of independence, a period of tensions, trials and wars were not unexpected, particularly in view of the determination to harm the Jews. In Kolbuszowa, for instance, the government had to intervene with the consequent murder by enraged peasants of Jews and of soldiers dispatched there to protect them. Other serious cases were also reported during that period. It is quite likely that similar incidents of lesser magnitude and consequences remained unrecorded or unknown. Of course, this goes not only for Poland.[28]

It is not yet known whether the 1919 accusations may have served as examples for the American ones. It is quite conceivable, however, that the hysteria and genuine fear of the dangers to Poland induced some clergymen who may have believed in the reality of ritual murder practices to utilize them for the homeland's defense. Their application to local identifiable persons and situations was probably viewed as a more effective weapon in the confrontation with the Jews. The desire to promote more effectively the anti-Jewish boycott and Polish communal solidarity may have served as another or additional inducement. The concentration of the blood libels in Massachusetts may even point to a possible consultation or collaboration among clergymen in the state. In vivid contrast, the Chicago hierarchy made serious efforts to calm the excited populace. Above all, it is important to be aware that anti-Semitism in Poland was the application under local conditions of prevailing European anti-Jewish ideologies and movements. These points as well as a more detailed treatment of the Polish-Jewish confrontation of 1918–20 will appear soon in my more extensive study on the subject with ample bibliographies.

Appendix

Document I[29]

The Clayton Incident

> Almost a Blood Libel In A Local *Shtetl* [Small Town]. A
> Christian Servant Girl Upon Seeing That Her Mrs Is
> Sharpening a Knife Raises The Outcry That The Jews
> Want To Kill Her

The insane agitation and the wild blood libels that the Black Hundreds in dark Russia are carrying on against Jews are felt right here in America and the household of Jacob Miller, a Jew from Clayton, Pa., lived through a terrible experience last Sabbath because of it.

A boy was born to Jacob Miller and he therefore wanted to celebrate the festive occasion with a repast for his friends and acquaintances. The *brit* (circumcision) was to take place on Sunday.

Saturday night came a *shohet* who killed a large number of ducks, etc. Mrs. Stein, the midwife, was the *sarver*[30] and was making the preparations for broiling and cooking the fowl. As she had not been able to manage by herself, she asked the Millers's Christian servant girl, Anna Hansel, to help her. The sixteen-year-old girl was from some small town and usually went home to sleep at her parents' every night after work. Her parents are Slavs.

The girl agreed to stay there overnight to help the midwife in her cooking and broiling. Mrs. Stein began to sharpen the knife for cutting the meat. When the Christian girl saw it, she reminded herself of all the wild tales that she heard about Jews and became frightened; she thought that the Jews wanted to offer her as a sacrifice.

In her wild fright she began to shout and cry that she wants to go home. Mrs. Stein took her hand to quiet her down, but the girl became even more frightened and ran out of the house with wild shouts.

Neighbors heard her shouts and a turmoil broke out, [much] running about. Someone pulled the fire alarm and the excitement was stirred up even [more]. The entire small town quickly came running hither. Because the girl, frightened, was hiding somewhere, the bigots began to shout that the Jews killed the Christian girl.

The Millers lived through a terrible night. On Sunday morning the girl was found hale and healthy, and the crowd calmed down.

Forverts, Wednesday, 5 February 1913.

Document II

The New York Incident

POLISH *GOYE*[31] MURDERS HER HUSBAND BECAUSE OF A BLOOD LIBEL

Shocking Murder on Pitt Street—Young Woman
Makes Accusation Against Her Husband That He Sold
Her Only Child To Jews For Passover And She Kills
Him For It[32]

Valerie Weszkowicz, 36, killed her husband in their apartment at 30 Pitt Street. Upon her arrest, she declared that the reason for the murder was that her husband sold their eleven-year-old boy to the Jews for Passover. "I have killed him because he sold my only child to the Jews, so that they could prepare their holiday with his blood. The Jews paid him for it with seven chickens and a five cent glass of liquor."

The Weszkowiczes were the housekeepers [janitors?] of the house that was fully occupied by Jews. They lived in three rooms in the basement. The detectives found the dead man lying on the bed with a split head. Near him was a long stick of wood stained with blood. The murder was probably perpetrated with that stick of wood. The murdered man was fifteen years older than his wife.

Later the detectives found the eleven-year-old son who was playing with Jewish children in the street. They asked him about his mother's assertion and he declared that he does not know what to say.

The woman was arrested on the charge of murder.

Forverts, 21 April 1913.

Document III

The Fall River Case

BOY'S TONGUE IS SLASHED BY MEN

Below-the-Hill Mother Tells Police That Blood From Her Son Was Taken For Use in Religious Rites

Slashing a boy's tongue for the purpose of receiving blood for a religious rite is alleged by a Below-the-Hill mother in a complaint to the police.

Four-year-old Joseph Karaszewski, 139 Spring Street, is the alleged victim. The parent charged that the deed was committed by two men who live in the vicinity.

The boy was playing in the yard a week ago yesterday afternoon and his mother, coming to the window, told him to go away. At about five, he shouted to his mother that he was going up the street to play with other children. About 20 minutes later, the boy returned with blood coming from his mouth and his clothing blood-stained. She immediately called Dr. S. Benjamin Kaufman, who found that the lad's tongue had been slashed.

When the boy had sufficiently recovered from the shock, he was questioned by his mother, who learned that a man had called him from the cellar of a nearby house and offered him money. The child was carried into the cellar and pennies were strewn on the table by another man. One of the men covered his eyes and told him to hold out his tongue, which he slashed.

She reported the case to officer McDermott, whose report to Police headquarters states that the boy was playing with two other boys who had a chain and that his tongue had been cut by the chain.

The case has been turned over to Inspector Westgate, who is investigating.

Fall River Evening Herald, Tuesday, 22 April 1919, p. 22.

Document IV

The Fall River Case

BLOOD LIBEL IN FALL RIVER, MASS.

The local Jews are very stirred up over a blood libel which was raised against them and which is being used by Polish anti-Semites and their priests to agitate against the Jews and to boycott them.

The story of the blood libel is as follows: In a fight, the day before Passover, between a six-year-old Polish boy and another Christian boy, the Polish one was so beaten up that he came home all bloodied. His mother went immediately to the Polish priest with the complaint that the Jews had extracted blood from her child for religious purposes.

Together with a detective the priest made an investigation about the complaint and, although both failed to find any evidence to back the libel, they announced in the local papers that the Jews tapped blood from the Polish boy for their religious purposes.

The local Poles utilized the libel to start a boycott and anti-Semitic incitement against the Jews.

At the beginning the local Jews made nothing of the libel. However, they came to realize that the boycott and the agitation were becoming increasingly serious and that something should be done about it.

For this purpose they held a mass meeting in the local synagogue and elected a committee, with the lawyer R. Radowski at its head, to locate the Christian boy who had injured the Polish boy and to go to the Catholic bishop and plead with him that he order the Polish anti-Semites and their priest to cease their baiting and boycott against the local Jews.

The bishop answered the Jewish committee that the priest is known to him as an honorable man and that he is certain that the priest would not make any contentions that are not true.

Having realized that the bishop is no better than the priest, the committee decided to seek other ways to expose the falseness of the blood libel and it began energetically to search for the guilty boy. Regrettably, their efforts were not crowned with the success they desired.

Der Tageblat (Jewish Daily News), 15 May 1919.

Document V

The Chicago Case

POGROM IN SOUTH CHICAGO IS GAINING STRENGTH

Blood Libelers Will Be Brought Today Before Judge [William N.] Gemmill[33]

Two *Goyes* Speak As "Witnesses" That They Heard The Polish Boy Cry And Beg Old Kohn Not To Kill Him.—Priests Preached Yesterday In The Churches Against Blood Libel. Poles Will Strike Today For Tom Mooney And It Is Feared That They Will Take The Murderous Feelings[34] Out On Jews.

The arrested Poles, at their head one Casimir Lata [Lota?] who led a mob of Poles and sought to make a pogrom against the Jews in South Chicago, argued that the Jewish businessman H. Kohn,[35] 8401 Buffalo Avenue, enticed a small Polish boy to his store, killed him and took his blood for religious purposes. As it was exclusively reported yesterday in the *Courier*, they will be brought today before Judge Gemmill who sits in the Municipal Court.

The warrant against Casimir Lata was taken out by Marcus Kohn, one of the sons of Mr. H. Kohn, whom the Pole approached with savage murder readiness, saying: "Return our child to us!" and without waiting for an answer, began to scream: "The *zhids*[36] should be killed!"

The policeman who arrested Lata is also a Pole and it is hardly believed that he will wish to tell the truth in court, because he argued in the station about the other arrested Poles that they were just boiling mad, but caused no harm to anyone.

The charges against Casimir Lata are not only of disorderly conduct, but also that he incited to riot. In order to develop the case properly the Kohns will request through their lawyer that the trial should be delayed.

At the same time, the Jews in South Chicago fear a pogrom and the Kohns are showing the greatest fear.

Jidisher Courier (The Daily Jewish Courier), Chicago, Monday, 7 July 1919.

Document VI

The Pittsfield Case

BAFFLING YOUTH'S STORY HE WAS DRAGGED
TO SYNAGOGUE AND CUT NOT BELIEVED BY
POLICE

The police are baffled by the case of George Nickols, the
seven-year-old son of Joseph Nickols of 102 Madison Avenue,
a shoemaker, who claims he was dragged to the basement of
the Synagogue of the Love of Peace Society on Robbins Avenue
Saturday noon and cut with a knife. The boy did not say anything about having been cut until Saturday night after he had
been to the street with his mother. When he reached home
that evening he was ill and investigation showed he had been
cut in the leg a considerable distance above the knee.

Neither the boy's pants nor his underclothing was cut, his
mother told the police. Dr. Harry A. Schneider attended the
boy and the cut was so serious the little fellow is still confined
to the bed.

The police do not believe the boy's story about having been
taken to the Synagogue because there were certain features
which he related and which they learned were incorrect.

Chief of Police John L. Sullivan, Inspector Daniel L. Mc-
Colgan and Officer W. J. Keegan have been investigating the
case.

Berkshire Eagle, Pittsfield, 30 October 1919, p. 14.

Document VII

The Pittsfield Case

BOY ADMITS THAT HIS STORY WAS UNTRUE.
YOUTH, WHO CLAIMED HE WAS ATTACKED IN
SYNAGOGUE, NOW SAYS HE FELL FROM TREE

The police have learned that the story of George Nickols,
aged seven years, of 102 Madison Avenue, to the effect that he
was dragged to the basement of the Love of Peace Society Synagogue on Robbins Avenue and cut in the leg was a complete
hoax. Joseph Nickols, the boy's father, called upon Chief of Po-

lice John L. Sullivan this morning and told him the little fellow had admitted that he was injured by falling from a tree onto a sharp stick. The reason there was no blood on his clothing is explained by the fact that the underclothing was driven into the wound in such a manner that he did not bleed until he undressed that evening.

The story that the boy had been dragged into the Synagogue was not believed by the police, but has caused such an uproar in that section of the city. Chief Sullivan devoted every means toward quickly clearing up the case. Chief Sullivan, Inspector Daniel J. McColgan, and Officer William J. Keegan worked on the case.

Berkshire Eagle, 31 October 1919, p. 2.

Document VIII

The Pittsfield Case

POLISH BLOOD LIBEL AGAINST JEWS IN AMERICA

Little Polish Boy in Pittsfield, Mass., Tells that Jews Have Locked Him Up In The Synagogue And Extracted From Him Two Bottles of Blood; A Local Paper Writes About It. A Springfield Newspaper Reprints It.[37]—A Policeman Comes To The Synagogue, Subjects The Hebrew Teacher[38] To A Hearing And Discovers Blood Stains On The Cellar Wall.—An Investigation Reveals That It Is Blood Of A Chicken.—The Boy Confesses That He Had Invented A Lie.—Jews Demand An Investigation, But German Jews[39] Say: It Is Not Necessary And It Should Not Be Done.

During the past few weeks the Jews of Pittsfield, Mass., have lived through a rather stormy and most disquieting time. They bore the burden of a blood libel with all its minutiae and are not as yet free from it even today.

The Pittsfield Jews have also suffered no little from the public preachments and private baiting of a Polish priest, who at every opportunity ordered his countrymen to boycott the Jews—Jewish storekeepers, Jewish landlords, etc. The worst, however, was still to come. The situation became much more

249

serious. As a Pittsfield reader of *The Day* reports, the following has taken place:

It happened a few weeks ago when the Pittsfield Jews read in a local English paper the following story:

"A Polish boy came home limping the previous Saturday. When his parents asked him what happened to him, he told that Jews seized him in the street, dragged him into the synagogue, and there extracted from him two bottles of blood."

The same news was reprinted on the following day in the responsible and respectable *Springfield Republican*.

On the same day a policeman walked into the Pittsfield synagogue. He encountered the *melamed* who was teaching the children.

"What are you doing with the blood of the children?" the policeman asked the teacher.

The teacher who is also a *mohel*[40] answered: "We do not have circumcisions in the synagogue."

The policeman, however, could not be gotten rid of so easily. "I mean the blood that you are extracting here from Christian children," the policeman added.

The teacher became more dead than alive. He swore to the policeman that such things have never happened, but that enemies of the Jews have invented it.

The policeman, however, was far from convinced.

"Come down with me to the cellar," he said.

The teacher went along and the policeman began to search and to examine the walls. After a long search, he suddenly stopped and pointing to red stains on the wall, asked the teacher:

"And where are these stains from?"

The teacher who in addition to being a *melamed* is also a *mohel* and a *shohet* [animal and fowl ritual slaughterer], answered that it was the blood of a chicken.

The policeman took a shrewd look at him and marched off. No arrests were made, probably because the so-called German *yahudim* of Pittsfield had heard of the blood libel before the other Jews. They have energetically taken the task of explaining the story. Two representatives of the Chicago "Anti-Defamation League,"[41] the organization that fights anti-Semitism in the papers and on the stage, also arrived.

Following the policeman's visit to the Pittsfield synagogue, several bricks were taken out of the basement wall, on which there were blood stains. The bricks were sent to a chemical laboratory for an analysis of the stains. The investigation proved that the blood was that of a fowl.

In the meantime the Jews of Pittsfield were pretty scared and began to search for ways of clearing themselves of the libel. The *yahudim*, however, warned them that they should not be in a turmoil and not raise any tumult. They, the *yahudim*, will clear up the libel before it will get out into the wider world, because no matter how ridiculous it is, not a few will be found who will believe it.

A few days later it became known that the Polish boy's parents were saying that the child confessed that the story about the blood extraction is a lie.

Pittsfield Jews are far from being satisfied with that. They wish that an open and thorough investigation be made as to who told the boy to invent the libel, so that this would serve as a warning for others. Incidentally, not a few Christians can be found who say that the Jews have bribed the Polish boy's parents to "suppress the scandal." The Jews therefore wish to have an investigation that would establish all the facts.

However, the *yahudim* are saying that it is not necessary and it is forbidden to attract the world's attention. The libel has been exposed. The Jews were not harmed at all. This is sufficient.[42]

Der Tog (The Day), 15 November 1919.

Notes

1. The initial stimulus of my interest in the American aspects of this rather gory and ancient theme dates back to 2 January 1923, my second day in this country. In his first briefing on America, my father, Asher Zelig, of blessed memory, *hazzan shohet* (cantor and ritual animal and fowl slaughterer) in Pittsfield, Massachusetts (1921–48), cautioned me on our way home from the Union Station about anti-Semitism in the United States. His telling example was a recent ritual murder accusation in Pittsfield.

I wish to thank Dr. Jacob R. Marcus, the Dean of American Jewish historians, for his great and indispensable help in locating the Yiddish originals of the news reports on the incidents, most of them hitherto unknown to me.

I also gratefully acknowledge the help of Dina Abramowicz, Head Librarian of the YIVO Institute for Jewish Research; Cyma Horowitz, Library Director and Archivist of the Blaustein Library of the American Jewish Committee; Professor Minerva Katz of the Library of Brooklyn College, the City University of New York; the Libraries of Columbia University, namely the General Library, Law Library, Lehman Library, Teachers College Library and the Microform Reading Room; The Jewish, Slavonic and American History Divisions, and the Newspaper Collection of the New York Library; the Library of the Polish Institute of Arts and Sciences in America; the Library of the Jozef Pilsudski Institute in America; the Library of the Jewish Theological Seminary of America; and many years ago, the Library and Archives of the Polish Roman Catholic Union in Chicago, now the Polish Museum.

To my dear sister, Mrs. Hilda Hadassah Levine, and her husband, Morris, of Ashley Falls, Mass., many thanks for dedicated legwork, telephoning, interviewing, and guidance in Pittsfield.

2. The standard study of the case is Alexander B. Tager's *The Decay of Czarism: The Beilis Trial . . . Based on Unpublished Materials in the Russian Archives* (Philadelphia: Jewish Publication Society of America [JPSA], 1935). It is followed up by Maurice Samuel's *Blood Accusation: The Strange History of the Beiliss Case* (New York: Knopf, 1967). Its free fictional presentation by Bernard Malamud, *The Fixer* (New York: Farrar, Strauss and Giroux, 1966), and its 1968 film version helped to popularize the theme. An interesting sidelight is E. Lifshutz's "Repercussions of the Beilis Trial in America," *Zion* 28, nos. 3–4 (1963): 206–22 (Hebrew, with English summary).

3. For the 1961–62 incidents, see *Jews in Eastern Europe* 2, no. 2 (May 1963): 34, and no. 3 (September 1963): 37–38; "New Blood Libels Unmasked: Significant Pattern Begins to Emerge," *Jewish Observer and Middle East Review*, May 31, 1963, 12–13. On Vilnius, see *loc. cit.* and *Jews in Eastern Europe* 2, no. 4 (February 1964): 28–30. Interesting is the handling of the accusations by the Soviet authorities. The same occurrences have been taking place in Moslem regions, and are very significant.

4. On its possible security police origins and management, see Stefan Korbonski, *Warsaw in Chains* (New York: Macmillan Co., 1959), pp. 22–23; Michael Checinski, "The Kielce Pogrom: Some Unanswered Questions," *Soviet Jewish Affairs* 1 (1975): 57–72. The perseverance of the belief in ritual murder can also be seen in the reply by the then (1946) Bishop and now (1978) Poland's Car-

dinal and Primate, Stefan Wyszynski, to a Jewish delegation's request that he join the protests against the pogrom. He answered that the Beilis trial failed to prove that Jews do not use blood for matzah. See Israel Ben-Dov, "Polish Antisemitism in the Years 1939 to 1946," *Enṣiḳlopedia shel galuyot* (Encyclopedia of Exile Communities), 12; *Warsaw, 3* (Jerusalem, 1973), p. 438 (article in Yiddish). My initial source is David Knaani's review in *Gal-Ed* (Witness Cairn) (Tel Aviv University) 2 (1973): 437. See also Samuel Shneiderman's *Between Fear and Hope* (New York: Arco Publishing Co., 1947), p. 117; Joseph Tenenbaum, *In Search of a Lost People: Old and New in Poland* (New York: Beechurst, 1948), pp. 240–42. Again, this was before the Vatican changes, the emergence of the Soviet Union's open anti-Semitic course and propaganda campaign under the guise of anti-Zionism, and before the forced exodus of communists of Jewish origin from Poland. The latest twist is a Masonic-Zionist plot against socialism and the Third World. The cardinal's present role in defense of religious liberty and in the opposition to racism is quite clear.

A particularly Polish factor is the belief in the truth of the 1759 Frankist accusation of ritual murder against the "talmudic" Jews. It left a lasting impression and was renewed from time to time, as for instance, on its hundreth anniversary in 1859 and on other occasions, including 1936. See Tadeusz Zaderecki, *O Zydach, Bolszewji, "mordzie rytualnym"* (About the Jews, Bolshevikdom, "Ritual Murder") (Lwow: A. Goldman, 1934), a defense of the Jews against Don Inigo's *Synowie Szatana* (Sons of the Satan). The book is based on a Russian work by the same name written by I. A. Rodionov. Don Inigo is the pseudonym of Ignacy Charszewski. See also n. 28.

A more recent example is Feliks Koneczny's posthumous, scurrilous, anti-Semitic work with footnotes, *Cywilizacja zydowska* (Jewish Civilization) (London: Towarzystwo Imienia Romana Dmowskiego [Society by the Name of Roman Dmowski], 1974), pp. 318–29, 340–42, and Jedrzej Giertych's (see introduction). The book bears the endorsement of some Polish dignitaries, including prominent clergymen, among them Americans.

The Jewish false messiah, Jacob Frank, and many of his followers (Frankists) underwent baptism in 1759 and after. Many of the latter continued as a mutual aid and protective enclave even after the abandonment of their belief in him as a messiah and world ruler. They disappeared through exogamous marriages at the end of the nineteenth, possibly also early in the twentieth century. See my "Polish Frankism's Duration from Cabbalistic Judaism to Roman

Catholicism and from Jewishness to Polishness," *Jewish Social Studies* [*JSS*] 25 (1963): 287–333; and my "Frankism as a Movement of Polish-Jewish Synthesis," in *Tolerance and Movements of Religious Dissent in Eastern Europe,* ed. Bela K. Kiraly (Boulder, Colo.: East European Monographs and Columbia University Press, 1975), pp. 133–64.

5. See Ibrahim Saada, "The Secret of the Blood Practice Israel Is Enjoined to Observe," *Akher Saa* (Last Hour—an illustrated weekly), 21 June 1967; "Arab Antisemitism—Blood Libel Revived," *Wiener Library Bulletin* (Summer 1967): 46ff. For 1971 (Lebanese and Iraqi propaganda), 1972, and 1973 (both in Cairo daily *Al Akhbar*), see D. F. Green, ed., *Arab Theologians on Jews and Israel: Extracts from the Proceedings of the Fourth Conference of the Academy of Islamic Research 1968* (Geneva: Editions de l'Avenir, 1974), p. 81.

6. See Yehoshafat Harkabi in Tel Aviv daily *Maariv* (Evening Time), 27 January 1978, on recent accusation in the Cairo *Octobre,* edited by Anis Mansour, a friend of President Anwar el Sadat. My source is A. M. Dover (pseud.), *Jidisher Kemfer* (Jewish Battler) (New York), 17 February 1978, p. 3. Mansour is also the author of a "documentary drama" on the canard. See Harkabi, *Maariv,* January 27, 1978, and Dover, *Jidisher Kemfer,* 24 February, p. 9.

7. On a speech in Quebec in 1913 about the Jews' use of Christian blood and the speaker's victory in a libel suit and subsequent defeat in an appeal in 1914, see Herman Abramowitz, "Samuel William Jacobs," *American Jewish Year Book* [*AJYB*], vol. 41 (Philadelphia: JPSA, 1939–40), pp. 97–98. On an accusation in the Winnipeg *Canadian Nationalist* and the injunction against it, see ibid., vol. 37 (1935–36), p. 168.

8. A good example is the special issue of Streicher's *Der Stürmer,* March 1, 1934. A reproduction of the front page by Raymond Apple appeared in *Jewish Chronicle* (London), 31 March 1972.

9. A child disappeared before Yom Kippur (Day of Atonement) but was found in nearby woods on the same day. However, the local Rabbi, B. Brenglass, was invited to the police station while a crowd of 300 to 400 persons gathered outside. See "Annual Report of the Executive Committee of the American Jewish Committee," *AJYP,* vol. 31 (1929–30), pp. 346–52; Saul S. Friedman, *The Incident at Massena: The Blood Libel in America* (New York: Stein and Day, 1978).

See also review by Boris Smolar, veteran journalist, who investigated the case on behalf of Louis Marshall in 1928, in *Jewish Week*–

American Examiner, week of 26 November 1978, p. 36. Incidentally, the first to mention the possibility of a ritual murder there was a person of Polish descent. See also, Friedman, *Incident at Massena,* pp. 61–62, who also holds a Greek to have been responsible for the spread of the rumor.

10. With the exception of the Massena case, the subject is not mentioned in any bibliographical listing, including the geographical card index of the Hebrew University and National Library in Jerusalem. Drs. Marcus and Nathan M. Kaganoff, librarian-editor of the American Jewish Historical Society, and Dr. Isidore S. Meyer, retired librarian-editor of the society, informed me that no such incident had come to their attention. Local historians may discover new information in the local press, police records, or from old people.

11. See Appendix, Document I. In this, as well as in the subsequent translations from Yiddish, I tried to retain the original flavor. Search in Philadelphia daily press and the local Clayton paper, if any, may locate more information.

Dr. Hyman Dicker of the Library of the Jewish Theological Seminary of America in New York did not find any references to this case in the microfilms of the Philadelphia Anglo-Jewish weeklies in the library. I owe him thanks for this ready cooperation.

12. See Appendix, Document II and n. 32 on the treatment of the murder in the New York press.

13. See Appendix, Document III. To Dr. Moshe Babin, of blessed memory, my former Chicago landsman, and later rabbi of Temple Beth El in Fall River, thanks are due for his kindness in locating and sending me photocopies of the news stories in the local paper. A follow-up in the police records and diocesan sources is recommended.

The case received national publicity, to judge by a report in the *Jewish Times* of Los Angeles, 29 May 1919. The *Boston Jewish Advocate* did not carry the news. The Boston Anglo-Jewish weeklies and Yiddish daily should be examined by local historians.

14. See Appendix, Document IV.

15. See Appendix, Document V.

16. There is no mention of the case in any of the local histories of the Jews in Chicago. It was not noted in the *Reform Advocate, The Israelite,* or in the *AJYB,* nor was it reported in the *Chicago Tribune* of the week. The person in Chicago on whom I relied failed to respond to my request on the treatment of the case in other newspapers and in the foreign language press, if any.

255

17. I wish to thank Rabbi Arthur D. Rulnick of Congregation Kenesset Israel for his kindness in looking up and sending me copies of the reports in the *Berkshire Eagle.* To Mr. Robert G. Newman, librarian of the Berkshire Atheneum–Pittsfield Public Library, thanks are due for sending me a copy of his father's necrology and for advice.

18. Mr. Newman, an outstanding civic leader and recipient of many rewards, who died at 81 in 1961, also held many offices of distinction in the Jewish community. Cf. his obituary in the *Berkshire Eagle,* 12 December 1961. According to Mr. Mendel Adlersheim (in a telephone conversation), the England brothers, department store owners, were also involved in trying to restore tranquility.

19. He was identified as the Reverend Joseph Stanczyk by a Polish friend of Mr. Irving Wolfe, secretary of the Pittsfield Lodge of the Independent Order B'nai B'rith, in 1977, and by Mr. Mendel Adlersheim.

20. See Pink Horwitt in collaboration with Bertha Skole, *Jews in Berkshire County* (Williamstown, Mass.: Dor Co., 1972).

21. See Appendix, Documents VI and VII.

22. See Appendix, Document VII.

23. See Jewish Telegraphic Agency, *Daily News Bulletin,* 3 June 1971. The dispatch is based on a report in the *Cleveland Jewish News.* The Ohio Bell Telephone Company explained that censorship of such telephone tape messages was against the law.

24. See William D. Sharpe, M.D., "Strange Murder of William of Norwich, 1144: Medicolegal Analysis of Thomas of Monmouth, De Vita et Passione Sancti Willelmi Martyris Norwicensis," *New York State Journal of Medicine* (November 1971): 2569–74.

25. See Edward R. Kantowicz, *Polish American Politics in Chicago, 1880–1940* (Chicago: University of Chicago Press, 1975), pp. 117–19; and my "Some Aspects of Polish-Jewish Relations in the United States after 1865," *Jewish Quarterly Review* 45 (1955): 529–39.

26. Space prevents the inclusion of a more detailed bibliography. Basic works on the interbellum situation of the Jews in Poland are Joshua A. Fishman, ed., *Studies on Polish Jewry, 1919–1939: The Interplay of Social, Economic, and Political Factors in the Struggle of a Minority for Its Existence* (New York: YIVO Institute for Jewish Research, 1974) (text in Yiddish and English); and Celia S. Heller, *On the Edge of Destruction: Jews of Poland Between the Two World Wars* (New York: Columbia University Press, 1977). For Jewish ideological positions and the pressure for minority rights

as well as the Peace Conference and treaties, see Oscar I. Janowsky, *The Jews and Minority Rights, 1898–1919* (New York: Columbia University Press, 1933). See also some works cited above. Moshe Landau, *Hayehudim Kemiut leumi* . . . (Jews as a National Minority during the First Years of Polish Independence, 1918–26) Ph.D. diss., Hebrew University, Jerusalem, February 1972), is an essential work which reached me after the article had been submitted.

27. Again the bibliography is limited. Basic on the history of the Poles in the United States are Joseph W. Zurawski, *Polish American History and Culture: A Classified Bibliography* (Chicago: Polish Museum of America, 1975); Alphonse S. Wolanin, *Polonica Americana: Annotated Catalogue of the Archives and Museum of the Polish Roman Catholic Union* (Chicago, 1960). The *Polish Review*, a New York periodical, contains useful contributions and book reviews for the non–Polish language readers and for scholars. Specialized treatments are: Stanley R. Pliska, "Polish Independence and the Polish American," a report of a Type C Project, D. Ed. Teachers College, Columbia University, New York, 1955, typescript; Ezekiel Lifschutz (Lifshutz) "The Pogroms in Poland in 1918–19: the Morgenthau Commission and the American State Department," *Zion* 23–24 (1958–59): 66–97, 194–218 (Hebrew); Zosa Szajkowski, "Relief Activities of American Jews for Polish Jewry, 1918–1923," *Zion* 34 (1969): 219–61.

28. Thus in 1920 Captain Wright, of the British Mission to Poland, viewed as its close friend, wrote in 1920 that "there is a general belief among all classes of Poles that Jews practice ritual murder." See *Report by Sir Stuart Samuel on His Mission to Poland*, miscellaneous, no. 10 (London: His Majesty's stationery office, 1920), p. 19. Morgenthau, the head of the Mission of the United States to Poland, reported on "the bloody riots in Kolbuszowa where eight Jews were killed on 7 May 1919, in consequence of agitation and an alleged ritual murder case in which the Jewish defendant had been acquitted." The authorities had been warned in advance and a company of soldiers came to protect the Jews. However, they were disarmed "after two soldiers and three peasants had been killed." A new detachment of soldiers was sent to restore order. One of the rioters, reported Morgenthau, "has since been tried and executed by the Polish Government." Riots were also reported from the nearby towns Rzeszow and Glogow. See Henry Morgenthau and French Strother, *All in a Life Time* (Garden City, N.Y.: Doubleday, Page & Co., 1923), appendix, p. 413.

Other ritual murder accusations were reported in 1919 from

Strzyzow, where two Jews charged with the alleged crime had been acquitted in Krakow, and in 1920 in Pizdry. Sir Stuart Samuel protested, 28 November 1919, to the Polish Foreign Office against a lecture by a Professor Tcherbak [Czerbak?] in which he accused the Jews of ritual murders. The Foreign Minister's assurance that there would be no recurrence failed to prevent his repetition of the charges in Tarnow on 26 December. There was also a report of a blood rumor with subsequent anti-Jewish disturbance in Ponevezh (Panevezye), Lithuania, 17 April 1920. Evidently, Poland was not the only country where such outbursts were arranged. See *AJYB* 22 (1920–21): 257, 258, 269.

29. I tried to convey the flavor of the Yiddish original in the translation. There are no capitals in Yiddish. Capitalization in the English translation follows the style of the period.

30. *Sarver*—person responsible for cooking, baking, setting the tables, and serving.

31. *Goye*—Gentile woman, plural *goyes.*

32. The coverage in the New York daily English-language press is of interest. Only the *New York Tribune* brought out the religious aspect of the demented women's bloody act in the issue of the same day, 21 April, p. 14. The sensational headlines, "Sold Son"; SLAIN BY WIFE/Got Chickens For Boy, She Says/Police Think She's Mad," were followed by more details. The husband was identified as Anton Maschkiewitz, 50, whose wife attacked him with a board from a fish crate. The woman spoke no English. "To a Polish interpreter she told a rambling story that her husband had sold her son Bobick, 11 years old, for seven chickens, with which he wished to make a sacrifice for the Passover, which is today." The police, reported the paper, believe that she is mentally unstable.

The *New York American* of the same day was less sensational. Nevertheless, it gave the incident prominent space on page 3, with the headline, "Killed Husband Believing He Had Sold Their Son." The name of the woman was given as Valeria Waszkiewicz; that of the arresting patrolman was Murphy. A third headline reported that the "Woman Would Not Believe The Man's Assertion That The Lad's Whereabouts Were Unknown." She claimed that the body was sold for seven chickens and a little whiskey, and "being told that the child was alive, she would not believe it." The *American* remarked that "perhaps the darkness of an enlightened city was never to be startingly proven as by the case of this woman who manifestly believed a boy could be sold and bought like ordinary chattel." The moral is an interesting one. The breach of enlightenment was not the belief in a hoary mass accusation against an entire people, but rather the woman's assumption that one had the right to sell children.

An interesting comment of the status of education among some immigrants was the concluding remark that "the boy said he never went to school but that he went every Sunday to St. Joseph's Church."

The *New York Times* similarly desisted from mentioning the ritual aspects in the demented woman's imagination. The story was headed by lurid headlines: "Kills Her Husband Saying He Sold Son Woman Tells Wild Story of Sacrifice, but Boy is Found to be Safe Used Piece of Firewood Then Makes a Confession—Son 11 Years Old Has Never Been Sent to School."

The *Times* refrained from comment. Among details added was the presence of three boarders in the menage. It was Patrolman Murray who answered the call. Another version of the name of the deceased was "Waschkavietz." The man was killed because "he had sold their boy for seven chickens and a nickel's worth of whiskey." The police got little out of the boy. As the other papers, the *Times* also reported that arrangements were made to place the boy under guardianship.

Three dailies, the *Post*, the *World*, and the *Sun* failed to mention the incident, nor did the *Brooklyn Eagle*. It would be worth while to check the reaction of the Polish press. Interestingly, no mention of the incident appeared in the *American Hebrew* or in the *AJYB*.

33. Only his family name was given in the *Forverts* in Yiddish characters. It had taken me some time to locate his full name and its pronunciation.

34. In the original, *retzikhe.*

35. H. Kohn is identified in the *Chicago Jewish Community Blue Book* (Chicago: Sentinel Publishing Co., 1918) as a representative of the "Bik.C.C.," very likely Bikur Cholim (Sick Visiting) Charity Committee. Abbreviations are not listed in the index.

36. From the Polish *Zydzi, Zydy*—Jews. Like its English counterpart, *Zydzi* can be used in derogatory sense. *Zydy* is always used so.

37. I regret that I was unable to obtain the cooperation of the Springfield person whom I asked to locate the item.

38. In the original, *melamed.*

39. In the original, *yahudim*, the term for the established Jews of German and periphery countries descent, used patronizingly by the East European Jews.

40. Circumcision performer.

41. The B'nai B'rith Anti-Defamation League (ADL) is a prime Jewish "defense" or community relations agency. To my inquiry about the record of the case Mr. A. Abbot Rosen, the ADL Director in Chicago, replied on 26 August 1976: "What we have on hand does not go back to that era." The league's New York head office also informed me that no such records are located there. The records of the Pittsfield B'nai B'rith Lodge have been retained by it only since 1940.

42. Reminiscences of local people help to round out the picture. Thus an authority who prefers to remain anonymous informed me as follows: "When I was a young boy, probably some time in the early 1920s, a story was circulated by sources unknown to me that blood stains had been discovered on the floor of a synagogue basement in Pittsfield and this circumstance was linked to a false rumor of an alleged ritual murder. The Jewish community was greatly concerned and the advice of . . . George A. Newman was sought as to what action should be taken. It is my understanding that he spoke with the then chief of police, John L. Sullivan. An analysis of the blood stains proved that they were of fowl. The rumor was thus apparently laid to rest." Mr. Harry Horelly reported that "the *melamed* interrupted his teaching when some "yente" (a gabby ignorant woman) came to have a chicken killed. The teacher dashed down to the cellar and killed it. Whereupon some kid who was looking in told the priest how he got the wound." The local historian, Mrs. Skole, a daughter of the *shamash* (sexton) of the large Orthodox synagogue Gathering of Israel and coauthor of *Jews in Berkshire County* (see n. 20), could not recollect the incident nor did she ever hear of it before my inquiry. I hope that she will follow it up. The police records are no longer in Pittsfield. They may perhaps be located in some central quarters. It may also be useful to look into the diocesan and other Roman Catholic records. I also recommend a more intensive interview with the octogenarian Mr. Mendel Adlersheim whom I was unable to visit while in Pittsfield, but had to be satisfied with a lengthy and informative telephone call much later.

The Feast of Purim and the Origins of the Blood Accusation

Most of the scholarship devoted to the blood libel legend consists of surveys of case histories in one or more countries. There has been relatively little speculation about the possible origins of the legend. One of the rare attempts at speculating on the difficult question of origins is that of Cecil Roth, a leading English Jewish scholar of the twentieth century. His suggestion that the blood libel legend may have arisen from the Christian misperception of the Jewish feast of Purim is often cited, but it is by no means clear that many writers on the subject of blood libel agree with his hypothetical origin theory.

Cecil Roth made other contributions to the study of blood libel. For example, he critiqued Isabella of Spain *(1931), written by William Thomas Walsh with specific reference to ritual murder. Walsh had argued that the historian was not obliged to make "wholesale vindication of all Jews accused of murder" and that "one must admit that acts committed by Jews sometimes furnished the original provocation." Outraged, Roth exclaimed, "It is the first time probably in living memory that the foul accusation has been made in this country [England]." See "Jews, Conversos, and the Blood-Accusation in Fifteenth-Century Spain,"* Dublin Review *191 (1932): 219–31. For Walsh's attempt at replying to Roth's charges, see "A Reply to Dr. Cecil Roth,"* Dublin Review *191 (1932): 232–52.*

A more important contribution to blood libel scholarship is Cecil Roth, The Ritual Murder Libel and the Jew: The Report *by Cardinal Lorenzo Ganganelli (Pope Clement XIV)*

Reprinted from *Speculum* 8 (1933): 520–26.

(London: Woburn Press, 1934), which not only contains an English translation of the 1759 Ganganelli report but an excellent discussion of blood libel by Dr. Roth.

Last year (1932) the Jewish carnival-feast of Purim, commemorating the triumph of Mordecai and Esther in Susa of old, happened to fall on Tuesday, 22 March, with an aftermath on the following day. Good Friday came immediately afterwards. The approximation is unusually close, but is neither unparalleled nor unsurpassed. For example, as recently as 1921, Purim actually fell on Good Friday itself. There is no need here to go into the causes of this calendrical vagary, with its paradoxical consequence of a Christian Easter which can fall a whole month before its Jewish prototype. It is sufficient to point out that (owing to the attempt of the Council of Niceae to prevent the exact coincidence between the two, or at least to secure that the Jewish celebration should fall after the Christian), Easter Sunday may occur as early as 22 March: while, when there is a supplementary month of Adar intercalated in the Jewish calendar (a device resorted to seven times in every nineteen years) Purim may be as late as 27 March. In consequence, it happens with relative frequency that the traditional Jewish carnival season—the sole occasion for a certain degree of licensed libertinism in the Jewish calendar—can coincide approximately with the most solemn period of the Christian year.

The motif of the Purim festival is familiar. It is the season of the downfall of Haman and the nullification of his knavish devices: and the enmity felt for that unfortunate worthy was symbolically revived year by year and vigorously expressed. Sir James Frazer has made us familiar with the idea that we have here simply a relic of the universally spread conception of the Scapegoat and its accompanying rites.[1] It is certainly the fact that the infliction of exemplary punishment on the effigy of their long-dead adversary was an ancient and almost universal Purim custom among the Jews.

The Roman Emperors Honorius and Theodorius forbade them to burn effigies of Haman "on a cross" at one of their festivals, and a formal abjuration of the practice was formerly obligatory on neophytes in the Greek church.[2] In Mesopotamia, we are informed, at the period which corresponds with the European Dark Ages, "the young men make an effigy of Haman four or five days before Purim, and hang it from the roof. On the day itself, they make a bonfire into which they cast the effigy, while they stand around it jesting and singing. At the same time they hold a ring above the fire and pass it from side to side through the flames."[3]

Similar customs continued to prevail throughout the Middle Ages, and after. Thus, in Italy, the Jewish children used to indulge in a battle of nuts, while the adults rode through the streets tilting at one another with fir branches. The festivities would close with a fanfare of trumpets round a doll or other effigy supposed to represent Haman, which would then be burned with all solemnity at the stake.[4] In Frankfurt am Main, down to a comparatively recent date, it was customary to stage a symbolical conflagration of waxen candles in the form of the villains of the Purim story, which would blaze merrily in the synagogue while the book of Esther was being read.[5]

All of this is not altogether unfamiliar. A point which has hitherto been overlooked—even by the omniscient Frazer—is that sometimes the Purim scapegoat was not necessarily an effigy. We hear of a remarkable episode in Provence, where up to the fourteenth century the Jews enjoyed a high degree of prosperity and autonomy. We are at Manosque, in the spring of 1306. The Jews of the city are indicted before the civil authority on the accusation that "in their presumptuousness, overlooking the respect due to God, and in contempt and dishonor of all Christendom," they had executed summary justice a short while before on one of their coreligionists. A certain Sahat (Saadiah?) described the circumstances. He informed the Court how on the feast called Purim many Jews had flogged naked through their *carrière* one Benedict, son of the Jewess Rassena, in punishment for his having been found with a certain woman. The case was not unique. Another Jew, named Nascassonus, had been treated by the Jews with hardly less contumely, for he was similarly driven through the streets dressed in women's clothes—another license which the Jews permitted themselves, as we know from other sources, only on Purim.[6]

Now, in that particular year, Purim had fallen on 3 March, and Easter exactly a month later. The Jewish ebullience could naturally be ascribed therefore to the prevailing carnival spirit. But, had the two celebrations coincided, matters would have been quite different. It would not have been surprising if, under such circumstances, unsympathetic Gentile observers had suspected that the Jews had simply been engaged in a blasphemous parody of the Passion. On the other hand, it would not have been altogether unnatural had the coarser spirits among the Jews themselves introduced into the proceedings a spirit of mockery of the religion in the name of which they were submitted to daily humiliation and suffering. If this were so, we would have the nucleus of a ritual murder story, centering upon a core of unimpeachable veracity, ready to hand.

Not that exact coincidence of dates was essential for the introduction of this element. Indeed, even in the harmless incident at Manosque, some religious feeling seems to have been aroused. Another case of the sort, with a Christian instead of a Jewish victim, and carried to a grimmer conclusion, took place at Bray, in northern France, in 1191. A certain vassal of the French crown had killed a Jew of the city. The dead man's coreligionists clamored for justice, and obtained permission from their suzerain, the Countess of Champagne, to execute the murderer with their own hands. It happened to be Purim, and the fact suggested to them the foolish idea of a ribald procession, in which their victim, preparatory to meeting his punishment, was to play the part of Haman. According to subsequent accounts (which can hardly be accepted implicitly) they tied his hands behind his back, placed a crown of thorns upon his head, and scourged him through the streets. The report reached the ears of the grasping Philip Augustus, king of France. The latter saw his opportunity. Sending an armed force over the border, he seized upon the Jews and had more than eighty of them burned at the stake (18 March 1191). Only children under thirteen years of age were spared, being apparently forced to embrace Christianity. Among the victims were the famous rabbis Jacob and Isaac of Bray remembered honorably in the annals of Hebrew literature.[7] It is obvious that Philip Augustus's move was motivated in part at least by political reasons; his principal object being to enforce his suzerainty over Champagne. Be that as it may, here is another instance in which the accusation of ritual murder could be raised with a certain degree of foundation, however distorted, in fact.

The same is probably the case with the prototype of the whole series—an episode reported by the fifth-century Church historian, Socrates, as having taken place about the year 415:

Now a little after this the Jews paid the penalty for further lawless acts against the Christians. At Inmestar, a place so-called, which lies between Chalcis and Antioch in Syria, the Jews were in the habit of celebrating certain sports among themselves: and, whereas they habitually did many foolish actions in the course of their sports, they were put beyond themselves [on this occasion] by drunkenness, and began deriding Christians and even Christ himself in their games. They derided the Cross and those who hoped in the Crucified, and they hit upon this plan. They took a Christian child and bound him to a cross and hung him up; and to begin with they mocked and derided him for some time; but after a short space they lost control of themselves, and so ill-treated the child that they killed him.[8]

It is almost universally agreed that this episode, if founded in fact, was merely an outrage committed by some drunken ruffians on the occasion of Purim. However, it is the earliest antecedent for the medieval ritual murder accusation on record, other than the grisly, but entirely academic, allegations made by Apion (Josephus, *Contra Apionem*, II, 8, §95) and

Democritus (as reported by the tenth-century lexicographer Suidas). Subsequent to it, the earliest instance of the allegation that has come down to us dates from more than seven centuries later. The lack of evidence does not conclusively prove, however, that it was not brought up in the meantime. That the general hatred against the Jew expressed itself in the intervening centuries in some grim accusation of the sort is not by any means unlikely. On the other hand, there were certainly some occasions (as we know from the early instances cited above) when the Purim sports, although not carried to an extreme, attracted the suspicions of oversensitive Christians.

It is, however, with the episode of William of Norwich, in 1144, that the continuous history of the ritual murder libel begins. Recent theory maintains that the child had died in a cataleptic fit and was buried alive by his relatives, who endeavored to shield themselves by putting the blame on the Jews. Whether or not this was the case, it must be noticed that many elements of the later blood accusation are missing. The connection with the Passover is only accidental. The day on which the murder was said to have been committed was the Wednesday in Holy Week, 22 March, which happened to be the second day of the Jewish feast. According to the envenomed oration made by the priest Godwin before the Synod, as reported by Thomas of Monmouth, the outrage was so fixed because of the incidence of the day not in the Jewish, but in the Christian calendar ("dominice passionis ebdomada") on which days the Jews were bound to carry out such practices ("ex dierum quibus tale quid a iudaeis fieri debuerit habitudine").[9] The murder of the child was thus in imitation of the Passion, with no ulterior motive. The apostate Theobald of Canterbury similarly asserted (if the account is correct) that every year the Jews "must sacrifice a Christian in some part of the world to the Most High God in scorn and contempt of Christ, that so they might avenge their sufferings on Him," the choice of place being made by a conference of rabbis which assembled at Narbonne; but he did not bring the outrage into connection with

266

the Passover.[10] Similarly neither in his unbalanced account, nor in any other portion of the record, is there any question of the use of the blood for any specific purpose. These two elements, therefore, had not yet made their appearance.

The ghastly accusation was repeated at Gloucester in 1168 before it had time to be imitated outside England. Contemporary records of the episode are vague and scanty. The child in question, one Harold, was reported to have been stolen by the Jews about 21 February, and hidden until 17 March, when he was circumcized (?) and murdered in imitation of the Passion.[11] Nothing is said regarding the customary or ritual nature of such offences. The dates given, however, are significant. That year, Passover fell on 26 March, Good Friday on 29 March; and twelve days before that date it was the Lenten season rather than the period of preparation for the Jewish feast which was most in evidence. However, 21 February approximated closely enough with Purim, which began on 24 February. Is it possible that in this whole story, with its inexplicable gap between the kidnapping of the child and his assassination, we have a ritual murder associated with Purim rather than with Passover, but deferred in execution so as to approximate with the Passion season? Whether this is so or not, the Passover element is lacking. It appears that this began to figure only at a later period, after the close general approximation of that festival with Easter, when the Jews were alleged to imitate the tragedy of the Passion on some helpless Christian (therefore, it may be presumed, a Christian *child*) began to impress the popular imagination.

In all that has preceded, there is nothing of the essential element of the blood accusation, i.e., that the supposed murderers employed the blood (or, for that matter, any part of the body) for some specific purpose, ritual or otherwise. This is, of course, an old conception, consistently advanced against any unpopular person or section of humanity. We meet it in the vampire legend, no less than in the story of Jack the Giant Killer. A typical piece of medieval Jewish folklore read some such motive into the persecutions in ancient Egypt; and, in the old Haggadahs, or Passsover liturgies, printed at

Venice in the seventeenth and eighteenth centuries, one is regaled with a woodcut of the arch-persecutor taking a bath in blood, with the couplet beneath (in Italian, printed in Hebrew characters):

> Faraò si lava con sangue per la lepra guarire;
> Perfino l'acqua si converte in sangue, e lo fa languire . . .

Similarly, in the fifteenth century, it was popularly credited that the transfusion of children's blood had been prescribed to save Pope Innocent VIII in his last illness; the results being fatal to both patient and victim. The person held responsible for this experiment (the first of its kind on record) was, as it happens, the Supreme Pontiff's Jewish body-physician. For it was inevitable that in an age when Jews enjoyed such unpopularity, combined with such renown in medical science, they should be associated with any ridiculous cure which the popular fantasy invented. There was an outstanding instance, in the winter of 1235, when a number of Jews at Fulda, in what is now Hesse Nassau, were put to death on a charge of murdering the five children of a miller living in the vicinity. Under torture, they were said to have confessed the crime, stating that they had committed it to obtain blood for the purpose of healing. It is true that the Emperor Frederick II set on foot an enquiry which completely absolved the Jews of all blame.[12] But the episode serves to show how the use of blood—not, indeed, with any specific religious motive—had become associated with the Jews in the general mind, not withstanding all the inherent improbabilities in the story. Here, then, we have a further component to add to the complex libel which was becoming evolved.

And the precise motive? Thomas of Cantimpré provided it, very shortly after, in his *Bonum Universale de Apibus*, II, 29, §23. In this work he alleged that, ever since the Jews had called out to Pilate, "His blood be on us and on our children" they had been affected with hemorrhoids. They had been informed by a wise man that they could be cured of this only by Christian blood ("solo sanguine Christiano")—i.e., that of the Messiah whom they had rejected. However, they followed this advice with wilful blindness, some congregation in every province slaughtering a Christian each year in order to obtain blood for distribution.

Once the two separate ideas of the systematic use of blood by the Jews for some purpose (the "blood accusation") and an outrage committed by them on the Passover, in mockery of the Passion or otherwise ("ritual murder") had been evolved, it was natural enough to merge the two. The Jews used wine—red wine—for their Paschal meal; they baked preposterous unleavened bread for their Passover fare. Assuredly, the blood must be used for the one or the other! So the popular mentality argued. Thus the various elements came to be combined, and associated essentially with the Passover season, as has continued to be the case to the present time.[13]

The view that the essential condition of the ritual murder was the parody, or imitation, of the Passion upon the person of some helpless Christian[14] child had one curious consequence. The victims were generally revered by the populace as martyrs; and in some instances the Church itself, somewhat unwillingly acquiesced. The cases of "St." William of Norwich, "St." Hugh of Lincoln, "St." Simon of Trent, and *El Santo Niño de La Guardia* immortalized by Lope de Vega will come readily to mind: yet they are only a few out of many. In these cases, there is one detail which appears supremely illogical. A child of perhaps three or four years, as yet unexposed to the trials and temptations of existence, can hardly have had the opportunity to show extraordinary perfection in his daily life. The mere fact that he was put to death at the hands of the Jews would not appear to give him per se a title to the adoration of the faithful, any more than falling in battle against the Saracen did to the average Crusader. If, however, the children were slain, not merely in a spirit of vengefulness or in order to obtain the blood, but as a quasi-religious ceremony in imitation of the Crucifixion, it is obvious that the case was different. Something of the divinity of Jesus himself descended upon the innocent boy (it may be noted, *en passant,* that the victim in early cases was never supposed to be a girl) who had suffered in a ceremonial reenactment of his Passion. Beatification, in the popular heart, at least, was thus a foregone conclusion.

It is thus possible to distinguish the following stages in the growth of the legend:

1. The Jews were considered enemies of the human race, and as such were capable of any crime, including that of murder (Apion, Democritus).
2. The Jews were in fact accustomed to commit in the early Spring, at the Purim season, some contemptuous formality in which an effigy of Haman figured. On occasion, this was transferred to the person of a human being—generally Jewish, exceptionally Christian.
3. This time of year falling very near Holy Week, and sometimes coinciding with it, the procedure was interpreted as an outrage against Christianity. Hence the *ritual* murder accusation (as distinct from that of ordinary murder) came into being.
4. But something more than pointless outrage was demanded by popular logic. An object also was desired. Hence it was suggested, first, that the blood was used for medicinal purposes (Fulda, 1235) or for celebrating the Easter communion (!) (Valréas, 1247).
5. Ultimately, the close coincidence of the Christian Easter and the Jewish Passover brought in another theory—that the blood was used for the celebration of the Passover rites. Subsequently, of course, the period of the year came to be beside the point.

What has just been said is largely in the nature of conjecture: borne out, indeed, by the original sources, but not definitely proved by them. The thesis is based to a large extent on the purely subjective consideration of the essential honesty of the human nature, which does not *invent* so much as *elaborate*. The ritual murder accusation, in its various aspects, has been responsible for untold misery for the Jewish people during the past centuries. That age of martyrdom has not yet passed: so little so, indeed, that a specific case has recently been raised even in the United States of America, that the general allegation has been repeated in an authoritative English work on fifteenth-century Spain, and that a trial based upon it took place not long ago in Czechoslovakia. But I cannot help feeling that the accusation was founded in the first instance, not so much on malice as on misunderstanding, not so much on hatred as on excess of zeal. There is in history that which may perhaps explain the origins of the ghastly libel, though indeed not providing the slightest justification for it. We have, as so often, not the melodrama of a struggle between right and wrong, but a Greek tragedy of a conflict in which both sides are prompted by a sense of justice, and in which even the fundamental error of the one has at its root a genuine misunderstanding. This assuredly makes the drama far more poignant.

Notes

1. Sir James Frazer, *The Golden Bough*, vol. 6, pp. 360ff., 392ff.

2. See the references ibid., pp. 392–93.

3. *Arukh*, s.v. *Shur*.

4. Abrahams, *Jewish Life in the Middle Ages*, ed. C. Roth (2d ed., 1932), p. 402.

5. Schudt, *Jüdische Merckwürdigkeiten*, vol. 2, p. 309.

6. Camille Arnaud, *Essai sur la condition des Juifs en Provence au Moyen-Age* (Forcalquier, 1879), pp. 48–49. For masquerading in female clothes, cf. Abrahams, *Jewish Life*, p. 261. An edict of Childebert referred to by Agobard (*apud* Migne, *Patrologia Latina*, CIV, 84–85), seems to imply that the Jews were accustomed to go in procession through the streets at Easter-tide: this may similarly refer to Purim. For further references which throw some light upon the points under discussion, see now Doniach, *Purim: An Historical Study* (Philadelphia, 1933), pp. 171ff.

7. Gross, *Gallia Judaica*, pp. 123–24.

8. *Historia Ecclesiastica*, VII, §16: cf. Augustus Jessopp and M. R. James, eds., *The Life and Miracles of St. William of Norwich*, pp. lxxii–lxxiii, for the translation here given.

9. Jessopp and James, *St. William of Norwich*, p. 44. The reference of the editors to the Passover Week in their introduction is not borne out by the wording of the text.

10. Ibid., p. 93. Joseph Jacobs, in his masterly article in the *Jewish Encyclopaedia*, vol. 3, pp. 260ff., assumes a reference to the

Passover which is again not justified by the text. It may be mentioned that the use of the same word *Pascha* for the Jewish Passover and for the Christian Easter, is responsible for a great deal of confusion in this respect.

11. See the sources in Jessopp and James, *St. William of Norwich*, pp. lxxiv–lxxv.

12. Graetz, *Geschichte der Juden*, vol. 7, n. 4.

13. The first combined case apparently dates to the middle of the thirteenth century, but in the face of late and confused evidence, it is not easy to tell with certainty. Without wishing to be dogmatic on the subject, in view of the enormous number of cases to be examined before any definite conclusions can be drawn, I am inclined to believe, that in those charges brought up by ecclesiastical authority or by some fanatical cleric the ritual murder motif predominated, whereas in those which resulted from popular prejudice the blood accusation tended to play a more important part. The differentiation between these two quite distinct elements is generally overlooked.

14. In only one medieval case (Majorca, 1435) was the supposed victim a Moslem or a Pagan.

MAGDALENE SCHULTZ

The Blood Libel:
A Motif in the History of Childhood

Another attempt at probing the possible origins of the blood libel legend tries to combine historical and a psychological approaches. Psychohistory, a blend of depth psychology and history, is an interdisciplinary effort to read history anew in the light of modern psychology.

In the present essay, Dr. Magdalene Schultz of Pädagogische Hochschule in Heidelberg looks at the history of blood libel accusations from a different perspective. Inasmuch as the victim of such ritual murders is almost always a small child, Schultz examines the historical record with respect to gauging parental attitudes toward small children. Certainly it is true that child abuse and infanticide have not received the scholarly attention they deserve. Schultz's novel approach does allow the reader to see the blood libel legend in quite a new light.

Investigations into prejudice in general and anti-Semitism in particular have so far not been able to demarcate the specific characteristics of the anti-Jewish blood libel from other and cognate calumnies, and to explain the well-known date of its first appearance. The point of departure of the present study is that, with regard to the blood libel, the child motif is so obviously striking that perhaps the psychohistorical approach is capable of clarifying these characteristics: that is, every child motif in history is a motif in the history of childhood. Starting from medieval accusations against Jews, the

Reprinted from *Journal of Psychohistory* 14 (1986): 1–24.

enquiry brings to light the ties between them and various phases in the history of European childhood. It also shows that the phenomenon is closely connected with how the majority of the population—and the minority within it— treated their own children.

An Overlooked Motif

A superficial perusal of only studies in psychohistory will show that it is one of the gravest problems in the investigation of the history of childhood how and where to unearth pertinent and authentic documents and illustrations older than two or three centuries: the farther one goes back into the past, the poorer and scarcer the sources. While this statement may sound trivial since, after all, it usually holds true for historical research in general, it carries additional weight in historical socialization research, one of whose best attested claims is the lack of interest in children before the seventeenth century, and hence the paucity of references to them.

It is, therefore, the more astonishing that one child motif has to date not been considered, although it is available in writings and drawings throughout the ages: I am referring to the rich literary and pictorial material concerning accusations of ritual infanticide which were raised ever since the founding of the earliest Christian congregations in Rome through the twentieth century:

> In the first centuries c.e. Christians were accused . . . of partaking, for ritual purposes, of the blood and flesh of nonChristians on the occasion of the Feast of Passover (respectively Easter, M.S.). This slander was the cause of extensive cruel persecutions of Christians which did not cease until Christianity had become the official religion of the Roman Empire. In the twelfth century for the first time and subsequently over and over again until most recent times, Jews and conversos, Christians, emperors, and even popes refuted the allegation innumerable times, but without success.[1]

The present enquiry will concentrate on the blood libel trumped up against Jews in the Middle Ages (from 1144 until approximately 1500), but for the sake of completeness some other and later important details will be adduced, too.

Let us begin by looking at the conclusion of a few authorities. In his overview of Jewish history, Heer states that in antiquity the Greeks imputed to the Jews the practice of ritual killing, and that the same libel experienced a revival in the Middle Ages on the eve of the Reformation, and again during the Counter-Reformation.[2] A Jewish source continues the sorry tale: "In the second half of the nineteenth century the slander of ritual murder was criminally used by the infamous (anti-Semites) Desportes and Rohling,"[3] while a historian of anti-Semitism mentions in passing that about two hundred years ago Christian missionaries in China were also held responsible for stealing children, cutting out their hearts and gouging their eyes out for the purpose of concocting charms.[4]

The number of such quotations could be augmented *ad lib* as very many historians have treated the topic. So far, scholars have dealt with it exclusively from the point of view of, and for the purpose of, enquiring into the history of the Jews in general and that of anti-Semitism in particular, whereas the very simple and obvious fact that almost every blood accusation concerned a *child* as the victim was neglected. Such an approach, therefore, can hardly be expected to contribute much to clarifying the origin and background of the child motif involved; how can the usual methods be fruitfully applied to the phenomenon of blood libel if the person figuring so prominently, though terribly, in its center is overlooked? This is where the psychohistorical theory may well play a role by shedding light on the detail discussed here as a part of the history of childhood. To quote one of the outstanding researchers in the field: psychohistory is the application of psychoanalytical and psychological principles to the study of historically significant groups, individuals, and events. Psychohistory aims at an understanding of history that is deeper than what the political and socioeconomic approaches have been capable of offering so far.[5]

275

The second point of departure of psychohistory is the recognition, emphasized by modern psychology, that the sort of care experienced by a person as a child determines the fashion in which he or she interprets in later life the behavior of people, political events, or, in a word, the world.[6]

Explanations Attempted by Anti-Semitism Research

Poliakov offers a number of explanations for the blood libel. According to him, it surfaces as soon as a society is confronted by disturbing and hated strangers.[7] This explanation seems inadequate: xenophobia, after all, may be observed in many periods of history and within the most variegated societies without the corollary of ritual murder accusations. With respect to medieval conditions, he says that one may well assume nascent Christianity not to have felt revengeful against Jews in this way because we do not find any trace of such accusations before the twelfth century. One may, therefore, conjecture that the antagonism originated in this form when it was encouraged by passions released by the Crusades.[8] Yet interpreting medieval anti-Semitism in such general psychological terms is of little use when one wishes to elucidate in what manner the calumny of bloody sacrifices by Jews of Christians differs from the many other accusations brought against them. Poliakov in fact owes the reader an explanation of three essential aspects.

First, he overlooks why the Jews were charged with abusing, mutilating, and killing children and not adults. Neither he nor any of the other authors of treatments of the subject—many of which, like the entry in the *Encyclopaedia Judaica*,[9] are excellent—account for this fact. The current argument that Christians sought to saddle the Jews with reenacting how they had martyred Jesus leaves the question open as to why, if so, they did not lay hands on a man in his thirties, the age at Jesus' crucifixion. Second, Poliakov also fails to establish why in different circumstances and other countries it was the Christians who were found to be guilty of the same crime and no other group. Women, for instance, could have served quite a plausible target if one recalls the ubiquitous witch hunts. Third, Poliakov does not show why blood libels occurred in certain periods and were absent in others.

On this last point, Poliakov has two tentative answers.[10] He surmises, for once, that the ancient legend might have been brought to Europe by the Crusaders on their return from the Orient. Alternatively, it could have arisen, so to say, of its own in the midst of the lower clergy or the monks, who used to remind their audiences in fervent and blood-thirsty sermons of Christ's passion. The listeners, conster-nated, confused, conscience-stricken, and eager to rid them-selves of this burden, projected it onto the Jews.

Poliakov's arguments are not convincing. The first leaves unanswered the question why other legends imported from the Near East did not trigger the same mass hysteria. As to the sermons, they may have intensified the popular view that Jews killed Christian babes, but could hardly have been its origin. Abounding with hate for the Jews and describing them as God-killers, enemies of Christianity, and the like long before the First Crusade, they were doubtless respon-sible for the Crusaders' slaughter of entire Jewish commu-nities in Germany on their route to the Holy Land, but never for the libel of child sacrifice raised against Jews when the Crusaders returned. Still less sufficient is the reference to general xenophobia: when the strangeness of the Jewish cult had first been felt as shocking and later as mysteriously fear-some, all disproof, so Poliakov, became of no avail.[11] If this were correct, then the rich evidence that Jews do not use blood on Passover, that they do not do so at all for ritual pur-poses, that they are expressly forbidden by their Torah even to eat one single drop of it, should have silenced even the fiercest among the accusers. But, unfortunately, the view held by the proponents of the Enlightenment, namely that truthful and rational arguments carry enough weight to dis-perse group prejudices, has proved illusory: people cling to those beliefs against their better knowledge. They do so since prejudices are located in the subconscious, and thus turn into problems precisely because they are inaccessible to the intellect and cannot be revised by it. They frequently originate in projections or transfers for the sake of defense against psychical injuries met in childhood. If a person does not succeed in later life in a realistic treatment of such experiences, the traumatization continues and may easily break through in his or her adult behavior as a projective reaction and thus influence later opinions and actions. But this goes even further. When others hold beliefs that are inimical to us and threaten our views, we often handle this situation by dehumanizing them by projecting onto our enemies all those negative characteristics in ourselves which we find unacceptable. At a certain point, we thus have become good and the enemy evil and vicious, and then the compunction regarding aggressive acts of our own is overcome.

I believe that the accusation of ritual murder is a case in point, and, therefore, see the psychohistorical theory as apposite for analyzing it. At the same time, I shall not overlook the well-known alternative theories advanced by researchers into anti-Semitism: on the contrary, I shall consider them trustworthy enough as a starting point, but I shall also try to complement them where they are at loss how to explain certain eventualities, for instance the specific child aspect of the theme under discussion.

The Psychohistorical Approach: Seven Hypotheses

In the following pages, the following hypotheses will be dealt with:
1. The accusation of ritual murder is a specific motif in the history of childhood, i.e., it is related to the treatment of children at given periods of history.
2. The accusation appears as a mass phenomenon whenever the treatment of children by the majority of the population is characterized by lack of care and understanding for a child's well-being and value.
3. It emerges when a new sensitivity for, and a new interest in, children is developing; in other words, when a new period is opening in the history of childhood. Killing a child

is bound to release a general demand to punish the killer as well as feelings of revenge only on the condition that the act is viewed by the public as a heinous crime.

4. This new sensitivity must have entered the consciousness of all strata of the population, especially the lower ones.

5. When the population is confronted with a minority the children of which enjoy higher esteem, guilt feelings develop within the majority which must be warded off. This is then effected through projection upon another group in relation to which one feels inferior in this respect.

6. Ritual murder is laid to the charge of a minority group which has formerly been cruelly wronged.

7. The projective character of the accusations is borne out by a typical behavior scheme consisting preponderantly of elements going back to not yet untangled childhood problems.

Let us now focus our interest on psychohistorical circumstances and ways of enquiry. Information about the legal treatment of these circumstances and their assessment may be looked up in the professional literature.[12]

Hypothesis 1: The Accusation of Ritual Murder —A Specific Motif in the History of Childhood

The nexus between the accusation and the child motif is so close and unambiguous that the denial up till now of the almost stringent association between the two can be understood only in itself as a sort of "warding off" on the part of the researcher as pointed out by Ende.[13] Further, it may not be impossible for the psychohistorical interpretation to clear up several patterns in which the course of ritual murder campaigns differs from pogroms erupting in the wake of alleged poisoning of wells and desecrating the Holy Host. One thus seems to be entitled to presume that here is a case of exactly what is depicted on the numerous period illustrations of Jews killing a Christian child: the relationship of Christians to Jews and the respective treatment of their children.

279

Hypothesis 2: Lack of Care on the Part of the Masses for the Child's Well-Being

It was when I searched for material regarding the concept of childhood among Jews, particularly within medieval Jewish society in Europe,[14] that I came across the topic of ritual murder and that it occurred to me to approach it from the point of view of psychohistory as persecutions of Jews, sparked off by this charge, which seemed to follow each other without cease. Upon reading descriptions thereof and files of juridical proceedings against the alleged perpetrators of the crime, I believe that an overall pattern became evident of how the mob incitements against Jews began.

The first case recorded in Germany, in Fulda in 1235, started as follows: "On Christmas, five boys, the children of a miller who lived beyond the town gate and who at the time attended church service together with his wife, perished miserably and their blood was collected for remedy . . . in wax-soaked pouches and their house set aflame."[15] This cannot but mean that the children were left alone and that their parents were held responsible for the accident that happened during their absence. If so, it constitutes a telling piece of evidence in favor of one of the most horrifying conclusions of historical socialization research, namely that lack of supervision of children was the rule in past centuries and that innumerable casualties were caused in this way (see ill. 1). How well founded this conclusion is emanates from a number of quotations taken from the protocols of ritual murder trials, all of which confirm that it was quite customary for parents to leave their children alone and unattended and to abandon them to their fate.

The first case of a ritual murder charge at all occurred in Norwich, England, in 1144: "When the corpse of a young apprentice was detected in a copse on Good Friday."[16] Only three years later, in 1147, in Würzburg, Germany, "the corpse of a Christian was found in the River Main . . . during a sermon calling people to join the Second Crusade."[17] The following are excerpts of various proceedings:

". . . a corpse was found" (Lauda, Germany, 1235).[18]

Symbolic representation of mishaps befalling a child by defenestration, a fall into a well, and death at the hands of a warrior. Woodcut by the Master of the Mirror of Consolation. Sixteenth century. From H. Boesch, *Kinderleben in der deutschen Vergangenheit* (Leipzig, 1900).

"In the well of a house belonging to the Jew Jopin . . . the corpse of an eight-year-old boy was found" (Lincoln, England, 1255).[19] "The corpse of a seven-year-old girl was found in the water." According to another (Christian) version, Jews had bought the child from an old Christian woman, which shows that the idea of a woman selling her child did not seem implausible at that time (Pforzheim, Germany, 1267).[20]

". . . the Jews were expelled under the pretext of having caused the disappearance of a little boy" (Berne, Switzerland, 1294).[21]

". . . in March, a boy was lost to his parents and was a few days later discovered dead in a well" (Überlingen, Germany, 1331).[22]

"Near the Kaiserstuhl, a family of beggars with two small boys asked in vain for overnight quarters until the wife of

281

Rabbi Elias offered them a barn for lodging. There, the children disappeared without leaving a trace, but their dead bodies were discovered there eight years later" (Endingen, Germany, 1462).[23]

"During the Holy Week, Little Simon, the Child of a tanner, met with a deadly accident" (Trent, Italy, 1475).[24]

"Henri Beil, a local shoemaker, had killed his stepchild. When arrested on his flight to Hanau, he admitted to the crime, adding, however, that he had brought the child's blood to a Frankfurt Jew named Gomchin upon which the latter was arrested together with one of his coreligionists" (Frankfurt, Germany, 1504).[25]

It is hard to mistake the above instances for anything else than attempts by those entrusted with a child's life and welfare to free themselves from guilt feelings and to escape punishment by means of projecting their own unpardonable conduct upon a minority. Thus, the report about the boy's body recovered from a well in Überlingen admits with much frankness that "the parents ran through the town and tried with loud shouts to incite the burghers against the Jews."[26]

As early as 1272 Pope Gregory VIII himself reprimanded Christendom in an encyclical for such excesses as follows:

> It happens occasionally that Christians lose their children and that enemies of the Jews charge the latter with having kidnapped or killed them in order to use their hearts and blood for sacrifice. Moreover, it also came to pass that parents hid their children and afterwards inculpate Jews for their disappearance so as to extort from them a certain amount of money for ransom. These things happen under the completely false pretence that the children were abducted and murdered by Jews, whereas, as is well-known, their laws clearly and universally forbid them to make blood sacrifices or to eat or drink blood.[27]

Hypotheses 3 and 4: A New Sensitivity Regarding Children and Their Rights

Precisely such a new phase was introduced in ancient Roman society when it met with Christianity. Deliberately exposing children to death and killing them was neither unusual nor

282

punishable in ancient Greek and Roman societies, but rather condoned or even recommended by thinkers such as Seneca and Plinius, until "a decisive change set in . . . with the rise of Christianity."[28] An analogous contrast existed between Greeks and Jews,[29] and it was no lesser a personage than Philo of Alexandria, the Jewish-Hellenistic philosopher, who more than anybody else used his authority for eradicating infanticide. Christianity's merit is to have inculcated the ancient world with the notion of human life being sacrosanct, a stance hitherto endorsed, if at all in antiquity, by a limited number of philosophers only. In the course of time, it permeated the consciousness of the plebs, of which early Christians in Rome, many of whom were slaves, were part. And when "ordinary" Romans encountered these new behavior orientations within their own day-to-day life framework, a reevaluation of their own practices must have taken place. A similar change of mind might have taken place in China, too, where infanticide was widely spread until it met, in the nineteenth century, the severe censure of Christian missionaries, and finally, through them, general opprobrium.[30]

When public opinion reaches such a stage, a weak minority becomes the best-suited object of projection: punishing it proves both one's own innocence as well as one's laudable insistence on justice being done. In consequence, and in accordance with what, psychologically speaking, may have been foreseen, the claim that Christians sacrificed children relapsed into silence when Christianity was proclaimed the religion of the Roman Empire. Keeping guilt feelings at bay through projecting the wicked deed on ruling circles would not only have been of very little relief, but would much rather have involved great risks for people of inferior political and religious status.

Moving ahead nine centuries, what was the situation in Central Europe around 1200 when blood libels were raised there against Jews for the first time? Research in historical socialization is quite poor in this respect. Among the few who contributed remarkably to it is Ariès with his studies in iconography. The data mentioned by him indeed substantiate the above hypothesis. After discussing how children were depicted in the Romanesque period, mostly in connection with biblical stories, he arrives at the conclusion that people living in the tenth and eleventh centuries paid little attention to the image of childhood which did not represent any reality to them.[31] He discerns a turn of affairs around the beginning of the thirteenth century: society's attitude to children must, therefore, have undergone a definite change between 1100 and 1200 so that from then on there existed several types of children, types which somewhat correspond to modern feelings.[32]

What did these "new" children look like? They are, as Ariès states, youthful angels and church attendants of different ages, starting from that of three years with the oldest ones being "big boys." Now it is surely impossible not to be struck by the observation that the alleged victims of Jewish blood sacrifices belonged exactly to the same age group: they were the first to be seen in the new light. Girls were only infrequently the purported victims and even more rarely were Jews said to have killed babies. On the contrary, most of those said to have been immolated had already been weaned and attained a certain independence. Children of this age are harder to supervise, which made the option of attributing to Jewish neighbors a mishap caused by the parents' negligence and resulting in death the more welcome.

Now, a similarly altered attitude can also be found in another subject in painting, namely Mary with the infant Jesus. Ariès draws attention to the fact that formerly Jesus was depicted as an adult in reduced size. Quite soon, though, artists chose to represent him with more empathy and realism. Thus, on a miniature of the second half of the twelfth century he is a little boy, standing and wearing a light and almost transparent shirt and embracing his mother's neck with both arms and holding her tight, cheek to cheek.[33] It may give the impression that this conception of Jesus contradicts what had been said above: that on paintings boys looked like three-year old choristers. The impression is erroneous. First, these "new" paintings of the Holy Virgin do in fact support the thesis that the mother-child relation had taken on a new ideal. Second, they imply more and more the responsibility of a mother for her child to such a degree that ritual killing of small children, if it had been committed at all, would invariably have been ascribed to the mother's lack of care and watchfulness.

Hypothesis 5: Confrontation with a "Better" Education

In the light of this hypothesis it is necessary to probe whether Jewish children in the Middle Ages were valued more highly and received more intense interest than those in Christian families. The answer depends on further research. Nevertheless, there are certain indications which already permit giving a tentatively affirmative answer. A number of circumstances make it quite probable that Jewish children were at least somehow better guarded from physical danger, though perhaps not treated with more empathy. For the time being— and until the problem under discussion is exhaustively investigated—let us enumerate several reasons for the above assumption. First, statistics from the beginning of demography prove that infant mortality among Jews was lower in Europe than among the non-Jewish population, even in the poorest and most crowded Jewish quarters. Second, illegitimate children enjoyed the same status as legitimate ones, and in any event their number was rather small. The history of childhood in Christian society shows that illegitimate children were its most neglected and ill-treated members. Third, it stands to reason that Jews were more careful than their neighbors in passing their children on to wet-nurses. Christians, especially in France, felt no compunction in committing their babies to wet-nurses far away in the countryside, which obviously must have drastically diminished the children's chance of survival. Fourth, children's furniture, such as benches and reading desks, existed in synagogues long before they were found in Christian localities. Fifth, the family fulfilled a much higher function and was, therefore, of greater significance, partly on religious grounds, partly because, aside from ready cash, it provided the only protection whenever one of the regularly occurring expulsions was decreed on a Jewish community. Sixth, respect for learning was greatly developed even among Jewish "simple folk" centuries before it came into existence among the same population-layer outside Jewish society. This cannot but have had a positive impact on the concept of childhood. And last, Jewish codes of behavior view a contribution to education and instruction as a more praiseworthy and pious undertaking than the erection of a synagogue.[34]

Hypothesis 6: Pogroms Are Preconditions for Blood Libels

The modern reader must first of all free himself of the notion that the Middle Ages were in the main an amorphous conglomerate of wars, superstitions, witch hunts, and religious schisms. He must try to disentangle the crowd of disjoined and nevertheless apparently senselessly joined facts into differentiated elements, and recognize the trace leading from one event to the other, from one psychological crisis to the next, and from one mass reaction to the following. The crucial *caesura* in the history of the Christian-Jewish symbiosis in the Middle Ages was the First Crusade. With it came to an end "that comparatively best state reached in the Middle Ages of free and in any case not massively and permanently impaired contact between a Christian majority and a Jewish (Ashkenazi) minority."[35]

In response to the call of Pope Urban II in 1095, the nuclei of Crusader armies assembled at various places in the West and marched east through Central Europe in order to liberate the Holy Land from the yoke of the Infidels. On their way, they annihilated Jewish communities wherever they met them. Their motives are defined by a historian as follows: "Both from one Christian and several Jewish reports . . . we learn of the Crusaders' reasoning for killing the Jews: to them it was incomprehensible why the Muslims should be fought and the Jews in France and Germany whom they regarded as God-murderers and much worse enemies of Christendom be spared. 'Let us begin with the Jews!' was the battle cry of the Crusaders when they asked the Jews to choose between baptism and death."[36] These wholesale massacres were the first committed by Christians against

Jews, yet their effects surpassed the physical extinction of the greater part of mid-European Jewry. In Güdemann's opinion, "the moral consequences of the violence endured destroyed a whole series of generations and their martyrology extends over centuries. It is no exaggeration to claim that these moral consequences last until our own time."[37]

The sad turning point led to a social and economic structure in which the position of the Jews had completely changed. More important perhaps, the self-image of both Christians and Jews had deeply changed, too, as well as their image of each other. This again induced either side to develop mutually deliminating tendencies such as had not been known before. No wonder that this recently strengthened Christian-Jewish antagonism disclosed itself fiercely and at once with the start of the Second Crusade (1147), the one much less characterized by the initiative and perhaps also the participation of the gentry. Güdemann thinks that "the atrocities of the First Crusade must have brought about, especially in the lower strata, much brutality and blunted all noble feeling."[38] His view is certainly well founded: if aggressions of such dimensions receive reenforcement and assent through impunity, worse may be expected in the future. And this is precisely what happened in the Second Crusade and lends additional force to the present argument: "Ever more accusations were raised against Jews for having evil designs on Christian lives. Maybe here one can speak of a projection inasmuch as one's own hate-feelings were imputed to the Jews. Yet it would have been only natural, after all the wrong done to them, to expect from Jews the most hostile attitude imaginable."[39]

It is, therefore, not a matter of chance that ritual murder accusations appeared after the First Crusade and not before it: the mass killings were the precondition for the need of projection and for the fear of reprisals. Incidentally, the persecutions of Christians by the Romans and the Chinese were also accompanied, and followed by, blood libels which makes the claim of a psychological nexus between the two phenomena the more persuasive. By contrast, in the slaughter of the First Crusade, there was little need for drawing an analogy between one's own behavior and that of the Jews: identifying contemporary Jews of any generation with the "Christ-killers" who lived one or two millennia earlier suffices to justify their punishment—with the Church condoning and consenting.

Hypothesis 7: The Projective Character of the Accusations

What distinguishes between the blood libel and all other accusations trumped up against Jews? Of the four principal ones, usury, poisoning of wells, desecration of the Sacrament, and ritual murder, the last is the farthest away from reality and the one most determined by projections. While there exist undeniable clues for the practice by Jews of usury,[40] the first charge was only tenuously and indirectly contiguous with prevailing conditions. In regard of the second, although it was never possible to prove that Jews tinkered with the water supply, Christians could not help noticing that Jews were excessively and incomprehensibly painstaking with the water they used. For instance, they never visited public baths, either because they were not admitted to them or because mixed bathing (which was quite customary) was forbidden to them by their religion; they also refrained from other uses of available water, among various reasons because water intended for the ritual immersion of women had to fulfill certain requirements. When Jews were seen scrupulously watching their own supply while preparing their kitchen and table utensils for Passover, their fuss about a simple commodity first puzzled non-Jews and was soon prone to raise suspicion and fear, particularly because for all these reasons Jews guarded their wells and cisterns most carefully.[41] The relation between the desecration of the Holy Wafer and reality is still more feeble inasmuch as it referred to a very ancient event, the crucifixion: Jews were supposed, in order to re-perform how they killed Christ, to steal the wafer and pierce it with knives until blood dropped from it.

Thus, concerning these three accusations, there might have been some extremely weak and farfetched cause observable in Jewish life or read about in the New Testament for breeding them. The charge of ritual murder, though, is not only totally disengaged from all reality, but, in addition, stands in absolute contrast to it. If there is anything in Judaism and within Jewry wholly unusable from the ritual point of view it is any sort of animal, and *a fortiori* human, blood. A central part of the Jewish dietary laws (kasherut) enjoins strict avoidance of blood and one of the requirements of making meat fit for consumption is that all blood be removed from it. Still more and stiffer dietary laws are in force during Passover, a fact, however, apt to have stimulated still stronger mistrust in this season.

The case in Rome against Christians, just as absurd as the one in Germany against Jews, nonetheless rested on slightly more understandable associations for spreading malicious rumors. Christians were known to believe in their redemption through the blood of a man whom they regarded as their God and savior and to remember with much fervor his passion on Good Friday. Moreover, their worship on Christmas centered around a child. Finally, because for the first three centuries Christianity was proscribed in Rome, congregations had to assemble for service in hiding in subterranean catacombs which might easily have increased the fears of non-Christians. Not so the Jews: it is true that in the story of the exodus from Egypt, the anniversary of which is celebrated on Passover, the Israelites had to touch their lintels and doorposts with a lamb's blood so that the "Angel of the Lord," about to destroy the Egyptian oppressors, would "pass over" their own houses. However, it is Jewish tradition going back thousands of years that this ceremony was to be performed exclusively on the eve of the exodus and was not to be repeated ever since. Also, the life of the Jewish community, its religious service, its studies and business, and also all sessions of its rabbinical court took place in the open, in full daylight and mostly in the synagogues, which were for the most part situated right in the town center. Nothing else can underline in stronger terms the purely projective character of the blood libel.

To properly conceive of this projective nature of this ac-

cusation and to permit its analysis, it seems profitable to define the ever-recurring stages of the blood libel campaigns.[42]
They were:

1. Around Easter (or, occasionally, on other Christian religious festivals)
2. a *dead body is found*
3. of a *boy.*
4. Jews are *immediately* accused of killing him,
5. but they deny the charge.
6. The *authorities* are *not consulted*/express disbelief/try
   to protect the Jews,
7. but a lower cleric *whips up the mob's frenzy* by means of
   anti-Jewish sermons and represents the *vox populi* before the authorities.
8. Proof is brought through evidence by *renegades* (baptized Jews) of the *use of blood for Passover ritual* and
   through a *miracle* whereupon
9. the Jews are *tortured.*
10. They never/rarely admit to their guilt, and if so, elderly
    people only, women or children do so.
11. The *entire community is then condemned* to death or
    expulsion,
12. its property is confiscated
13. with the authorities participating in apportioning the
    spoils
14. and the murdered child is paid deep *reverence as a
    martyr.*

There is hardly one single constituent in this scheme that
would not refer, beyond the dry facts, to a suppressed energy
potential. To corroborate this assertion, those steps, the potential of which allows one to surmise for them an origin in
early childhood experiences and an attempt at overcoming
the latter, are italicized as childhood specifying elements.
Persons involved may of course go through them from the
standpoint of adults as well as of children.

A few observations are in place with respect to the
above list.

ad 2: For the connection between the stimulus for the ritual

murder accusation and the contemporary educational praxis,
see under Hypothesis 2.

ad 3: The higher esteem enjoyed by male offspring may account for the greater grief felt on the occasion of a boy's
death than on that of a girl. In Christian hagiography, too,
boys figure much more prominently than girls. In any case,
girls could not have met with fewer accidents for they were
probably treated with even less alertness than boys.

ad 4: That Jews were immediately inculpated is not hard to
explain: their image as the enemy *par excellence,* preached
for centuries, had prepared the ground. The undistanced
emotional overreaction against them demonstrates imma-
turity and is therefore another proof of an action which is
rooted in infancy.

ad 6: This stage recalls the behavior of children who wish to
conceal a transgression from their parents. In many cases
the population preferred never to lodge a complaint with the
authorities and instead lynched the suspects on the spot and
at once.[43] We learn from various reports that the spiritual
and temporal authorities, while convinced of the Jews' innocence, were unwilling or too weak to assert themselves
against the fanatical rabble, particularly when the lower
clergy supported the outrage. What happened in Norwich, as
described by Dubnov, is typical.[44]

ad 7: It is again the infantile level ("being under age") that
explains how easy it was to influence the populace to take to
violence.

ad 8: Having recourse to signs lacking reality and to lies—
see Hypothesis 7—represents a denial of the reality principle, another infantile, or imaginary, way out of a conflict.
Here are two examples:

> Upon the complaint of a fisherman, the corpse was laid down
> on a river bank in the presence of Rudolphe I, margrave of
> Baden. It was recognized that the girl must have been mur-
> dered. And now, a miracle happened: the dead body rose, ex-
> tended its hand to the margrave and then sank again down to
> the ground. Those present understood at once that the dead

child wished by this strange conduct to demand expiration of the wicked deed committed against it. Suspicion fell promptly on the Jews.[45]

The corpse was carried to the house of the Jews where its wounds began to bleed again. This persuaded the citizenry of the guilt of the Jews."[46]

ad 9: Many modern investigations show that parents who batter their children were battered children themselves. This refers not only to the attitude within the family toward corporal punishment as a means of education, but also to whether such measures were admissible and justified in general. Fromm elaborates the point in his reflections on maternal love: "A woman can be a truly loving mother only if she can love; if she is able to love her husband, other children, strangers, all human beings. The woman who is not capable of love in this sense . . . is never a truly loving mother."[47]

ad 11: In practically all cases the punishment was not meted out on the one person allegedly guilty, but on the entire group of which he was a member:

"All members of the Jewish community. . . ."[48]
"All Jews were chased away."[49]
"All Jews were burnt in their synagogue."[50]
"Several Jews were broken on the wheel, others hanged."[51]
"Some were burnt at the stake, some baptized."
"Three were ground and burnt, the rest expelled."[52]

The disproportion between a crime purported to have been committed and which, if committed, may have cost one single life, and the punishment once more attests to the projective character mentioned: what is at stake is not the triumph of justice but working off juvenile feelings of inadequacy, impotence, and revenge.

ad 14: Examples for the elevation of the dead child to the rank of a martyr abound. Two, Simon of Trent and Werner of Bacharach were beatified, the coffin of the little girl of Pforzheim is preserved in the castle church, Norwich became a place of pilgrimage, Berne erected a "Childeater's

Well," and in Endingen a "Judenspiel" was performed for a very long time.

What is so arresting about the incidents described when seen within the context of the history of childhood is the inequality between the value rank attributed to the children once they were "killed" and the rank and everyday treatment accorded to their living contemporaries. By way of *pars pro toto*, people appear to have expiated their actual behavior toward children through confirming in public the children's right to attention and through punishing comparable faults of omission on others. By ostentatiously taking the part of the bereaved family, one diverts with much ease any reproach from oneself.

A different sort of projection finds its expression in a woodcut depicting the murder of Simon of Trent (Nuremberg, 1494; see ill. 2). Of the four injuries suffered by the boy, only one is inflicted upon him with a knife, his blood being collected in a dish: the wound is on his penis. The purpose that suggests itself is clear: to remind the viewer of circumcision, to hint at its violent performance on an innocent Christian babe, and to associate it with the uncounted forcible baptisms. Even less wonder that in blood libels most of the alleged victims were males: how relieving it is to project one's own reprehensible doings on a helpless and guiltless minority. This interpretation finds further support in many other contemporary pictorial materials. Among them are illustrations 3 and 4, where the fixation upon circumcision manifests itself particularly by the stress upon the utensils necessary for performing the operation.

Two more elements of the listed pattern deserve some attention, although they are not explicitly childhood-specific. That Jewish property was confiscated on the occasion of pogroms, either as their side effect or their purpose, is so well known that it need not be discussed here. The dates, however, when the pogroms happened are different. Without going into the details of every single instance of the long register of blood libels in the Middle Ages, it may be stated with much certainty—since most cases are well documented— that the "killings" occurred most frequently on Christian

Murder of the child Simon of Trent. Woodcut by Wohlgemuth. From G. Liebe, *Das Judentum in der deutschen Vergangenheit* (Leipzig, 1903).

religious holidays or on other ecclesiastical occasions. It makes sense that they "happened to happen" on Easter because this festival often (but never fully) coincides with Passover when, as rumor had it, Jews were more than ever in need of blood for their occult ceremonies. Yet data concerning ostensible killings on Christmas after a sermon had been delivered to recruit volunteers for the Second Crusade [53] indi-

Colored woodcut, Germany, c. 1475. From I. Shahar, *The Judensau* (London, 1979).

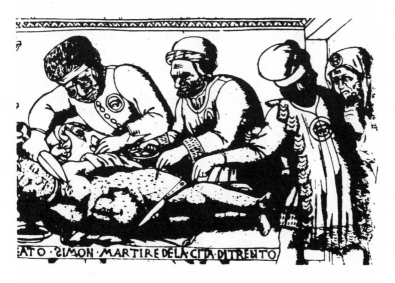

Engraving, probably from Florence, c. 1475–1485. From I. Shahar, *The Judensau* (London, 1979).

cate that the matter was not so simple. Thus, Haverkamp pointed out in a detailed enquiry that attacks on Jews used to fall on certain days of the week.[54] Can it be a chance effect that these days coincided with ecclesiastical events? It surely makes better sense to ascribe this peculiarity to local clerics and their sermons delivered from pulpits on these days in order to instigate the listeners against the Jews. The names of a number of these preachers are actually on record. When, for instance during the Passion Week, the audience's anti-Jewish mood had been inflamed, city councils such as that of Frankfurt am Main decided they had better lock up the ghetto for a couple of days for the Jews' protection from the violence of the masses.

The Jewish Reaction

How did the Jews react to the terrible hardships they had to suffer? Among the many dirges, legends, execrations, and other ways by means of which they tried to take a stand vis-à-vis their martyrdom,[55] one only, as far as I have been able to ascertain, stands in direct contact with the blood libel—and with the child motif as well. In many editions of the so-called *Haggada*, a Hebrew booklet recited by Jews at their domestic Passover ceremony and meal, illustrations (see ill. 5) can be found of the Egyptian Pharaoh sitting in a tub while Egyptian soldiers are killing Hebrew babes. It is an allusion to an ancient Jewish legend[56] which relates that Pharaoh had contracted leprosy and had been advised by his courtiers to bathe twice daily in the blood of 150 Hebrew babes to find a cure for his affliction. "One may well see in such pictures a reply by medieval Jews to the blood libel,"[57] an interpretation which is fully convincing: to assign the true responsibility for the afflictions of the Jews to the Christians would have been fatal; but to portray Pharaoh—the symbol of oppression—as the perpetrator thirsting for the blood of Jewish children provided some relief. It drew attention to an evil, and was yet unobtrusive.

Yahuda Haggadah, Germany (South), 1450–1500, fol. 13, Israel Museum Jerusalem. From *Index of Jewish Art*, 1978/3/68.

The Revival of the Accusation

Since the history of Jewish childhood, the research project which the present article is part of, covers only the Middle Ages, I shall not touch upon blood libels of a later period except in passing. Among them no little support is found for the hypotheses submitted so far. Let two examples stand for many others.

A boy by the name of Anderl was said to have been murdered by the Jews of Rinn (Austria). He was canonized in 1755, three centuries after his martyrdom. How can bestowing this honor at so late a date be understood psychohistorically? Was it a direct attempt at indirectly resurrecting an old lie? And why was it bestowed upon the poor child exactly at that time and not before? Heer's view is that the year 1755 was exceptionally critical for European Christendom:

the foundations of Catholic and Protestant belief in Providence were severely shaken when it became known that the earthquake in Lisbon took the lives of many women and children.[58]

The same decade saw another turn in the world of ideas and sentiments in Europe: Elisabeth Badinter dates this as the juncture of a new attitude of mothers to their children, in precisely 1760. According to her own words, it may surprise one that she gives such an exact date for the change having come about, as if everything had taken a different course in a single year, when Ariès has shown that it took a long time for a feeling to develop and strike root. The royalist society of the seventeenth century had not yet acknowledged the reign of the child-king, the center of the family world. But the reign of the child began loudly to be celebrated in the rising population layers of the eighteenth century, especially from the years 1760–70 on.[59]

The change observed by Badinter seemed this time to have affected the higher, or a better term is, the rising classes. This notion, though, stands in contrast to the assertion made under Hypothesis 4, that the new understanding of children had become finally noticeable on the other end of the social spectrum before a group was accused of having harmed an infant or youth. Yet this contradiction is only an apparent one: the recent accusation was not new, but rather one resuscitated and taken up again by the better situated. The clergy, competent of issuing encyclicals and similar decrees, may surely be counted among these. A further coincidence corroborates this impression: the reference to the earthquake and its numerous young victims. The new attitude toward a child's life, it is true, had at that time not yet permeated the peasantry and parallel parts of the population. All the same, considerations like *la raison d'état* had already sensitized the gentry in regard to the life of the individual. Badinter adduces another characteristic for 1760: the issue was now to produce human beings so that the state's wealth might increase. For this purpose, wasting human material had to be avoided at any cost: children must remain alive. The state was now interested in those who were formerly left to perish and strove to preserve them from death.[60]

Another phase in the history of childhood was reached in the nineteenth century. The idea of childhood as a social age *sui generis* had finally pervaded all strata. Historian Edward Shorter sets the date for this turning point at 1850,[61] when, perhaps not so surprisingly any longer, a new wave of blood libels occurred; the most notorious of them were those prompted by Desportes and Rohling.[62] (It would be a rewarding task to find out how these two were treated by their own parents.)

Be it as it may, many more important aims than the one just proposed remain to be pursued in this field of childhood history. A revision is needed of the course taken by the typical medieval blood libel in the light of the revival it experienced in later periods, when, as an additional variable, the religious allegiance of the accusers to the Catholic and Protestant Churches, respectively, must be taken into account. For the time being, the impression is gained that the phenomenon remained restricted within Catholic countries: one meets canonizations and expressions such as "the Baroque of the Counter-Reformation," a list of "Ritual Killings" which was printed in *Civiltà Cattolica* in 1881 and in *Osservatore Romano* in 1892; a manifest on the subject was published by English Catholic circles in 1901; Desportes was a monk and Rohling a canon.[63] These references are interesting insofar as the difference between the educational patterns of the two main branches of Christianity, as realized in their respective geographical regions, are well documented. It might be instructive for the history of childhood in general and of the blood libel in particular to follow up the seven hypotheses mentioned to see if and how they correspond with denominational differences.

The least to be concluded from the foregoing discussion is that every child motif in history is a motif in the history of childhood and that it cannot satisfactorily be interpreted unless the ways of how children were treated at given times are reckoned with.

Notes

All translations from German by the author.

1. G. Herlitz and Br. Kirschner, eds., *Jüdisches Lexikon*, (Berlin, 1927), vol. 1, col. 1085.

2. Fr. Heer, *Gottes erste Liebe: Die Juden im Spannungsfeld der Geschichte*, 2d ed. (Berlin, 1981), p. 109. Cf. English translation, *God's First Love* (London, 1970).

3. See n. 1.

4. L. Poliakov, *Geschichte des Antisemitismus*, vol. 1: *Von der Antike bis zu den Kreuzzügen*, 2d ed. (Worms, 1979), p. 49. Cf. English translation, *History of Antisemitism* (London, 1974).

5. A. Ende, "Geschichte und Kindheit: Über den gegenwärtigen Stand der Psychohistorie," *Kindheit* 2 (1980): 135–45, esp. p. 135. This approach is cognate to that of the "History of Mentality," which focuses on human attitudes towards, and ways of mental processing of, historical events during a given period. Cf. F. Graus, "Historische Traditionen über Juden im Spätmittelalter (Mitteleuropa)" in *Zur Geschichte der Juden im Deutschland des späten Mittelalters und der frühen Neuzeit*, ed. A. Haverkamp, Monographien zur Geschichte des Mittelalters, vol. 24) (Stuttgart, 1981), pp. 1–26, esp. p. 2.

6. L. DeMause, *Über die Geschichte der Kindheit* (Frankfurt am Main, 1979), pp. 117f.

7. Poliakov, *Geschichte des Antisemitismus*.

8. Ibid.

9. *Encyclopaedia Judaica*, ed. C. Roth et al. (Jerusalem, 1971), vol. 4, cols. 1120–31. The author of the entry is Yehuda Slutzky.

10. Poliakov, *Geschichte des Antisemitismus*, p. 51.

11. W. Eckert, "Zum Wert der bildlichen Darstellung als Geschichtsquelle: Überlegungen zur Ikonographie der Juden im Mittelalter" in *Juden in Deutschland: Zur Geschichte einer Hoffnung. Historische Längsschnitte und Einzelstudien*, ed. P. v. Osten-Sacken (Berlin, 1980), pp. 115–26, esp. p. 120.

12. See n. 1; Heer, *Gottes erste Liebe*, pp. 606–7; Graus, "Historische Traditionen," p. 17, n. 84 (see n. 5).

13. Ende, "Geschichte und Kindheit," p. 137.

14. This enquiry (still unpublished) concerns Jewish childhood in Central Europe from the Middle Ages until the Emancipation.

15. J. Aronius, *Regesten zur Geschichte der Juden im fränkischen und deutschen Reiche bis zum Jahre 1273* (Hildesheim and New York, 1970), p. 207 (no. 474).

16. Poliakov, *Geschichte des Antisemitismus*, p. 50.

17. Ibid.

18. B. Rosenthal, *Heimatgeschichte der badischen Juden seit ihrem geschichtlichen Auftreten bis zur Gegenwart* (Buhl, 1927; rpt. Mamstadt-Stuttgart, 1980), p. 12.

19. *Jüdisches Lexikon* (see n. 1), vol. 2, col. 1048.

20. Rosenthal, *Heimatgeschichte*, p. 14.

21. Poliakov, *Geschichte des Antisemitismus*, p. 54.

22. Rosenthal, *Heimatgeschichte*, p. 13.

23. Ibid., p. 15.

24. Eckert, "Zum Wert der bildlichen Darstellung," p. 120.

25. T. Krakauer, *Geschichte der Juden in Frankfurt am Main* (Frankfurt, 1927), 2:246ff.

26. Rosenthal, *Heimatgeschichte*, p. 13.

27. Encyclica of 7 October 1272, quoted from Poliakov, *Geschichte des Antisemitismus*, p. 68.

28. W. L. Langer, "Infanticide: A Historical Survey," *History of Childhood Quarterly, Journal of Psychohistory* 1, no. 3 (1974): 353.

29. J. C. Sommerville, *The Rise and Fall of Childhood* (London and New Delhi, 1982), p. 35.

30. Interestingly enough, P. Ariès speaks in one breath of the "insensitivity of the Roman and Chinese societies who practised exposure of children"; *Geschichte der Kindheit*, 3d ed. (Munich, 1980), p. 99. Cf. *Centuries of Childhood*, trans. from French by R. Baldick (New York, 1962).

31. Ibid., p. 93. This change in the attitude towards children is confirmed by Mary Martin McLaughlin in "Überlebende und Stellvertreter: Kinder and Eltern zwischen dem neunten und dreizehnten Jahrhundert," in *Hört ihr die Kinder weinen*, ed. Lloyd deMause (Frankfurt, 1977), p. 202. Cf. English translation, *The History of Childhood* (New York, 1974).

32. Ibid., p. 94.

33. Ibid.

34. M. Güdemann, *Geschichte des Erziehungswesens und der Cultur der Juden in Frankreich und Deutschland* (Vienna, 1880; rpt. Amsterdam, 1966), 1:117.

35. D. Mertens, "Christen und Juden in Deutschland zur Zeit des ersten Kreuzzugs," in *Die Juden als Minderheit in der Geschichte*, ed. E. Schulin and B. Martin, 2d ed. (Munich, 1982), pp. 46–67, esp. p. 62.

36. B. Stemmberger, "Geschichte der Juden in Deutschland von

den Anfängen bis zum 13. Jahrhundert," in Osten-Sacken, *Juden in Deutschland*, pp. 15–50, esp. 33.

37. Güdemann, *Geschichte des Erziehungswesens*, pp. 127ff.

38. Ibid., p. 136.

39. Stemmberger, "Geschichte der Juden," p. 39.

40. As this point does not directly touch upon the present topic, a few marginal remarks must suffice. The term *usury* was loosely used in the Middle Ages for taking interest in general. Rates were in any case quite high and reached between 40 and 200 percent. Since a monetary economy had only just begun, ordinary people were rarely able to fulfill their pledges. That such high rates were demanded by non-Jews, too, is confirmed by many witnesses. Thus, for example, Luther in one of his table talks upbraids the burghers of Leipzig with being worse usurers than the Jews, and Bernard of Clairvaux was almost lynched in Mayence when he reprimanded Christians for taking high interest rates. On these two details, see Mertens, "Christen und Juden." In addition, because of the special (and often arbitrarily changed) taxes imposed upon Jews and because appeal against them was impossible, Jews had only one way open to deal with the pressure, namely by passing it on to their debtors. In 1544, the Emperor himself justified in writing the higher rates of interest taken by Jews in view of the heavier taxation they had to bear (*Jüdisches Lexikon*, vol. 2, col. 108). Finally, since numerous professions were forbidden to them and expulsions were very frequent, ready cash was the best investment which contributed of course to the expansion of monetary business.

41. M. Metzger and Th. Metzger, *Jüdisches Leben im Mittelalter nach illuminierten hebräischen Handschriften vom 13. bis 16. Jahrhundert* (Freiburg, 1983), p. 76.

42. How useful it is to encode events in a pattern was demonstrated by Haverkamp's study regarding the persecutions of the Jews during and in the wake of the Black Death. See A. Haverkamp, "Die Judenverfolgungen zur Zeit des Schwarzen Todes im Gesellschaftsgefüge deutscher Städte," in Haverkamp, *Zur Geschichte der Juden*, pp. 27–93.

43. See Aronius, *Regesten zur Geschichte der Juden*, p. 242; Rosenthal, *Heimatgeschichte*, p. 15.

44. S. M. Dubnov, *Die Geschichte des jüdischen Volkes in Europa*, vol. 4: *Das frühe Mittelalter* (Berlin, 1926), p. 304. Cf. English translation, *History of the Jews* (New York, 1967–73).

45. See n. 18.

46. Ibid.

47. E. Fromm, *The Art of Loving* (New York, 1963), p. 44.

48. Dubnov, *Die Geschichte des jüdischen Volkes,* p. 293.

49. See n. 21.

50. See n. 18.

51. Ibid.

52. Ibid.

53. See n. 17.

54. Haverkamp, "Die Judenverfolgungen," pp. 51ff.

55. Poliakov, *Geschichte des Antisemitismus,* pp. 80–85. See also H. H. Ben Sasson, *Geschichte des jüdischen Volkes—Vom 7.–17. Jahrhundert: Das Mittelalter* (Munich, 1979), 2:36–45.

56. *Midrash Shemot Rabba; Pirké de R. Eliezer,* trans. G. Friedländer (London, 1916), p. 48.

57. Eckert, "Zum Wert der bildlichen Darstellung," pp. 119ff.

58. Heer, *Gottes erste Lieben,* p. 110.

59. E. Badinter, *Die Mutterliebe—Geschichte eines Gefühls vom 17. Jahrhundert bis heute* (Munich, 1981), p. 35.

60. Ibid., p. 114.

61. E. Shorter, "Der Wandel der Mutter-Kind- Beziehungen zu Beginn der Moderne," *Geschichte und Gesellschaft* 1 (1975): 157–87.

62. *Jüdisches Lexikon.*

63. Heer, *Gottes erste Liebe,* p. 110; *Jüdisches Lexikon,* col. 1083.

The Ritual Murder Accusation:
The Persistence of Doubt
and the Repetition Compulsion

Among those few psychoanalysts who have tried to decipher the meaning of the blood libel legend is Ernest A. Rappaport, an alumnus of the University of Vienna Medical School and a survivor of the Buchenwald concentration camp. In his posthumously published book Anti-Judaism: A Psychohistory *(1975), he devotes a chapter to the blood libel legend. A practitioner of psychoanalysis in Chicago, Rappaport, despite a somewhat rambling discursive style of writing, manages to apply several tenets of psychoanalytic theory to the legend. For example, he borrows the Freudian concept of "repetition compulsion," which refers essentially to a neurotic obsessive wish to repeatedly reenact some particular form of behavior. Rappaport tries to see the repeated instances of the ritual murder accusation as a type of repetition compulsion related, he suggests, to the Christians need to reenact the crucifixion of Christ. The reader may judge for himself or herself how successful Rappaport's idiosyncratic version of psychoanalytic theory is with respect to illuminating the blood libel legend.*

For an alternative psychoanalytic reading of the legend, see Stanley Rosenman, "Psychoanalytic Reflections on Anti-Semitism," Journal of Psychology and Judaism 1, no. 2 *(1977): 3–23 (see esp. p. 19), and the same author's "Psychoanalytic Knowledge, Jewish Identity and Germanic Anti-Semitic Legends,"* American Journal of Psychoanalysis 42 *(1982): 239–48.*

Reprinted from Ernest A. Rappaport, *Anti-Judaism: A Psychohistory* (Chicago: Perspective Press, 1975), pp. 94–115.

The anxiety-provoking reality from which the doubter tries to escape is the reality of death. He turns the fear of death into a phobia because a phobia leaves open the possibility of doubt whether the inhibitions and restrictions which he has voluntarily imposed upon himself need to be kept. These restrictions are applied to logical thinking which is replaced by miraculous thinking. The original anxiety is so overwhelming that every loosening of the phobic restriction of rationality, every upsurge of doubt in miracles is followed by an immediate increase in anxiety. The next maneuver is the conversion of anxiety itself into a phobia, the Christophobia, which however again is associated with doubt, not in regard to the lurking reality of death, but in the belief in Christ and the crucifixion as the precondition for the resurrection and the promise of survival. But the crucifixion and resurrection took place only once, what if this was the last time and there will be no more of it? Christ died so that those who believe in him should live, but if He is not dying any more how could His believers go on living?

The anxiety grows into a panic, especially since it now also leads into doubting the career of Christ, a doubting which is blasphemy for which the penalty would be death and damnation to hell. But here, just in time, comes the redemption. It was the Jews who crucified Christ because they did not accept him. They still refuse to accept Him, thus they are compelled to repeat crucifying Him.

> Of all the bizarre charges against the Jewish people the one that has enjoyed the hardiest tenacity and the utmost notoriety, and has produced the direst consequences, is the so-called ritual murder accusation.[1]

Medieval Christians (and some modern ones, too) believed that Christian children were seized and tortured to death by the Jews during the Passover season. This myth appears in a complete form for the first time in *The Life and Miracles of St. William of Norwich*, a Latin work written about 1173 by Thomas of Monmouth, a contemporary of the events which

305

he relates. The story of the ritual murder of the boy William in 1144 is virtually the first of a long series of such accusations, a series that has not yet come to an end.[2]

At the beginning of Lent in 1144, William, a twelve-year-old boy who had been boarded out to a master furrier at the early age of eight and supposedly was known to the Jewish fur traders as a skillful apprentice, had disappeared in Norwich, England. A monk by the name of Theobald, who was a Jewish convert and probably as a child had been abducted by Christians, baptized, and put into a monastery, swore that the Jews of Norwich had seduced the Christian boy William into the home of one of their elders and had killed him in observance of a Passover blood ritual. A massacre of the Jews was avoided at the last moment when the dead body of the boy was found and showed no evidence of murder. Nevertheless, a cult of William, the supposed martyr of Norwich was started, the boy was sainted and enshrined in his hometown church; and the diligent chronicler failed to delete any of the gory details of the boy's crucifixion by the heartless and cruel Jews. According to his report there was in the house of the rich Jew, Eleazar, "instead of a cross a post set up between two other posts, and a beam stretched across the midmost post and attached to the other on either side." As was discovered afterwards, "from the marks of the wounds and of the bands, the right hand and foot had been tightly bound and fastened with cords, but the left hand and foot were pierced with two nails. Now the deed was done in this way, lest it should be discovered from the presence of nail-marks in both hands and feet, that the murderers were Jews and not Christians, if eventually the body were found." After additional "many and great tortures they inflicted a frightful wound in his left side, reaching even to his inmost heart, and, as though to make an end of all, they extinguished his mortal life so far as it was in their power. And since many streams of blood were running down from all parts of his body, then, to stop the blood and to wash and close the wounds, they poured boiling water over him."[3]

We notice that doubt even crept into the repetition compulsion to resolve the doubt. He had the Jews hammer nails not into both hands and feet but only into the left (sinister) ones. The tortured body of the dead boy was found without any wounds but this was because the Jews cunningly had closed the wounds with boiling water.

In spite of, or maybe because of, the fact that the Jews of Norwich were not punished for the crime they allegedly had committed, identical charges were brought up at Gloucester in 1168 where the boy Harold was supposed to have been carried away secretly by Jews on 21 February, kept hidden until 16 March, then "tortured with immense tortures" in front of the assembled Jews of all of England, and made into a glorious martyr to Christ. Marcus reports the ritual murder accusation levied against the Jews of Blois near Orleans in France in May 1171. One of the ca. forty Jews who had settled there "rode up to water his horse;" when "a common soldier . . . was also there watering the horse of his master. The Jew bore on his chest an untanned hide, but one of the corners had become loose and was sticking out of his coat. When, in the gloom, the soldier's horse saw the white side of the hide, it was frightened and sprang back, and it could not be brought to water. The Christian servant hastened back to his master" and told that he saw a Jew throw a little Christian child, whom the Jews had killed into the river. When the ruler of the city, count Theobald V, heard about it he had all the Jews of Blois seized and thrown into prison. Attempts were made by the friends of the Jews to collect money to pay a ransom to the mayor, but a cleric appeared and on his instigation thirty-one of the Jews were burnt alive. At Bury St. Edmonds ritual murder charges were made against the Jews in 1181, at Pontoise, Braisne, and Saragossa in 1182, at Winchester in 1192, and once again at Norwich in 1235.

The harassment of the Jews in England reached its climax in 1255 with the classical case, as Cecil Roth calls it, of "Little St. Hugh" of Lincoln. A large number of Jews were in Lincoln at the time to attend the marriage of Belaset, daughter of Magister Benedict Ben Moses. The day after the wedding the body of a boy, who had been missing for over three weeks, was discovered in a cesspool into which he had probably fallen while at play. But a more dramatic explanation of his death immediately suggested itself. Matthew Paris, whom we know already from his chronicle of the Wandering Jew Ahasver, describing the alleged murder, related how "the child was first fattened for ten days with white bread and milk, and then how almost all the Jews in England were invited to the crucifixion." The Jew Copin was forced to confess that the boy was crucified *in injuriam et contumeliam* (for the injury and derision) *Jesu*. Nearly one hundred Jews were arrested, of whom nineteen, including Copin, were hanged without trial. The rest, after being convicted and sentenced, were ultimately released when Richard of Cornwall, who held the Jewry of the Kingdom in mortgage and was naturally anxious to protect his property, interceded in their behalf.[4] St. Hugh was also enshrined in the church for the attraction of pilgrims. The final expulsion of the Jews from England was ordered by King Edward at the instigation of his bigot mother and without affirmation of the Parliament in 1290.

In the same year as the accusation at Norwich, the first accusation was made in Germany against the Jews of Lauda a.d. Tauber and in the next year in Fulda. On 1 July 1267 a child was killed and its blood collected on folded pieces of linen in Pforzheim. In Weissenburg on 29 June 1270, Jews were accused of suspending a Christian child by the feet and opening every artery in its body in order to obtain all its blood. Jews were accused of kidnapping a child in Munich in October 1285. In 1286 in Oberwesel "the good Werner" was allegedly slowly tortured to death by Jews for three days. A year later a boy, Rudolph, was tortured and his head cut off in Bern, and in Krems at the Danube the Jews supposedly killed a boy "in order to get his blood."

By 1400 the epidemic had spread to Poland where Jews, refugees from the marauding crusaders in the Rhine valley, had settled as early as 1100 and, welcomed with open arms by the Polish nobility as culture bearers, had become prosperous. A ritual murder charge against the Jews was whipped up by the clergy into a hysteria that swept all Poland. Casi-

mir IV tried to reassure the uneasy Jews, but the Roman
Catholic clergy, alarmed at the heretical trends sweeping the
West, needed reassurance for the Church and linked the Jews
to the new heresies to overcome their own heretical doubts.
Host desecration charges were leveled against both Jews and
Protestants. The first pogroms, that is organized attacks
against Jews, broke out in Poland around 1500. Stronger
kings, not intimidated by the clergy, restored temporarily
the former order. Both Sigismund I and Sigismund II de-
nounced the charge of the desecration of the Host as a fraud,
and Sigismund II declared frankly: "I am shocked at this hideous villainy, I am also not that much devoid of common
sense as to believe there could be any blood in the Host."[5] Of
course, the king knew that common sense is uncommon
sense, especially in comparison with the *credo quia absur-
dum* demanded by the Church. It also facilitated the repetition compulsion if the accusers did not have to wait to find a
dead boy as a stand-in for the martyred Christ, but could
claim that the Eucharist, the "transubstantiated" Christ had
been crucified by the Jews. The doctrine of the transubstantiation, decreed in the twelfth century, maintained that in
the communion by drinking wine and eating a wafer, i.e.,
the Host, the communicant was drinking the blood of Christ
and eating the actual flesh of Christ. Again the doubt crept
in whether the communicant should with his teeth and
tongue masticate the flesh of Christ or should swallow the
body of the God whole.

Even through the Age of Enlightenment the blood accusation persisted into so-called modern times. In fact, it reached
another climax in the nineteenth century. Cecil Roth gives
special significance to the Damascus Affair of 1840, because
it initiated a new era in foreign affairs and confirmed Occi-
dental Jewry in its position of leadership. On 5 February of
that year, Father Thomas, Superior of the Franciscan Convent at Damascus, mysteriously disappeared, together with
his servant. By means of the bastinado, a beating with a stick
or cudgel on the soles of the feet, a sort of confession was
extorted from a poor Jewish barber to the effect that a ritual

murder had been meditated. In consequence several members of the community were arrested and put to torture. A general massacre seemed imminent.

When the news reached Europe and America, public opinion was deeply stirred. Meetings of protest, attended by Christians as well as Jews, were held at the Mansion House in London, as well as in New York and Philadelphia. Sir Moses Montefiore (who had been sheriff for the City of London upon the accession of Queen Victoria, when he had been knighted) proceeded to the East together with Adolphe Cremieux, the famous French lawyer, and Solomon Munk, the well-known Orientalist. At Alexandria, they obtained an order without difficulty from Mehemet Ali, governor of Egypt, for the release of the survivors. In Constantinople, the delegates were received in audience by the Sultan, from whom they elicited a firman, unconditionally acquitting the accused persons, pronouncing the ritual murder a gross libel, and confirming the inviolability of the persons and the property of Jews throughout the Ottoman Empire.

Maurice Samuel enumerates besides the above case in Damascus, those of Saratov, Russia (1857), and Tisza-Eszlar, Hungary (1882), and in the twentieth century among others the case of Blondes, a Jewish barber of Vilna, and Mendel Beiliss (1911), an employee in a Kiev brick factory.[6] The last two have attracted little attention outside Russia, despite the fact that the trial of Beiliss was particularly shocking and frightening because for the first time the action was carried through not merely by provincial authorities but was sponsored by the Russian national government which so far had disclaimed responsibilities for pogroms, though unconvincingly. Samuel expresses regret that the Beiliss case has fallen nearly into oblivion, even in Russia, in contrast to the Dreyfus case in France which, with all the fantastic accusations against the Jews, had made no allusion to a Jewish addiction to cannibalism with exclusive preference for Christian blood. Samuel's remarks were stimulated by the simultaneous appearance of the novel *The Fixer* by Bernard Malamud, a fictional version of the Beiliss case. Mendel Beiliss was at length exonerated, but not before his show trial had served its purpose. He died at age sixty in obscurity in New York in 1934 just when publicity given to his martyrdom would have accelerated the slow opposition against Hitler. I agree with Samuel that none of the grotesque manifestations of anti-Judaism must be omitted from memory because there is no time for complacency in spite of the general revulsion from the hideous crimes that the Nazis committed against the Jews. For this reason we now turn our attention to the Austrian-Hungarian Monarchy and its German fragment, the Austrian Republic, as a bastion of clericalism and anti-Judaism.

In 1883 a Jew by the name of Joseph Scharf was brought to trial in Tisza-Eszlar in Hungary for presumably having murdered a fourteen-year-old girl by the name of Esther Solymossy for ritual purposes. The anti-Jewish press of all countries discussed the case with great gusto and a special anti-Jewish congress took place in Dresden at which the Hungarian agitator and member of the *Landtag* Geza von Onody appeared. He brought an oil painting of the new martyr Esther Solymossy done from memory for the purpose of agitation.[7] The Jewish people watched the events with great tension. Sigmund Freud[8] discussed the psychiatric diagnosis of the principal witness in the trial. Naturally he was gratified at the successful outcome of the case, but he had no hope it would do much towards diminishing the prevailing anti-Judaism. He was only too right, the synagogue at Tisza and the house of the caretaker were destroyed. In Pressburg, Hungary, a town close to Vienna, riots against the Jews were taking place, and in the entire monarchy anti-Jewish propaganda once again was on the increase.

The premier minister Count Egbert Belcredi, known for his abolishment of the Constitution and in fear of liberal movements, gave money to the arch-reactionary Ernst Schneider of the Morgenpost for agitation against the Jews. The clergy, the aristocracy, and certain circles of the Court, among them the Archduchess Maria Theresa, the namesake of the notorious Jew-hating lady on the imperial throne (1740–80), anticipated that their hour had come, especially when the agitation against the Jews found a popular leader in the Mayor of Vienna, Karl Lueger, *der "schöne Karl."*

The Professor of Catholic Theology at the University of Prague, August Rohling, was called to give the agitation against the Jews a pseudoscientific veneer. He had published a pamphlet against the Talmud which had reached an enormous circulation and had already seventeen editions in spite of the devastating critique of Christian talmudic experts. After Rohling's appointment at the University of Prague he had offered himself as an expert to courts of law with respect to the truth of accusations of ritual murder. At a people's gathering in Vienna (1882) a speaker, referring to Rohling's pamphlet, challenged the Jews to battle. He was put under charge in court, but the judge declared: "I cannot deny that this particular statement can be found in the Talmud." For the Jews of Vienna it was a critical day of the first order. It was a mood like that in Susa when Haman's charge became known. The Talmud was the conversation of the day in all of Vienna and the Jews had to get prepared for the worst. Then, in the midst of this stifling heat before the storm a voice sounded like that of David challenging Goliath to battle. In a much-circulated Viennese newspaper, Rohling, the k.k. ("imperial and royal") Professor, was deprived of every moral adequacy and scientific capacity, and the author of the essay offered to pay three thousand fl. if Rohling would show his ability to read only one page in the Talmud. It was Rabbi Bloch, a young Talmud student from Galicia who after a childhood and youth in dire poverty had ministrated in some small communities as a rabbi and was now employed in this function in Floridsdorf, a suburb of Vienna. He was equipped with a talmudic knowledge which even in the Talmud-soaked Galicia was sensational. He also had acquired a brilliant style and quick repartee which enabled him to smash to bits the pseudoscientific arguments and the arrogant mendacity of the anti-Semitic agitator. Rohling kept silent, but not for long. In the struggle of the nationalities for superiority in the Austrian-Hungarian Empire, the Jews had always emphasized their preference for the German language and for German cultural values, even when after the defeat of the Austrians in the war with Prussia in 1866 the German chauvinistic propaganda in Austria suffered a setback. The Jews were not rewarded with gratitude; on the contrary, the German National Party under the infamous Georg Ritter von Schönerer joined forces with the clerical party and at times even surpassed it in the practice of rabid anti-Judaism. One of their agitators, Franz Holubek, at a meeting of Christian tradesmen at the Three Angels, a large beer and dance hall in Vienna at that time, accused the Talmud of inciting the Jews to the vilest aggressions against their Christian neighbors. Now Rohling offered himself to the courts to swear under oath that the Jews must be criminals on account of their religion. Bloch, however, stamped this publicly as an offer to perjury, and forced Rohling, who had to maintain a government position, to accuse him of defamation.

Bloch had called his opponent a habitual liar and had to prove the truthfulness of his statement. All the slanderous accusations against the Talmud had to be disproved by recognized experts as witnesses. They had to be not only beyond reproach and of great erudition but first of all Christians. Naturally they could not be found in Austria and two German professors, Nöldke and Wünsche, had to be chosen by the court as experts. The material was put together with great effort in the next two years, the date of the trial was already set when Rohling suddenly withdrew his charge. The Jews were jubilant.[9]

Again Freud's pessimism proved correct. In 1899 a Jew by the name of Hilsner was tried and convicted of killing a Christian boy and using his blood for the making of matzah for Passover. The trial took place in the town of Polna, Bohemia, and the anti-Judaism that was stirred up in Prague and in the country, especially by the *Sudetendeutschen*, the predecessors of the party of Konrad Henlein, the pacemaker of Hitler in Bohemia, approached the boiling point. It was at that time that the Emperor Franz Josef received the rabbi of Prague, Alexander Kisch, in audience and uttered the following words: *"Ich bin sehr empört über diese Roheiten"* ("I am very indignant about these rudenesses"). He also gave the permission that this spontaneous remark may be reported to the press. It did indeed find an echo far beyond the frontiers of the monarchy and aroused a demagogical attack against the ruler in the Bohemian *Landtag*. Guido Kisch who reports this incident states that a similar sharp and energetic rejection of anti-Semitism in public to his knowledge has never taken place by the ruling chief of a European country. Obviously he has not read about Sigismund II of Poland, but as far as Franz Josef is concerned it is known that the emperor twice refused to confirm the election of Lueger to Mayor of Vienna and that he admonished him with the words: *"Lassn's meine Juden in Ruh"* ("Leave my Jews in peace").[10]

Returning to Maurice Samuel's warning that there is no time for complacency, it deserves to be pointed out that even in the post-Hitler era and in the second half of the twentieth century Austria has not freed herself from souvenirs of the most repugnant medieval libel against the Jews. There is in Eastern Tyrol the town of Lienz, which on account of its beautiful natural surroundings has become a tourist center. One of its sights is the St. Andreas church about which even a little guide book has been published (Munich and Zurich: Schnell & Steiner) in which one can read on page 13 that in the left wing of the church a memorial stone dedicated to Ursula Boeck is attached to the wall. On the stone plaque one can read the following inscription:

HERE REST THE BONES OF THE INNOCENT CHILD
URSULA BOECK WHO AT THE AGE OF FOUR YEARS ON
GOOD FRIDAY 1443 WAS MARTYRED BY THE JEWS.

This plaque had not been forgotten, it was not even part of the original possessions of the church but was attached only a hundred years ago. Not enough with this, it was in consideration of the increasing number of visitors, natives and from abroad, that the plaque was even renovated in the year—1960.

Kurt R. Grossmann, to whom I owe this report,[11] makes particular mention of the native guide from whom the visitor will hear the story of the unfortunate child which the Jews have ritually slaughtered, recited with full conviction because the parish priest has only recently given a sermon about the poor Ursula. Then the visitor is directed to the sacristy where pamphlets are for sale, published by the Catholic Printing Company and Bookstore in Brixen, which on page 7 gives a detailed account of the atrocity committed on the four-year-old Ursula by the Jews in the Judengasse of Lienz in the year 1443. In contrast to the rapidity with which the clerical authorities usually put a publication which is not quite acceptable to their moral sensitivity on the Index, it is remarkable that here the Catholic press itself has published a tale of fiction in which a perverse murder is described with full obscene details. Several organizations have made urgent appeals to the Church to remove this memorial stone, but these appeals were rejected by the Church authorities with the strange explanation that "the removal of the memorial stone would alienate the populace and would arouse even greater attention to the ritual murder."

There is one more such memorial in Tyrol, which in a special anthem is praised as the Holy Land Tyrol. This memorial has been discovered by Simon Wiesenthal while searching for traces of Eichmann in this area. He reported about a stone in the church of Rinn near Innsbruck called the Jew-stone on which the bloody tale of a ritual murder is recorded in relief. In the year 1462 (thus nineteen years after the case of Ursula Boeck) a boy named Anderl was allegedly murdered by Jews traveling through. Not only is the stone still preserved, annual pilgrimages are arranged to give full religious honors to the boy, St. Andreas, after whom the church is named and to whom it is dedicated after Pope Benedict XIV (1740–58) issued a bull on Blessed Andrew of Rinn (*Beatus Andreas*) in 1755. This explains why protests against the pilgrimages and against the spread of the legend itself were in vain, especially why Wiesenthal's approach to Cardinal Innitzer and Bishop Rusch were without success. Bishop Rusch even wrote in his response that "the Jewish letter goes much too far if it means to assert that Jews never had done such things."[12]

315

In Tyrol clericalism and German borderland chauvinism have been holding hands already since the days of Napoleon's invasion of Austria. Another celebrated Andreas was a guerilla fighter against the French, who were hated for bringing with them some of the heritage of the French Revolution, such as equal opportunity for the Jews. It was Andreas Hofer who was executed by the French in Mantua as a terrorist but has been glorified as an Austrian patriot and is now the model hero for the terrorists of the Iselberg Bund who drive the Italian carbinieri to desperation. The terrorists of the Iselberg Bund want to force Italy to return South Tyrol, which was annexed by Italy from Austria in accordance with the Treaty of Versailles. The anti-Jewish policies of the Bund are fortuitous and would seem to bear no necessary relation to its rampant nationalism except that they once again illustrate the close compatibility between the ultranationalist temper and anti-Semitic prejudice.[13]

We can only guess why Hitler, who insisted on the abrogation of all border revisions of the Treaty of Versailles, neglected the desire of the South Tyrolian Nazis to return home into the Reich—it was as a favor to Mussolini. Trent, at the river Adige (German *Etsch*), is in South Tyrol and was the scene of the celebrated case of Simon of Trent in 1475. The boy reputedly was killed "to the accompaniment of curses and spells" two days after the beginning of Passover, when his death could no longer have had any connection with the Passover ceremonial; Jews are alleged to have admitted that they required "fresh Christian blood" because it was a jubilee year (which it was in the Christian calendar; Jews have not counted or celebrated the Jubilee year since early biblical times, if at all).

Bavaria, though not a part of Austria but bordering on it and just as Catholic, should not be forgotten for her carefully preserved relics of inhumanity. All Jews of the town of Deggendorf in the Bavarian Forest were killed in 1337 under the pretext of a rape of the Hostia. The exciting event was demonstrated in twelve pictures, one for each month of the year, which decorate the presbytery of the Mission Church. Only the explanatory text to the pictures was removed on account of an ordinance of the bishop of Regensburg, while the pictures themselves remained. They are skillfully exploited for tourism, and in a public announcement of the parish as recently as 1964 under the title "A Bavarian Destination for a Six-Day Pilgrimage," the origin of the miraculous capacity of these images is elucidated in the following words: "They were occasioned by a sacrilege to the Hostia which was committed in 1337. Even if the details of it cannot all be proven historically, it was a sacrilege nevertheless and the expiation for it was a historical fact."[14]

To make the register complete, it should be mentioned that the blood libel has spread to the United States. Only forty-seven years ago in 1928 in Massena, New York, the rabbi of the town was questioned on the blood ritual when a little girl happened to disappear. The girl was found unharmed the next day and the mayor, the instigator of the questioning, made a public apology. A booklet published in Birmingham, Alabama, in 1962 (Arnold Leese, *Jewish Ritual Murder*), still gives credence to the charge.

The classical ritual murder accusation consists in the kidnapping and ritual slaughter of a Christian boy and the use of the drained-off blood for the preparation of matzah. An important vicissitude of the crucifixion theme is the injury inflicted upon the Eucharist, the Charity of Christ, i.e., the transubstantiated wafer or Host, and the bleeding of this martyred or crucified miniature matzah by the Jews. Common sense will object to the assumption that a lifeless object such as a wafer can bleed. We are reminded of the psychiatrist who tries to convince the schizophrenic patient, who steadfastly maintains that he is dead, that dead people do not bleed, whereupon the patient cuts himself with a knife to show the psychiatrist triumphantly that dead people do bleed. Of course, the irrational content of the assertion that unleavened wafers can bleed must also have dawned upon the stubborn clergy, therefore the Jews were supposed to rub the blood of the boy selected as a stand-in for Christ into the dough for the matzah to soak them in the blood that the matzah were expected to pour out when crucified as once again stand-ins for Christ. It was also a variation of the

317

theme of the Jewish usurer as a sponge, soaked full with Christian money (blood) and then squeezed out by the clergy who were not supposed to touch money.

One may assume that the bleeding of Christ on the cross was only an accessory to the crucifixion, but the predominant place that it occupies in the ritual murder accusation contradicts this assumption. The crucifixion can be left out and the bleeding can be made that much more significant, for instance, if the victim is put into a head-down position like a slaughtered animal in a butcher shop, as the case in Weissenburg in 1270 is depicted. In all cases the alleged murderers with great eagerness collect the blood, even after Passover when matzah are no longer made, as in the Trent case.

The paradox of the blood accusation is that the Jews are accused by the Christians of consuming blood, which is in accordance with Christian ritual tradition but is trespassing the Mosaic law. In other words, it is silently taken for granted that they are already converted to Christianity so that they are charged with a crime which is a Christian sacrament. The kosher butcher, by making sure that the food animal is completely emptied of its blood, performs a ritual service to the Jewish community but arouses thereby the curiosity and bewilderment of uninformed or misinformed Christian observers.

According to the standard psychoanalytic interpretation, Yahweh's injunction to Moses to forbear from eating or touching blood betrays a strong repression of an archaic wish. Since blood was considered by all people as the essential fluid of life, their gods in order to preserve their immortality needed an uninterrupted supply of it, and so blood was also poured daily upon the altar of Yahweh in the Temple of Solomon in Jerusalem. Primitive man to compete with God by sharing the magic properties of the divinity, especially its omnipotence and immortality, wanted to acquire them by the more primitive form of transfusion, the ingestion, of the immortal blood of the god. If it is not overt cannibalism and the blood originates from an animal, it is still not contradictory to the cannibalistic meaning, considering that all archaic gods originally have been animals, such as the lamb

318

Jesus, the bull Jehovah, and the bull Zeus, until the animal was reduced in its status to a mere representation of the divinity. The Jewish God in the invisible and amorphous form of cosmic energy of which no images can be made, and which He was forced to adopt after His Temple was destroyed, had become a god whose power could no longer be acquired by simple ingestion. Consequently, His prohibition of the consumption of blood is not only the repression of an archaic wish, it is the enforcement of the painful modesty of reality. The Galileans on the other hand, were forced to regress in the compulsive pursuit of proselytizing savage tribes and as a concession to the ancient totemistic practices of these tribes.

From the time of the Gospels there is a preoccupation with blood which is typical of Christian writing and which has persisted throughout the centuries. The Jews, allegedly collecting the blood of the stand-in Christ, were not aware that they continued the efforts of "the Angels during Christ's Passion who reverently collected the Holy, Divine Blood as it trickled down"; or that they followed the old tradition which relates how "Joseph of Arimathea, a pure elect soul, immediately after the death of Christ on Calvary, came with the Holy Grail or chalice, fashioned out of a ruby that fell from out of the crown of Lucifer, the prince of the Angels, to receive in it during the washing of Christ's Body the Sacred Blood thereupon remaining. This Blood, not taken up again by Christ at His resurrection, became the precious Relic which Joseph of Arimathea guarded in Jerusalem according to the old tradition."

These words are quoted from the Foreword to the *Sanguis Christi* Play, performed since 1938 (Leuven: "Opbouwen," 1947) in memory of the first Holy Blood Procession in Brugge, Belgium, in 1303, when Diederich of Alsace, Count of Flanders, returned from his crusade and brought from the Holy Land a few drops of the most Precious Blood presented to him by the Patriarch of Jerusalem through the mediation of Baldwin III, King of Jerusalem. The open air performance on the market place of Brugge begins with a prolonged laudation of the Holy Blood:

Choir:

Sanguis Christi
O Blood Divine
that outpoured for us
still pulses with love;
O Blood Divine,
glowing magnificat
of redemption:
Blood
that calls
like a cry
of ceaseless pain
over the wilderness
of the stricken soul:
. . . . .

. . . . .
Sanguis Christi
bright ruby
of flame-like beauty,
pearl
in the mouth of Thy wounds
which call and scream
and laugh in endless pain
and in joy
at our redemption;

Christe Jesu,
from Thy gaping wounds
did Arimathea
the drops of blood collect
in the holy grail,
and our fathers
with valiant deed
strong
as the Belfry
that in this city stands
have testified
to that far land
where Thy tomb yet stood
as memorial
of all Thy suffering.
[etc.]

Jesus is once again placed on trial before Pilate who appears on the balcony of the Belfry facade. The Jews are represented by a shouting and ranting, infuriated mob.

Pilate:

What does this people want of me?

Jewish People (like a sudden hurricane let loose from the confines of hell):

Blood, Blood, the Law, Jesus of Nazareth,
Blood, False Prophet, Blood!
Law! Death! Death! Death!
Hail Pilate!

(Pilate, phlegmatic and motionless, his arm resting on the balcony, waits until the shrieking and hissing below him stops and then announces in a skeptical tone):

Pilate:

I find no fault in this man.

Jewish People (cry aloud):

Ah. Woe.

(A swarm of raging figures rises up, pushing and jostling in an ugly way. The whistling and clamor increase to a delirium of excitement and threats. The soldiers, in their struggle to keep order, thrust down groups of people with their lances.)

Pilate (feverishly and vehemently):

What must I do with your Jesus of Nazareth?

Jewish People (unanimously):

Crucify Him. Crucify Him. Crucify Him.

Pilate:

You shed innocent blood.

Jewish People (a terrible ominous laugh which runs like a shiver over the darkening atmosphere. Then suddenly, with hands raised on high, and fingers outspread, they cry out):

His blood be upon us and upon our children.

An Invisible Choir (calls out immediately in counterpoint from out the mysterious heights of the tower, which stands illuminated by a somber green light):

Ah. Woe.

(and this lament of the choir floats down over the thousands of people in poignant complaint. But immediately the crowd call out a second time still more emphatically):

Jewish People:

His blood be upon us and upon our children.

The Play of the Holy Blood in Brugge is one of the Passion Plays held during Holy Week; another one even more famous is the Passion Play of Oberammergau in Bavaria. As repetitious mass performances, the task of these Passion Plays is the reinforcement of the belief in the original Passion Play, to keep up its slackening popularity, and to make the repetition compulsion also highly remunerative for the commerce of the town or village. Adolf Hitler was well aware of the anti-Jewish propaganda of the Oberammergau production, therefore in July 1942 he underscored the importance of the play to the Nazi movement in these words: "It is vital that the Passion Play be continued at Oberammergau; for never has the menace of Jewry been so convincingly portrayed as in this presentation of what happened in the times of the Romans. There one sees in Pontius Pilate a Roman racially and intellectually superior, there he stands out like a firm, clean rock in the middle of the whole muck and mire of Jewry."

Of course, we know that this is a complete misrepresentation of history and that the Jewish King and the Roman authorities remained unmoved by the *paranoia querulans* of a tentmaker's son, eager to sell his megalomanic delusions and hallucinations. We also learn from Phil Baum's report to the American Jewish Congress that Oberammergau acquired notoriety as *das sündige Dorf*, the sinful village, because of the crass commercialism of the play and its perversion of religious views.[15] In 1934, that is a year after Hitler came to power, the income of the play was something over three million marks, and after the individual players were paid, part of the surplus was used to build an outdoor municipal swimming pool, described as the largest in Bavaria. Therefore it will need many more repetitions of the play to wash the village clean from this new doubt in its immaculate belief in the Passion of Christ. No wonder that all protests against further unpurged performances of this anti-Jewish play are intentionally ignored by the village fathers.

The play, a seven-hour marathon, has been put on in Oberammergau almost without fail every ten years since 1633 for a hundred performances between May and September. It is naïve to expect that a revision of the text will take out the anti-Jewish propaganda from a strictly anti-Jewish play, but even the presumption of eradicating the most vicious sentences such as "His blood be upon us and upon our children" (Matt. 27:25) met the embittered resistance of the village board preparing for the 1970 series, and Cardinal Julius Döpfner, the archbishop of Munich, declared that he would not let himself be put under pressure from any direction. When orders for tickets from the United States and Canada were canceled, the Jewish "protest business" was accused by Herr Bauer, the publicity director, as maliciously interfering with the anti-Jewish theater business of the village.

In regard to bloodthirsty fantasies deriving from the crucifixion motif, two English poets of the seventeenth century, both Catholics, deserve to be quoted here.[16]

. . . . . .
Shoot, like a flash of fire, to th' ruby wine,
His precious blood, transcendently Divine.
(How poor those costly pearls were, drunk by some)
My Lord, drink Blood to me. Let it to th' world's health come.

This toast is from a poem called "Theophila's Love Song" by Edward Benlowes, who wrote that his pen "was dipped i' th' standish of thy Blood." Richard Crashaw wrote in his "Hymn

323

to the Adorable St. Teresa" about the "milky soul" of this "soft child":

> She never undertook to know
> What death with love should have to do;
> Nor has she e'er yet understood
> Why to show love she should shed blood;
>
> Yet though she cannot tell you why,
> She can love and she can die.
> Scarce has she blood enough to make
> A guilty sword blush for her sake;
>
> . . . . . .
>
> . . . . . .
>
> So shall she leave amongst them sown
> Her Lord's blood, or at least her own.
> [etc.]

We are not surprised that in the holy land Tyrol of little Urschl of Lienz, of the holy Anderl of Rinn, and holy little Simon of Trent a whole mountain village is called *Heiligen-blut* ("Holy Blood"). The preoccupation with the Holy Blood fostered by the Catholic clergy, finally was adopted in Rosenberg's mythus of the blood and Hitler's and Streicher's concern over the purity of the Holy Aryan Blood. Then Himmler preached his sermons of Blood and Soil and founded the blood order for the bearers of the blood medal.

But Trachtenberg writes, "It seems to have been a common belief that the Jews made use of the flesh of the victims too." According to this, Shakespeare's *Merchant of Venice* is a ritual murder accusation. Again we have here the repetition of the drama of the crucifixion with the gentle, self-sacrificing Antonio in the role of Christ and Shylock representing the stereotype of the unscrupulous, cruel Jew. Bernard Grebanier proposes that just as Shakespeare's dramatic gifts towered above those of his contemporaries, so did his humane spirit tower above the bigotry of his time.[17] Shakespeare was innocent of Jew hatred because considering that England was *Judenrein* (the Jews had been expelled in 1290 and were not readmitted until 1655), he did not know any Jews and naïvely used the word "Jew" only as a synonym

for "usurer." The play is not about Jewish-Christian relations but the conflict between Love and Hate.

Shylock is a chilling and discordant presence in a sunny,
idealized society. He displays a significant distaste for music
and laughter with which this society abounds. Unlike his
adversaries, he is grimly purposeful, thrifty, and business-
like. By contrast Antonio and Bassanio are impulsively gen-
erous and loving. The tension between Shylock's wretched,
life-destroying avarice and the magnanimous spirit of Antonio and Bassanio is the substance of the play.

Sir Arthur Quiller-Couch[18] refers to many aspects of what
he calls poor workmanship in Shakespeare's writing of the
Merchant of Venice.

> We have a perfect setting of romance in Portia's garden but the
> atmosphere is heartless and chilling. Barring the Merchant
> himself, a merely static figure, and Shylock, who is meant to
> be cruel, every one of the Venetian dramatis personae is either
> a "waster" or a "rotter" or both, and cold-hearted at that.
> There is no need to expend ink upon such parasites as sur-
> round Antonio . . . The evil opposed against these peculiar
> Christians is specific; it is Cruelty; and, yet again specifically,
> the peculiar cruelty of a Jew. To this cruelty an artist at the top
> of his art would surely have opposed mansuetude, clemency,
> charity, and, specifically, Christian charity. Shakespeare misses
> more than half the point when he makes the intended victims,
> as a class and by habit, just as heartless as Shylock without
> any of Shylock's passionate excuse. It is all very well for Portia
> to strike an attitude and tell the court and world that

> The quality of mercy is not strain'd
> It droppeth as the gentle rain from heaven . . .

> But these high-professing words are words and no more to us,
> who find that, when it comes to her turn and the court's turn,
> Shylock gets but the "mercy" of being allowed (1) to pay half
> his estate in fine, (2) to settle the other half on

> the gentleman
> That lately stole his daughter,

> and (3) to turn Christian. (Being such Christians as the whole
> gang were, they might have spared him *that* ignominy.)

Returning to the ritual murder libel, like the Play of the Holy Blood it proved effective in keeping the cross and the blood from becoming victims of skepticism and enlightenment. There are, however, a number of questions which intrude upon us: Why does the victim, as a rule, have to be a child, preferably a small boy? Why does the drained blood have to be used, of all things, for the making of matzah? And the related questions of why the crime has to take place at Passover or Easter?

To answer the first question is easiest. The kidnapping of the Christian child is, of course, the reversal of the Christian practice of stealing Jewish children and baptizing them without their parents' knowledge. If a Christian child disappeared, it usually was a runaway child who no longer was willing to tolerate its hostile environment, as for instance in the case of William of Norwich, who lost his mother or was taken away from his mother at the early age of eight to learn a craft as an apprentice. It can also be a battered or misunderstood child who ran away from its own parents and got killed by accident. The responsible parent would then love nothing more than to put his own guilt for the dastardly murder of an innocent child on the Jews. To terrorize the child by threatening to sell it to a Jewish peddler who would put it into the sack that he carried on his back used to be a frequent practice of mothers dealing with a naughty child, especially if it was a child born out of wedlock and was, therefore, an unwelcome child.

The use of the drained-off blood from the body of a Christ stand-in for the making of matzah is the acting out by the Jews of the papal doctrine of the transubstantiation. The act of the offertory or oblation refers to any offering (*ob*—in place of) and in place of Jesus it could have been the lamb of God or the fish meaning Iesos Chrystos Theos; the offering of unleavened bread was in reference to Passover. It also was the challenging assertion that the Eucharist, the miniature matzah, not merely brings Christ vividly to mind, in a metaphorical symbolic sense, understood in the words "this is my body . . . this is my blood," but that it IS the flesh and blood of Christ, which met with mounting resistance. If the

Jews, however, as they were accused really mixed blood into the dough for the unleavened bread they *nolens volens* confirmed the object of doubt. Therefore, as much as the popes welcomed the persecution of the perfidious Jews and the massacres they incurred on account of the ritual murder accusation, they were confronted with the same dilemma as in regard to the witness people theory: if they did not want to lose the involuntary cooperation of the Jews for the maintenance of the doctrine of the transubstantiation they were forced to protect the Jews from complete annihilation. Hence a number of popes, whom Flannery enumerates, issued bulls to exonerate Jews of the charges, but, as Flannery adds, to little avail.

Only recently, after five hundred years and owing to the untiring investigation of Verwaltungsrat Karl Kurrus in Freiburg im Breisgau, were the executed Jews of Endingen and other small towns at the upper Rhine rehabilitated. It was on 22 April 1470 that in Endingen three brothers, Elias, Eberlin, and Merklin, accused of the ritual murder of two children and two adults in the year 1462, after having confessed and supposedly without undergoing torture, were burnt to death outside the town. The bodies of their alleged victims were exhibited publicly in the church of Endingen, the two children in a glass case and the adults in a closed case. The two "innocent children" were worshipped as local saints, and their martyrdom at the hands of the Jews told and retold in local church and secular chronicles, in an inscription on the church bell from 1773, and in the Endingen *Judenspiel* ("Jew-Play"). At last in June 1967, under the pressure and protest of various agencies, including two articles by Tonie Oesner in the *Aufbau* (16 December 1966 and 25 August 1967), the town priest Gäng removed the glass case with the bodies of the children and replaced it with a baroque figure of Jesus in the grave. Toni Oesner writes that "Pope Gregory X revealed the true situation unmistakably by pointing out that in many cases in which Christian children perished without explanation, Christians hostile to Jews made 'false assertions' against the Jews or were even hiding Christian children to extort money from the Jews by means of torture, and he ordered the setting free of all Jews captured under such circumstances." This was in 1272. Martin V, according to Flannery, took a similar stand in 1422, which was forty-eight years prior to the Endingen incident. The epidemic had been endemic in Germany since 1235. Why were there only two popes in 235 years who tried to stop the epidemic? Is it possible that Rome could have been that powerless?

We proceed to answer the question why the ritual murder was to be committed at Passover or about that time. Passover is a Jewish national holiday, it is the Jewish Bastille Day called *Z'man Cheruseinu*—the time of our freedom. It was and in some countries still is celebrated as a holiday of national redemption by a people in servitude and anguish and therefore is based on the hope for deliverance from servitude as it happened once before under the leadership of its Messiah Moses from the bondage in Egypt. It is also a holiday celebrated in the anticipation of a national rebirth, a Zionist holiday with the motto "Next year in the land of Israel." Purim and Chanuka are also national holidays of similar meaning but they represent nothing else and are of much younger date. Passover lasts seven days and is the only Jewish holiday during which ordinary bread is abolished from the table as well as from the whole household and unleavened cakes, or matzah, are eaten. The house has to be emptied carefully of all leavened bread and is on the evening before the first seder even ceremoniously searched by the father carrying a candle and being followed by the mother carrying a spoon for any traces of *chomets* (ordinary bread). The custom clearly points to the intention of starting a new life, a life of freedom. Freud referred to this spring cleaning as the removal of all *Geseres* from the house in favor of the *Ungeseres*, a wordplay based on a slight distortion of the German word *gesäuert*, i.e., leavened, to *Geseres*, Yiddish, meaning laments, and *ungesäuert*, i.e., unleavened, changed to a new word coined by Freud, *Ungeseres* meaning free from lamenting, i.e., rejoicing. The reason for the eating of matzah is explained in the Haggadah that there was not sufficient time for the dough to leaven before the Holy King of the kings, etc. appeared unto the Israelites and "redeemed them" . . . or "it was not leavened because they were thrust out of Egypt and could not tarry" (Ex. 12:39). This sounds more like an expulsion than a liberation and we also wonder about the ambivalent attitude toward the matzah implied in the biblical definition as "the bread of affliction, which our ancestors ate in the land of Egypt." One of the four questions of the *Manish-Tanoh* asked by the youngest of the family at the beginning of the celebration of the Seder is why bitter herbs are eaten on this particular night, and he is told that it is symbolic of the bitterness of life in bondage, which is another reference to Pesach as the festival of the urgently hoped for national liberation. However, there is a whole display of herbs on the Seder dish, lettuce, parsley, and horseradish, and the Haroset, a mixture of ground nuts with fruits and wine; all this pointing to a different origin of the celebration.

Pesach was celebrated in Palestine as an agricultural festival related to the grain harvest in spring beginning with the cutting of barley and ending with the reaping of the wheat. It was called *Chag Ha-Matzot*, the feast of the matzah, and consisted of two ceremonies: the removal of the *chometz*, which was the leaven of the past year's crop, and the *omer*, the first sheaf of newly cut barley offered to the priest on the first day of the harvest as a gift to God. In the observance of the Seder, beginning at a later period of history, it was the *afikomon*, half of the first matzah on the plate, which was broken off at the start of the Seder and preserved. In Eastern Europe a special type of matzah was baked and carefully guarded, the *matzot shel mitzwoh* ("matzah of charity").[19]

It is interesting that none of the four questions of the *Manish-Tanoh* refers to the shank bone of roasted lamb on the Seder plate, as if the memory of its meaning had fallen into repression. The most archaic feature of the Pesach ceremony is the tribal totem festival of the nomadic shepherds in the desert, which was observed with the sacrifice of a lamb or kid not more than a year old, one for each family or clan, which ushered in spring in the month when the kids and the lambs were born. This also explains the display of

329

the hard-boiled egg on the Seder plate, as an indicator that
the repressed real content of the questions of the *Manish-Tanoh* is the basic question of where the babies come from.

Considering nomads who lived in the open wilderness, we
understand the tradition of serving only roasted meat, and
that all the flesh of the animal had to be eaten before day-
break when the caravan moved on. The prohibition of breaking the bones of the totem animal was to guarantee the in-
tactness of the skeleton for the rebirth of the totem. All this,
of course, had nothing to do with Judaism, which developed
in the diaspora when Pesach became the national liberation
festival as described but when the mixture with archaic customs and traditions could no longer be disentangled from it.

Even before the *Manish-Tanoh*, the master of the household uncovers the matzah, holds up the Seder plate, and, in
the early Middle Ages, even stepped out in the street to in-
vite neighbors and out of town visitors to join the meal and
the festivities. This was the threat of Pesach to the Christian
clergy who feared that their flock would give up the Nazarean
heresy and return to the Jewish mother's fold. The council of
Nicaea (325 C.E.) formally decreed that Christians should not
celebrate Passover with the Jews but met with little success,
so that the issue had to be taken up again by the council of
Antioch (341) and again at the Council of Laodicea (343–81),
both of which clearly prohibited this custom. The calendar
was carefully manipulated so that the new Passover would
no longer coincide with Jewish Pesach. In the Teutonic
countries it now coincided with the festival of the goddess
Austro, the light-bearing goddess of spring, therefore the
name Easter (German Ostern).[20] On the other hand, the Jewish Pesach rituals were thoroughly studied and converted
into anti-Jewish rituals and accusations.

The Messianic hope for national redemption from oppression and servitude was turned into a promise for universal
redemption from the original sin, and the Zionist expectation of return to the national home was changed into a general expectation of resurrection and return from the dead.
The savage totemistic concept was lifted out of repression;
the Messiah was placed on the Seder plate as the totem God

Jesus and the Jews were accused of having killed Him and of eating Him. The red wine on the Seder table was turned into the blood, and the matzah into the body of Jesus Christ, who thus was eaten in two manifestations, as the lamb and as the unleavened bread, the Eucharist.

The matzah as "the bread of affliction" is a reminder of the liberation from the affliction in Egypt, but the Eucharist is not a mere reminder or substitute of the afflicted Christ but his real flesh and blood. Therefore, the Christian boy whom the Jews had to steal to make him into a Eucharist (matzah) was not a substitute for Christ but Christ Himself, and therefore a welcome proof and confirmation of the continued grace and effectiveness of the cross.

The monk Isidor, a predecessor of the legendary Eternal Jew, who in his former secular life was married and had made his wife spit out the holy wafer that the Catholic neighbor woman had given her, was punished for this sacrilege with uncontrollable eternal weeping. It was, of course, the reverse, she was a Catholic woman Judaizing at the Jewish neighbor on Pesach, and the monk had forced her to spit out the matzah. To counter the appeal of Passover to their flock the clergy introduced a miniature Passover for daily consumption, the Holy Mass.

In the offertory or oblation, the service of the Eucharist, the priest offers wine and unleavened bread at the altar mumbling the words of consecration ("This is my body . . . This is my blood"). After the ceremonies of the *Agnus Dei* ("Lamb of God") and others the communicants kneel at the railing of the altar. Each of them has been at confession and is now waiting for the *oblata* (ob—in place of) or Host, a flat dry paper-thin wafer of the size of a fifty-cent piece, and is muttering, "I am not worthy of the body and the blood of God (I have been doubting)." Then the priest comes with a gold platter and the communicant raises his chin and tilts his head backward. The priest makes the sign of the cross indicating the presence of Christ and puts the wafer into the communicant's mouth, whereupon the communicant makes the sign of the cross confirming the presence of Christ. He goes back to his pew, kneels down, makes again the sign of the cross and covers his head with his hands and tries to swallow the Host, which is difficult because it is sticking to the roof of the mouth. The commandment is to swallow it as a whole because the body of Christ must go into the intestines as a whole (the bones of the lamb of God must not be broken). The communicant is not supposed to put a finger into the mouth and to touch God, for the same reason he is not allowed to eat or to drink water before the communion and two hours after it so that God's body would not be mixed with ordinary food. A patient reported that as a child when she was sitting next to somebody who just had communion, she felt so awed by the person who had God inside her that she believed that she was sitting next to God. On the other hand, she often was plagued by the doubt whether God's body inside her could turn into excrement.

Theodor Reik interpreted the ritual murder tale as a "displacement and generalization" of the reproach that the Jews had killed and eaten Christ, who was substituting for the father god. "It is easy to see," he added, "that the reproach derives from an unconscious feeling of guilt accomplished by means of projection. If one keeps in mind that Jesus takes the place of the father god here, the connection is within easy grasp; mankind as far as it has turned Christian confesses in this legend without any disguise the old tendency to deicide. One might say that this process is equivalent to the argument between two brothers who have together murdered the father and now want to shift the guilt each to the other."[21]

I have to disagree with Reik. The ritual murder accusation coincides with the Passover season and is stimulated by it. God instructed His people to smear the blood of a lamb on the "lintels and on the two side posts" of the doors so that when He would be executing the tenth plague on the Egyptians, which was slaying their first-born sons, He would recognize the houses of His people and pass them over. This is what gave the festival the name Passover, and the lamb whose blood was being used the name "paschal lamb." Passover does not refer to deicide but to infanticide or respectively to the saving of the lives of infants. Moses had to be

332

hidden as an infant because his life was threatened by the infanticide ordered by the Pharaoh, Jesus had to be hidden because of the infanticide ordered by King Herod, and the larger half of the first matzah on the Seder plate is being hidden at the beginning of the Seder as the *afikomon*. As mentioned before, in Eastern Europe a special type of matzah was baked for this purpose and carefully guarded, the *matzo shel mitzvoh*, matzah of charity—in ecclesiastical terminology "grace," i.e., Christ. The Jewish custom, usually practiced by the children, was boring a hole in the *afikomon* and hanging it up as a charm in the synagogue or the home, but the Christians saw in the harmless holiday custom of the Jews once again their secret repetition of the crucifixion of Christ. Now they had proof for the Jewish sacrilege of pushing a needle or nail into the Eucharist *matzot shel mitzvoh* to make it bleed, which was a favorite accusation hurled against the Jews. Father Flannery states that "it is not outside the confines of possibility that an odd superstitious Jew may have indulged in the sacrifice, the falsity resides in the attribution of the crime to Judaism itself."[22] We see from this statement how immensely important it still is for the clergy to hold on at least to the "possibility" of a Jewish documentation of the doctrine of the transubstantiation.

It is not apparent from the English word "Host," but the gender of the Latin word *Hostia* from which it derived is feminine. *Hostia* means both sacrificial animal and sacrificial virgin. *Immolare hostiam* is Ciceronic Latin for killing a virgin. This explains why by a failure of repression the victim of a ritual murder often turns out to be a girl. It also explains why Jews were not permitted to be on the street or stand at a window while the *hostia* was carried in a procession. I call this the *Lady Godiva Injunction*. In Germany the Jews were accused of *Hostienschändung*, i.e., rape of the *hostia*, literally bringing shame upon the *hostia* by robbing her of her virginity. Again we have a reversal here, the incited mob was eager to rape helpless Jewish girls.

Actually the real host is the person who gives hospitality to his guest, providing him with food and shelter and, according to archaic traditions, with a female companion for the night, the *Hostia*. The stranger, the guest, may be a god in disguise whose embrace would increase the fecundity and temporal prosperity of the *Hostia* and her family. But the syllable *hos-* is ambivalent, it appears not only in hospitality but also in hostility, a host is also an army, and the Latin *hostis* means enemy. *Pesach* is a feast of hospitality and the matzah is the token of Jewish hospitality which the clergy managed to turn into a token of Christian hostility.

The custom of providing a virginal bed companion for the visiting god, the *jus primae noctis*, can be brought into one line with the sacrifice of the firstling of the lambs, the first sheaf of the newly cut barley, or the first matzah on the Seder plate. Then the blood of the sacrificed lamb, or the matzah, and the blood from the defloration of the virgin are all stand-ins for the Holy Blood of the crucified Christ.

The child who had opportunity to observe the mother bleeding as a rule interprets the menstruation as the result of a sadistic attack (crucifixion) by the father. He could see undeniable pieces of evidence in the bloody pieces of linen with which she covered the same area where he saw the bloody loin cloth of Jesus.

By committing the ritual murder, the Jews are to act out the doctrine of the transubstantiation by mixing the blood into the host; in committing the rape of the host, they confirm the presence of blood in the host by squeezing it out, and by pricking the wafer they prove the bisexuality of the host or Eucharist. By the reference to Passover and the paschal lamb, the ritual murder is acknowledged as infanticide whose repetition is desired for the acquisition of the unlimited life expectancy of the paschal lamb, the eternal infant on the eternal lap of the eternal virgin, the opposite manifestation of Christ on the Cross.

Notes

1. Joshua Trachtenberg, *The Devil and the Jews* (New Haven: Yale University Press, 1943), p. 124.
2. Jacob R. Marcus, *The Jew in the Medieval World* (New York: Meridian, 1960), p. 121.

3. Ibid., pp. 121–24.

4. Trachtenberg, *Devil and the Jews*, pp. 131–32.

5. Max I. Dimont, *Jews, God and History* (New York: Simon and Schuster, 1962), p. 243.

6. Maurice Samuel, "Blood Accusation," *Midstream* 12, no. 7 (August–September 1966).

7. Joseph S. Bloch, *My Reminiscences* (Vienna and Berlin: R. Löwit, 1923), p. 16.

8. Sigmund Freud, *An Autobiographical Study*, trans. J. Strachey (London: Hogarth Press, 1935), p. 16.

9. Max Grunwald, *Geschichte der Wiener Juden* (Vienna: Selbstverlag der Israelitischen Kultusgemeinde, 1926).

10. Guido Kisch, "Kaiser Franz Josef und die Juden," *Aufbau*, 8 December 1961.

11. Kurt R. Grossmann, "Ritual-Denkmal in Lienz—1960 erneuert," *Aufbau*, 28 July 1961.

12. Simon Wiesenthal, "Tiroler Ritualmord Märchen," *Aufbau*, 11 May 1951.

13. Phil Baum and Carol Weisbrod, "Neo-Nazis and Extremists, Austria—Lingering and Shadows," *American Jewish Congress* (special issue) 23, no. 12 (12 September 1966).

14. Herbert Liebmann, "Wie lange noch Deggendorfer 'Hostienschändung'?" *Aufbau*, 30 September 1966.

15. Phil Baum, *American Jewish Congress*, 19 February 1968.

16. Michael Williams, *The Book of Christian Classics* (New York: Liveright, 1933).

17. Bernard Grebanier, *The Truth About Shylock* (New York: Random House, 1962).

18. Arthur Quiller-Couch, *Notes on Shakespeare's Workmanship* (New York: Henry Holt & Co., 1917), pp. 79–84.

19. Hayyim Schauss, *Guide to Jewish Holy Days* (New York: Schocken Books, 1964).

20. Friedrich Kluge, *Etymological Dictionary of the German Language* (London and New York: George Bell & Sons and MacMillan & Co., 1891).

21. Theodor Reik, "Der Eigene und der fremde Gott," *Imago Bücher IV* (Leipzig: Internazional Psychoanalytischer Verlag, 1923), p. 129.

22. Edward H. Flannery, *The Anguish of the Jews* (New York: Macmillan Co., 1965), p. 296, chapter 5, n. 44.

The Ritual Murder or Blood Libel Legend: A Study of Anti-Semitic Victimization through Projective Inversion

So much has been written on the blood libel legend that one might despair of being able to say anything about the legend that had not already been said before. In the following essay, I try to interpret the blood libel legend by using a psychoanalytic concept I call "projective inversion." I also draw on much of the previous scholarship—including many of the essays included in this casebook. The reader will have to form his or her own conclusion as to whether my utilization of projective inversion succeeds in illuminating both the possible cause and content of this insidious legend. It is my fervent hope that any understanding of any of the contributing factors in the formation of bigotry and prejudice may help in the constant struggle against bigotry and prejudice. That is what led me to carry out my research on such a horrible and dastardly legend in the first place.

If one were to poll most folklorists as to whether or not folklore was on the whole a positive force in human culture, I suspect there would be considerable consensus that indeed it was. A tale well told, a song well sung ordinarily give pleasure to the performers themselves and almost certainly to those in the performer's audience. Esthetically speaking, it would appear to be a safe generalization that life is more pleasant because of the charm of folk costume and the de-

Reprinted from *Temenos* 25 (1989): 7–32.

light in participating in a favorite calendrical festival. Shorn of its folkloristic dress, daily life would be ever so much more drab and dull than it otherwise is. Yet it is important to keep in mind that there is some folklore which is highly pernicious and even life-threatening. I am thinking of various forms of racist and sexist folklore. Social scientists are normally reluctant to attach value judgments to the data they study, but it is my contention that one can make a convincing case for the label "evil folklore" for selected individual items of tradition.[1]

Among the prime candidates for placement under the rubric of the folklore of evil, I would rank at or very near the top of the list the so-called blood libel legend. Other phrases designating this vicious legend include *blood accusation* and *ritual murder (accusation)*. These terms are used almost interchangeably but there are several scholars who have sought to distinguish between ritual murder and blood libel, arguing that ritual murder refers to a sacrificial murder in general whereas the blood libel entails specific use of the blood of the victim.[2] In the case of alleged Jewish ritual murder, the blood motivation is nearly always present which presumably accounts for the equally common occurrence of both ritual murder and blood libel as labels.

The relevant motif is V361. Christian child killed to furnish blood for Jewish rite. The typical gist of the story line is that one or more Jews murder an innocent Christian infant or child, supposedly to obtain blood required for ritual purposes, e.g., to mix with unleavened bread or to make matzah. The legend has been in constant circulation in oral and written tradition from the twelfth to the twentieth centuries, often leading to deadly consequences for Jews accused of the crime. Like all legends, the blood libel story is traditionally told as true, that is, as an actual historical happening.

Joshua Trachtenberg begins his chapter of *The Devil and the Jews* devoted to a discussion of ritual murder as follows: "Of all the bizarre charges against the Jewish people the one that has enjoyed the hardiest tenacity and the utmost notoriety and has produced the direst consequences, is the so-called ritual-murder accusation. In its popular version, it foists upon Jewish ritual the need for Christian blood at the Passover. The subject of much study and infinitely more polemics, its absurdity has been conclusively established, but the true nature of the accusation has never been made sufficiently clear."[3] Salomon Reinach made a similar comment: "Of all the accusations which fanaticism and ignorance have used as a weapon against Judaism, there is none which can be compared in terms of improbability and absurdity to that of ritual murder."[4] Max Grunwald, the pioneer of Jewish folklore studies, had this to say: "Of all the attacks on Jews, there could scarcely be one capable of inflicting a deeper or more painful injury than the blood-lie."[5] Another major figure in Jewish folkloristics, Moses Gaster, in a strong letter to the London *Times* of 2 October 1888 remarked: "Baseless and without foundation as these legends are, they are dangerous even in normal times; how much more in abnormal? Who can foresee to what terrible consequences such a superstition might lead, when the people fanatic with rage and terror, get hold of it and wreak their vengeance on innocent men?"[6] Finally, American ballad scholar Francis James Child used the following language: "And these pretended child-murders, with their horrible consequences, are only a part of a persecution which, with all moderation, may be rubricated as the most disgraceful chapter in the history of the human race."[7]

Anglo-American folklorists are reasonably familiar with the plot, in part because it occurs in ballad form, namely as "Sir Hugh, or, The Jew's Daughter," Child Ballad 155. It has many titles in oral tradition, e.g., "Hugh of Lincoln" or "Little Sir Hugh" among others. In the ballad, a Jewish temptress induces a young Christian boy to enter her garden where she brutally murders him, often taking special care to catch the blood in a basin or cup.[8]

The narrative is also well known because it is one of Chaucer's celebrated *Canterbury Tales:* the Prioress's Tale. The murder of Hugh of Lincoln supposedly occurred in 1255; Chaucer's tale was written near the end of the fourteenth century. The earliest subtype of the legend, according to the standard typology, goes back to before the year 1200 and contains the following elements:

1. A boy sings the responsorium "Gaude Maria" as he passes daily along a street in which Jews dwell, thereby provoking their resentment.
2. He is slain (either by a single Jew or by a group of them in conspiracy), and his body is buried under the earth in the Jew's house, in his garden, in a trench beside the door, in a stable under the manure, etc.
3. The boy's mother, in her search for him, passing by the Jew's door, hears the voice of her child, and with the assistance of friends, a crowd of citizens, forces an entrance.
4. The boy is dug up from the earth alive and unharmed.
5. In consequence of this miracle, the Jew (or Jews) according to most versions is converted.[9]

In other versions of the legend, the boy's body is thrown into a latrine. When the body is recovered, it miraculously continues to sing praise to the Virgin Mary, typically until a Christian priest removes a seed from under the child's tongue whereupon the singing stops (cf. motif V254.7: Murdered boy still sings "Ave" after his death).

It would be one thing if this classic bit of anti-Semitic folklore existed only in ballad or legend form, but the sad truth is that what has been so often described in legend and literature is also alleged to have occurred in life. There have not been tens, but hundreds of actual cases of blood libel tried in various courts in various countries. The map of Western and Eastern Europe and the Near East is profusely dotted with sites where ritual murders were said to have occurred.[10] Moreover, one must keep in mind that many of these allegations led to lengthy trials (often involving torture to extract "confessions" from the accused Jews) and eventual executions. "In 1171 at Blois, after due trial, thirty-eight Jews were burned at the stake; in 1191, at Bray-sur-Seine, the number of victims reached one hundred."[11] Trials occurred in England, France, Czechoslovakia, Germany, Hungary, Italy, Poland, Russia, Spain, and elsewhere. There is no comprehensive or definitive list of all the alleged instances of ritual murder, despite the fact that many of the numerous books devoted to the subject consist of little more than synopses of reported instances. For example, Frank (1901) reviews 172 cases. Monniot (1914) in a chapter entitled "The Facts" discusses more than 100 separate purported cases. Manzini (1930) lists 137 examples. Folklorist Peuckert (1935–36) gives some 175 examples in chronological order while Lïutostanskii (1934) summarizes 144 instances. Trachtenberg gives a round number of 150 charges of ritual murder but suggests these are not more than a "fraction" of the whole.[12]

Although one might have logically assumed that this strange medieval legend might have died out over time and that the number of recorded cases might have declined over the centuries, this does not appear to be the case at all. One observer noted that there seem to have been almost as many blood accusations in the nineteenth century as in all the previous centuries combined and that, for example, between 1887 and 1891, there were twenty-two indictments in Europe alone with some fifty cases of blood libel reported between 1870 and 1935.[13] It should also be remarked that compared to the large number of Jews actually brought to trial on the basis of blood libel or ritual murder charges, only a tiny percentage of the anti-Semitic accusers were ever themselves brought to trial.[14]

Some readers may find it hard to believe that Jews were dragged in front of tribunals accused of having performed ritual murder, often having been first tortured on several occasions so as to elicit a confession of guilt from them. But a considerable number of monographic studies have detailed these heinous trials which have sometimes ended with condemning the "guilty" Jew(s) to death. Some of the trials, especially those which took place in the nineteenth and early twentieth centuries attracted international notice.

One of the earliest trials was in Norwich, England, in 1144. Some even go so far as to claim that it was in England that the ritual murder charge first appeared,[15] and that it was with this account that "the continuous history of the Ritual Murder libel begins."[16] In fifteenth-century Spain, we find "El Santo Niño de la Guardia."[17] It was said that a group of

Jews and Catholic converts (from Judaism) had ritually murdered a child at La Guardia, near Avila, in imitation of the Passion of Jesus. This version of the blood libel legend, incidentally, was apparently used as part of the pretext to expel Jews from Spain in 1492.[18] (The infant was supposedly murdered in 1488 with the trial held in 1490 and 1491.) If this is so, then it would demonstrate the extraordinary power of folklore in general and legend in particular to effect political events. An annual ten-day holiday in La Guardia is said to continue to the present day and local clergy are not anxious to close down the La Guardia festival because it is the major village holiday and it brings in valuable income from tourist-pilgrims.[19] This instance of a festival springing up from a legend shows that the blood libel story remains alive and that it is even celebrated annually in the twentieth century. Unfortunately, this is not an isolated instance. For example, the Domingo del Val cult is widespread in Spain. According to tradition, little Domingo was a choir boy whose singing hymns so enraged Saragossa Jews in the 1250s that they secretly crucified him and buried his body. However, his body began to glow mysteriously, and in the twentieth century he is known as the patron saint of choir boys in Spain; in the Seo Cathedral in Saragossa, there is a brightly lighted chapel devoted to him, a chapel which actually serves as a site of destination for modern pilgrimages.[20]

The blood libel legend is not only the basis of ongoing festivals, but it has also been memorialized in church decoration. Legends proclaiming the Jewish "ritual murder" of Christian children or the profanation or desecration of holy wafers are celebrated in various European towns in such artistic form as tapestries or stained glass church windows. For example, there are such windows or pictures or tapestries ornamenting the choir of the Saint Michael–Saint Gudule Cathedral in Brussels, a ceiling fresco in the small Tyrol village of Judenstein, paintings in a church sanctuary in the Vienna suburb of Korneuberg, and a stained glass window in a Paris church chapel.[21] These artistic renderings of the legend provide daily reminders in such locales of the existence (and by extension presumably the truth or historicity) of the story.

One might think that in modern times there would have been protests against festivals or stained glass representations of the legend, but that is not the case. In only a few instances have campaigns waged against this blatantly anti-Semitic folklore had any success. In the Judenstein case, we have perhaps a typical situation. A French Jew, Jean Hauser, whose brother died at Auschwitz, tells of a vacation trip in 1952 in Austria not far from Innsbruck when he took an unexpected detour to an apparently idyllic hamlet of Judenstein (the name meaning, of course, the stone of Jews).[22] Entering the village church, he found in the nave, near the altar, in front of a tapestry, three figures made of wood or wax in a menacing pose with knives in hand surrounding a stone upon which was stretched out a supplicating infant garbed in white. The scene purportedly commemorated the ritual murder of Andrew of Rinn at Judenstein, as Hauser soon discovered when he purchased souvenir postcards in the shop located conveniently and immediately across from the church. He later learned that for nearly two centuries, Judenstein had been a place of pilgrimage where children led by their parents could see for themselves the reconstruction of the assassination by three Jews of a small child of about their own age.[23]

Interestingly enough, the Judenstein site had been noted a year earlier in 1951 by famed Nazi-hunter Simon Wiesenthal who wrote a short essay "Tiroler Ritualmord Märchen" in protest. In that report, Wiesenthal voices his dismay at seeing full cars and busloads of school children making annual pilgrimages to Rinn under the tutelage of their religious instructors to see the ritual murder lie depicted as a historical event. Wiesenthal was sufficiently concerned to bother to write a letter of protest about these pilgrimages to Cardinal Innitzer via Innsbruck Bishop Rusch, but he was rebuffed by the latter when he replied that ". . . the Jewish writer goes much too far if he meant to claim that Jews had never done such things."![24] Prejudice and bigotry die hard if at all. Part of the problem is clearly that of trying to disprove the negative. As one report of Bishop Rusch's response to a protest from the Jewish community of Linz reads: "The Jews have not up to the present time ever proved that they never committed a parallel crime [of ritual murder]."[25]

After several repeated unsuccessful attempts to halt the pilgrimages, a plaque was finally put up in 1961 in the Judenstein church by a secret order of Pope John XXIII. The plaque stated that the case of Andrew of Rinn was nothing other than a legend and that "it is clear that the event had nothing to do with the Jewish people." Pope John also directed that the cult of Andrew be suppressed and that the various tableaux, statues, and frescoes be removed from the church. But the villagers of Rinn became incensed. If the statue of the martyred Andrew were removed, they would openly revolt against the church. So despite the papal order, the statue was left intact, and a large fresco on the ceiling of the church showing a group of Jews in the act of burying little Andrew was similarly left alone. Moreover, the pilgrimages continued with the statue of the infant martyr surrounded by flowers and candles left by those who came to pray from near and far.[26] It may be concluded from this that it is not easy to legislate folklore out of existence. Since the Austrian authorities decided not to suppress the artwork celebrating the legend or to remove the statue of the martyr,[27] it remains to be seen if the installation of the plaque can succeed in defusing a legend which has circulated and flourished for centuries. (Andreas Oxner of Rinn was said to have been killed by Jewish merchants on the "Jew-stone" in 1462 and although he was never officially beatified or canonized by the Catholic church, a plenary indulgence for pilgrims to Rinn was granted on 15 January 1754.)[28] All this attests to the remarkable staying power of folklore. While folklore's resistance to censorship may be deemed a positive thing, e.g., when folklore opposes political repression or social injustice, this very same strength of tradition also means that dangerous and pernicious racist folklore cannot really be checked or halted either.

There have been so many famous cases and trials involving ritual murder that it is simply not possible to recount them all in a brief overview. In 1840, the Jews of Damascus were accused of the ritual murder of a Capuchin friar, Father Tommaso. To obtain "evidence" that it was a case of ritual murder, some seventy Jews were tortured to secure the necessary confessions.[29] There was a concerted surge of international protest and it did have some effect.[30] The Sultan Abdul Mejid issued a firman or proclamation which said in part:

> An ancient prejudice prevailed against the Jews. The ignorant believed that the Jews were accustomed to sacrifice a human being, to make use of his blood at their feast of Passover. . . . the religious books of the Hebrews have been examined by learned men, well versed in their religious literature, the result of which examination is that it is found that Jews are strongly prohibited not only from using human blood but even that of animals. It therefore follows that the charges made against them and their religion are nothing but pure calumnies. . . . we cannot permit the Jewish nation (whose innocence of the crime alleged against them is evident) to be vexed and tormented upon accusations which have not the least foundation in truth.[31]

The sultan's words—like the words uttered by various popes—proved to be insufficient to put the legend to rest.

It should be noted that there were a number of papal bulls on the subject of ritual murder, e.g., in 1247, 1259, 1272, 1422, 1540, as well as Cardinal Ganganelli's famous investigative report of 1759.[32] Although a number of popes did honestly seek to repudiate and deny the blood libel legend, it is also true that the semi-official Vatican periodical, the *Civiltà Cattolica* from 1881 to 1914 promoted and systematically "documented" the legend,[33] and this was the case as well with other nominally Catholic periodicals, e.g., *La Croix*, in the late nineteenth century.[34] In some instances, Catholic priests cleverly used the ritual murder accusation as a weapon against Jews.[35]

In his oft-cited report of 1759, Cardinal Ganganelli, the future Clement XIV (1769–74), reviewed a large number of the alleged ritual murder cases and rejected them all with the exception of Andrew of Rinn (1462) and Simon of Trent (1475). In Ganganelli's words, "I admit, then, as true the fact of the Blessed Simon, a boy three years old, killed by the Jews in Trent in the 1475 in hatred of the faith of Jesus

Christ. . . . I also admit the truth of another fact, which happened in the year 1462 in the village of Rinn. . . . in the person of the Blessed Andreas, a boy barbarously murdered by the Jews in hatred of the Faith of Jesus Christ."[36] Ganganelli generously adjudged his own findings as being generally an exculpation of the Jews. In his own words, "It should then be concluded that, among so many infanticides imputed by writers to the Jews in hatred of our Holy Faith, only two can be said to be true, since these two only can be said to be proved by authentic proofs after much diligent search and a considerable lapse of time. . . . I do not believe, then, that by admitting the truth of the two facts . . . one can reasonably deduce that this is a maxim, either theoretical or practical, of the Jewish nation; for two isolated events are not enough to establish a certain and common axiom."[37] Vacandard plausibly suggests that Ganganelli's views of these two cases was very probably influenced by the political fact that there had been previous papal decisions authorizing the cults of Simon and Andrew and the miracles attributed to these martyrs.[38]

Among the more famous cases of the late nineteenth and early twentieth centuries are that of Tisza-Eslar, Hungary (1882);[39] the murder of a nineteen-year-old Christian girl, Agnes Hruza, on 29 March 1899, in the Grzina Forest near Polna in Czechoslovakia,[40] a case which fortunately was influenced by the critical intervention of T. G. Masaryk, then a professor at the Czech university in Prague, who would later (1918) be elected as the first president of Czechoslovakia;[41] the ritual murder case in Kiev in 1911 involving a twelve-year-old boy, also known as the Beilis case, which came to trial in 1913;[42] and a case in Massena, New York, in 1928.[43] Many of these and other cases are discussed at length in detailed essays and book-length monographs, many of which reprint actual trial transcripts.[44]

Even in those instances where the accused was eventually found innocent, the very fact that a trial took place in which the basis of the accusation was essentially the existence of the legend demonstrates the undeniable tenacity of the story. Some well-known individuals went on record to state their conviction that the ritual murder story was true. The celebrated traveler and amateur anthropologist-folklorist Sir Richard Burton in his book, *The Jew, the Gypsy and El Islam,* published posthumously in 1898, ends his supposedly objective ethnographic description of the Jews with a list of "what *history* [my emphasis] tells us concerning the Jews, their crimes, and their condemnations,"[45] a list which includes numerous alleged instances of ritual murder. The editor of this curious volume claims he elected to suppress Burton's special "Appendix on Human Sacrifice among the Sephardim or Eastern Jews," the data for which Burton was said to have gathered during the period from 1869 to 1871 when he served as British Consul in Damascus, although one anti-Semitic source claimed that the appendix in question had been suppressed through pressure from influential Jews.[46] The important point is that Burton evidently considered blood libel legends as "history," not fiction.

Unfortunately, the research of folklorists has on occasion been utilized to "prove" the existence and veracity of ritual murder. Toward the middle of the nineteenth century, the Russian Ministry of Foreign Affairs set up a special secret commission to investigate the supposed "use by Jews of the blood of Christian children" and this commission enlisted the aid of folklorist V. I. Dal. He wrote a book in 1844 on ritual murder based upon fieldwork carried out among the so-called Old Believers.[47] Apparently, Dal was himself persuaded by his informants of the truth of the custom and his research was cited in the Kiev trial of Beilis in 1913.[48] It may or may not be a total coincidence that Dal's book was reprinted in 1913.[49]

In similar fashion, Sir James George Frazer's writings were also cited in the Kiev trial. When Frazer learned of this, he immediately wrote a letter to the London *Times* protesting the citation of his research in such a trial. The particular passage from "The Scapegoat" volume of *The Golden Bough* which had been quoted in the trial was actually published in the *Times* of the day preceding, that is, 10 November 1913. However, a close reading of both the passage itself and Frazer's letter of protest of November 11 reveal considerable equivocality on Frazer's part. The upshot is that he does not really deny the possibility of Jewish ritual murder. His position is rather that if ignorant lower-class Jews did commit such crimes on occasion, that was no reason to hate all Jews. In other words, Frazer's anti-Semitism was tempered by typical British class consciousness: It wasn't Jews who committed the crime, but lower-class Jews. "If all the charges of ritual murder which have been brought against the Jews in modern times are not, as seems most probably, mere idle calumnies . . . the extraordinary tenacity of life exhibited by the lowest forms of superstition in the minds of ignorant people, whether they are Jews or Gentiles, would suffice to account for an occasional recrudescence of primitive barbarity among the most degraded part of the Jewish community."[50] Frazer acknowledges the debate about the issue of historicity, but he hedges by saying, "Into this troubled area I prefer not to enter; I will only observe that, so far as I have looked into the alleged cases, and these are reported in sufficient detail, the majority of the victims are said to have been children and to have met their fate in spring, often in the week before Easter."[51] That statement could hardly be taken as any kind of a repudiation of the truth value of the ritual murder legend! Shortly thereafter, he again fails to take a stand. "If deeds of the sort alleged have been really done by Jews—a question on which I must decline to pronounce an opinion—they would then interest the student of custom as isolated instances of reversion to an old and barbarous ritual which once flourished commonly enough among the ancestors both of Jews and Gentiles. . . . Such customs die hard."[52]

In his letter to the *Times*, Frazer does not alter his position: ". . . while I discuss hypothetically the possibility of an occasional crime instigated by superstition among the dregs of the Jewish as of the Christian population, I stigmatize such accusations against the Jewish people as 'a monstrous injustice,' and speak of all the charges of ritual murder as '*most probably*' mere idle calumnies, the baneful fruit of bigotry, ignorance, and malice" [emphasis mine].[53] The continued and insistent use of such words as "occasional" crime and "probably" certainly strongly suggest that

Frazer may have harbored some personal conviction that Jewish ritual murder was in part a historical reality.

Some twentieth-century folklorists apparently believe in the historicity of the blood libel legend, e.g., Caro Baroja of Spain[54] and Peuckert of Germany. The latter called for a scientific study to determine which cases were false and which were fact. After having compiled a considerable chronological list of cases, Peuckert comments, "There remains only one question to be answered in connection with this shocking list: For what purpose did the Jews use the blood?"[55] Moses Gaster, in his review of the volume of the *Handwörterbuch des Deutschen Aberglaubens* in which Peuckert's extensive entry on "Ritualmord" appeared, remarked scathingly, "It is unfortunate that this volume should be disfigured by a disgraceful article on the foul blood-libel accusation of which author, publisher, and editors ought to be thoroughly ashamed."[56]

If folklorists considered the blood libel legend credible, then it is no wonder that various folk groups did so as well. It is, however, disheartening to realize that the legend has continued to exert its maleficent influence well into the twentieth century. A book published in Russia in 1917 recapitulating the Beilis trial in Kiev in 1913 made the following shameful statement: "The fanatic murder committed by the *Zhidi* [Yids] in order to obtain Christian blood is not a legend even in the twentieth century; it is not a blood libel; it is a terrible reality."[57] The lie and legend also surfaced in the United States. Besides the Massena incident of 1928, among others, there was also a pamphlet which claimed that the 1932 kidnapping of Charles A. Lindberg's baby was an instance of Jewish ritual murder.[58]

The striking revival or perpetuation of the blood libel legend in the twentieth century was very much nurtured by Nazi Germany. The legend was obviously made to order for anti-Semitic propaganda efforts. Leaflets circulated in Berlin and Dresden in 1933 telling of ritual murder accusations and calling for the prosecution of Jews.[59] A special ritual murder of *Der Stürmer* was published in May of 1934. The campaign of hate continued throughout World War II. Nazi researcher

Hellmut Schramm compiled a massive 475-page collection of blood libel legends entitled *Der jüdische Ritualmord*. Published in 1943, the book struck a responsive chord. Here is part of a letter dated 19 May 1943, and addressed to SS Gruppenführer Dr. Kaltenbrunner, chief of police in Berlin:[60]

> Dear Kaltenbrunner,
>   I have ordered a large number of copies of the book *Jewish Ritual Murder* and I have distributed them to individuals up to the rank of *Standartenführer* [SS colonel]. . . . We should proceed to investigate ritual murders among the Jews with respect to those who have not yet been evacuated. Every case discovered should be submitted to me. We will organize then several trials for this category of crime. The problem of ritual murder ought to be treated by experts in such countries as Rumania, Hungary, and Bulgaria. I have the idea that we could pass on these ritual murder cases to the press in order to facilitate the evacuation of Jews from these countries. . . .
>   [The letter concludes:] In short, I am of the opinion that we could give anti-Semitism an incredible virulence with the help of anti-Semitic propaganda in English and perhaps even in Russian by giving huge publicity to ritual murders.
>
> [Signed] Heil Hitler!
Heinrich Himmler

But the blood libel legend did not end with the end of World War II either in Germany or anywhere else where anti-Semitism flourishes. In November of 1960, Golda Meir, addressing Israel's Knesset specifically protested against blood libel charges appearing in the official newspaper of the Soviet Republic of Daghestan, which accused Jews of using the blood of Moslem children for ritual purposes—Moslems being the predominant group in Daghestan. Soviet authorities apparently ignored a delegation sent to Moscow seeking a retraction.[61] The legend may have been Christian in origin but it also can function in a Moslem context. In 1985, Mustafa Tlas, then Defense Minister and Deputy Prime Minister of Syria, holder of a law degree and at one time a doctoral candidate at the Sorbonne, published a book in Arabic entitled *The Matza of Zion*, a two-hundred-page book which revives the 1840 Damascus legend. A quote from the book provided by the Simon Wiesenthal Center in Los Angeles, which sought to alert people about the existence of this updated version of the legend, reads: "From that moment on every mother warned her child: Do not stray far from home. The Jew may come by and put you in his sack to kill you and suck your blood for the Matza of Zion."

It is not my purpose in this essay to document all the countless cases of blood libel which have occurred or even to demonstrate how the legend may have encouraged prostitutes or unwed Christian mothers to practice infanticide and then blame Jews for the crime. There is evidence that the victims of child abuse or child murder may have been "planted" on Jewish property.[62]

My interest lies in other questions. Why did such a legend arise in the first place? Why has it continued to be popular? Why should it have been believed to be true for at least eight centuries? There isn't a shred of evidence whatsoever to indicate that Jews ever killed Christian children to obtain blood for sacrificial or ritual purposes. We are dealing here not with fact, but with fiction, not with history but with folklore, not with life but with legend. But how could such a bizarre legend have come into existence to be used as a continuing basis for cruel prejudice and as a charter for anti-Semitic sentiments?

Psychology is necessary, I submit, for the analysis of fantasy material. Most of the writers who have studied the blood libel legend have tried to treat it historically or rather have tried to show that the legend lacks historicity. I have no quarrel with those of a historical turn of mind, but I remain convinced that historical analysis alone cannot fully explicate the content of fantasy. The question can then be phrased: Why should Christians think that Jews murder innocent children to obtain blood to mix with their matzah?

Some scholars have recognized the need for psychological interpretation in connection with the challenge of illuminating the blood libel legend. Isidore Loeb writing in 1889 remarked that savants searching for a historical origin of the blood accusation would search in vain. "The problem is not one of history, but one of psychology."[63] Among the earliest psychoanalytic interpretations of the blood libel legend was that proposed by Theodor Reik in 1923.[64] According to Reik, the legend represented a displacement of the reproach that the Jews had killed and eaten Christ who was substituting for the father god. The reproach "derives from an unconscious feeling of guilt accomplished by projection. Mankind insofar as it has turned Christian confesses in this legend without any disguise the old tendency to deicide."[65] It is equivalent to the argument between two brothers who have together murdered the father and now want to shift the guilt to each other. But it is not immediately obvious—at least to me—why we are obliged to interpret the legend as an example of killing a *father* figure, especially keeping in mind that in the vast majority of reported instances, it is specifically a child or infant who is ostensibly murdered.

In a later (1967) psychoanalytic reading of the legend, Seiden argues along similar Oedipal lines to explain ritual murder by suggesting that Christian sons want to kill Jewish fathers—Judaism did historically give rise/birth to Christianity—claiming that this is why the Jew is "the monstruous father who threatens or destroys the lives of his innocent primordial children. He is the guilt-ridden father who must be punished by his imaginary Christian son."[67] In a further articulation of the Oedipal model, Seiden claims, "As a ritual murderer of little children, the medieval Jew thus personifies and reflects the unconscious fear of 'the primordial male child': the child's fear that his father, whose rival he is for the latter's wife (and consequently for his own mother), may one day castrate him."[68] One difficulty here is that the "plot" of the blood libel legend rarely involves a battle for a female mother-wife figure. Moreover, the hypothetical suggestion that Christians want to kill their father-figure Jews would *not* seemingly elucidate such details of the blood libel legend as the Jews requiring Christian infant blood to make matzah.

Rappaport argues in 1975, in yet another psychoanalytic reading of the legend, that "by committing the ritual murder the Jews are to act out the doctrine of the transubstantiation by mixing the blood into the host. . . . By the reference to Passover . . . the ritual murder is acknowledged as infanticide whose repetition is desired for the acquisition of the unlimited life expectancy of the . . . eternal infant on the eternal lap of the eternal virgin."[69] But it is by no means clear why ritual infanticide committed by Jews would ensure eternal life for the infant Jesus.

Finally in 1982, Rosenman suggests that the blood libel legend gives "expression to the adult's desire to destroy enviable youth."[70] Adults thus do to infants what they think infants will want to do to adults. According to this formula, adults believe that infants want to devour their (adult) blood and so to forestall that, the adults devour the infants' blood. Supposedly this parental hatred for their children is projected onto Jews. In addition Rosenman contends, "Also projected upon the Jew in the blood libel is envy of the young sibling who drains all the mother's nuturant fluids, leaving the mother too depleted to succor the subject." Here we find the standard psychoanalytic arguments based upon the familiar parent-child as well as sibling rivalries. Yet the semantic fit, if any, between conventional psychoanalytic theory and the actual details of the blood libel legend seems a bit contrived or forced. A Jungian as opposed to a Freudian reading of the legend offers even fewer specifics insofar as a Jungian might simply label the legend as a reflection of the dark or shadow side of man.[71]

I am persuaded that a more appropriate and revealing approach to the legend lies in the Christian need for a Jewish scapegoat and in the psychological process I have termed "projective inversion."[72] In a brilliant analysis of the legend of the Wandering Jew, Hyam Maccoby has proposed that Christians needed a dead Jesus to worship, but that they also needed someone to kill Jesus, to take the blame or bear the guilt for committing the crime.[73] Although Jews did not kill Jesus (who, of course, was himself a Jew—the Romans did), Christian folklore insists that the Jews were Christ-killers. In this context, the blood libel is simply another example of the same kind of Christian folklore. Christians blame Jews for something which the Christians needed to have happen, a thing which the Jews never did.

Projective inversion refers to a psychological process in which A accuses B of carrying out an action which A really wishes to carry out him or herself. Otto Rank described this process (but without calling it projective inversion) in his path-breaking *The Myth of the Birth of the Hero* in 1909. In standard Indo-European biographies, the father tries to kill his own son. According to Rank, it is the son who wishes to kill his own father (along Oedipal wish-fulfillment lines), but since this is a taboo thought, it is expressed in folklore the other way round, namely that the father wishes to kill his son.

This psychological process of "blaming the victim" is also found in female terms. A girl would like to remove or kill her own mother (so as to have her father for herself), but this is a taboo thought. So in fairy tales, it is invariably the mother who tries to remove or kill her own daughter. In the tale of Hansel and Gretel (Aarne-Thompson tale type 327), it is really Gretel's story. It is a girl-centered tale and therefore it is about a girl's struggle with her mother. In the original *oral* tale, it is actually Gretel's *mother* who sends the children out to the forest to die, but the Grimms altered the tale and changed "mother" to "stepmother."[74] The fight for nourishment involves Gretel and the witch (an evil mother imago) who seduces the children with the orally attractive gingerbread house so that she can eat the children. The struggle ends when Gretel dupes the witch/mother into being burned up in her own oven—a symbol which suggests both the production of food and the production of infants—to have "a bun in the oven" is a conventional euphemism for pregnancy. Or in other fairy tales, the girl's taboo wish to marry her own father is transformed through projective inversion into a father who wishes to marry his own daughter.

In the case of majority-minority group relations, it is typically the minority group which is victimized by the majority group's stereotype or image of the minority group. Blacks are victimized by having to conform to white stereotypes of blacks; women are victimized by having to conform to men's stereotypes of women; and in the present instance, Jews are victimized by having to conform to Christian stereotypes of Jews.

Let us be absolutely clear about this. I am saying that it is Christians, *not* Jews, who would like to commit the blood libel and in a way they do. It is, after all, Romans, *not* Jews, who killed a savior and it is Christians who use his blood in *their* ritual. The Eucharist is one of the central rituals of Christianity and this is so whether one believes that the bread and wine actually turn into the body of Jesus Christ or simply commemorate Jesus' last supper. Either way, it is an act of patent cannibalism. To incorporate the blood and body of one's savior is at the very least symbolic cannibalism. The doctrine of transubstantiation as found in Roman Catholicism and the Orthodox Eastern churches would seemingly entail literal rather than figurative cannibalism.

The Eucharist is a fairly complex symbolic ritual for it entails not only cannibalism, but also the male usurpation of the female nurturant role. It is men who give their body and blood (no milk is available from males) to nurture their followers. That is presumably why women are not permitted to give the Eucharist. It is a purely male ritual involving the imitation of female nurturance.[75]

For the commission of an aggressively cannibalistic act, participants in the Eucharist would normally feel guilt,[76] but so far as I am aware, no one has ever suggested that a Catholic should ever feel any guilt for partaking of the Host. Where is the guilt for such an act displaced? I submit it is projected wholesale to another group, an ideal group for scapegoating. By means of this projective inversion, it is not we Christians who are guilty of murdering an individual in order to use his blood for ritual religious purposes (the Eucharist), but rather it is you Jews who are guilty of murdering an individual in order to use his or her blood for ritual religious purposes, making matzah. The fact that Jesus was Jewish makes the projective inversion all the more appropriate. It is a perfect transformation: Instead of Christians killing a Jew, we have Jews killing a Christian![77]

Another indication that projective inversion underlies the blood libel legend comes from the supposed motivation for Jews to commit ritual murder. Almost invariably, the anti-Semitic tract will proclaim that the Jews killed the innocent Christian infant because Jews hate Christians.[78] In the language of the 1759 report of Cardinal Ganganelli, infants Simon and Andrew were killed by the Jews "in hatred of the faith of Jesus Christ."[79] We know that in standard projective inversion, "I hate you" becomes transformed into "You hate me." By transposing subject and object, the initial party is left free to hate his or her enemy and furthermore to be totally absolved of feelings of guilt therefor. So the Christian hatred of Jews is neatly transformed into Jews' hatred of Christians. (Another modern example of this kind of projective inversion occurs when men accused of raping women claim that the women victims actually wanted sexual activity. The undoubted power of this projective inversion is such that rape victims are sometimes made to feel that they, not the rapists, are on trial.)

Projective inversion also serves to illuminate the curious detail in which Jews are alleged to need Christian blood to make matzah. First of all, Jews are not supposed to consume blood. Genesis 9:4: "Only you shall not eat flesh with its life, that is, its blood." Leviticus 3:17: "It shall be a perpetual statute throughout your generations, in all your dwelling places, that you eat neither fat nor blood." Leviticus 17:12: "There I have said to the people of Israel, No person among you shall eat blood." As many authors have pointed out, Jews are expressly forbidden to incorporate blood and this is why Kosher butchers take great care to drain blood from any animal to be eaten.[80] English folklorist Venetia Newall goes so far as to suggest that it may have been the non-Jew's misunderstanding of such ritual rules of blood-letting that led to the formation of the blood libel legend in the first place.[81]

The consistency of the Old Testament rule prohibiting the eating of blood may perhaps be usefully contrasted with the New Testament words of Jesus (John 6:53–56): "Truly, truly, I say to you, unless you eat the flesh of the Son of man and drink his blood, you have no life in you; he who eats my

355

flesh and drinks my blood has eternal life, and I will raise him up at the last day. For my flesh is food indeed, and my blood is drink indeed. He who eats my flesh and drinks my blood abides in me, and I in him." The point is obvious: Whereas Jews are specifically forbidden to drink blood, Christians are specifically ordered to do so. This is why Rappaport is correct when he says, "The paradox of the blood accusation is that the Jews are accused by the Christians of consuming blood which is in accordance with Christian ritual tradition, but is trespassing the Mosaic law."[82] But now thanks to the device of projective inversion, we can understand this paradox. In a *Christian* projection, the Jews operate under Christian, *not* Jewish, terms. One has only to compare the highly *negative* image of evil Jews standing with basins waiting to collect the blood from the slain innocent child with the very *positive* image in Christian iconography of Joseph of Arimathea who used a chalice (the Holy Grail) to collect the precious blood from the body of Jesus![83]

The fundamentally Christian aspect of the projection also explains why, as Maccoby reminds us, "the accusation is associated with the Christian festival of Easter, *not* with the Jewish festival of Passover; it was at Easter-time that these alleged crimes took place."[84] Since Easter is the time of crucifixion (as well as resurrection), this might be a period of maximum or intensified guilt feelings on the part of Christians for eating the body and blood of their god. Other evidence that projective inversion is involved comes from the celebrated case of Simon of Trent in 1475 when Jews were alleged to have admitted that they required "fresh Christian blood" because it was a "jubilee year," but as Trachtenberg astutely observes, it was a jubilee in the *Catholic* calendar, but not in the Jewish calendar.[85] The Jews under duress and torture had to confess their "crime" in strictly Christian terms.

What about the blood being used or needed to make matzah? If the story needed a functional equivalent for the Christian Eucharist which involved wine (blood) and a wafer, then obviously the nearest thing in Jewish ritual to the Eucharistic wafer is the matzah. The obvious parallels between the Eucharist and the ritual murder/blood libel were pointed out

356

by earlier writers, but were explained solely from a Christian perspective in terms of the Jews intentionally seeking to mock the Passion.[86] Maccoby puts it this way: "The Jews . . . were pictured as doing in reality what the Christian worshipper was doing in fantasy, i.e., killing a child and drinking its blood.[87]

We can now better understand why the blood libel legend so often gets mixed up with related legends of profaning the host.[88] Using blood to make matzah is in symbolic terms not all that different from making the host bleed. The belief that Jews pierced the wafers making them bleed apparently goes back at least to the end of the thirteenth century.[89] Reports indicate that Jews were persecuted and burned as punishment for this alleged miraculous crime.

Again in terms of projective inversion, it is Christians who profane the Passover meal by claiming that Jews use blood to make matzah. The Last Supper was in all probability a Passover meal, but that historical fact has little to do with the projective fantasy. The Jews did not and do not profane Christian Eucharistic ritual. It is the underlying Christian guilt for orally incorporating the blood and flesh of their god, commonly perceived as the Christ *child*, which makes them project that guilt to the convenient Jewish scapegoat.

As Maccoby observes in his analysis of the Wandering Jew, Christians want Jews to accept the role assigned to them by Christian fantasy, e.g., as killers of Christ.[90] Recall that in the summary of the major subtype of the Prioress's Tale, the story ends with the Jews being converted. This is straight, unadulterated wishful thinking on Christians' part. The guilty Jew should accept his punishment and be converted to Christianity. This is perhaps why so many blood libel legends involve converted or apostate Jews in their plots. When Jews resisted acting out their assigned part in this overt Christian fantasy, Christians became angry, very angry—just as whites become angry if blacks don't conform to the white stereotype of blacks and just as men become angry if women won't conform to the men's stereotype of women.

The blood libel legend is clearly *not* a significant part of Jewish folklore any more than the legend of the Wandering

Jew is part of Jewish folklore.[91] The blood libel legend and the legend of the Wandering Jew are part of the Christian folklore about Jews. Unfortunately, because of the very nature of the legend genre—that is, a story set in the modern, postcreation world and told as true—the blood libel legend has had a devastating effect upon Christian-Jewish relations in Europe and elsewhere.

There is yet one more piece of evidence to be adduced in support of the interpretation of the blood libel legend proposed here. To what extent is it reasonable to assume that the Christian celebration of the Eucharist is perceived as a form of ritual cannibalism or murder? Has this perception existed in a documentable form? Relevant here is the fact that it was the Christians themselves who in the earliest years of Christianity were accused of killing infants to obtain their blood to be used for sacrificial purposes.[92] Presumably, the accusation was made by non-Christians who recognized the bloody cannibalistic underpinnings of the Eucharist, although not everyone agrees with this explanation.[93] These charges were leveled very early in the history of Christianity. Pliny the Younger writing the Emperor Trajan circa A.D. 110 commented that he had interrogated Christian prisoners who adamantly denied that they had murdered children and drunk the blood.[94] Tertullian, born in the middle of the second century, who became one of the most important early Christian writers, referred to Pliny's letter in his famous *Apologeticus*, written near the end of the second century, before articulating the charges in somewhat gory detail. He begins his seventh chapter: "We are called abominable from the sacrament of infanticide and the feeding thereon." Then after directing some well-chosen criticisms at rumor, which is what he aptly labels the blood accusation, he tries in the next chapter to show the absurdity of the rumor by recounting it: "Come, plunge the sword into an infant who is no one's enemy, guilty of no crime, the child of all: or if such bloodshed is another's duty, do you merely stand by a human dying before he has really lived; wait for the flight of the new life; catch the scarce-formed blood; with it soak your bread, and enjoy your meal." Tertullian even imagines someone in charge of the ritual murder giving verbal instructions: "You have need of a little child, still soft, with no knowledge of death, who will smile under your knife; also bread, in which to gather the blood sauce."[95] This enables us to understand a wave of persecutions of Christians in southern France in A.D. 177 in which mobs accused Christians of cannibalism. Reports of the Eucharist led to rumors that Christians had consumed someone's blood and flesh.[96]

Anyone the least bit familiar with the simplistic attempts of small children to counter insults by turning the very same insults back upon the initial insulters ought to be able to see how Christians might try to deflect the blood libel accusations aimed at them by claiming that it was instead another group which was guilty of performing ritual murder. In one scholar's words, "Unfortunately Christians, after the Christian religion became dominant, directed against others the calumny once directed against themselves."[97] As we have noted, through projective inversion, it was not Christians who were guilty of murdering the Jewish son of a Jewish father god, but it was Jews who were guilty of murdering a Christian innocent (usually a boy).

Before the advent of psychoanalytic theory and the identification or formulation of such concepts as projective inversion, as defined here, some scholars did intuitively understand the basic psychodynamics of the blood libel legend. The Dutch jurist and philosopher Hugo Grotius, in a letter dated 12 December 1636, suggested that the ritual murder accusation derived simply from the Christian hatred of the Jews and that the accusation was strangely similar to comparable accusations made against the early Christians themselves.[98] Isidore Loeb who was one of the first to recognize that the problem was one of psychology, not history, spoke astutely about the popular obsession with the mystical idea of blood. "Those who accuse the Jews accuse or betray themselves. The Jew is there only to put into action the dream [nightmare] they carry within themselves. They burden them [the Jews] with playing in their place the drama which simultaneously attracts and terrifies them."[99] Loeb appears to have understood that the blood libel legend is a Christian fantasy in which Jews were forced to act against their will.

In much the same way, twentieth-century scholars have understood the issue even if they fail to utilize such psychoanalytic concepts as projective inversion. For example, René Girard in his provocative 1987 essay "Generative Scapegoating" does not make specific mention of the blood libel legend, but he speaks eloquently of the "imaginary crimes and real punishments" of victims, and more to the point, he draws attention to the role reversal of victimizer and victim: "The victimizers see themselves as the passive victims of their own victim, and they see their victim as supremely active, eminently capable of destroying them."[100] So many Christians saw and for that matter still see the Jews.

The sad truth about the blood libel legend is not so much that it was created—the need for such a psychological projection on the part of Christians is evident enough—but that it was believed to be true and accepted as such and that the lives of many individual Jews were adversely affected by some bloodthirsty Christians who believed or pretended to believe in the historicity of the blood libel legend.

Let me end as I began by remarking once again that not all folklore constitutes a positive and constructive force in human society. Folklore is powerful fantasy material and it unfortunately has the capacity to act as a dangerous and all too potent force for evil. I wish I could be sanguine about the blood libel legend's eventually dying out. But the undeniable persistence of this pernicious legend for the past eight centuries must give one pause. Louis Ginzberg, the celebrated student of Jewish legends, probably summed up the problem best in the first sentence of his unpublished 24-page "A Reply to Mr. Pranaitis," inspired by the Beilis case in Kiev: "August Dillmann, the famous oriental scholar and Professor of Hebrew at the Berlin University, once remarked, 'I do not see any use in refuting the Blood-Accusation; those who spread it do not believe it, and the fanatical who believe it do not read the refutation, nor would it have any weight with them if they would read it.'"[101]

Notes

1. See Rysan 1955.
2. Cf. Cohen 1982:244; Cohen 1983:1n.2. Trachtenberg also devotes separate chapters to ritual murder (1966:124–39) and to the blood accusation (1966:140–55).
3. Trachtenberg 1966:124.
4. Reinach 1892:161.
5. Grunwald 1906:5.
6. Gaster's letter is cited in full in Newall 1975:198–200.
7. Child 1962:240–41.
8. There is considerable scholarship devoted to this ballad. See Michel 1834a and 1834b; Halliwell-Philips 1849 (drawn largely from Michel); Hume 1849; Jacobs 1893–94; Gresham 1934; Beckwith 1951; Woodall 1955; Ridley 1967; Hippensteel 1969; Bebbington 1971; and Langmuir 1972. It should be noted that the blood libel was the subject of folksongs in other countries as well, e.g., Germany. See Lewin 1906 and Hsia 1988:59–60. For a general account of the image of the Jew in German folksong, see Kynass 1934.
9. This summary follows the research of Brown 1906. For a further consideration of Brown's typology, see Statler 1950. For an entrée into the scholarship on the Prioress's Tale, see Morris 1985. Chaucerians have argued to what degree Chaucer himself was anti-Semitic as opposed to poking fun at anti-Semitism (cf. Friedman 1974; Archer 1984; Rex 1984; and Boyd 1987:43–50).
10. For such a map, see Ben Sasson 1971:1125–26.
11. Poliakov 1974:60. There is some question about the exact number of victims in the Blois incident. See Chazan 1968:15n.4 who mentions thirty-one or thirty-two martyrs.
12. Trachtenberg 1966:125.
13. Kubovy 1964:23–24.
14. Cf. Bloch 1973:121, 353.
15. Roth 1933:523; cf. Schultz 1986:6. For discussions of William of Norwich, see Berger 1897; Anderson, 1964; Langmuir 1984.
16. Maccoby 1936.
17. See Loeb 1887; Lea 1889; and Baer 1966:398–423.
18. Trachtenberg 1966:134; Baer 1966:423; and Shepard 1968:78.
19. Anon. 1975:284.
20. Ibid., 283–84; cf. Bishop 1974:105.
21. Anon. 1975:283.

22. Hauser 1969:120–22; Anon. 1975:284.

23. Hauser 1969:123.

24. Wiesenthal 1951.

25. Despina 1971a:22.

26. Ibid., 26–27. The plaque at Judenstein is reminiscent of similar plaques installed at other sites of martyrs allegedly the victims of Jewish ritual murder. For example, a notice at the shrine of Little Saint Hugh in the Cathedral Church of Saint Mary in Lincoln reads: "Trumped-up stories of 'Ritual Murders' of Christian Boys by Jewish communities were common knowledge throughout Europe during the Middle Ages and even much later. These fictions cost many innocent Jews their lives. Lincoln had its own legend, and the alleged victim was buried in the cathedral in the year 1255.

Such stories do not redound to the credit of Christendom, and so we pray: Remember not, Lord, our offenses, nor the offenses of our Forefathers." See Boyd 1987:vii.

27. Braun 1973. The importance of such artwork is also attested by Mary Anderson's account of how her curiosity was piqued by a damaged painting she noticed on the roodscreen of an East Anglian church in the village of Loddon and how it led her to write a book on the "Strange Death of William of Norwich." Again the scene depicted three Jews murdering a child. One has pierced the child's side with a knife and is holding a basin to catch the blood. See Anderson 1964:14. For a striking series of illustrations of the martyrdom of Simon of Trent evidently printed in 1475, the same year of his death, see Tessadri 1974:164–65. Similar illustrations appear in children's textbooks. For example, one popular booklet in Spain designed to prepare children for their first communion contains the story of Saint Domingo de Val accompanied by a picture of four Jews and a child. Two Jews are nailing the child to a wall while the other two catch his blood in wineglasses. See Shepard 1968:74n.8. See also Bishop 1974 for comparable materials in Italian and French teaching materials.

28. Despina 1971a:17. One may compare this case with that of the cult of Simon of Trent (1475) which was not officially abrogated until October of 1965 when the Archbishop of Trent relayed such a notification from the Vatican Commission for Religious Customs and Observances. See Z. 1967. Cf. the removal of the Werner relief from the Werner chapel in Oberwesel in 1968—the relief celebrated the ritual murder of "Good Werner of Bacharach" in 1287. See Petzoldt 1986:41. For other accounts of Andrew of Rinn, see Hruby 1960–62; and Hauer 1985.

29. Hyamson 1952:49. The Damascus incident of 1840 inspired J. B. Levinsohn to compose a fictional dialogue between a Greek Orthodox Priest and a Rabbi in which the blood libel is discussed at length. See Levinsohn 1841.

30. Ezekiel 1900; Jacobs 1902; Meisl 1930; and Helfand 1980.

31. Hyamson 1952:70, 71.

32. For the papal bulls, see Anon. 1900; Strack 1909:250–59; for an English language text of Cardinal Ganganelli's 1759 report, see Roth 1934; for additional references to Ganganelli's findings, see Szajkowski 1963:207n.33.

33. Klein 1974.

34. Sorlin 1967:296n.114.

35. Cohen 1982:43–44; cf. Burbage 1916.

36. Roth 1934:83.

37. Ibid., p. 85.

38. Vacandard 1912:353, 359; cf. Poliakov 1974:272.

39. Wright 1883; Handler 1980.

40. Nussbaum 1947; Rychnovsky 1949.

41. For details of Masaryk's involvement, see Rychnovsky 1949.

42. This is one of the best-known cases of ritual murder in the twentieth century. The best account is to be found in Tager 1935. For other discussions, see Polak 1949; Szajkowski 1963; Rogger 1966; Samuel 1966; Zeitlin 1968; and Giffin 1980. The case was the inspiration for Malamud's novel *The Fixer* (1966), which in turn was the basis for an American (MGM) film with the same title released in 1968. There is a long history of ritual murder trials being the source of poems, novels, and dramas. The Endingen incident of 1470, for example, evolved into a full-fledged folk drama. Trachtenberg 1966:149 claims that the Endingen *Judenspiel* was one of the most popular German dramas of the seventeenth century. See also Hsia 1988:36–40 for more detail. In the same way, the La Guardia incident in Spain in 1490 inspired a drama by Lope de Vega. For a discussion of this 1605 play, see Shepard 1968:71.

43. See Friedman 1978; Jacobs 1979. For other American instances of blood libel, see Duker 1980.

44. There are simply too many individual case studies to list. See, for example, Chazan 1968 for Blois (1171); Molinier 1883 for Valréas (1247); André-Michel 1914 for a case in 1297; Esposito 1938 for Savoy (1329); Kracauer 1888 and Hsia 1988:14–41 for Endingen (1470); and Menestrina 1903; Eckert 1964; and Tessadri 1974 for the case of Simon of Trent (1475), etc. For a sample of the enormous bibliography devoted to the subject, see Chwolson 1901 and Hayn

1906, who lists 121 separate items, mostly from German sources. For later German references, see Lehr 1974 and Hsia 1988. For Russian cases, see Lĩutostanskii 1934; Wolpe 1961; and Slutsky 1972.

45. Burton 1898:120; for the list, see 120–29.

46. Ibid., xv; Monniot 1914:315; see also Holmes 1979:49–62; and Holmes 1981:269–70.

47. Slutsky 1972:1129; Baer 1972:26.

48. Polak 1949:265.

49. Baer 1972:26.

50. Frazer 1913b:395–96.

51. Ibid., 395.

52. Ibid., 396.

53. Frazer 1913a; cf. Holmes 1981:282n.27.

54. Shepard 1968:74.

55. Peuckert 1935–36:734.

56. Gaster 1937:324.

57. Tager 1935:225.

58. Anon. 1938:8; Jacobson 1948:127–28.

59. Tager 1935:xviii.

60. For the full text of the letter, see Poliakov and Wulf 1959:292.

61. Wolpe 1961:22; Newall 1973:113.

62. Anderson 1964:97; Rappaport 1975:109. For a consideration of the blood libel legend from the perspective of parental treatment or mistreatment of children, see Schultz 1986 (pp. 273–303 in this volume). For discussion of how "evidence" can be trumped up, see Strack's "The Pretended Evidence of History for Jewish Ritual Murder" 1909:169–235; or Bloch's "Attempts at Fabricating 'Ritual Murder'" 1973:365–73; or the intricate details of the effort to frame Beilis in Tager 1935.

63. Loeb 1889:184.

64. Reik 1923:128–129.

65. Ibid., 129; cf. Rappaport 1975:113; Rosenman 1977:21.

66. Reik 1923:129; cf. Rappaport 1975:113–14.

67. Seiden 1967:78.

68. Ibid., 145–46.

69. Rappaport 1975:115.

70. Rosenman 1982:243.

71. Liefmann 1951:494.

72. Dundes 1976.

73. Maccoby 1982:167; cf. Hasan-Rokem and Dundes 1986: 245–46.

74. Ellis 1983:73.

75. This feature of the Eucharist was overlooked by Schuster 1970 in his psychoanalytic consideration of the ritual.

76. Rosenman 1977:19 mentions "the discomfiture that the Mass, so close to the parricidal crime, calls forth in its celebrants" in connection with the legend of the Jewish desecration of the consecrated wafer, but not with the blood libel legend.

77. Schultz 1986:13 does rightly insist that the blood libel is the product of projection, but she does not explain the legend in terms of projective inversion.

78. For a typical statement, see Desportes 1889:277–85.

79. Roth 1934:83.

80. Cf. Strack 1909:124 for additional biblical citations regarding the prohibition against consuming blood. The lack of Old Testament or talmudic sanctions for Jews requiring Christian blood posed no problem for the true anti-Semite. The sanctions came, supposedly, by means of a secret oral tradition passed on from generation to generation. Cf. Desportes 1889:252–53.

81. Newall 1973:114. This speculation is somewhat analogous to Roth's conjecture that the blood accusation arose from Christian misunderstanding of the Jewish feast of Purim. See Roth 1933.

82. Rappaport 1975:103.

83. Cf. Bebbington 1971:33.

84. Maccoby 1982:153.

85. Trachtenberg 1966:137.

86. Roth 1933:525; Trachtenberg 1966:131.

87. Maccoby 1982:159, 155.

88. Cf. Browe 1926; Despina 1971b.

89. Strack 1909:59.

90. Maccoby 1982:167; Cohen 1983.

91. But see Noy 1967 and Alexander 1987 for Jewish texts of the blood libel legend. There is also the curious figure of the Golem (Motif D1635), a clay anthropoid mannikin which in Prague was thought to have been created by a rabbi who employed it to expose ritual murder accusations against Jews and to apprehend the instigators of these blood libels. Cf. Bloch 1925:37; Goldsmith 1981; and Sherwin 1985. I am indebted to Professor Dan Ben-Amos of the University of Pennsylvania for these references.

92. Levinsohn 1841:171; Labriolle 1913; Schultze 1953–54; Cohn 1977:1–9.

93. Cf. Harris 1914:200. Cohn 1977:8, however, is confident of this interpretation when he says, "As it happened, there was one feature of Christian ritual which could easily be interpreted as can-

nibalistic: the Eucharist." In the light of the argument of the present essay, I am very tempted to see a possible correlation between the point in time when the doctrine of transubstantiation first arose and the initial flourishing of the blood libel legend in the twelfth century. The basic idea of transubstantiation apparently existed as early as the ninth century but it was not fully adopted until the Fourth Lateran council in 1215. Strack (1909:59) suggests a connection between the doctrine and the legends of Jews desecrating the host, but not the blood libel legend itself.

94. Pliny 1925:168 (letter XCIV).
95. Tertullian 1917:25, 29.
96. Schuster 1970:231.
97. Strack 1909:283.
98. Balaban 1930:88.
99. Loeb 1889:184–85.
100. Girard 1987:87, 91.
101. Pranaitis was an obscure Catholic priest who had written a pamphlet purporting to prove that the practice of ritual murder was advocated by Jewish religion and he had been called as an expert witness in the trial of Beilis in 1913. For details, see Tager 1935:199–212; Polak 1949:266; and Samuel 1966:87. A copy of Louis Ginzberg's unpublished essay is located at the Jewish Theological Seminary of America in New York City.

Selected Bibliography

Alexander, Tamar. 1987. "A Legend of the Blood Libel in Jerusalem: A Study of a Process of Folk-Tale Adaptation." *International Folklore Review* 5:60–74.

Anderson, M. D. 1964. *A Saint at Stake: The Strange Death of William of Norwich, 1144.* London: Faber and Faber.

André-Michel, R. 1914. "Une accusation de meurtre rituel contre les Juifs d'Uzès en 1297." *Bibliothèque de l'Ecole des Chartes* 75:59–66.

Anon. 1882. *Christliche Zeugnisse gegen die Blutbeschuldigung der Juden.* Berlin: Walther & Apolant.

Anon. 1883. *The 'Blood Accusation,' Its Origin and Occurrence in the Middle Ages: An Historical Commentary on the Tisza-Eszlar Trial.* London: Jewish Chronicle.

Anon. 1900. *Die Päpstlichen Bullen über die Blutbeschuldigung.* Munich: August Schupp.

Anon. 1913. *Der Fall Justschinski: Offizielle Dokumente und private Gutachten.* Berlin: R. Boll.

Anon. 1934. *Zur Ritualmordbeschuldigung.* Berlin: Philo Verlag und Buchhandlung.

Anon. 1938. *The Ritual Murder Accusation.* Chicago: Fireside Discussion Group of the Anti-Defamation League B'nai B'rith.

Anon. 1967. "Arab Antisemitism—Blood Libel Revived." *Wiener Library Bulletin* 21, no. 3: 46–47.

Anon. 1975. "Persistence of Ritual Libel Charges." *Intellect* 103: 283–84.

Apple, Raymond. 1972. "Pesach and the Blood Libel." *Common Ground* 26, no. 1: 12–15.

Archer, J. 1984. "The Structure of Anti-Semitism in the 'Prioress Tale.'" *Chaucer Review* 19: 46–54.

Baer, Joachim T. 1972. *Vladimir Ivanovič Dal' as a Belletrist.* The Hague: Mouton.

Baer, Yitzhak. 1966. *A History of the Jews in Christian Spain.* Vol. 2. Philadelphia: Jewish Publication Society of America.

Balaban, Majer. 1930. "Hugo Grotius und die Ritualmordprozesse in Lublin (1636)." In *Festschrift zu Simon Dubnows siegzigstem Geburtstag,* ed. Ismar Elbogen, Josef Meisl and Mark Wischnitzer, pp. 87–112. Berlin: Jüdischer Verlag.

Bebbington, Brian. 1971. "Little Sir Hugh: An Analysis." *Unisa English Studies* 9: 30–36.

Beckwith, Martha W. 1951. "The Jew's Garden." *Journal of American Folklore* 64: 224–25.

Beilis, Mendel. 1926. *The Story of My Sufferings.* New York: Mendel Beilis Publishing Co.

Ben-Sasson, Haim Hillel. 1972. "Blood Libel." *Encyclopedia Judaica,* vol. 4, pp. 1120–28. Jerusalem: Keter Publishing House.

Berger, S. 1897. "Le prétendu meurtre rituel de la Pâque juive (II)." *Mélusine* 8: 169–174.

Bischoff, Erich. 1929. *Das Blut im jüdischen Schriftum und Brauch: Eine Untersuchung.* Leipzig: L. Beust.

Bishop, Claire Huchet. 1974. *How Catholics Look at Jews: Inquiries into Italian, Spanish and French Teaching Materials.* New York: Paulist Press.

Bitton-Jackson, Livia. 1982. *Madonna or Courtesan? The Jewish Woman in Christian Literature.* New York: Seabury Press.

Bloch, Chayim. 1925. *The Golem: Legends of the Ghetto of Prague.* Vienna: The Golem.

Bloch, Joseph S. 1973. *My Reminiscences.* 2 vols. New York: Arno Press.

Boyd, Beverly. 1987. *A Variorum Edition of the Works of Geoffrey Chaucer*, vol. 11, *The Canterbury Tales*, pt. 20, *The Prioress's Tale*. Norman: University of Oklahoma Press.

Braun, Roger. 1973. "La fin d'une legende de crime rituel: Une plaque à Judenstein." *Rencontre: Chrètiens et Juifs* 8:34–36.

Browe, Peter. 1926. "Die Hostienschändungen der Juden im Mittelalter." *Römische Quartalschrift für christlische Altertumskunde und für Kirchengeschichte* 34:167–97.

Brown, Carleton. 1906. "Chaucer's Prioress' Tale and Its Analogues." *Publications of the Modern Language Association* 21:485–518.

Burbage, Thomas H. 1916. "Ritual Murder Among the Jews." *Catholic Bulletin* 6:309–14, 354–60, 434–41.

Burton, Sir Richard F. 1898. *The Jew, The Gypsy and El Islam*. London: Hutchinson & Co.

Chazan, Robert. 1968. The Blois Incident of 1171. *Proceedings of the American Academy for Jewish Research* 36:13–31.

Child, Francis James. 1962. *The English and Scottish Popular Ballads*. Vol. 3. New York: Cooper Square Publishers.

Chwolson, D. 1901. *Die Blutanklage und sonstige mittelalterliche Beschuldigungen der Juden: Eine historische Untersuchung nach den Quellen*. Frankfurt: J. Kauffmann.

Cohen, Jeremy. 1982. *The Friars and the Jews: The Evolution of Medieval Anti-Judaism*. Ithaca: Cornell University Press.

Cohen, Jeremy. 1983. "The Jews as the Killers of Christ in the Latin Tradition, From Augustine to the Friars." *Traditio* 39:1–27.

Cohn, Norman. 1977. *Europe's Inner Demons*. New York: NAL Penguin.

Corvé, Karl Ignaz. 1840. *Ueber den Ursprung der wider die Juden erhobenen Beschuldigung bei der Feier ihrer Ostern sich des Blutes zu bedienen*. Berlin: L. Fernbach.

Dal', V. I. 1844. *Ob ubivanii evreiami khristianskikh mladentsev*. Moscow.

Despina, Soeur Marie. 1971a. "Le Culte d'Andreas de Rinn historique et situation actuelle." *Rencontre: Chrétiens et Juifs* 5:8–27.

Despina, Soeur Marie. 1971b. "Les accusations de profanation d'hosties portées contre les Juifs." *Rencontre: Chrétiens et Juifs* 5:150–70, 179–91.

Desportes, Henri. 1889. *Le Mystère du sang chez les Juifs de tous les temps*. Paris: Albert Savine.

Duker, Abraham G. 1980. "Twentieth-Century Blood Libels in the United States." In *Rabbi Joseph H. Lookstein Memorial Volume*, ed. Leo Landman, pp. 85–109. New York: KTAV Publishing House.

Dundes, Alan. 1976. "Projection in Folklore: A Plea for Psychoanalytic Semiotics." *Modern Language Notes* 91 : 1500–1533.

Eckert, Willehad Paul. 1964. "Beatus Simoninus—Aus den Akten des Trienter Judenprozesses." In *Judenhass—Schuld der Christen?!* ed. W. P. Eckert and E. L. Ehrlich, pp. 329–58. Essen: Hans Driewer Verlag.

Ehrman, Albert. 1976. "The Origins of the Ritual Murder Accusation and Blood Libel." *Tradition* 15, no. 4: 83–89.

Ellis, John M. 1983. *One Fairy Story Too Many.* Chicago: University of Chicago Press.

Esposito, Mario. 1938. "Un Procès contre les Juifs de la Savoie en 1329." *Revue d'Histoire Ecclésiastique* 34 : 785–801.

Ezekiel, Jacob. 1900. Persecution of the Jews in 1840. *Publications of the American Jewish Historical Society* 8 : 141–45.

Frank, Friedrich. 1901. *Der Ritualmord vor den Gerichtshofen der Wahrheit und Gerechtigkeit.* Regensburg: G. J. Manz.

Frazer, Sir James George. 1913a. "Dr. Frazer's Disclaimer." *Times,* 11 November, p. 8.

Frazer, Sir James George. 1913b. *The Scapegoat. The Golden Bough: A Study in Magic and Religion.* 3d ed. Vol. 9. London: Macmillan.

Freimut, Bernardin. 1895. *Die jüdischen Blutmorde von ihrem ersten Erscheinen in der Geschichte bis auf unsere Zeit.* Munster: Adolph Russel's Verlag.

Friedman, Albert B. 1974. "The *Prioress's Tale* and Chaucer's Anti-Semitism." *Chaucer Review* 9 : 118–29.

Friedman, Saul S. 1978. *The Incident at Massena: The Blood Libel in America.* New York: Stein and Day.

G[aidoz], H[enri]. 1892–93. "Le prétendu meurtre rituel de la Pâque juive (I)." *Mélusine* 6 : 169–171.

Gaster, Moses. 1937. Review of *Handwörterbuch des Deutschen Aberglaubens.* Vol. 7. *Folklore* 48 : 322–24.

Giffin, Frederick C. 1980. "American Reactions to the Beilis Case." *Social Science* 55 : 89–93.

Girard, René. 1987. "Generative Scapegoating." In *Violent Origins,* ed. Robert G. Hamerton-Kelly, pp. 73–105. Stanford: Stanford University Press.

Goldsmith, Arnold L. 1981. *The Golem Remembered, 1909–1980: Variations of a Jewish Legend.* Detroit: Wayne State University Press.

Gresham, Foster B. 1934. "The Jew's Daughter: An Example of Ballad Variation." *Journal of American Folklore* 47:358–61.

Grunewald, Max. 1906. *Zur Psychologie und Geschichte des Blutritualwahnes.* Vienna: L. Beck & Sohn.

Halliwell-Phillips, James Orchard. 1849. *Ballads and Poems Respecting Hugh of Lincoln, A Boy Alleged to have been Murdered by the Jews in the Year MCCLV.* Brixton Hill: for private circulation only.

Handler, Andrew. 1980. *Blood Libel at Tiszaeszlar.* East European Monographs no. 68. Boulder, Colo.

Harris, J. Rendel. 1914. "The Blood-Accusations against the Jews in Southern Russia." *Expository Times* 25:199–200.

Hasan-Rokem, Galit, and Alan Dundes. 1986. *The Wandering Jew: Essays in the Interpretation of a Christian Legend.* Bloomington: Indiana University Press.

Hauer, Nadine. 1985. *Judenstein: Legende ohne Ende.* Vienna.

Hauser, Jean. 1969. "A propos de l'accusation de meurtres rituels: La legende d'Andre de Rinn." *Rencontre: Chrétiens et Juifs* 3:117–27.

Hauser, Jean. 1973. "Les Legendes ont la vie dure." *Rencontre: Chrétiens et Juifs* 8:37–40.

Hayn, Hugo. 1906. *Uebersicht der (meist in Deutschland erschienen) Litteratur über die angeblich von Juden verübten Ritualmorde und Hostienfrevel.* Jena: H. W. Schmidt's Verlagsbuchhandlung.

Helfand, Jonathan I. 1980. "A *Megillah* for the Damascus Affair." In *Rabbi Joseph H. Lookstein Memorial Volume,* ed. Leo Landman, pp. 175–84. New York: KTAV Publishing House.

Hellwig, Albert. 1914. *Ritualmord und Blutaberglaube.* Minden: J. C. C. Bruns.

Hippensteel, Faith. 1969. " 'Sir Hugh': The Hoosier Contribution to the Ballad." *Indiana Folklore* 2:75–140.

Holmes, Colin. 1979. *Anti-Semitism in British Society, 1876–1939.* London: Edward Arnold.

Holmes, Colin. 1981. "The Ritual Murder Accusation in Britain." *Ethnic and Racial Studies* 4:265–88.

Hruby, Kurt. 1960–62. "Der Ritualmord von Rinn—Zusammenhänge und Hintergründe." *Der Judenchrist* 7, no. 3:6–16; 8, no. 1:10–12; 8, no. 2:10–14; 9, no. 1:12–15; 9, no. 2:10–14.

Hruby, Kurt. 1964. "Verhängnisvolle Legenden und ihre Bekämpfung." In *Judenhass—Schuld der Christen?!* ed. W. P. Eckert and E. L. Ehrlich, pp. 281–308. Essen: Hans Driewer Verlag.

Hsia, R. Po-chia. 1988. *The Myth of Ritual Murder: Jews and Magic in Reformation Germany*. New Haven: Yale University Press.

Hume, Abraham. 1849. *Sir Hugh of Lincoln; or, An Examination of a Curious Tradition respecting the Jews, with a notice of the Popular Poetry connected with it*. London: John Russell Smith.

Hyamson, Albert M. 1952. "The Damascus Affair—1840." *Transactions of the Jewish Historical Society of England* 16:47–71.

Jab. 1889. *Le Sang Chrétien dans les rites de la synagogue moderne*. Paris: Henri Gautier.

Jacobs, Joseph. 1894. "Little St. Hugh of Lincoln: Researches in History, Archaeology and Legend." *Transactions of the Jewish Historical Society of England* 1:89–135.

Jacobs, Joseph. 1902. "The Damascus Affair and the Jews of America." *Publications of the American Jewish Historical Society* 10:119–28.

Jacobs, Samuel. 1979. "The Blood Libel Case at Massena—A Reminiscence and a Review." *Judaism* 28:465–74.

Jacobson, David J. 1948. *The Affairs of Dame Rumor*. New York: Rinehart and Company.

Kennan, George. 1913. "The 'Ritual Murder' Case in Kiev." *Outlook* 105:529–35.

Klein, Charlotte. 1974. "Damascus to Kiev: *Civiltà Cattolica* on Ritual Murder." *Wiener Library Bulletin* 27:18–25.

Kracauer, Isidor. 1887. "Accusation de meurtre rituel portée contre les Juifs de Francfort au XVIᵉ siècle." *Revue des études juives* 14:282–89.

Kracauer, Isidor. 1888. "L'Affaire des Juifs d'Endingen de 1470: Prétendu meurtre de chrétiens par des juifs." *Revue des études juives* 16:236–45.

Kubbovy, Myriam. 1964. "Matzoh, Red Wine and the Eucharist." *Jewish Spectator* 29 (November):21–25.

Kurrein, Adolf. 1900. *Brauchen die Juden Christenblut?* Prague: J. Brandeis.

Kynass, Fritz. 1934. *Der Jude in deutschen Volkslied*. Greifswald: E. Panzig & Co.

Labriolle, Pierre de. 1913. "Le meurtre rituel." *Bulletin d'ancienne littérature et d'archéologie chrétiennes* 3:199–203.

Landau, Jacob. M. 1973. "Ritual Murder Accusations in Nineteenth-Century Egypt." In Jacob M. Landau, *Middle Eastern Themes: Papers in History and Politics*, pp. 99–142. London: Frank Cass.

Langmuir, Gavin I. 1972. "The Knight's Tale of Young Hugh of Lincoln." *Speculum* 47:459–82.

Langmuir, Gavin I. 1977. "L'absence d'accusation de meurtre rituel à l'ouest du Rhône." In *Juifs et Judaisme de Languedoc*, Cahiers de Fanjeaux 12, pp. 235–49.

Langmuir, Gavin I. "Thomas of Monmouth: Detector of Ritual Murder." *Speculum* 59:820–46.

Lea, Henry Charles. 1889. "El Santo Niño de la Guardia." *English Historical Review* 4:229–50.

Lehr, Stefan. 1974. *Antisemitismus-religiöse Motive im sozialen Vorurteil: Aus der Fruhgeschichte des Antisemitismus in Deutschland 1870–1914*. Munich: Chr. Kaiser Verlag.

Levinsohn, J. B. 1841. *Éfés Dammîm: A Series of Conversations at Jerusalem Between a Patriarch of the Greek Church and a Chief Rabbi of the Jews, Concerning the Malicious Charge against the Jews of using Christian Blood*. London: Longman, Brown, Green, and Longmans.

Lewin, Adolf. 1906. "Die Blutbeschuldigung in oberbadischen Liedern aus dem 15. und 16. Jahrhundert." *Monatsschrift für Geschichte und Wissenschaft des Judentums* 50:316–33.

Liefmann, Else. 1951. "Mittelalterliche Überlieferungen und Antisemitismus: Ein tiefenpsychologischer Beitrag zu seinem Verständnis." *Psyche* (Stuttgart) 5:481–96.

Līūtostanskii, Ippolit Iosifovich. 1934. *Die Juden in Russland*. Vol. 2, *Jüdische Ritual-morde in Russland*. Berlin: Deutsche Kultur-Wacht.

Loeb, Isidore. 1887. "Le Saint Enfant de la Guardia." *Revue des études juives* 15:203–32.

Loeb, Isidore. 1889. Un Mémoire de Laurent Ganganelli sur La Calomnie due Meurtre Rituel. *Revue des études juives* 18:179–211.

Loge, Christian. 1934. *Gibt es jüdische ritual-morde? Eine sichtung und psychologische klärung des geschlichtlichen materials*. Graz: Ulrich Moser.

Maccoby, Hyam. 1982. *The Sacred Executioner: Human Sacrifice and the Legacy of Guilt*. London: Thames and Hudson.

Maccoby, S. 1936. "Ritual Murder: The Growth of an Anti-Jewish Legend." *Jewish Chronicle Supplement* 168 (April):vii–viii.

Malamud, Bernard. 1966. *The Fixer*. New York: Farrar, Straus and Giroux.

Manzini, Vincenzo. 1930. *La Superstizione Omicida e i Sacrifici Umani con particolare riguardo alle accuse contro gli ebrei*. 2d ed. Padua: CEDAM.

Marcus, Jules. 1900. *Étude médico-légale du meurtre rituel.* Paris.

McCaul, Alex. 1840. *Reasons for Believing That the Charge Lately Revived Against the Jewish People Is a Baseless Falsehood.* London: B. Wertheim.

Meisl, Josef. 1930. "Beiträge zur Damaskus-Affäre (1840)." In *Festschrift zu Simon Dubnows siebzigstem Geburtstag,* ed. Ismar Elbogen, Josef Meisl, and Mark Wischnitzer, pp. 226–36. Berlin: Jüdischer Verlag.

Menestrina, Giuseppe. 1903. "Gli Ebrei a Trento." *Tridentum* 6:304–16; 348–74; 385–411.

Michel, Francisque. 1834a. "Ballade Anglo-Normande sur le meurtre commis par les Juifs sur un enfant de Lincoln." *Mémoires de la Société Royale des Antiquaires de France* 10:358–92.

Michel, Francisque. 1834b. "Hugues de Lincoln: Recueil de Ballades anglo-normades et écossaises relatives au meurtre de cet enfant commis par les Juifs en MCCLV." Paris: Sylvestre.

Molinier, Auguste. 1883. "Enquête sur un meurtre imputé aux Juifs de Valréas (1247)." *Cabinet historique* 29:121–33.

Monniot, Albert. 1914. *Le crime rituel chez les Juifs.* Paris: Pierre Téqui.

Morris, Lynn King. 1985. *Chaucer Source and Analogue Criticism: A Cross-Referenced Guide.* New York: Garland.

Newall, Venetia. 1973. "The Jew as a Witch Figure." In *The Witch Figure,* ed. Venetia Newall, pp. 94–124. London: Routledge & Kegan Paul.

Newall, Venetia. 1975. "The English Folklore Society Under the Presidency of Haham Dr. Moses Gaster." In *Studies in the Cultural Life of the Jews in England,* ed. Dov Noy and Issachar Ben-Ami, pp. 197–225. Folklore Research Center Studies 5. Jerusalem: Magnes Press.

Noy, Dov. 1967. "Alilot Dam b'sipurei Ha'eidot." *Mahanayim* 110:32–51.

Nussbaum, Arthur. 1947. "The 'Ritual-Murder' Trial of Polna." *Historia Judaica* 9:57–74.

Petzoldt, Leander. 1986. "The Eternal Loser: The Jew as Depicted in German Folk Literature." *International Folklore Review* 4: 28–48.

Peuckert, Will-Erich. 1935–36. "Ritualmord." *Handwörterbuch des deutschen Aberglaubens* 7:727–39. Berlin: Walter de Gruyter.

Pliny. 1925. *The Epistles of Pliny.* Trans. William Melmoth, ed. Clifford H. Moore. Boston: Bibliophile Society.

Polak, I. R. 1949. "Mendl Bejlis." In *Thomas G. Masaryk and the Jews: A Collection of Essays*, pp. 257–68. New York: B. Pollak.

Poliakov, Léon. 1974. *The History of Anti-Semitism*. New York: Schocken Books.

Poliakov, L., and J. Wulf. 1959. *Le IIIᵉ Reich et les Juifs*. 3d ed. Paris: Gallimard.

Rank, Otto. 1959. *The Myth of the Birth of the Hero*. New York: Vintage Books.

Rappaport, Ernest A. 1975. *Anti-Judaism: A Psychohistory*. Chicago: Perspective Press.

Reik, Theodor. 1923. *Der Eigene und der Fremde Gott: Zur Psychoanalyse der Religiosen Entwicklung*. Leipzig: Internationaler Psychoanalytischer Verlag.

Reinach, Salomon. 1892. "L'accusation du meutre rituel." *Revue des études juives* 25: 161–80.

Rex, Richard. 1984. "Chaucer and the Jews." *Modern Language Quarterly* 45: 107–22.

Ridley, Florence H. 1967. "A Tale Told Too Often." *Western Folklore* 26: 153–56.

Rogger, Hans. 1966. "The Beilis Case: Anti-Semitism and Politics in the Reign of Nicholas II." *Slavic Review* 25: 615–29.

Rokonitz, Heinrich. 1913. "Die Analyse des Ritualmordglaubens." *Der Wage* 16, no. 47: 1088–1093.

Rosenman, Stanley. 1977. "Psychoanalytic Reflections on Anti-Semitism." *Journal of Psychology and Judaism* 1, no. 2: 3–23.

Rosenman, Stanley. 1982. "Psychoanalytic Knowledge, Jewish Identity, and Germanic Anti-Semitic Legends." *American Journal of Psychoanalysis* 42: 239–48.

Roth, Cecil. 1933. "The Feast of Purim and the Origins of the Blood Accusation." *Speculum* 8: 520–26.

Roth, Cecil. 1934. *The Ritual Murder Libel and the Jew: The Report by Cardinal Lorenzo Ganganelli (Pope Clement XIV)*. London: Woburn Press.

Rowan, Steven. 1985. "Luther, Bucer and Eck on the Jews." *Sixteenth Century Journal* 16: 79–90.

Rychnovsky, Ernst. 1949. "The Struggle Against the Ritual Murder Superstition." In *Thomas G. Masaryk and the Jews: A Collection of Essays*, pp. 154–243. New York: B. Pollak.

Rysan, Josef. 1955. "Defamation in Folklore." *Southern Folklore Quarterly* 19: 143–49.

Samuel, Maurice. 1966. *Blood Accusation: The Strange History of the Beiliss Case*. New York: Alfred A. Knopf.

Schramm, Hellmut. 1943. *Der jüdische Ritualmord: Eine historische Untersuchung.* Berlin: T. Fritsch.

Schultz, Magdelene. 1986. "The Blood Libel: A Motif in the History of Childhood." *Journal of Psychohistory* 14:1–24.

Schultze, W. 1953–54. "Der Vorwurf des Ritualmordes gegen die Christen im Altertum und in der Neuzeit." *Zeitschrift für Kirchengeschichte* 65:304–6.

Schuster, Daniel B. 1970. "The Holy Communion: An Historical and Psychoanalytical Study." *Bulletin of the Philadelphia Association for Psychoanalysis* 20:223–35.

Seiden, Morton Irving. 1967. *The Paradox of Hate: A Study in Ritual Murder.* New York: Thomas Yoseloff.

Shepard, Sanford. 1968. "The Present State of the Ritual Crime in Spain." *Judaism* 17:68–78.

Sherwin, Byron L. 1985. *The Golem Legend: Origins and Implications.* Lanham, Md.: University Press of America.

Slutsky, Yehuda. 1972. "Blood Libel in Russia." *Encyclopedia Judaica,* vol. 4, pp. 1128–31. Jerusalem: Keter Publishing House.

Sorlin, Pierre. 1967. *La Croix et les Juifs (1880–1899).* Paris: Éditions Bernard Grasset.

Statler, Margaret H. 1950. "The Analogues of Chaucer's *Prioress Tale:* The Relation of Group C to Group A." *Publications of the Modern Language Association* 65:896–910.

Stauf von der March, Ottokar. 1933. *Der Ritualmord: Beitrage zur Untersuchung.* Vienna: Hammer Verlag.

Strack, Hermann L. 1909. *The Jew and Human Sacrifice [Human Blood and Jewish Ritual].* New York: Bloch Publishing Co.

Tager, Alexander B. 1935. *The Decay of Czarism: The Beiliss Trial.* Philadelphia: Jewish Publication Society of America.

Tertullian, Q. Septimi Florentis. 1917. *Apologeticus.* Cambridge: Cambridge University Press.

Tessadri, Elena. 1974. *L'arpa di David: Storia di Simone e del processo di Trento contro gli ebrei accusati di omicidio rituale, 1475–1476.* Milan: Campironi.

Thompson, Stith. 1955–58. *Motif-Index of Folk-Literature.* 6 vols. Bloomington: Indiana University Press.

Trachtenberg, Joshua. 1966. *The Devil and the Jews.* New York: Harper Torchbooks.

Tugendhold, Jakob. 1858. *Der alte Wahn vom Blutgebrauch der Israeliten am Osterfeste.* Berlin: Weit & Co.

Utikal, Gerhard. 1943. *Der jüdische Ritualmord: Eine nichtjüdische Klarstellung.* Berlin: Widukind-Verlag.

Vacandard, Abbé Elphège. 1912. "La Question du Meurtre Rituel Chez les Juifs." In *Études de Critique et d'Histoire Religieuse,* 3d ser., 2d ed., pp. 311–77. Paris: Librairie Victor Lecoffre.

Wiesenthal, Simon. 1951. "Tiroler Ritualmord-Marchen." *Aufbau* (New York) 17, no. 19 (May 11): 40.

Wolpe, Gerald I. 1961. "Russia and the Blood Libel." *Jewish Spectator* 26 (April): 20–22.

Woodall, James R. 1955. "'Sir Hugh': A Study in Balladry." *Southern Folklore Quarterly* 19: 77–84.

Wright, Charles H. H. 1883. "The Jews and the Malicious Charge of Human Sacrifice." *Nineteenth Century* 14: 753–78.

Z., G. 1967. "End of a Blood Libel." *Jewish Observer and Middle East Review* 16, no. 5: 17.

Zeitlin, Solomon. 1968. "The Blood Accusation." *Jewish Quarterly Review* 59: 76–80.

Selected Bibliography

Index

A Selected Bibliography:
Suggestions for Further Reading
on the Blood Libel Legend

Alexander, Tamar. "A Legend of the Blood Libel in Jerusalem: A Study of a Process of Folk-Tale Adaptation." *International Folklore Review* 5 (1987): 60–74. An interesting discussion of Jewish (as opposed to Christian) versions of the blood libel legend, with five full texts presented in the appendix.

Chwolson, D. *Die Blutanklage und sonstige mittelalterliche Beschuldigungen der Juden: Eine historische Untersuchung nach den Quellen.* Frankfurt: J. Kauffmann, 1901. This 362-page work, originally published in Russian in the late nineteenth century, offers a comprehensive overview of the blood libel legend.

Despina, Soeur Marie. "Les accusations de profanation d'hosties portées contre les Juifs." *Rencontre: Chrétiens et Juifs* 5 (1971): 150–70, 179–91. An excellent, scholarly discussion of the desecration of the Eucharistic host legend.

Friedman, Saul S. *The Incident at Massena: The Blood Libel in America.* New York: Stein and Day, 1978. A book-length treatment of the most famous blood libel case in the United States, at Massena, New York, in 1928.

Handler, Andrew. *Blood Libel at Tiszaeszlar.* East European Monographs no. 68. Boulder, Colo., 1980. A full account of the Tiszaeszlar, Hungary, case in 1882.

Hayn, Hugo. *Uebersicht der (meist in Deutschland erschienen) Litteratur über die angeblich von Juden verübten Ritualmorde und Hostienfrevel.* Jena: H. W. Schmidt's Verlagsbuchhandlung, 1906. An old but still valuable bibliographical listing of 121 separate books and monographs on the subject of ritual murder or desecration of the host.

Hsia, R. Po-chia. *The Myth of Ritual Murder: Jews and Magic in Reformation Germany.* New Haven: Yale University Press, 1988. A detailed and scholarly discussion of the blood-libel tradition in fifteenth- and sixteenth-century Germany.

Langmuir, Gavin I. "The Knight's Tale of Young Hugh of Lincoln." *Speculum* 47 (1972): 459–82. A thorough review of the Hugh of Lincoln incident of 1255.

Lehr, Stefan. *Antisemitismus-religiöse Motive im sozialen Vorurteil: Aus der Fruhgeschichte des Antisemitismus in Deutsch-*

land 1870–1914. Munich: Chr. Kaiser Verlag, 1974. Although not indicated in the title of this valuable dissertation, there is an important discussion of ritual murder (pp. 52–125) in late-nineteenth- and early-twentieth-century Germany with a superb bibliography (pp. 253–91).

Loeb, Isidore. "Le Saint Enfant de la Guardia." *Revue des études juives* 15 (1887): 203–32. One of the best and most methodical debunking efforts in blood libel case reporting.

Maccoby, Hyam. *The Sacred Executioner. Human Sacrifice and the Legacy of Guilt.* London: Thames and Hudson, 1982. A brilliant exegesis of myth-ritual theory applied to the role of Jews in Christian thought arguing that Christians needed a Jewish scapegoat to take on the guilt of killing Christ. The blood libel legend is also discussed in particular (pp. 152–60).

Reinach, Salomon. "L'accusation du meurtre rituel." *Revue des études juives* 25 (1892): 161–80. A useful overview of the subject of ritual murder.

Roth, Cecil. *The Ritual Murder Libel and the Jew: The Report by Cardinal Lorenzo Ganganelli (Pope Clement XIV).* London: Woburn Press, 1934. Ganganelli's 1759 investigative report of numerous blood libel cases is required reading for anyone seriously interested in the subject and Roth's excellent introductory remarks remain valuable.

Rychnovsky, Ernst. "The Struggle Against the Ritual Murder Superstition." In *Thomas G. Masaryk and the Jews: A Collection of Essays,* pp. 154–243. New York: B. Pollak, 1949. A long and detailed account of the Polna case of blood libel of 1899 including a translation of the trial transcript and a description of the important intervention of Professor Thomas G. Masaryk.

Strack, Hermann L. *The Jew and Human Sacrifice [Human Blood and Jewish Ritual].* New York: Bloch Publishing Co., 1909. A translation from the German of one of the most important single books on the blood libel legend. Written by a Christian theologian, the book consists of a comprehensive Frazerian survey of folkloristic practices involving blood.

Tager, Alexander B. *The Decay of Czarism: The Beiliss Trial.* Philadelphia: Jewish Publication Society of America, 1935. A remarkable account of the incredible intrigues involved in the famous Beilis trial in Kiev in 1913.

Trachtenberg, Joshua. *The Devil and the Jews.* New York: Harper Torchbooks, 1966. This important book, whose subtitle is "The Medieval Conception of the Jew and Its Relation to Modern Anti-semitism," contains chapters on ritual murder (pp. 124–39) and the blood accusation (pp. 140–55).

Vacandard, Abbé Elphège. "La Question du Meurtre Rituel Chez les Juifs." In *Études de Critique et d'Histoire Religieuse*, 3d ser., 2d ed., pp. 311–77. Paris: Librairie Victor Lecoffre, 1912. A sober and insightful survey of the blood libel legend.

Index

Index